Augustine and Politics as Longing in the World

ERIC VOEGELIN INSTITUTE
SERIES IN POLITICAL PHILOSOPHY

# AUGUSTINE
# AND POLITICS AS
# LONGING IN
# THE WORLD

 John von Heyking

University of Missouri Press • Columbia and London

Library of Congress Cataloging-in-Publication Data

Heyking, John von.

   Augustine and politics as longing in the world / John von Heyking.

     p.   cm.

   Includes bibliographical references and index.

   ISBN 0-8262-1349-9 (alk. paper)

   1. Augustine, Saint, Bishop of Hippo—Contributions in political science. I. Title.

JC121.A8 H48 2001

320'.092—dc21                                  2001027169

Text Design: Stephanie Foley

Jacket Design: Susan Ferber

Typesetter: Bookcomp, Inc.

Printer and Binder: Thomson-Shore, Inc.

Typefaces: ITC Giovanni and Stone Sans

The University of Missouri Press offers its grateful acknowledgment for a generous contribution from the Eric Voegelin Institute in support of the publication of this volume.

*For on whatever place one has fallen,*
*on that place one must find support*
*so that one may rise again.*

—AUGUSTINE, *De Vera Religione*

I greeted every scrap of news with the feeling that each located friend had been resurrected from the Beyond. . . . I was at Werner's for the last time, when by chance, Ursula, his children's nurse, dropped in. A soldier had left her a piece of paper for me last September, and that piece of paper was somewhere. . . . Here . . . she found it. My hand shook with joy and excitement. It was in my husband's handwriting! The note consisted of only a few lines legibly written on the dark grey cardboard, dated the second of September 1945. . . .

How was it possible? How could they have kept this jewel, this *everything* away from me for all this time? . . . A soldier had found this piece of paper near the railway tracks at the main train station, tied onto a small, dry biscuit along with the following instructions: "I beg the finder of this letter to take it to the above address. As thanks, I can only offer this biscuit."

—MARTHA VON ROSEN, "The Reminiscences of Martha von Rosen," in *A Baltic Odyssey: War and Survival,* ed. Elvi Whittaker

# C O N T E N T S

T HIS BOOK examines the political thought of Augustine of Hippo, a
fourth-century bishop of the Christian Church. It is not so much about
the political thought of a religious thinker (which, of course, Augustine was)
as it is an exposition of the political thought that accounts for human beings'
participation in diverse realms of being, from the vegetative, to the animalistic,
passionate, rational, and to that which philosophical anthropology signifies as
the ground of being, or the divine ground of being. It explicates the essential
attitude toward politics that one can take from the perspective of one who
reflectively participates in all of those strata of being. The study is one of political
philosophy, and not of theology, although certain problems of the latter discipline are necessarily discussed as they bear on the issues at hand. It considers
primarily the resultant way of considering politics, articulated mostly in the *City
of God* (but also in his other writings), that one with Augustine's philosophical
anthropology had. A full explication of his philosophical anthropology would
require an exegesis of his great meditations, the *Confessions* and *On the Trinity*,
which is a task best left for another time. This study refers to those works,
but focuses more on Augustine's presentation of the insights, gained from his
meditations, in his political *City of God*, which he wrote for posterity as his
account of politics and theology. Thus, the reader skeptical of the truth of those
meditations will have to determine their veracity for himself. This study more
modestly presents the view of politics that accompanies those meditations and
attempts to judge the coherency of that view.

This study attempts to explicate Augustine's political thought to the fullest
extent in a way that is sympathetic but not hagiographic, critical but not
unnecessarily suspicious. However, it was born out of a serious criticism of

the ways Augustine's thought has been transmitted to us from the past. It is commonplace to observe that Augustine's *City of God* was inspired by the collapse of Rome. His political world collapsed, and he, like similarly situated great thinkers such as Plato or Bodin, used the political and spiritual upheaval to think through the foundations of political life that peace and security might otherwise obscure. The twentieth century witnessed great wars and political and spiritual disruptions of a similar magnitude. However, those disruptions had causes that were different from the vices, imperialism, and barbarism that brought about Rome's collapse. The twentieth century had to deal with totalizing ideologies that coercively sought to perfect human beings. They exhibited the kind of rebellion that, as Albert Camus noted, was unthinkable before Christianity. For Camus and for others, modern ideologies presuppose a Christian worldview that includes a personal God and a vision of perfection foreign to the ancient Greeks and even to non-Western cultures. The moral and political uncertainties that followed the cold war share a passing resemblance with those about which Scipio lamented after the destruction of Carthage, Rome's enemy that had formerly inspired it to virtue. However, the current uncertainty does not rule out the possibility of future disruptions similar to those of the past, and the present situation fortunately enables people to work to build a more robust and just political life. Whatever the future brings, Augustine appears to have played no small part in the creation of the conditions in which ideologies may spring: his massively successful critique of classical culture had the effect of aggravating tendencies that either undermined political life or promoted the creation of a sacred empire as the only option for the European civilization. The tradition tells us that Augustine left politics either in a moral vacuum or as having to be dominated by the Church, leaving human beings to fill politics with their own gods when they strayed from the Church. Either way, his construction of a historical narrative, according to which the Church apparently becomes the exclusive bearer of truth in history, had the ironic effect of combining sacred and profane histories, which he had otherwise tried to keep separate.

This study is not a historical or genealogical inquiry. Rather, it considers whether Augustine's political thought transcends the version we think we have inherited. Entering into conversation with Augustine enables us to enter into his meditations, or at least into the results of his meditations, about the heights and depths of human existence and longing. By doing so, we can gain a better understanding of the promise and limitations of such longings. Perhaps we can reawaken ourselves to the possibilities of our aspirations and find the true meaning of wisdom and friendship with those who seek it with us. This is the true calling of political philosophy, a calling Augustine perhaps knew better than anyone.[1]

Isidore of Seville said that anyone who claims to have read all of Augustine's writings lies. One incurs numerous financial, professional, and personal debts to avoid mendacity. The University of Notre Dame and its Department of Government and International Studies provided me with generous financial support, as did the National Broadcasting Corporation's coverage of civil religion. The Erasmus Institute allowed me to complete a crucial stage of the project. Rainer Knopff of the University of Calgary patiently allowed me to make "soft" money even more pliable, which permitted me to complete the manuscript. The *History of Political Thought* published part of Chapter 3 in its winter 1999 issue.

I thank Jean Bethke Elshtain and Charles Matthewes for serving as external reviewers for the manuscript. Amy McCready, Joanna Vecchiarelli Scott, Andrew Murphy, Enid Bloch, Gerson Moreno-Riaño, Clarke Cochran, Marianne Sawicki, Brad Lewis, and Frederick Crosson provided helpful comments at earlier stages of preparation. Valerie Snowdon provided helpful editing, and Barb Hodgson came through when the fabled gods of technology fled Rome. Walter Nicgorski, John Roos, and Fred Dallmayr served as critical and patient readers at the dissertation stage. I am profoundly grateful to my dissertation supervisor, E. A. Goerner, for his wisdom, counsel, generosity, and patience. He shepherded me over several peaks and through many more valleys. Barry Cooper first awoke my interest in what Augustine had to say about love, and how a civil religion like Canadian hockey could manifest it. A. J. Parel gave me the resolve to reject academic fads, and to pursue work on such a neglected thinker.

Jeanne Heffernan, Erin Joyce, and James Old provided me with delightful friendship while writing, and the last helped me to understand why the third wave is the biggest. I thank Marie Pannier for her love, proving that love can indeed be requited beyond expectation and desert.

My parents, Rolf and Karin von Heyking, deserve the greatest thanks. This study pays tribute to their testimony of their Great Trek. The book is lovingly dedicated to them.

---

1. On this point, see Gerhart Niemeyer, "Augustine's Political Philosophy?" 284.

# ABBREVIATIONS

CA   *Contra Academicos* (Against the Academics). Trans. John J. O'Meara. Ancient Christian Writers, vol. 12. New York: Newman Press, 1951. Citations show book, chapter, and paragraph numbers.

CD   *De Civitate Dei* (City of God). Trans. G. E. McCracken et al. Bilingual ed. 7 vols. Cambridge: Harvard University Press, 1969–1988.

   *De Civitate Dei* (City of God against the Pagans). Trans. R. W. Dyson. Cambridge: Cambridge University Press, 1998. Citations show book and chapter numbers.

Conf.   *Confessions.* Trans. F. J. Sheed. Indianapolis: Hackett Publishing, 1970.

   *Confessions.* Trans. William Watts. Bilingual ed. 2 vols. Cambridge: Harvard University Press, 1989. Citations show book and chapter numbers.

DDC   *De Doctrina Christiana.* Trans. R. P. H. Green. Oxford: Clarendon Press, 1995. Citations show book and paragraph numbers.

DGL   *The Literal Meaning of Genesis.* Trans. John Hammond Taylor, S.J. Ancient Christian Writers, vols. 41–42. New York: Newman Press, 1982. Citations show book, chapter, and paragraph numbers.

DLA   *De Libero Arbitrio.* "The Free Choice of the Will." In *The Teacher, the Free Choice of the Will, Grace and Free Will*, trans. Robert P. Russell. Fathers of the Church, vol. 59. Washington, D.C.: Catholic University of America Press, 1968.

   *De Magistro, De Libero Arbitrio.* Ed. F. J. Thonnard. Oeuvres de Saint Augustine. Bilingual ed. Paris: Bibliothèques Augustinienne, 1941. Citations show book, chapter, and paragraph numbers.

DM   *De Musica.* "On Music." In *Writings of Saint Augustine*, trans. Robert Catesby Taliaterro. Fathers of the Church, vol. 2. New York: Cima Publishing, 1947. Citations show book, chapter, and paragraph numbers.

DO      *De Ordine.* "Divine Providence and the Problem of Evil." In *Happy Life, Answer to Skeptics, Divine Providence and the Problem of Evil, Soliloquies,* trans. Robert P. Russell, O.S.A. Fathers of the Church, vol. 1. New York: Cima Publishing, 1948. Citations show book, chapter, and paragraph numbers.

DT      *De Trinitate* (On the Trinity). Ed. W. J. Mountain. Corpus Christianorum Series Latina, vols. 50–50A. Turnholti, Belgium: Typographi Brepols Editores Pontificii, 1968.

        *The Trinity.* Trans. Edmund Hill, O.P. Brooklyn: New City Press, 1991.

        *The Trinity.* Trans. Stephen McKenna. Fathers of the Church, vol. 45. Washington, D.C.: Catholic University of America Press, 1963. Citations show book, chapter, and paragraph numbers.

DVR     *De Vera Religione.* "On True Religion." In *Augustine: Earlier Writings,* trans. John H. S. Burleigh. Philadelphia: Westminster Press, 1953. Citations show chapter and paragraph numbers.

EnP     *Enarrationes in Psalmos* (Expositions on the Book of Psalms). Trans. A. Cleveland Coxe. Nicene and Post-Nicene Fathers, vol. 8. Grand Rapids, Mich.: Wm. B. Eerdmans Publishing, 1989. Citations show sermon, chapter, and paragraph numbers, where applicable.

Ep.     *Epistolarum* (The Confessions and Letters of St. Augustin). Trans. J. G. Pilkington and J. G. Cunningham. Grand Rapids, Mich.: Wm. B. Eerdmans Publishing, 1994.

        *Epistolarum Classes Quatuor.* Opera Omnia, vol. 2. Paris: Apud Gaume Fratres, 1836.

        *Letters.* Trans. Wilfrid Parsons et al. Fathers of the Church, vols. 9–13. New York: Fathers of the Church, 1951. Citations show letter, chapter, and paragraph numbers, where applicable.

Serm.   *Sermons on the Liturgical Seasons.* Trans. Sister Mary Sarah Muldowney, R.S.M. Vol. 17. New York: Fathers of the Church, 1959.

83Q     *Eighty-three Different Questions.* Trans. David L. Mosher. Fathers of the Church, vol. 70. Washington, D.C.: Catholic University of America Press, 1982. Citations show question and paragraph numbers, where applicable.

Augustine and Politics as Longing in the World

# INTRODUCTION

C ONTRARY TO the way Augustine's political thought has usually been interpreted by modern readers, this study shows that Augustine possessed a "right-by-nature" understanding of politics. Instead of arguing that politics is based on sin, he actually considered political life a substantive good that fulfills human beings' longings for a kind of wholeness. Instead of supporting the Christian Church's domination of politics, he actually held a more nuanced account of the relationship between religion and politics that preserves the independence of political life. Instead of basing his politics on a natural law ethic or on one whereby authority is conferred by direct revelation, Augustine actually held to an understanding of political ethics that emphasizes practical wisdom and judgment in a mode that resembles that of Aristotle and Cicero rather than of Machiavelli. This study provides a fresh reading of Augustine and helps us to begin thinking about how his thought speaks to our current political situation, without "updating" Augustine to fit our time and thereby learning nothing from him.

As Jean Bethke Elshtain asks: "Why Augustine? Why Now?"[1] The first and immediate reason is that he is one of the founders of the Western intellectual tradition, and Western civilization takes its form, at least in part, from his thought. His thought informs the Western Christian faith tradition. Both Roman Catholics and Protestants call him their own. Moreover, some have argued that modern civilization is a secularized version of Augustine's account of the city of God and the city of man. According to this view, Enlightenment, romantic, and Hegelian symbolizations of historical progress

---

1. Elshtain, *Augustine and the Limits of Politics*, 1–18.

and human agency replace the Augustinian distinction of sacred and profane histories (according to which only the sacred—that is, nonpolitical—is progressive) and the Augustinian understanding of human being as oriented by the *amor Dei*.[2]

Except for wanting to understand our historical inheritance, this is an insufficient reason for reexamining Augustine's political thought. The choice to study him might be surprising or even quaint to some. For instance, what can someone who lived fifteen hundred years ago possibly teach us about politics? It is true that Augustine did not know the modern state, liberalism, technology, and the other hallmarks of modern politics. However, the student of politics will know that the flux of actions and events does not rule out the possibility of an inquiry into their first principles. In fact, recognizing multiplicity might actually confirm their existence, and this study shows how Augustine's reasoning on political matters enables us to move up to those first things. It may also provide a way to think about how to alleviate the aggravated tension our civilization experiences between instrumental political rationality and proceduralism (which inhibits our thinking about the right and the good), on the one hand, and various types of political romanticism that attempt to inject meaning into political life, on the other hand.

The choice to study Augustine's political thought may also be frightening. For example, as a Father of the Christian Church, was he not a propagandist for a particular worldview responsible for many of the problems we currently face? It is true he was an apologist and a polemicist whose writings have been taken to justify certain forms of repressive political rule, intolerant ecclesiology, and the Inquisition. However, his substantive thought rises above his polemics and provides a nuanced account of politics. The choice of Augustine may also be frightening because Augustine ominously justified the coercion of heretics. This may be the most vexing problem in all of Augustine's political thought, but the final chapter shows that he supported coercion for only violent heretics and their leaders who incited violence (indeed, he counseled clemency for them), and that his at times violent language can be understood as part of a peculiar Roman political rhetoric common in his time. The problem of

2. Vladimir Lossky contends that the elements of negative theology in Augustine's thought mean that Eastern Christians cannot easily dismiss him as the source of dogmatic accounts of God ("Les éléments de 'Théologie négative' dans la pensée de saint Augustin"). The literature on Augustine's relationship with modernity is extensive. See Carl L. Becker, *The Heavenly City of the Eighteenth-Century Philosophers.* The classic critique of the "progressivist" thesis was made by Karl Löwith *(Meaning in History)* and Eric Voegelin *(The New Science of Politics).* See also Pierre Manent, *The City of Man,* and Hans Blumenberg's rejoinder to Löwith *(The Legitimacy of the Modern Age).*

coercion is a problem that any political thinker, including the most tolerant, must face.

As a Christian, Augustine also theorized about politics within a framework of revelation. Christianity is about the miraculous birth and resurrection of Christ. One of the difficulties that political philosophers working in the Judeo-Christian tradition have faced is how one can articulate transpolitical or transhistorical principles where those very principles seem to be suspended or changed by God's will. For example, how can one's laws prohibit killing when Abraham himself was specifically commanded by God to kill his son? The relationship between reason and revelation, and nature and grace, is complicated, and a full treatment lies outside the scope of this study.[3] What is important for this study is that Augustine's Christian theological commitments and so-called metaphysical baggage do not lead him to undermine political life. Augustine did not advocate priestly rule because he rejected political rulership as the proper function of priests, and was thus skeptical of their political claims. Politics for Augustine is not simply the administration of the natural law or the divine will.

Augustine's account of reason and the passions in politics is the primary focus of this study. Its main theme as suggested in the title, *Augustine and Politics as Longing in the World*, signifies two of its central themes. The first is that Augustine understood human beings in terms of their longings, that what they long for is what defines them. *Longing* signifies neediness in our incomplete natures and the fullness of experience more accurately than other words such as *craving* or *loving*, for example. The second theme that this study shows is that, as a virtue thinker, Augustine regarded the world as the appropriate locus for this longing. His political thought is based on his understanding of virtue as ordinate loving *(ordo amoris) (CD* 15.22). As such, his much quoted and misinterpreted dictum to "love and do what you will" *(ama et fac quod vis)* includes within its meaning that the intellect guides one's love. It is not a blank check for moral sadism and other forms of extremism. The appropriate way to understand Augustine's theory is to consider it in terms of the proper way for human beings to live in

---

3. Augustine's theology and metaphysics are left to those better equipped to interpret them. The works of Frederick J. Crosson, John Milbank, and Rowan Williams are especially helpful in this regard, as each shows how Augustine synthesized wisdom *(sapientia)* with knowledge *(scientia)* in a way that is comparable to Aristotelian *episteme* (Crosson), that is decidedly un-Cartesian (Williams), and that resists being characterized as what is generally taken as metaphysical dualism (Milbank) (Crosson, "Religion and Faith in St. Augustine's *Confessions*," "Show and Tell: The Concept of Teaching in St. Augustine's *De Magistro*," and "Structure and Meaning in St. Augustine's *Confessions*"; Williams, "*Sapientia* and the Trinity: Reflections on the *De Trinitate*" and "The Paradoxes of Self-Knowledge in the *De Trinitate*"; Milbank, *Theology and Social Theory* and "Sacred Triads: Augustine and the Indo-European Soul").

the world, and whether they love different objects ordinately or inordinately. Augustine is usually said to deny the goodness of the world, the created order, and to advocate an ethic of asceticism. This study attempts to show that this view is false when it comes to Augustine's views on politics. Instead, it considers how our longings can be formed or made ordinate in order to cultivate a good politics. His theory differs from those of ancient Greek and modern political philosophers because it is situated within a framework of reason and revelation, or nature and grace. For Augustine, virtue depends on the love of God and of neighbor. Thus, his moral and political thought depends on his philosophical anthropology that clarifies human beings' participation in these parts of reality. As explained more thoroughly below, however, Augustine's theory turns out to be consistent with what has come to be known as a right-by-nature theory of politics.[4] This study tries to show that the claims of revelation do not overturn those made by natural reason. It also avoids trying to "naturalize" Augustine by turning him into a kind of deist.

By focusing on longing, this study addresses the topic on which Augustine's meditations prove most compelling. When considering the objects of our love, we risk, in a sense, remaining unrequited lovers. Our restless hearts rest only in God, as Augustine maintains, in the beginning of his *Confessions* (1.1). Groping our way through the dark of our mortality, we confront the mystery of not knowing and not being ensured of our end. Augustine has a reputation for thinking that no earthly good can give us happiness and that human life is merely an ascetic time of waiting for redemption. However, this view overlooks other parts of his thought in which he states that "he approaches *(propinquat)* being a blessed human being who desires well whatever he desires; when he obtains what he desires, then he will be blessed" *(DT* 13.6.9). We can never be perfectly happy by our own efforts in this mortal life. However, we have our own kind of happiness that approaches perfect happiness if we persevere. At best we can characterize such happiness as an approach. Still, confronted

---

4. This sort of argument can be found in the ethical and political theories that right and morality have standards and criteria but their application is never simply deductive. Such theories concentrate on natural right or "right-by-nature" *(physei dikaion)* instead of natural law, virtue as a good internal to a practice, and judgment as a faculty rather than as deduction. They usually start from Aristotle's observation that objective rules of right are, at best, generalizations that are not universally valid but are changeable according to circumstance (*Nicomachean Ethics* 5.7). Important twentieth-century versions include: Leo Strauss, *Natural Right and History,* and Voegelin, *Anamnesis.* Also notable are Alasdair MacIntyre's efforts to theorize about practical wisdom within a Thomistic tradition *(After Virtue* and *Whose Justice? Which Rationality?),* and Hannah Arendt's efforts to articulate political judgment in terms analogous to aesthetic judgment rather than according to rules *(Lectures on Kant's Political Philosophy).*

with this mystery, we risk lashing out and putting faith in easy answers such as triumphalist religiosity, technological dreams, revolutionary ideology, or some other idol. A thorough political theory is one that helps us understand our existence by teaching us how to persevere through this darkness without lashing out or without giving up and proclaiming that the end is whatever we make it to be. Augustine's political thought provides such thoroughness.

By considering Augustine as a right-by-nature thinker, one challenges the view that Augustine understood political ethics simply as a matter of applying exceptionless rules—whether natural or divine—to political rule. Right-by-nature as considered here has two characteristics. First, it treats politics as the highest practical activity for human beings. Human being is the political animal and a polity his little world. As Eric Voegelin notes, political society "is as a whole a little world, a cosmion, illuminated with meaning from within by the human beings who continuously create and bear it as the mode and condition of their self-realization."[5] Augustine does not use the term *cosmion*, but he theorizes about politics in terms equivalent to the way defined by the political theorists who use them.

Augustine is generally seen to reject the classical view of politics. Thus, Robert Markus, the author of the benchmark study of Augustine's political thought, argues that political authority for Augustine has its roots in sin: " 'Control of the wicked within the bounds of a certain earthly peace' remained Augustine's fundamental thought about the purpose of government."[6] If political life is to be moral, subpolitical civil society institutions such as the family or churches, not statesmanship or the political process, can supply that morality. An older

---

5. Voegelin, *New Science of Politics*, 27. Voegelin elaborates the meaning of the cosmion elsewhere: "[T]he political cosmion provides a structure of meaning into which the single human being can fit the results of the biologically and spiritually [productive, procreative] energies of his personal life, thereby [relieving] his life from the [disordering aspects] of existence that always spring up when the possibility of utter senselessness of life ending in annihilation is envisaged" (*History of Political Ideas*, vol. 1, *Hellenism, Rome, and Early Christianity*, 226). See also Yves R. Simon, *A General Theory of Authority*, 28–29. Likewise, Leo Strauss emphasizes the role that politics plays in promoting the life of excellence when he describes politics as "the field on which human excellence can show itself in its full growth and on whose proper cultivation every form of excellence is in a way dependent" (*Natural Right and History*, 133–34).

6. Markus, *Saeculum: History and Society in the Theology of St. Augustine*, 96. He quotes from *DGL*, 9.9.14. Markus also argues that political authority and slavery have the same origins (see *Saeculum*, app. B). Most modern interpreters share Markus's view in attributing a minimalist, even proto-Hobbesian, conception of politics. See Herbert Deane, *The Political and Social Ideas of St. Augustine*; Peter Brown, "Political Society"; Oliver O'Donovan, "Augustine's *City of God* XIX and Western Political Thought"; Reinhold Niebuhr, "Augustine's Political Realism"; Elshtain, *Limits of Politics*; Paul J. Weithman, "Toward an Augustinian Liberalism"; and Rowan Williams, "Politics and the Soul: A Reading of the *City of God*."

interpretation deriving from Giles of Rome and Gregory VII, called "political Augustinianism," imputes moral content to political life but ascribes salvational meaning to political life and thus leads to a fusion of church and state. This view of politics was admirably expressed also by Charlemagne, who, in his *livre de chevet* (bedside book), referred to the *City of God* 5.24 when he cried out to his people at the great assembly at Aix-la-Chappelle: "My beloved brethren . . . attend! We have been sent here for your salvation, to exhort you to follow the law of God exactly and convert you in justice and mercy to the laws of this world."[7] In other words, for Charlemagne and subsequent commentators who hold this type of view, political activity is seen to become the imperial activity of converting souls to the Creed. Whether interpreters take this or the former view, Augustine's political thought appears incapable of achieving a middle ground between securing a minimalist peace and security or a sacralized regime.

Second, right-by-nature theories of politics emphasize practical wisdom instead of viewing politics simply as a matter of applying universal rules to political life. Justice requires, in extreme and rare circumstances, breaking what is generally taken to be the just in a way that preserves the just without collapsing into a flimsy moral relativism or a calculus of expediency. As Strauss observes, "There is a universally valid hierarchy of ends, but there are no universally valid rules of action."[8] Augustine is generally thought to fail miserably on this score. He is regarded either as a natural or eternal law thinker or as relying dangerously on divine inspiration to justify exceptions to such laws that might inspire false prophets to destructive acts.[9] Either way, he is seen to lack a rigorous articulation of the grounds that enable someone who is not a prophet to act

7. Quoted in Robert R. Barr, "The Two Cities in Saint Augustine," 228. Citation taken from Gustave Combès, *La Doctrine Politique de Saint Augustin* (Paris, 1927), 415. Combès's reference is to *Patrologia Latina*, vol. 97, cols. 239–42. In general, see H.-X. Arquillière, *L'Augustinisme politique: Essai sur la formation des theories politiques du moyen âge*. On medieval appropriations of Augustine, see M. S. Kempshall, *The Common Good in Late Medieval Political Thought*, 19–25. Modern Thomistic and postmodern commentators regard Augustine's failure to affirm politics as a natural good or to give politics its own autonomous space as problematic. See MacIntyre, *Whose Justice? Which Rationality?* 158; and William Connolly, *The Augustinian Imperative: A Reflection on the Politics of Morality*. More recently, John Milbank has argued that Augustine's theology and ecclesiology can replace the "ontology of violence" inherent in ancient and modern understandings of social life (*Theology and Social Theory*, 398–434). The Church would thus take a more direct political role along the lines of the ideal of Christendom.

8. Strauss, *Natural Right and History*, 162.

9. For the former view, see Connolly, who sees Augustine building an asphyxiating web of rules whose observance makes action difficult (*Augustinian Imperative*, 68–69); Deane argues that ethics is based on the negative version of the Golden Rule (as it is with Hobbes) (*Political and Social Ideas*, 87). See also Anton Chroust, "St. Augustine's Philosophical Theory of Law." For the latter view, see John M. Rist, *Augustine: Ancient Thought Baptized*, 296. E. L. Fortin argues that Augustine presents a "primitive" right-by-nature teaching that allows for only certain kinds of exceptions ("Political

justly in situations that require one to set aside the usual just norm in order to serve justice.

Commentators have missed the right-by-nature basis of Augustine's political thought in part because they have taken Augustine's antipolitical and other-worldly rhetoric at face value and have attributed contradictions in his thought merely to his own indecision and lack of rigor. For instance, Markus contends that Augustine's overblown antipolitical rhetoric lacks rigorous logic:

> Augustine's identification of the Roman state with the earthly city is as clear in his writings as is his refusal to abide by this identification. His logic is the logic of late antique rhetoric rather than modern formal logic. "Babylon" is both the city of the impious, and the secular sphere in which good pious Christians may discharge important functions. Without the least sense of inconsistency, Augustine will assert that Rome, or the *res publica*, is the earthly city, or assume this equation, and then go on to speak in ways which imply the contrary.[10]

Markus regards Augustine's antipolitical rhetoric as normal, but then does not take seriously Augustine's statements that contradict that rhetoric. This approach overlooks the care that Augustine took in writing, which had been better noticed by his medieval readers such as John of Salisbury.[11] By doing so, Markus and other modern interpreters fail to distinguish whether Augustine's view is essentially antipolitical or whether he more narrowly reserves his criticism for those who would falsely seek complete happiness in political and in mortal life. Augustine's antipolitical rhetoric and ironic praise for the Romans is directed to those with inordinate loves. One can push this point further and observe a deeper irony that lies beneath the irony he displays toward the Romans. It is directed toward those, such as Eusebius or Orosius (for example, see *CD* 18.52), who have allowed Augustine's antipolitical rhetoric to flatter them into believing that Christianity negates politics, or, in Platonic terms, that it solves the political problem of trying to harmonize wisdom with political power. The interpretation that sees the Church subsume politics assumes wisdom can easily wield political power, and the "minimalist" interpretation removes wisdom from the equation. Either way, both versions

Idealism and Christianity," in *Collected Essays*, 2:46; "Augustine and the Problem of Goodness," 184–86; "St. Augustine," 189–90). See Chapter 4, below.

10. Markus, *Saeculum*, 59. Peter S. Hawkins, on the other hand, points out that Augustine's use of symbolic dualities (that is, cities of God and of man) has an internal consistency about them ("Polemical Counterpoint in *De Civitate Dei*").

11. See John of Salisbury, *Policraticus*, 7.2.

claim that Augustine solved or thought he solved the political problem when he actually did neither.

Claiming Augustine to be a right-by-nature thinker does not contradict his having been a Christian believer and bishop. Christianity, for him, does not overturn classical right-by-nature teaching, but, rather, gives it greater public force.[12] Augustine differs from the classical thinkers by demanding greater attention to justice in politics, and writing for a wider audience. His consistency with them is difficult to prove in light of his characterization of Christians as pilgrims in the earthly city, and because the classical position asserts the polis as human beings' only home. Even if it can be shown that Augustine affirms the naturalness of politics, he makes it explicit for citizens that political life pales in the light of life in the Church. Classical right-by-nature, however, also affirms the arbitrary character of any given regime, and it was the task of the classical political philosophers to articulate a kind of natural theology to serve the city.[13] Plato's noble lie that tells citizens that they, like plants, have grown from a common stock out of the earth veils the arbitrariness that chance and human choice confer onto political life. Plato's *Laws* constitutes his own effort to articulate a natural theology to guide the city, and Augustine praises Varro and a few other virtuous Romans who longed for one.

It may be argued that Augustine's achievement in making such arbitrariness explicit undermines the salutary and crucial stories that bind societies, and that debunking such stories unravels society. This is true in part. However, Augustine was not a revolutionary, and Chapter 1 shows that Augustine's apparent antipolitical and anti-Roman rhetoric was actually quite conservative. Even so, Augustine, in keeping with classical right-by-nature, recognized that all human beings always have intimations, or what the classical political philosophers called divinations, of the eternal whole that forms the subsisting basis of all their opinions about the right and the good. Such experience leads everyone to long for wholeness, and Augustine argued that such longing logically means that our longing for happiness intimates a longing for eternal happiness. Politics is part of the flux of becoming, and cities cannot be eternal. For Augustine, people's longing for eternal happiness can be realized only in their participation

12. A useful consideration of Saint Thomas Aquinas and right-by-nature (as opposed to natural law) is presented by E. A. Goerner, "On Thomistic Natural Law: The Bad Man's View of Thomistic Natural Right"; "Thomistic Natural Right: The Good Man's View of Thomistic Natural Law." See also James V. Schall, S.J., "A Latitude for Statesmanship? Strauss on St. Thomas," and James M. Rhodes, "Right by Nature," who suggests that right-by-nature is equivalent to the biblical concept of righteousness.

13. See Strauss, *Natural Right and History,* 132.

in the sacramental life of the Church. The Church provides an account of eternal happiness for all believers, which Plato, Aristotle, and Cicero maintained was fleetingly available to only a few philosophers. Furthermore, Augustine's understanding of the Christian Church as the primary representative of the city of God on earth does not contradict classical right-by-nature. He preserves the standard that political ethics requires a multiplicity of means to a universally valid hierarchy of ends. As will be shown in Chapter 6, Augustine affirms natural virtue that is not exclusive to the Christian Church.[14]

Despite the schizophrenia between political minimalism and sacralism that Augustine scholars have generally attributed to his thought, major political philosophers and thinkers in this century have drawn from his thought in their own recoveries of order. Some major thinkers of the twentieth century from outside the Christian tradition have drawn from Augustine in order to guide them through the century's political confusion. For example, Hannah Arendt derived her concepts of natality, life between past and future, and the unifying power of love from her dissertation on Augustine. Her doctoral work provided her with the conceptual categories with which to criticize such twentieth-century phenomena as totalitarianism. She called Augustine her "old friend" throughout her life, and she regarded his thought sufficiently important to begin revising her dissertation for republication.[15] Arendt defined natality as the experience of one's creatureliness that inspires gratitude. She regarded this concept as a counterbalance against the views of her teacher, Martin Heidegger, who saw human beings as anxiously tending toward death. She learned from Augustine how human beings are embedded in the world, which gives them a ground in the past and also gives them hope for the future. Finally, at the end of

14. Some scholars see Augustine affirming politics as a positive good. See Peter J. Burnell, "The Problem of Service to Unjust Regimes in Augustine's *City of God*" and "The Status of Politics in St. Augustine's *City of God*"; D. J. MacQueen, "The Origin and Dynamics of Society and the State according to St. Augustine"; and Voegelin, *History of Political Ideas: Hellenism, Rome, and Early Christianity,* 1:217–19. Fortin notes that Augustine's *On the Free Choice of the Will* supports the view that governmental structure would have been required in Eden ("Political Idealism and Christianity," in *Collected Essays,* 2:52 n. 18). Milbank makes a similar observation about the educative aspect of Edenic political life (*Theology and Social Theory,* 406).

15. Arendt, *Love and Saint Augustine,* 115–211. It is probably not an overstatement to claim that existentialism would have been inconceivable had it not been for the interest in Augustine in German universities in the first part of the twentieth century. It showed its mark on Arendt's other teacher, Karl Jaspers, and in the development of Heidegger's formulation of Dasein, despite the limitations of what he took as Augustine's "platonizing" and his historical context. Heidegger also taught a course titled "Augustine and Neo-Platonism" in 1921 (Heidegger, "Augustinus und der Neuplatonismus"). See also Theodore Kisiel, *The Genesis of Heidegger's "Being and Time,"* 101–8, 191–219. Another student of Heidegger, Hans Jonas, wrote his first book on Augustine (*Augustin und das paulinische Freiheitsproblem*).

her last work, *The Life of the Mind*, she reintroduces, after having long neglected it, the healing concept of love on the will as the way of uniting thought and action. She learned from Augustine that no matter how miserable the world becomes, no matter how wearisome, it is always the place of new beginnings.

In a similar vein, Augustine was important for Michael Oakeshott because he offered an account of politics based on realistic assumptions about its capabilities. Augustine's "politics of skepticism" provided a useful counterweight to the "politics of faith" that so dominated the ideologies of the twentieth century. He interpreted the intermingling of the cities of God and of man as the permanent character of political activity, necessitating a practically minded approach to politics that emphasizes it as a process-guided *societas* rather than as a "teleocratic" corporate *universitas*. Oakeshott found Augustine's account of *ordo amoris* useful, going so far as to compare his own concept of *societas* to *civitas peregrina*, Augustine's characterization of the intermingling of the cities of God and man, in which (according to Oakeshott) partners associate in a prudential manner, and not on account of a common desire to satisfy substantive wants.[16] Oakeshott concludes *On Human Conduct* with a portrait of the Augustinian character upon which *societas* is based:

> And since men are apt to make gods whose characters reflect what they believe to be their own, the deity corresponding to this self-understanding is an Augustinian god of majestic imagination, who, when he might have devised an untroublesome universe, had the nerve to create one composed of self-employed adventures of unpredictable fancy, to announce to them some rules of conduct, and thus to acquire convives capable of "answering back" in civil tones with whom to pass eternity in conversation.[17]

The Augustine from whom Oakeshott draws is one for whom *ordo amoris* is imagined to entail loving God and neighbor for their own sakes instead of other "outcomes [that] are preferred to adventures and satisfactions to wants." Modern

16. Oakeshott, *On Human Conduct*, 243. The symbol of *peregrina* is drawn from CD 18.1; Oakeshott refers to Brown, *Augustine of Hippo*, chap. 27.

17. Oakeshott, *On Human Conduct*, 324. In a letter to a friend, Oakeshott elaborated Augustine's importance to his understanding of the character upon which *societas* is based: "I have gone back to 'theology'—or rather, to reflection upon religion. . . . This ambition came to me, partly from my rereading all that St. Augustine wrote—St. Augustine and Montaigne, the two most remarkable men who have ever lived. What I would like to write is a new version . . . of Anselm's *Cur deus homo*— in which (amongst very much else) 'salvation,' being 'saved,' is recognized as [having] nothing whatever to do with the *future*" (quoted in Patrick Riley, review of *Morality and Politics in Modern Europe: The Harvard Lectures* and *Religion, Politics, and the Moral Life*, 747; emphasis in original). See also Glenn Worthington, "Michael Oakeshott and the *City of God*."

life had aggravated mankind's desire for political "outcomes," and Oakeshott saw in Augustine a conversant who appreciated what Oakeshott characterized as the adventure of political life.

The novels of Albert Camus are highly regarded for their insightful criticisms of modern spiritual alienation and for their honest attempts to articulate a nuanced and nondogmatic account of the human condition. His work reflects a double movement toward and away from Christianity: he appreciated, in its Augustinian form, articulation of longing and the mystery of God, but rejected the dogmatism found in its apparent "providentialism" and creationism. Much of his attitude is first found in his dissertation, in which he argued that Augustine constituted the culmination of Christianity's evolving synthesis of itself and of Greek philosophy. For Camus, Augustine helped to relax or to "supple up *(assouplissement)* reason" so as to articulate religious experience, and, in turn, to protect faith from degenerating into dogma. Camus regarded Augustine's synthesis as a failure because it could not hold together Christianity with Greek philosophy. However, he concludes his examination by arguing that "it is possible to consider Augustinianism as a second revelation; the Christian metaphysical one after the one of evangelical faith. The miracle is that the two may not be contradictory."[18] Camus took from Augustine, however, a way of articulating the tension between wisdom and the mystery of the human condition, which would structure his later novels and essays.

Eric Voegelin often used Augustinian categories to describe modern political religions, and he uses a quotation from Augustine as the epigraph to *Order and History:* "In the study of creature one should not exercise a vain and perishing curiosity, but ascend toward what is immortal and everlasting" (*DVR* 29.52). For Voegelin, as for Augustine, history consists in the "existential exodus from the pragmatic world of power—*incipit exire, qui incipit amare* [he begins to leave who begins to love]—and, consequently, conceived the 'intermingling' of the *civitas Dei* with the *civitas terrena* as the In-Between reality of history."[19] Voegelin at one point thought that Augustine gave form to modern politics because his history of human salvation was secularized as the modern notion of progress. For Voegelin, Augustine's characterization of the epoch after Christ as *saeculum senescens,* the old age of the world, denies the world's inner goodness, and implies that history is just a boring time of waiting before the return

18. Camus, "Entre Plotin et Saint Augustin," 1306 (my translation). According to the editors, different copies of the dissertation had different titles, including *Hellénisme et Christianisme, Plotin et saint Augustin,* and *Métaphysique chrétienne et Néoplatonisme* (1223). They also single out his novel *Mythe de Sisyphe* as manifesting the aforementioned double movement.

19. Voegelin, *The Ecumenic Age,* 172.

of Christ. The perception of the world's emptiness gave rise to impatient attempts to give it meaning through various forms of millenarianism, alchemy, gnosticism, and revolutionary ideology. Voegelin later modified his position by returning to Augustine's recognition of the meaningfulness of earthly existence, as evidenced by the above quotation. He too learned from Augustine the reasons to practice patience.[20]

Arendt, Oakeshott, Voegelin, and even Camus, to an extent, rediscovered Augustine so as to articulate a nonreductive anthropology open to the heights and depths of human longings that are otherwise perverted by scientistic Enlightenment accounts of human beings. As thinkers who were not especially committed to the Christian religion, their reflections were intended not to "bring religion into politics," as such reflections are often accused of, but to provide an account of politics that both is robust and allows human longings to flourish and to be expressed constructively. In this sense, they looked to this religious figure to help them articulate a moderate, yet elevated, politics.

This study examines how Augustine affirmed political life as a positive good. Chapter 1 demonstrates that Augustine's apparent antipolitical rhetoric is not as extreme as it is usually taken to be. Behind Augustine's rhetoric lies his substantial agreement with his Roman philosophical interlocutors on virtue and politics. His antipolitical rhetoric is meant to tame the lust for domination of Roman patriots by showing that lust can never be satisfied by political goods. By opposing extreme "worldliness" with extreme "otherworldliness," Augustine appears to reject politics as a natural good. The rest of the book attempts to show that this is not the case, and that Augustine affirms politics as a natural good.

The second and third chapters demonstrate Augustine's affirmation that politics is a natural good. It will be shown that he recognized political life as the mode by which human beings satisfy their longings for a kind of wholeness, that political society serves as a kind of microcosm of the way its citizens perceive reality. The cosmion or political city constitutes a conceptual space

20. The Augustinian character of Voegelin's *zetema*, as he called it, also drew from Max Scheler's philosophical anthropology (see William Petropulous, "The Person as *Imago Dei*: Augustine and Max Scheler in Eric Voegelin's *Herrschaftslehere* and *Political Religions*"). Scheler characterized his project of philosophical anthropology as delivering "the kernel of Augustinianism from the husklike accretions of history. . . . When this has been done, natural theology will more and more clearly reveal and demonstrate that *immediate* contact of the soul with God which Augustine, from the experience of his great heart, was striving with the apparatus of neo-Platonism to capture and fix in words. Only a theology of the *essential experience of divinity* can open our eyes to the lost truths of Augustine" (*On the Eternal in Man*, 13).

between Augustine's well-known categories of the city of God and the earthly city. Neither the city of God, which is governed by the love of God, nor the earthly city motivated by the lust for domination, the political city is the best practical regime as understood and governed by natural reason. Like the Church, the political city experiences what Augustine refers to as the intermingling of the cities of God and of man. That is, it experiences both the best and the most vicious passions of human beings, and serves a different purpose from that of the Church. Chapter 2 also demonstrates that Augustine considered the basis and origins of political authority as natural. It shows that political life exists even in Eden, which indicates that its origins are separate from the origin of sin. Chapter 3 examines Augustine's statement that better passions make for a better regime. It shows how his reformulation of Cicero's definition of a republic remains consistent with the original in maintaining that politics plays a role in securing the good life. The chapter concludes by examining Augustine's understanding of the hierarchy of different regimes and their loves, such as the loves of virtue, honor, wealth, and freedom, and the love of domination that rules the tyrant.

Chapter 4 shows how Augustine's understanding of political ethics emphasizes practical wisdom and judgment in right-by-nature, and virtue as ordinate loving *(ordo amoris)*, rather than either natural law or grace. It examines three cases of moral reasoning in extreme circumstances (lying, adultery, and tyrannicide and rebellion) and shows that Augustine adopts a right-by-nature style of practical reasoning in each case. In extreme circumstances, according to Augustine, the purpose of what appears as a universal rule or commandment can be better fulfilled by breaking the prohibition. The chapter shows how his emphasis on practical wisdom preserves the moral life while maintaining the flexibility necessary for a robust political life and avoiding the pitfalls of a Machiavellian ends-justify-the-means political calculus.

Chapter 5 takes a closer look at Augustine's understanding of the love of glory, the preeminent political love. Contrary to the way he is usually understood, the chapter shows how he affirms the ordinate love of glory, which he sees as a necessary means of forming civic virtue and community.

The final two chapters show how Augustine relates religion to politics. Chapter 6 demonstrates that, for Augustine, the love of God is a virtue and is not reducible to adherence to a code. This suggests that non-Christians are capable of worship in a manner equivalent to Christians and can cultivate equivalent political virtues. Chapter 7 examines his justification of the coercion of heretics, because this is usually taken as the place where his virtue teaching collapses and where he appears to rely on law-abidingness to preserve order. It shows instead that Augustine's justification of coercion must attend to the particular circumstance and that he justifies the coercion for those whose beliefs manifest themselves in violence (as did those of the Donatists).

This rereading of Augustine's political thought shows how his affirmation of politics as the way for humans to fulfill their longings for a kind of wholeness discloses a deeper affirmation of a more meaningful, pluralistic, and robust political life than his interpreters have hitherto appreciated.

This study examines Augustine's political thought and asks the types of questions about human beings and political order that events in the twentieth century forced scholars of political philosophy to ask with added urgency. This approach is slightly unusual because most people who study his thought tend to be classicists, historians, and theologians; the interest of Augustine to their fields is obvious. Studying Augustine's political thought is challenging because one cannot examine it as a topic separate from his theology. This is especially true since he never actually wrote separate political treatises. For him, God, man, world, and society form an intimate community of being, so it is simply impossible to speak of politics as an autonomous entity outside of God's providence. This intimate relationship necessitates not an antipolitical attitude that has often been ascribed to him, but quite the reverse. The community of being necessitates a view of politics as natural because politics entails building a little world for human beings within that community, in which political society is, in the words of John Milbank, "nothing but a sequence of mediations between individuals, households, and cities," and that such a "finite series," embedded as it is within the community of being, "continues indefinitely towards an infinite and unfathomable God." Thus, to view all of politics essentially as *propter peccatum* and as alienated from this community of being, as exemplified by the sins of the Romans that Augustine gleefully recounts, would entail the removal of an essential partner in that community, which contradicts Augustine's view of reality. This study focuses on political life as a partner of that community by treating political topics as interconnected with his explications of theological topics, but it does so without entering into elaborate discussion of theological points. As such, this study takes a position similar to that which Peter Brown, his modern biographer, found himself, "led along the side of a mountain-face: I found myself, for instance, above the plains of Augustine's routine duties as a bishop, and far below the heights of his speculations on the Trinity."[21] This study

21. Milbank, *Theology and Social Theory*, 405; Brown, *Augustine of Hippo*, 9.

focuses on the mountain face of Augustine's thought, in between concern over the day-to-day situations of contemporary political life and the highest points of theological speculation, which, while ever present in lived experience, recede indefinitely "towards an infinite and unfathomable God." Or, to repeat the point made in the Preface, this study considers the results of his meditations without providing the details of those meditations.

The study concentrates on the *City of God* but draws from other works as well. This focus is somewhat unorthodox because it runs the risk of over-looking the ways that Augustine changed his mind from one period of his career to the next. For instance, he is generally seen to change his mind re-garding the naturalness of politics between his so-called Neoplatonic period before 400 and later in his career, when he wrote the last twelve books of the *City of God*. Although his affirmation of politics appears diminished in the *City of God*, I attempt to show that his later views are consistent with the earlier ones. Also, the anti-Pelagian polemics that he wrote late in his life, and from which he gained his reputation as the dour "doctor of grace," are referred to sparingly. Some have argued that this period reflects his growing pessimism and that he rules out any basis for seeing political rule as natu-ral. He is called the "doctor of grace" because he argues virtue exists only by grace and not by nature. Space constraints prevent incorporating these writings into the work. Attempting to do so would overburden the study with the task of distinguishing Augustine's rhetoric in these works from his theological position, which is problematic because these arguments are in the form of polemics and letters to his Pelagian interlocutors. They believed that human nature could secure complete human happiness; Augustine objected by arguing that the will cannot heal itself and by emphasizing human beings' radical dependence on God's grace. Therefore, I shall speak of Augustine's position as the one he held until he completed the *City of God* around 426. However, it should be noted that in the anti-Pelagian writings he distinguishes redemptive or subsequent grace from preceding grace, which one might also symbolize as "nature."[22]

Augustine provides a useful lens with which to understand politics because he reflected about the heights and depths of human longings, and incorpo-rated his understanding of the possibilities of human action into his political

---

22. Augustine, "Against Two Letters of the Pelagians," in *Anti-Pelagian Writings*, 2.10.21–22, written ca. 420 A.D.; see also *CD* 8.11.

writings. This study provides primarily a commentary on his political thought, but includes some side glances to general problems about contemporary politics. It has not been bogged down with numerous discussions of contemporary problems because a conversation with one such as Augustine should not produce a "crib" to politics or a political training that attempts to act as a substitute for a political education (to borrow Oakeshott's phrase). Rather, if one eschews the language of "production" in favor of one that focuses on the way that delightful conversation is reflected in political life, then one can say that this study attempts to recover the fundamentals of political order, which can go a small way in assisting the reader to exercise better judgment about political life. The reader will draw his or her own conclusions about the utility of Augustine's thought in understanding the current problems that plague our society.

Two preliminary observations can be suggested, however. The first is that Augustine's thought should lead us neither to despise liberal democracy nor slavishly to celebrate it as the final achievement of human beings. Augustine's thought provides us with a critical lens to understand the corruption brought on by inordinate loves of pleasure and wealth, for example. However, Augustine was always a political minimalist because he understood human beings' capabilities for evil. Thus, anything good that can be obtained, such as liberal freedoms, ought to be cultivated and maintained. Human beings can find a thousand ways to destroy themselves and the things that make them happy, and thus finding a political order that at least provides clean drinking water and functioning public utilities should be maintained and cherished. Considering all that can go wrong (especially when politics is expected to do more than it can handle), Augustine teaches us to be thankful indeed when something goes right. This leads to the second conclusion: Augustine's political thought teaches political moderation and gratitude by teaching patience in light of the human condition where we can be sure of neither our origin nor our future. The freedoms obtained by liberal democracies are dizzying indeed because they leave so much room for things to go wrong. But Augustine provides a way for us to persevere while acknowledging the unknown.

# 1

## POLITICAL RHETORIC

*Of course, the affairs of human beings are not worthy of great seriousness; yet it is necessary to be serious about them. And this is not a fortunate thing. But since we're here, if somehow we would carry out the business in some appropriate way it would perhaps be a well-measured thing for us to do. But whatever am I saying? Someone would perhaps be correct to take me up in this very way.*

—Plato, *Laws*

A UGUSTINE was the professor of rhetoric in Milan before he became a Christian and then a bishop. He had his famous conversion while he held this post, and he tells us in his *Confessions* that he thought it was right to finish out the term before resigning his post and withdrawing from the earthly city. Many of his works, such as the *Confessions* and sermons, are regarded as rhetorical masterpieces, and his *De Doctrina Christiana* constitutes his attempt to synthesize Ciceronian and biblical rhetoric. Despite the extensive scholarship that has been done on the rhetoric of Augustine's theological works, comparatively little has been done on his political rhetoric in the *City of God* beyond demonstrating Augustine's antipolitical rhetoric. One of the reasons for this neglect is that his rhetoric appears so straightforward. He heaps scorn on any and all kinds of political pretensions and leaves little room to doubt that his antipolitical rhetoric is qualified in any way. As a result, modern readers assume that Augustine's work is complete after he "deconstructs" Rome and its morality. However, modern readers overlook his ongoing and implicit conversation with classical philosophers who would also appreciate his antipolitical rhetoric and ironic "praise" of Roman virtues. This and subsequent chapters show that his antipolitical rhetoric of Roman practice veils a deeper affirmation of politics that modern readers overlook when they allow his rhetoric to flatter their own belief that Christianity has solved the political problem of reconciling wisdom and power.[1]

Another possible reason for this neglect is that the *City of God* is a treatise and was written after Augustine had abandoned writing dialogues. The dialogue replicates the dialectical activity of philosophy whereby the words can at best signify only a portion of the truth of the whole, and the unspoken drama of the dialogue communicates as much if not more about the truth than can any individual utterance. Christian revelation in Scripture is often (inaccurately) seen to overcome these limitations of words because the Gospels tell the story of the Word Incarnate. Indirect speech seems to be no longer required because Christ's speech proclaims the truth. The *City of God* appears to replicate Christ's speech in this regard. After Christ, speech, including political speech, no longer seems restricted to Plato's cave, and can be expressed openly and according to the rule of faith (*CD* 10.23, 15.7). Thus, Augustine speaks from the perspective of the forms, as it were, by referring to justice only as supreme justice, meaning that imperfect political justice cannot be justice in the full sense of the word.[2] The truth of the city of God shines out in stark contrast to the utterances and truth claims of the reprobate earthly city whose inhabitants may either repent and accept the truth or reject it.

On the other hand, human existence remains enshrouded in mystery, meaning that language remains a means of signification of realities beyond itself. Our knowledge of the two cities remains perspectival until their final separation, and whatever knowledge we have of the two derives from comparing and contrasting them, and requiring each to regard the other as a model. As Peter S. Hawkins argues:

1. The literature is cited below. Fortin is among the few to notice the constructive role that the philosophically minded play as part of Augustine's audience, and that his argument "presupposes an understanding of political philosophy or of political things as they appear to unaided reason." He also observes that Augustine employed the "art of concealing the truth" ("St. Augustine," 176–79).

2. Fortin explains: "Strange as it may seem to us, Augustine's habit of equating 'justice' with the supreme justice, *summa iusititia* (*CD* 2.21) and 'city' with the perfectly just city has nothing unusual about it. It merely conforms to the general principle that the unqualified noun designates the perfected object. A thing is called good to the extent that it has all that belongs to it by reason of its nature. . . . To speak of a chair *tout court* is the same thing as to speak of a good chair, inasmuch as a defective chair is not a chair in the full sense of the word" ("Justice as the Foundation of the Political Community: Augustine and His Pagan Models (Book IV.4)," 51–52).

Thus, while the force of Augustine's polemic relies on the perception of absolute and "mystical" opposition—of God against gods, of true City against false—he is obliged to admit a countercurrent of confusion. This lies not only in the fact that the two cities occupy a common space and time *in hoc saeculo*, but in the unexpected revelation that the reprobate dominion is, in fact, "something of a model" for the redeemed. Not only do sheep and goats pasture in the same field; the sheep are given an image of themselves as they ought to be in none other than their capric opposites![3]

The former type of interpretation, which is rooted in the forms, explains why Augustine sounds so antipolitical and otherworldly, and the latter, which speaks around the forms, as it were, explains why, in Markus's words, Augustine can, "[w]ithout the least sense of inconsistency . . . assert that Rome, or the *res publica*, is the earthly city, or assume this equation, and then go on to speak in ways which imply the contrary." Further, the former refers to concrete realities or loves whereas the ontological status of the latter's "mystical" or "ideal" types appears unclear precisely because it speaks around them. As Johannes Van Oort explains, this type of interpretation is rooted in the German Protestant tradition of biblical hermeneutics, which emphasizes allegory over literalness and can lose the connection between the two strata of meaning: "In his expositions on the two cities, however, Augustine was not concerned with mere allegories or ideas, nor with a myth, but with real entities. The city of God is the actually existing society of good angels and true believers; its antipole is the truly existing city of Satan, the fallen angels and the unbelievers."[4] This latter method of reading Augustine appears more consistent with Augustine's own description of reading Scripture (discussed below) and would avoid the danger that comes with assuming that one's perspective is that of the forms, a perspective that Augustine warns is that of the demons if it is not also accompanied by love.[5] Yet, Fortin is correct to observe that Augustine's perspective points to a concrete reality that can escape the view of the latter method of interpretation. Thus, this chapter shows how Augustine can simultaneously speak from the perspective of the forms, as it were, and from within the flux of becoming.

3. Hawkins, "Polemical Counterpoint," 97, quoting *CD* 5.18. See also Jeremy Duquesnay Adams, *The "Populus" of Augustine and Jerome: A Study in the Patristic Sense of Community*, 131–35; and Jean-Claude Guy, S.J., *Unité et structure logique de la "Cité de Dieu" de saint Augustin*, 31.
4. Markus, *Saeculum*, 59; Van Oort, *Jerusalem and Babylon: A Study into Augustine's "City of God" and the Sources of His Doctrine of the Two Cities*, 117. For Van Oort, the location of the political city and thus the character of Augustine's political rhetoric is found in what Augustine means by calling the two cities *mystice*, because the question of the goodness of a political city will depend on its relation to these two cities.
5. See *CD* 9.21 and Augustine, *Homilies on the Gospel of John*, 6.21.

Augustine's antipolitical rhetoric is meant to form the passions of identifiable types of people among his readers. His political speech is intended to form the inordinate passions into ordinate love. His rhetoric appears immoderately antipolitical because he considered most of his audience's passion for political glory inordinate and deformed, and his rhetoric is meant to illuminate goods that transcend politics and to demonstrate how political glory insufficiently secures eternal happiness. Augustine shows how the inordinate desires of his audience degenerate into the lust for domination (*libido dominandi*) if the goals of these desires are taken as the greatest human good. This is not the full story of his political teaching, however. This chapter shows how Augustine criticizes the inordinate political passions of his audience. His criticism does not exhaust his substantive political teaching. His affirmation of an ordinate love of political things is examined in subsequent chapters.

The aim of Augustine's antipolitical rhetoric is to tame inordinate political passions and ambitions. He utilizes a dialectic of excess over excess to warn the ambitious of the extremes to which their excessive ambition leads. In so doing, he provides some clues to indicate that he does not deny the goodness of political life altogether. His purpose and hope is to give his readers nothing more than a Platonic education in recognizing the limitations of political life with the hope that they can return to their political duties with moderated ambitions and expectations.

## PASSIONS OF AUDIENCE

Augustine wrote the *City of God* in the midst of the destruction of a world. The haunting image of Augustine dictating the book within earshot of the invading Vandals is a common one. Although he is generally regarded as antipolitical and otherworldly, his immediate purpose in writing the *City of God* was meant to be very much of this world and pastoral. The work was written to answer pagan charges that Christianity was the cause of Rome's collapse. However, Augustine's more immediate concern was generally to console the suffering who wondered why the just and unjust suffer alike, and specifically (*praecipue*) the women who had been raped by the invaders (*CD* 2.2; see also 1.19). Pagan ethics would have shamed these women, and required them to follow the example of Lucretia whose shame at having been raped drove her to commit suicide. Augustine argues that a woman's soul remains pure even if someone defiles her body. He argues that what counts is a pure will, which, in turn, enjoins Christians to cherish and take care of the body, not to commit suicide.

Augustine's justification, however, sounds otherworldly to modern ears because it seems to enjoin a radical interiority by appearing to discount the good of the body as long as the soul remains intact. His political rhetoric suggests an analogous relationship: political peace merely secures bodily goods that have no essential relationship with the soul: "As for this mortal life, which ends after a few days' course, what does it matter under whose rule a man lives, being so soon to die, provided that the rulers do not force him to commit impious and unjust acts?" (CD 5.17).[6] This perception of radical interiority is abolished, however, when we consider the relationship of the will and the body in suffering: "when the good of holy continence does not yield to the impurity of fleshly lusts, it sanctifies the body itself" (CD 1.18). The *City of God* was intended to explain why the just and unjust suffer equally. Incapable of providing a concise philosophical answer, he provides pastoral consolation to the afflicted by telling them that their suffering not only is temporary and minute in the light of the glorious city of God, but also, just as concretely, reorients them within the world. An examination of whether Augustine's attitude to suffering is adequate must lie outside the bounds of this study. It is merely important to note that he responds to this vexing mystery not by advocating withdrawal and "otherworldliness," but by advocating a radical reorientation that affirms one's existence within the world. This general rhetorical strategy then affects his particular political strategy. Forcing his insufferably ambitious audience to suffer (repeatedly, as will be seen) through his long polemic is, analogously, his first step in having them make this turn.

Augustine intended to tame the inordinate love of political glory with his rhetoric. The inordinate love of glory decomposes in several directions such as the love of wealth and the love of domination. Therefore, Augustine directs his attention to several dimensions of the love of glory in order to channel his readers' loves toward a higher good that better secures the ordinate love of glory. The term *gloria* derives from *clara*, meaning clear or shining. Augustine defines it as "clear knowledge together with praise *(clara cum laude notitia)*."[7] God deserves full glory although human beings may be glorified insofar as they imitate God and teach others to imitate God. He tells his audience to love glory by bringing themselves and others to God: " 'it is that [purpose for which] they may glorify your father who is in heaven,' and that they may

6. See Markus, *Saeculum*, 70. For a critique of Markus's position, see Burnell, "Status of Politics," 20.

7. Augustine, "Answer to Maximinus the Arian," 2.13.2.

turn to him and become what you are *(conversi fiant quod estis)"* (*CD* 5.14, paraphrasing Matt. 5:16). The lover of glory is tempted to replace his function of letting his works shine before others as a testimony to the glory of God with an assertion of his own glory. For Augustine, glorying in oneself is actually the lust for domination *(libido dominandi)*, because it causes one to assert oneself over others and to attempt to turn them into one's own exclusive image, instead of that of God. Chapter 5 will present a fuller account of Augustine's understanding of the love of glory and its political dimension. This chapter focuses instead more generally on the passions of his audience, of which glory and the lust for domination are the two most important. Augustine's audience is characterized by five types of love that spring from the inordinate love of glory: (1) the lust for domination, (2) the love of glory proper, (3) Roman patriotism as expressed in their piety for their gods and for the achievements of ancient Rome, (4) the love of glory in the mythologists (my term used for those whom Augustine identifies as opposing Christianity even though they no longer believe the Roman myth nor care for Roman virtues), and (5) the pagan philosophers' love of wisdom. He understood these passions to lie on a continuum between the most inordinate passion, the lust for domination, and the most ordered passion, the love of wisdom. Identifying these passions allows one to see how Augustine attempts either to form those passions (as in the case of the first three passions) or to speak directly to his philosophic friends in the audience.

Augustine focuses on the lust for domination into which the love of glory is in danger of degenerating. He exposes the Romans' pretended love of glory as covering their lust for domination. He admits that the Romans originally had not been ruled by the lust for domination, as their original glory consisted in seeking liberty against their oppressors. This love of liberty was short-lived, however, as the glory of liberty degenerated into the lust for domination when, after successfully defending Rome from external attack, they charged onto the offensive (*CD* 5.12). This lust for domination was present from the beginning and infected the rest of Rome's history. Augustine quotes a fragment of Sallust's criticism of the lust for domination that succeeded early man's life without greed:

> When [Sallust] has touched upon and briefly praised those earlier days when men lived their lives without cupidity and each was satisfied with what he had, he says, "But afterwards, when Cyrus in Asia, and the Lacedaemonians and Athenians in Greece, began to subdue cities and nations, and to consider a lust for domination *(libidenem dominandi)* sufficient ground for war, and

to think that the greatest glory belongs to the greatest empire *(maximam gloriam in maximo imperio)."*[8] *(CD* 3.14)

The Romans, according to their own sources, came to find glory in domination rather than in virtuous deeds.

Augustine quotes Virgil's assertion that the lust for domination became incorporated into the Roman mind. Virgil is important as the most famous and admired of all poets *(omniumque praeclarissimus atque optimus) (CD* 1.3; see also 4.11, 5.12, 8.19, 10.1, 10.27, 15.9, 21.6).[9] Augustine's use of Virgil in this regard is significant because Augustine, at the beginning of the *City of God,* sets up Virgil as the mouthpiece for the earthly city and its hypocrisy. In the preface to book 1, Augustine brings together two similar quotations from the Epistle of James and from the *Aeneid* concerning the necessity to restrain the proud and to pity the humbled. From James 4:6, he quotes: "God resists the proud but gives grace to the humble." He continues: "Indeed, it is this definition, which belongs to God, that the inflated spirit also affects, and dearly loves to be praised for these attributes: 'To spare the fallen and subdue the proud.'"[10] Augustine observes that the earthly city, dominated by the lust for domination, aims at replacing God as the highest good. He concludes here that: "I cannot, in so far as the plan of my understanding demands and my own ability permits, pass over in silence that earthly city which, when it seeks for mastery, though the nations are its slaves, has as its own master that very lust for mastery *(ipsa ei dominandi libido dominantur)."*[11]

These passages from the preface of the *City of God* only set up the problem of the lust for domination, however. Elsewhere, he quotes Virgil giving voice to Jupiter:

> Even the envious Juno
> Who now vexes the sea and the lands and the sky with her terror,
> Shall for the better change her intent, and with me be protectress
> Unto the toga-clad race, the Romans, the masters of all things.

---

8. Quoting Sallust, *"The Conspiracy of Catiline,"* in *"Jugurthine War" and "The Conspiracy of Catiline,"* 2.2.

9. See Harald Hagendahl, *Augustine and the Latin Classics,* 2:458 n. 1. Hagendahl also notes that Augustine in his sermons (see especially *Serm.* 105.7.10) accuses Virgil of flattery and for "selling words to the Romans" (416–17; see also 457). However, Hagendahl also notes that Augustine could treat Virgil as a proto-Christian (388).

10. Quoting Virgil, *The Aeneid* 6.853. These words conclude the speech by Anchises, Aeneas's father, who addresses Aeneas and his men in the Eleusian fields.

11. Hagendahl emphasizes the equation of Rome and the earthly city, dominated by the lust for domination (*Latin Classics,* 2:409–12).

> Thus it is decreed. For an age shall come as the years glide onward
> When Assaracus' house shall enslave the land of Achilles,
> Famous Mycenae to servitude bring, and be lord over Argos.[12]
>
> (*CD* 5.12)

He takes Virgil as a spokesman for Roman aims and ambitions to demonstrate the lust for domination replacing the love of liberty as Rome's highest goal. The lust for domination is reiterated by another passage in Virgil: "The same thought is again expressed in the famous passage of the same poet where, above the arts of the other nations, he gives first place to the peculiarly Roman art of reigning and commanding and subjugating and beating down *(regnandi atque imperandi et subiugandi ac debellandi)* nations in war" (*CD* 5.12). He then quotes Virgil from Anchises' speech that was quoted above:

> Others with tenderer touch shall beat out the bronze to be lifelike.
> That I must grant, for faces that live shall they draw from the marble,
> Cases at law with more eloquence plead, and the pathways of heaven
> Trace with the compass, predict as they rise both the stars and the planets.
> Thy task, O Roman, remember: to rule by thy sceptre the nations.
> Here are the arts to be yours, all the folkways of peace to establish,
> To spare the fallen and to beat down the proud.[13]

The last line repeats the quote from the *Aeneid* that Augustine provides in the preface to the *City of God*. These lines show how Augustine understood the Romans to be dominated by the lust for domination and to believe that domination was their highest glory. The quotations also show that Augustine viewed Roman piety as problematic, for he observes that Jupiter, through the voice of Virgil, commanded these deeds, which meant that Roman civil religion itself made the Romans unjust. I shall examine this point in further detail below when I examine Augustine's treatment of Roman civil religion.

Despite Augustine's emphasis on the lust for domination in the Roman soul, it is doubtful that he thought the Romans purely dominated by it or that this lust was exclusively expressed through the inordinate love of glory. Augustine uses the case of Nero to illustrate that rejecting glory can actually beget the lust for domination and that, perhaps, the love of glory actually prevents worse vices:

---

12. Virgil, *The Aeneid* 1.279–85. Translation taken from *City of God*, Loeb edition. Augustine appears to capture accurately the meaning of the passage. He cites Virgil giving voice to Jupiter proclaiming that the Roman Empire will know no bound, and that there would be born Julius, "whose empire shall reach to the ocean's limits, whose fame shall end in the stars" (1.287–88).

13. Ibid., 6.847–53.

But he who is a despiser of glory, but is greedy for domination *(Qui autem gloriae contemptor dominationis est avidus)*, exceeds the beasts in the vices of cruelty and luxuriousness. Such, indeed, were certain of the Romans, who, though they had lost interest in their reputation, still were not free from their lust for domination; and that there were many such, history testifies. But it was Nero Caesar who was the first to reach the summit, and, as it were, the citadel, of this vice; for so great was his luxuriousness, that one would have thought there was nothing manly to be dreaded in him, and such his cruelty, that, had not the contrary been known, no one would have thought there was anything effeminate in his character. (*CD* 5.19)

The lust for domination culminates in the figure of Nero, who lost his interest in glory and thought himself free from all constraint to impose cruelties on others. This is the point at which the lust for domination eclipses the love of glory, which is a love that, at the very least, made Romans love the judgments of other men (*CD* 5.12), and reinforced a moral code that kept them virtuous and capable of great deeds. The Roman soul, however, appeared vulnerable to being overcome by the lust for domination, because whatever glorified them and led them to be virtuous could not outweigh the lust for domination (however, see Chapter 5).

Turning to the way that Augustine understands his audience to be lovers of glory, one finds that glory is a central theme of the *City of God*. It is proclaimed in the opening words of the work: "Most glorious is and will be the city of God." In the words of Peter Brown, "The *City of God* is a book about 'glory.' "[14] Augustine distinguishes between the glory that human beings owe to God and the glory sought by Romans (including those who sought it inordinately and those who sought it by the true way): "Glory they most ardently loved: for it they wished to live, for it they did not hesitate to die" (*CD* 5.12). He quotes the historian Sallust's assessment: "they were 'greedy of praise, liberal with money, desirous of great glory, and happy with riches honorably gained' " (*CD* 5.12).[15] He observes that the love of glory improves desires in two ways. First, at a minimum this love prevents shameful acts. He quotes Horace advice on how to curb the lust for domination:

> [T]o curb the lust for domination, [Horace] sang:
> Wider will be your realm if you conquer

14. Brown, *Augustine of Hippo*, 311.
15. "[L]audis avidi, pecuniae liberales erant, gloriam ingentem, dividtias honestas volebant," quoting Sallust, *"The Conspiracy of Catiline"* 7.6.

> Greed in your heart, that if to distant Gades [Spain]
> Libya you should join, and the two Punic peoples
> Give to one master.[16]

(CD 5.13)

At a minimum, loving glory can curb the lust for domination. Augustine repeats this observation elsewhere: "Nevertheless, they who restrain baser lusts, not by the power of the Holy Spirit obtained by the faith of piety, or by the love of intelligible beauty, but by desire of human praise, or, at all events, restrain them better by the love of such praise, are not indeed yet holy, but only less base" (CD 5.13). Augustine observes that the love of praise, as a part of the love of glory, can perform a form of social sanction in preventing people from engaging in shameful acts.

The love of glory, however, also accompanies the love of virtue. Citing Sallust again, Augustine asserts: "Praise of a higher kind was bestowed upon Cato, for he says of him, 'The less he sought glory, the more it followed him.' We say praise of a higher kind; for the glory with the desire of which the Romans burned is the judgment of men thinking well of men" (CD 5.12).[17] This leads Augustine to warn his readers that virtue is not to be sought for the sake of glory, although he adds that virtue should be sought by means of glory. Augustine elsewhere provides examples of Roman noble deeds that serve as models of sorts for Christians to follow (CD 5.18), which suggests that the love of glory can motivate virtuous deeds in addition to restraining shameful desires. One might also point to the example of Regulus as a Roman who practiced virtue and loved and received due glory (CD 1.24). The relationship between virtue and glory, with specific reference to Regulus, is explored further in Chapter 5. For now, a sketch of the love of glory of Augustine's audience is the focus of

---

16. Quoting Horace, *The Odes in Latin and English* 2.2.9–12. Augustine's interpretation of this passage appears accurate. Horace advocates virtue because it teaches a man to stand firm against his desires: "And laurel wreath / to him alone / Who can a treasured mass of gold / With firm *(inretorto)* / undazzled eye behold" (26–28). Hagendahl argues that Augustine took Horace as a moral authority: "Augustine attached special importance to the contents of the passages quoted. He was evidently an admirer of the general sayings and moral maxims wherein Horace excels" (*Latin Classics,* 2:465).

17. Citing Sallust, *"The Conspiracy of Catiline"* 54.6. Augustine slightly distorts the meaning of the text. This is the entire sentence from which Augustine quotes only the second clause: "[Cato] preferred to be, rather to seem, virtuous; hence *(ita)* the less he sought glory, the more it followed him." Sallust does not state that Cato did not seek glory, but rather that being virtuous was more important for Cato than appearing virtuous. This does not mean that Cato did not seek glory as a good that accompanies true virtue. Sallust earlier had stated that one of the goods that Cato sought was propriety *(decor)*, which means gracefulness and nobility, and would constitute the public expression of virtue, that is, glory.

discussion. Glory is indeed a good (but not the highest good), and so can be sought viciously and can be transformed into the lust for domination, as shown above. Augustine cites Sallust, who claims that glory can be gained either by virtue or by vice: " 'For glory, honor, and power are desired alike by the good man and by the ignoble; but the former,' he says, 'strives onward to them by the true way *(vera via)* while the other, knowing nothing of the good arts, seeks them by fraud and deceit' " *(CD* 5.12; see also 5.19).[18]

Augustine also appeals to the piety of his audience by relating it to their love of glory:

> This, rather, is the religion worthy of your desires, O admirable Roman race—the progeny of your Scaevolas and Scipios, of Regulus, and of Fabricius. . . . If there is in your nature any eminent virtue *(Si quid in te laudabile naturaliter eminet)*, only by true piety is it purged and perfected, while by impiety it is wrecked and punished. Choose now what you will pursue, that your praise may be not in yourself, but in the true God, in whom is no error. . . . Awake more fully *(evigila plenius)*: the majesty of God cannot be propitiated by that which defiles the dignity of man. *(CD* 2.29)

Augustine uses the Roman love of glory to suggest that Christianity is a religion worthy of the esteem of the great noble Romans. The strategy of claiming that a certain principle or act is becoming of someone of a noble family was one of the ways ancient Romans persuaded each other to practice virtue. For example, J. E. Lendon notes: "[T]he greater a man's honour, the higher his position in society, the more people watched him, and the more he felt his actions hemmed in by his own rank. . . . To remind a man of the glory of his family and his need to act in accord with it was a usual way of pressing him on to action; the unwelcome requests of a distinguished man could be beaten off by sharply pointing out that they did not accord with his dignity."[19] According to Lendon, the Roman world was bound together by a web of patronage and benefactions, and the place and power of any one individual depended on the honor bestowed on him. Augustine appears to take advantage of this dimension of the Roman love of glory to show how dishonorable the Roman civil religion was.

Augustine also appealed to the Roman veneration and piety of their gods and their ancestors. For example, in the above quotation, he appeals to the Roman's veneration of their ancestors in order to show that Christianity is a religion worthy of the honor of their families and of Roman piety in general.

---

18. Quoting Sallust, *"The Conspiracy of Catiline"* 11.1–2.
19. Lendon, *Empire of Honour: The Art of Government in the Roman World,* 39.

Augustine appeals to the Romans' patriotism and religious piety to show that he acknowledges the virtue of his audience. First, he acknowledges their pride in their past by choosing Sallust, who glorified the early history of Rome, for his source of Roman history. He praises Sallust for being a great historian renowned for his veracity *(nobilitatae veritatis historicus) (CD* 1.5). Sallust argued that Rome began its degeneration after it began to grow, due to lust for empire and wealth.[20] Augustine notes Sallust's saying of the ancient Romans: "the just and the good *(ius bonumque)* prevailed among the Romans not more by force of laws than of nature" *(CD* 2.17).[21]

Along with their piety toward their ancestors, Augustine appeals to the piety that the Romans held toward their gods. Brown observes of Augustine's audience: "Like men who put their money in a safe foreign bank, these last pagans were anxious to invest their beliefs in a distant, golden past, untroubled by the rise of Christianity. . . . These men were deeply religious. They could compete with the Christians in their firm belief in rewards and punishments after death."[22] Augustine attempts to direct their piety toward Christianity (the source of true glory for Augustine) by making them recognize the depravity of current Roman religious practices. He ridicules debased Roman ceremonies. He describes how Berecynthia (also called Rhea, or Cybele), the mother of the gods, was worshiped by the singing of songs whose obscenity would have embarrassed the mothers of the singers had they heard them *(CD* 2.4). Augustine points out that even though Scipio Nascia was chosen by the Senate as the citizen most worthy to receive the image of Berecynthia, he would not have wished even to have had his mother receive the "honors" that she would receive were she a goddess:

> Surely he would desire that his mother should enjoy such felicity were it possible. But if we proceeded to ask him whether, among the honours paid to her, he would wish such shameful rites as these to be celebrated, would he not at once exclaim that he would rather his mother lay stone-dead, than survive as a goddess to lend her ear to these obscenities? Is it possible that he who was of so severe a morality, that he used his influence as a

20. Augustine's admiration for Sallust's abilities as a historian and as a moral teacher seem genuine despite Sallust's tendency to give Roman origins a whitewash. Hagendahl thought that Sallust provides Augustine "with a moralizing interpretation of Rome's history, which suited him so much that he made it entirely his own" *(Latin Classics,* 2:637).

21. Quoting Sallust, *"The Conspiracy of Catiline"* 9.1. Augustine caustically adds that this equity and virtue must have led them to rape the Sabine women. This passage is discussed in more detail below.

22. Brown, *Augustine of Hippo,* 301.

Roman senator to prevent the building of a theatre in that city dedicated to the manly virtues, would wish his mother to be propitiated as a goddess with words which would have brought the blush to her cheek when a Roman matron? Could he possibly believe that the modesty of an estimable woman would be so transformed by her promotion to divinity, that she would suffer herself to be invoked and celebrated in terms so gross and immodest, that if she had heard the like while alive upon earth, and had listened without stopping her ears and hurrying from the spot, her relatives, her husband, and her children would have blushed for her? Therefore, the mother of the gods being such a character as the most profligate man would be ashamed to have for his mother, and meaning to enthral the minds of the Romans, demanded for her service their best citizen, not to ripen him still more in virtue by her helpful counsel, but to entangle him by her deceit. (CD 2.5)

He contrasts the base mother of the gods with the magnanimous (*magnae indolis animus*) Scipio Nascia. This statement shows Augustine appealing to the piety of Rome's great men toward their city, families, and virtue in order to teach them that their civil religion undermines their own virtue.

Behind the political men stand the mythologists and ultimately the philosophers. Mythologists include the historians and poets who use, create, and defend the false civil religion, and the philosophers are those who love wisdom but prudently mute their criticism of the civil religion. These two groups are crucial members of Augustine's audience because his treatment of their loves indicates how he understands the relationship between the love of glory and the love of wisdom. Mythologists glory in their own achievement, and philosophers glory in wisdom. Their loves disclose the extent to which the pagan mind could practice virtue according to Augustine. Their importance is indicated in a letter to Firmus, who circulated the *City of God:* "As a scholarly man you are not unaware how much repeated reading helps one to understand what is read. For there is no difficulty in understanding or at least very little, where there is ease in reading, and this becomes greater as the text is used over and over again" (*Ep.* 231A).

Augustine distinguishes between the passions that motivate mythologists and those of the philosophers. Mythologists included Rome's literati and perhaps also Rome's historians. Augustine states that their glory resides in the supposed benefits that they claim they bestow onto men: "There are most learned and acute men who glory (*gloriantur*) in the great benefit that they have performed, because they have written books which teach men to know why each god should be supplicated and what is to be sought from each"

(*CD* 6.1).[23] Such mythologists prefer human glory to wisdom. They are further troublesome because they blame the Christian religion for the collapse of Rome and other calamities, and they stir up the uninstructed to attack Christians. Their problem, as Augustine saw it, was that their glorying in their vanity outweighed their love of truth: "For it is esteemed the glory of vanity *(gloria vanitatis)* to concede nothing to the force of truth even when he who is dominated by so gross a fault perishes thereby. The disease remains unconquered despite all the industry of the physician, for the patient is incurable" (*CD* 6.pref.; see also *CD* 2.1, 4.1, 5.26, 18.51). He considered their misuse of reason to be rooted in their preference to glory in vanity rather than wisdom and virtue.

Evidence suggests that Augustine believed the presence of this vice prevents non-Christians from practicing true virtue. He appears to admit that non-Christian philosophers, as opposed to mythologists, truly love wisdom and truly seek to improve the morals of their fellow human beings. Indeed, philosophers appear to be the most important members of his audience, the ones who deserve the greatest attention (*CD* 6.1, 10.1). Augustine states of Plato: "But among the disciples of Socrates, Plato was the one who shone with a glory *(gloria claruit)* which far excelled that of the others, and who, not unjustly *(non quidem inmerito)*, eclipsed them all" (*CD* 8.4). This statement is important because it shows that Plato's glory was just. It is also significant because, as far as I have been able to determine, Augustine never states that Plato (as distinguished from his followers) actually sought glory at the expense of virtue. Plato's true virtue is reflected in Augustine's comment that the philosopher is the one who loves God: "[N]othing shines forth *(flagrat)* more than that in those sacred scriptures" (*CD* 8.11). Plato's glory resembled that of Cato: "The less he sought glory, the more it followed him" (*CD* 5.12). Similarly, the Platonists are "praised as having most closely followed Plato, who is rightly preferred to all the other philosophers of the Gentiles" (*CD* 8.4; see also 8.6). Augustine argues that unlike the teachings of the mythologists who portray themselves as upholding popular morals, Plato's dialogues were really meant to improve the morals of the Athenians. He points out that Plato, in his *Republic*, removes the poets and prohibits the worship of demons from his republic; he observes too that Plato often concealed his true views (*CD* 8.21; see also 8.4, 14).

The virtue of the philosophers is rare, as it depends on their ability to purify their souls to understand things as they are. Although Augustine does not write

23. Augustine also calls Varro "most skilled and acute," but, as shown below, he appears to exclude Varro from the category of mythologist.

for a secret sect, he appears to assume that some readers, by their virtue, will be able to apprehend truth spiritually:

> For God speaks with a human being not by means of some audible creature dinning in his ears, so that atmospheric vibrations connect Him that makes with him that hears the sound, nor even by means of a spiritual being with the semblance of a body, such as we see in dreams or similar states; for even in this case He speaks as if to the ears of the body, because it is by means of the semblance of a body He speaks, and with the appearance of a real interval of space—for visions are exact representations of bodily objects. Not by these, then, does God speak, but rather by the truth itself, if anyone is prepared to hear with the mind *(mente)* rather than with the body. For He speaks to that part of man which is better than all else that is in him, and than which God Himself alone is better. *(CD* 11.2; see also 16.6)

The ability of a few to understand in this mode requires Augustine to engage in a different form of communication from that which he uses for other readers. Discussing the same problem in Augustine's *On the Trinity,* John Cavadini describes the sort of reader, one of the "few," whom Augustine addresses:

> These people, some of whom can be glimpsed by name in the Letters, would know (or in Augustine's view be capable of knowing) that "knowledge" or "understanding" of that which is uncreated and eternal consists in a sort of intellectual "seeing" or "vision" of it, one which involved a mode of thinking completely free of images or of any mental construct applicable to the creature, much as Augustine himself had learned from his first reading of Plotinus. The "few" would also realize (or at least be expected to grasp) that the mind could be "exercised" in this image-free thought through a process of step-by-step ("gradatim") "ascent" from the consideration of physical things, to that of finite spiritual things, to the eventual vision of things eternal. Such an "ascent" would also represent a turning inward as one passes from bodily things to the things of the soul and mind. In short, the "few" whom Augustine expected might understand his treatise would be those familiar with a standard Plotinian and especially Porphyrian characterization of the "return" of the soul to contemplation or noesis.[24]

Augustine, then, acknowledges real philosophers in his audience who seek, in their way, the salvation of their souls, and perhaps would, like him, help to constitute the city of God in its pilgrimage on earth.

---

24. Cavadini, "The Structure and Intention of Augustine's *De Trinitate,*" 104–5.

This is not to say that the ascent described in *De Trinitate* culminates in perfect knowledge. Cavadini, for instance, argues that Augustine's description of the ascent is meant to demonstrate that such attempts to understand God will fail. The wisdom gained, however, is not negligible. As Rowan Williams suggests, Augustine argues that "the *image* of God in us, properly so called, is not 'the mind' in and to itself (whatever that is—he will effectively dismiss such a notion in the final stages of his argument) but the mind of the saint—the awareness of someone reflectively living out the life of justice and charity." For Augustine, "God cannot be sought without the seeker seeking and finding, wanting and holding to, the creaturely incompleteness, the exigence and expectancy, that *eros* represents. Before we can want God, we must know and want our wanting nature."[25] Williams's second statement is consistent with the position developed below in Chapter 6 that Augustine thought non-Christian philosophers could maintain this reflection on eros even though his criticisms of pagan philosophers indicate that they are sorely tempted to leap out of this tension and proclaim they know God (see *CD* 8.5).

## STRATEGY OF DIALECTIC OF EXCESS OVER EXCESS

Turning now to Augustine's rhetorical strategy of forming these passions, we see that Augustine employs a strategy of using excessive rhetoric in order to demonstrate to certain members of his audience how their own immoderation undermines their own attempt to find happiness. He employs this strategy because he thought that the Roman loves for political glory (by statesmen and "mythologists"), their past, and their gods (expressed as piety) degenerate or are vulnerable to degeneration into the lust for dominion *(libido dominandi)*. This leads him to draw the sharpest contrast between political ends (possibly identifying them with the earthly city) and the transcendent end of the city of God, while implicitly admitting that they are not so distinct.[26] It leads him to argue that the Roman civil religion is false while admitting his agreement with some pagan philosophers.

Augustine speaks in two voices when he discusses the city of God and the earthly city. Generally speaking, he defines the city of God as the city that

25. R. Williams, "Paradoxes of Self-Knowledge," 131, 133.

26. This strategy can be profitably compared with what he elsewhere calls the principles of Christian healing, the principles of similarity and contrariety (*DDC* 1.27). These principles are examined with reference to coercion in Chapter 7.

glorifies God, and the earthly city as that which glorifies itself. Before identifying either of the two cities with any institution, Augustine identifies them with their corresponding loves. One loves God for his own sake, the other loves itself and uses God (or its gods) for its own purposes:

> The two cities then were created by two kinds of love: the earthly city by a love of self *(amor sui)* carried even to the point of contempt for God *(contemptum Dei)*, the heavenly city by a love of God *(amor Dei)* carried even to the point of contempt for self *(contemptum sui)*. Consequently, the earthly city glories in itself while the other glories in the Lord. For the former seeks glory *(gloriam)* from men, but the latter finds its greatest glory in God, from the testimony of conscience. (*CD* 14.28)

The two cities are rooted in the order of loves.

That being the case, Augustine occasionally identifies the city of God with the Church *(ecclesia)*, and he often speaks of "our God" and "our authors" in opposition to "their gods" and "their authors" (*CD* 8.24, 11.1, 13.16, 15.26, 16.2; see also 17.4, 20.11). Augustine speaks in this way to suggest that true virtue and true worship exist only in the Christian Church and only as a result of worshiping Christ. He often contrasts the city of God as *ecclesia* with the earthly city as the political city (in other words, including actual cities such as Rome). For example, he often compares Rome with Babylon, which is the paradigmatic earthly city.[27] Hagendahl observes that in the first ten books of the *City of God* (generally interpreted by scholars as the "critical" part of the work compared with the last twelve books that are more expository), Rome is the earthly city: "In the first ten books the *civitas terrena* is the heathen *imperium Romanum*; from the eleventh book onwards, this conception, although not entirely absent, falls into the background and gives way to a conception of a *genus hominum qui secundum hominem vivunt* ('a type of human being who lives according to human beings') in opposition to those *qui secundum Deum vivunt* ('who live according to God')."[28] Augustine also calls Cain the founder of the earthly city and compares this founding with that of Rome by Romulus and Remus, going so far as to call both foundings an archetype of crime: "So that we cannot be surprised that this first specimen, or, as the Greeks say, archetype of crime, should, long afterwards, find a corresponding crime at the foundation of that city which was destined to reign over so many nations, and be the head of this earthly city of which we speak" (*CD* 15.5).

27. In general, see Van Oort, *Jerusalem and Babylon*, 127–31.
28. Hagendahl, *Latin Classics*, 2:410–11.

Despite appearing to identify the two cities with the *ecclesia* on the one hand and the political city on the other hand, Augustine speaks of this *saeculum* as the time when the two cities are intermingled and intermixed, which implies that the two cities coexist both in the Church and in the political city. For example, he argues: "In truth, these two cities are entangled together in this world, and intermixed until the last judgment effects their separation" (*CD* 1.35). Later, he says: "And now, in fulfillment of the promise I made in the first book, I shall go on to say, as God shall aid me, what I think needs to be said regarding the origin, history, and deserved ends of the two cities, which, as already remarked, are in this world intermingled and intermixed *(invicemque permixtas)* with one another" (*CD* 10.32; see also, 11.1, 11.34, 12.1, 14.28, 15.1, 15.22, 16.11, 18.1, 18.54). He also observes that the "mystery of iniquity" refers to the number of wicked people and hypocrites who are in the Church, which shows how the Church itself is mixed (*CD* 20.19, quoting 2 Thess. 2:1–12).

The meaning of the two cities relates to Augustine's rhetorical strategy, which he derives from Scripture. In the *City of God*, he imitates Scripture in illuminating and glorifying the city of God in contrast to the earthly city. Neither, according to Augustine, presents a comprehensive historical account. Scripture's account of the two cities is governed by figurative, not literal, meanings. Commenting on whether there were righteous persons outside the biblical narrative of the generations from Noah to Abraham, he asserts:

> I do not conclude that there were none; but it had been tedious to mention everyone, and would have displayed historical accuracy *(historica)* rather than prophetic foresight *(prophetica providentia)*. The object of the writer of these sacred books, or rather of the Spirit of God in him, is not only to record the past, but to depict the future, so far as it regards the city of God; for whatever is said of those who are not its citizens, is given either for her instruction, or as a foil to enhance her glory. Yet we are not to suppose that all that is recorded has some signification; but those things which have no signification of their own are interwoven for the sake of the things which are significant. It is only the ploughshare that cleaves the soil; but to effect this, other parts of the plough are requisite. (*CD* 16.2)

This passage indicates that Augustine saw the purpose of the biblical narrative, and thus the purpose of his own account of the two histories, not exclusively as a historical retelling of events, but as a way of glorifying the city of God in contrast to the earthly city.

Augustine's theory of signification, which the above passage reflects, lies well beyond the scope of this study, but it is necessary to comment on how it affects his understanding of the two cities as mystical. His understanding clarifies the passions of his audience and the rhetoric he uses to communicate to his audience. His symbols of the two cities would be meaningless if they were merely ideal, unrealizable types (the type criticized by Van Oort, as described above), meant exclusively to glorify the city of God instead of also signifying it. Their use would be merely polemical and not substantive because the glory of the city of God would arise merely from the degeneracy of its opposite type. If Augustine were merely using the symbols as ideal types, his rhetorical strategy as a political strategy would have the same substance as ideological movements that define themselves in opposition to their "counter-idea," as Voegelin once called it, that, as the source of evil, define the ideological movement while constantly threatening it.[29] The motivating force of this construction would be resentment, as Nietzsche puts it in his *Genealogy of Morals,* rather than the love of God.

Augustine's motivations can be better understood by examining his statements on his method of writing. He claims to have written the *City of God* according to the "rules of faith" that are more constrictive than methods governing the dialogic writings of the philosophers: "For philosophers use words freely *(liberis),* and in matters that are most difficult to understand they are not overly careful to avoid giving offence to religious ears *(religiosarum aurium).* But religion requires me to follow a fixed rule *(certam regulam)* in my use of language, for fear that some verbal licence may give rise to a mistaken view, contrary to religious truth, of the matters to which the words refer" (*CD* 10.23; see also 15.7). He states that he must obey the fixed rules of faith by which one writes according to piety rather than in a philosophic way that may give rise to impious opinions.[30]

Augustine's rhetorical strategy is reflected in his calling the two cities "mystical *(mystice)"* (*CD* 15.1); he calls Jerusalem a mystical name, and he speaks of mystical Babylon (*CD* 18.11, 18.41). The term *mystice* means generally secret or hidden (for example, see *CD* 20.19), and he speaks of the mystic foreshadowings of God's truth (*CD* 10.24, 10.32, 11.23, 11.33, 17.6, 17.10, 17.14, 18.11, 18.23,

---

29. Voegelin, *Race and State,* 2.7.

30. Augustine discusses the rules of faith in *On Christian Teaching.* It is important to note, however, that these rules of faith are not themselves literal statements. Commenting on *DDC,* Mark D. Jordan states: "So the rule of faith must stand outside the circle of literal and figurative, of signs and things. Nothing can be taught without signs; no sign can be recognized as such without knowing the thing it signifies. The rule of faith, to escape this regress, must be a *thing which teaches itself.* This is what was implied above in saying that God made Himself our way to beatitude. The rule of faith must be transparent, self-proclaiming" ("Words and Word: Incarnation and Signification in Augustine's *De Doctrina Christiana,"* 190–91; emphasis in original).

20.10) as well as pagan mystical rites and significations (*CD* 2.8, 8.27, 10.21). He equates mystical meanings with figurative meanings in his *On Christian Teaching*: "An unfamiliarity with numbers makes unintelligible many things that are said figuratively *(translate)* and mystically *(mystice)* in scripture" (*DDC* 2.62). In the *City of God*, he specifies the purpose of literal and figurative expressions: "For in the style of prophecy, figurative and literal expressions are mingled, so that a sober examination may be useful and salutary labour attain to the spiritual meaning, while carnal sloth or the sluggishness of an uninstructed and unexercised mind may be content with the superficial and literal meaning and think that nothing deeper need be sought" (*CD* 20.21). Literal and figurative expressions are meant to exercise the mind, making it better able, through purification, to understand spiritual meanings.

Augustine describes the process of purification in *On Christian Teaching*. He outlines seven steps of spiritual ascent whereby the mind is cleansed to the point that it reaches true wisdom. Fear of God constitutes the first step: "This fear will necessarily inspire reflection about our mortality and future death, and by nailing our flesh to the wood of the cross as it were crucify our prideful impulses *(superbiae motus)*" (*DDC* 2.16). As we shall see, fear of God and, along with it, dread of one's mortality lie behind Augustine's rhetorical strategy, which is meant to inspire reflection on human limitations. As shown above, Augustine addresses the "prideful impulses" of his readers. The prideful are not restricted to the utterly reprobate. They include those whose inadequate intellectual and moral virtue prevents them from completely understanding the figurative meaning of Scripture and loving God. Augustine is more likely to address those who are neither wholly vicious nor wholly virtuous, but rather, like most of us, struggle with our sinfulness to live a virtuous life. These are the carnal auditors. Such people require a multiplicity of rhetorical devices to teach and inspire them. Augustine identifies three types of style: grand, restrained, and moderate (*DDC* 4.104). Grand style is intended to drive unwilling auditors to action, restrained style teaches, and moderate style praises. The *City of God* utilizes all three types of rhetoric, and Augustine invokes the grand style to inspire readers to the life of virtue. He explains how Scripture utilizes these kinds of methods by, for example, symbolizing God as wrathful and thus changeable: "But if Scripture were not to use such expressions, it would not come home so intimately, as it were, to all mankind, for whom it chooses to take thought. For only in this way can it frighten the proud, arouse the remiss, keep the curious occupied and provide nourishment for the wise; nor would it succeed in doing this if it did not first incline and come down, as it were, to the lowly" (*CD* 15.25). Elsewhere, Augustine not only says that God speaks directly to one's mind and does not use images and sights, but also says that God thundered *(intonare)* his prohibition against worshiping false gods in his law (*CD* 19.23). Using tropes such as wrath and thunder is rhetoric in the grand style.

In the ascent to true wisdom, the mind is increasingly purified until the sixth stage is reached wherein the reader is so "single-minded and purified that he will not be deflected from the truth either by an eagerness to please men or by the thought of avoiding any of the troubles which beset him in this life" (*DDC* 2.23). Of the seventh and final stage of wisdom, which few reach, Augustine states simply that it is "enjoyed by those who are calm and peaceful." He elsewhere describes such a person's prodigious wisdom and knowledge of Scripture:

> Therefore a person strengthened by faith, hope, and love, and who stead-fastly holds on to them, has no need of the scriptures except to instruct others. That is why many people, relying on these three things, actually live in solitude without any texts of the scriptures. They are, I think, a fulfillment of the saying "If there are prophecies, they will lose their meaning; if there are tongues, they will cease; if there is knowledge *(scientia)* that too will lose its meaning." (*DDC* 1.93, quoting 1 Cor. 13:8; see also, *Conf.* 13.15)

Augustine argues that the person who has painstakingly gone through Scripture, and who has ascended to wisdom, can dispense with Scripture because he or she knows its mystical meanings, and perhaps embodies the city of God. By the grace of God, such a person would understand truth intellectually rather than in the form of sounds or bodies (*CD* 11.2; see also 16.6).

Augustine's two ways of speaking of the city of God and the earthly city make sense in light of the distinction among his readers. Carnal readers dominated by the lust for domination will more likely have to be told that the city of God is the Church because that holds out the best hope for taming their prideful ambitions. They will hear that happiness consists not in politics but only through submission to Christ and community in the Church. More virtuous readers will learn that the two cities actually refer to the dominant loves and that the two cities intermingle in the Church and the political city. The latter group constitutes a greater hope that the political city might be more justly governed. This strategy of speaking in two different ways (though speaking the same substantial truth) accords with Augustine's statement in the *Confessions* on the character of perfect writing: "Certainly—and I say this fearlessly and from my heart—if I had to write with such vast authority I should prefer to write that my words should mean whatever truth anyone could find upon these matters, rather than express one true meaning so clearly as to exclude all others, though these contain no falsehood to offend me" (*Conf.* 12.31). By identifying the differing virtues and vices of his readers, and the degree to which they can understand spiritual truths, Augustine writes in a way he hopes is accessible to everyone and conveys (by different means) the truth to everyone (see also *DDC* 3.59). He does not restrict the truth to a small, mystical sect by closing off truth to everyone else. Rather, his rhetoric is meant to be directed toward people possessing differing degrees of intelligence and different passions. Most important, for Augustine, the message delivered to the spiritually minded and that delivered to the carnally minded are of the same essence, so his audience cannot be divided into an inner elite and a manipulated mass of outsiders.[31] Indeed, he criticizes the Romans for engaging in this practice (*CD* 2.6). Thus, Augustine's strategy of taming the lust for domination by contrasting the glory of the city of God with the evil of the earthly city does not replace one form of lust for domination with an ecclesiastical lust for domination, one that serves the interests of an inner elite. Having examined Augustine's two kinds of usages of the cities of God and the earthly city—one that appears to identify the two cities with a corresponding institution or set of institutions, and the other treating each city as signifying a specific love (and thus not identifying any one institution with each love)—I turn to the strategy he employs to reform love of glory.

Augustine tends to downplay the goodness of glory. For example, he states that even though the love of glory inspired the Romans to perform awesome deeds, the love of praise at best prevented certain vices from arising: "However,

31. The difference between Augustine's rhetoric and that found in ideological states requires emphasis given the preponderance of ideological thinking in the twentieth century. Kenneth Minogue calls the latter the "onion" theory of totalitarian party organization in which the "language of the ideology is designed to have different meanings according as it is addressed to an inner core guiding the movement, the rank and file of party members, a peripheral layer of fellow travelers, or the world outside" (*Alien Powers: The Pure Theory of Ideology*, 123). For Augustine, virtue is not identified with any one institution, and in the case of which truths the virtuous discern and which the less virtuous receive, the difference is not in different truths each group receives, but in figurative and literal meanings. Figurative and literal meanings differ not in the essence of the truth conveyed, but rather in the manner they are communicated. This being the case, Augustine's rhetorical strategy helps to guard against the other side of ideologies (according to Minogue) that consists in a perpetual removal of mystifications and masks: "[Ideologies] consist in revealing discernible truths which others would prefer us not to know. The general secret revealed by ideologies is that all relationships within the chosen structure are fundamentally power relationships" (124). Minogue identifies Marx as the practitioner par excellence of this art: "At every level, Marx is a master of the occult revelation, and it emerges most clearly in that parade of familiar metaphors about ripping off masks, revealing what things reflect or represent, seeing through smokescreens and penetrating veils" (127). These comments help us to view Augustine's own metaphors of removing masks in context (see below).

men who do not obtain the gift of the Holy Spirit and bridle their baser passions by pious faith and by love of intelligible beauty, at any rate live better because of their desire for human praise and glory *(melius saltem cupiditate humanae laudis et gloriae)*. While these men are not saints, to be sure, they are less vile *(minus turpes sunt)*" *(CD* 5.13). The love of human praise and glory prevented vices such as luxuriousness from arising, but it does not appear to be a true virtue. Later, Augustine states that "to him who possesses virtues it is a great virtue to despise glory" *(CD* 5.19) because such a desire for glory can lead to lust for domination: "[I]t is an easy step for one who finds excessive delight in human glory to conceive also an ardent affection for domination. . . . It follows that anyone who covets glory either strives 'by the true path,' or at least 'pushes ahead by treachery and deceit,' wishing to appear good though he is not" *(CD* 5.19; see also 5.12).[32] Instead of loving human glory, it is better to love God and to despise glory: "And therefore virtue is better, which is content with no human judgment save that of one's own conscience. Whence the apostle says, 'For this is our glory, the testimony of our conscience' " *(CD* 5.12, quoting 2 Cor. 1:12). Augustine's rhetoric suggests that virtue consists of despising human glory. Later, evidence will be shown that this is not the case. At this point, however, he appears to deny the possibility of such an ordinate love and instead indicates that the love of human glory is in continual danger of degenerating into the lust for domination.

This rhetorical skepticism explains Augustine's apparent rejection of politics as a natural good. We find an example of this apparent rejection in his discussion of an anecdote that he borrows from Cicero's *De Re Publica* (3.14.24; see *CD* 4.4). The anecdote relates an alleged encounter between Alexander the Great and a pirate he seized. Augustine argues that their conversation teaches a political lesson. Alexander is said to have asked the pirate why he wrongfully took possession of the sea. The pirate answered: "The same as you when you molest the world! But I do it with a little ship, and I am called a thief *(latro)*; you do it with a great fleet, and are called an emperor." The anecdote appears to disclose the nature of politics:

> And justice removed *(Remota itaque iustita)*, what are kingdoms *(regna)* except great robberies *(latrocinia)*? For what are robberies themselves, but little kingdoms? The band is made up of men; it is ruled by the authority of a prince, it is knit together by the pact of confederacy; the booty is divided by the law agreed on. If, by the admittance of abandoned men, this evil

32. Quoting Sallust, *"The Conspiracy of Catiline"* 11.1–2.

increases to such a degree that it holds places, fixes abodes, takes possession
of cities, and subdues peoples, it assumes the more plainly the name of a
kingdom. (*CD* 4.4)

In one masterful stroke, Augustine reduces the greatest pretensions to glory of
the emperor to the same essence as that of the schemes of a petty pirate by
calling both of their establishments robberies. This reflects his principle in *On
Christian Teaching* that the fear of God requires that one's prideful impulses
be undermined, as Augustine here provides a mirror for the emperor, and the
emperor is forced to see a petty and inglorious pirate. Augustine also in one
broad stroke appears to characterize the foundation and history of political
societies as a history of robberies that are legitimated by their own successes.
There are many historical examples that substantiate his point.

However, that is not the whole story. For instance, it is significant that
Augustine begins the passage quoted above with a condition: "And justice
removed." His treatment of Rome and of politics in general indicates that justice
is never completely removed. In fact, even though he later appears to agree
with Cicero's Scipio that the Roman republic was never a republic because it
never possessed perfect justice, he admits that a "more plausible" definition
of a republic would include semblances and degrees of justice (*CD* 2.21). As
shown below, that admission opens the door to the possibility that the passage
quoted above is rhetorical and meant to temper the inordinate love of glory by
stripping the emperor of his robes and exposing the pirate outfit underneath.

Augustine undermines Roman piety toward its ancestors, history, and great
historical achievements by providing evidence, including the statements of its
own authors, that early Rome was corrupt, despite the pious view that Rome
became corrupt only during the imperial period. As Milbank observes, the *City
of God* deconstructs Roman history and morality by showing how it fails to live
up to even its own standards.[33] Augustine quotes a passage from Sallust that
taints the glory of the early Romans:

> I will therefore pause, and adduce the testimony of Sallust himself, whose
> words in praise of the Romans (that "equity and virtue prevailed among
> them not more by force of laws than of nature") have given occasion to this
> discussion. He was referring to that period immediately after the expulsion
> of the kings, in which the city became great in an incredibly short space of
> time. And yet this same writer acknowledges in the first book of his *History,*

---

33. Milbank, *Theology and Social Theory,* 389.

in the very exordium of his work, that even at that time, when a very brief interval had elapsed after the government had passed from kings to consuls, the more powerful men began to act unjustly, and occasioned the defection of the people from the patricians, and other disorders in the city. (*CD* 2.18)

Augustine observes that even the great historian Sallust, the great proponent of the view that early Rome was virtuous, notes its degeneracy during its alleged glorious period. Augustine continues by quoting Sallust's narrative of Rome's degeneracy after the destruction of Carthage: " 'Yet, after the destruction of Carthage, discord, avarice, ambition, and the other vices which are commonly generated by prosperity, more than ever increased.' If they 'increased,' and that 'more than ever,' then already they had appeared, and had been increasing." Then Augustine provides Sallust's reason for this "increase":

> "For," he says, "the oppressive measures of the powerful, and the consequent secessions of the plebs from the patricians, and other civil dissensions, had existed from the first, and affairs were administered with equity and well-tempered justice for no longer a period than the short time after the expulsion of the kings, while the city was occupied with the serious Tuscan war and Tarquin's vengeance." You see how, even in that brief period after the expulsion of the kings, fear, he acknowledges, was the cause of the interval of equity and good order. (*CD* 2.18)

Augustine concludes his commentary with this passage: "You see what kind of men the Romans were, even so early as a few years after the expulsion of the kings; and it is of these men he says, that 'equity and virtue prevailed among them not more by force of law than of nature' " (ibid.).

Fear was the root of Rome's "equity and virtue" in its glorious period, and the myths and histories that detailed its subsequent glories masked this core fear with tales of Rome's early justice. In this way, Augustine undermines Roman piety toward its past by showing how its past, its traditions, were based upon injustice. He elsewhere criticizes the desire to see perfection in the past when he comments on Ps. 33: "Do you not complain every day, saying: 'How much longer are we to put up with all this? Every day things go from bad to worse; in our parents' times the days were happier and better.' Oh, if you were to ask those parents of yours, they would make the same complaint about their days. . . . It is not here that he must look for good days. He is looking for a good thing, but not in the right direction" (*EnP* 33.2.17). The myths and histories of the Roman past are based on this kind of seeking of a "good thing," but they look in the wrong direction. Because the illusion of a Roman glorious past governed by equity and virtue masked present injustices and made them seem just, Augustine provides evidence that such a past never existed. He states: "Away with these fallacious cloaks and deceptive whitewashes that the facts may be inspected by a sincere examination" (CD 3.14). Part of Augustine's strategy is to "deconstruct" Roman history. He strips bare the Roman myths about its past and reveals the truth by showing how the mythmakers themselves, Sallust for example, masked the original lust for domination (and makes explicit their implicit admissions that the past contained numerous injustices).[34]

Augustine, however, does not merely "deconstruct" the Roman past. In the case just treated concerning the question of the justice of early Rome, Augustine qualifies his dismissal of its injustice by admitting that some of its rulers possessed true virtue, but that, unlike in the city of God, this virtue was limited to a few individuals. Commenting on Cato's speech quoted by Sallust, Augustine asserts: "There were only a few, then, whose character was praised even by Cato, men who climbed to glory, honor and power by the true path, that is, by virtue alone. That was the source of the hard work at home that Cato mentioned, which aimed to have a full treasury but to keep private wealth small. Hence, in the opposite case, when morals had degenerated, he sets it down as a vice that the state was poor and private citizens rich" (CD 5.12).[35] Augustine qualifies his previous observation of Sallust's work that even the early Roman republic was a tyranny because it was dominated by those who persecuted the plebs. Augustine's comment on Cato's praise of a few simultaneously confirms Augustine's judgment about the early republic and confirms that there were some Roman statesmen who sought glory by the true path of virtue.

Augustine continues his strategy by showing how the worship of their gods led the Romans to commit injustices. His treatment of the Roman civil religion has received differing interpretations. The most widely held view is offered by Brown: "Augustine feels challenged to employ to the full the approach of a true radical faced with the myths of conservatism—he will indulge in the great

---

34. Here and elsewhere, Augustine makes Sallust refute himself (see Hagendahl, *Latin Classics*, 2:639). I have not found any place where Augustine indicates that Sallust contradicted himself knowingly, although he frequently notes the method of another historian, Varro, of veiling his own views. Sallust appears to have been more willing to express his views about the injustices of the Roman past. Augustine comments, after having quoted Sallust (*The Histories* 1.12): "[I]f those historians thought it the privilege of honourable freedom not to be silent about the blemishes of their state, which in many places they have been forced loudly to praise since they had no other more genuine city (one whose citizens are to be selected for all time), what is it incumbent on us to do, whose freedom ought to be greater as our hope in God is better and surer?" (CD 3.17). Paganism placed the historians into the dilemma of veiling their views concerning the injustices of early Rome and of praising them anxiously out of a lack of having a praiseworthy model of perfect justice.

35. Quoting Sallust, *"The Conspiracy of Catiline"* 53.2–5.

pleasure of calling a spade a spade." Eric Voegelin similarly criticizes Augustine for his act of "deconstruction" but argues that Augustine overlooks the importance of spiritual substance in animating political society, which is seen in his failure to appreciate the spiritual experience rooted in civil religion: "His attitude toward Varro's civil theology resembled that of an enlightened intellectual toward Christianity—he simply could not understand that an intelligent person would seriously maintain such nonsense." Voegelin concludes: "What St. Augustine could not understand was the compactness of the Roman experience, the inseparable community of gods and men in the historically concrete *civitas*, the simultaneousness of human and divine institution of a social order. For him the order of human existence had already separated into the *civitas terrena* of profane history and the *civitas coelestis* of divine institution."[36] According to Voegelin, Augustine's criticism of Roman history and the corruption caused by the gods is the result of his failure to appreciate the formative order of the civil religion. This was not exclusively a misunderstanding of the political function of the civil religion, of providing Roman citizens a civil myth by which to live their lives in a way that would not be as austere or difficult as the life spent philosophizing. Rather, Augustine's view of the cosmos led him to overlook the close contacts of human beings and gods that one finds in pagan literature. For Augustine, grace had separated radically from nature, leaving nature, and thus the political city, devoid of any orientation toward the divine.

On the other hand, Fortin argues that such attempts to treat Augustine as an iconoclastic Enlightenment radical are overstated and overlook the indirect and even conservative nature of his criticism.[37] He observes that Augustine's reliance on Varro is suspect because Varro's treatise was drastically outdated, perhaps even at its publication a couple of hundred years before Augustine's time. The treatise was also largely ignored during Augustine's time: "More importantly, we have no assurance that the quaint deities which Augustine dredges up with Varro's help . . . were even remembered, let alone revered, by the pagans themselves." As a result, Augustine "was hardly meeting head-on major concerns of his more thoughtful opponents." Fortin argues that Augustine adopted this strategy because he recognized that the complete deconstruction of the Roman civil religion would only further disrupt an already chaotic Roman empire, and that Christianity was not in a good position to fulfill a civil function.

---

36. Brown, *Augustine of Hippo*, 305; Voegelin, *New Science of Politics*, 87.
37. Fortin, "Augustine and the Roman Civil Religion: Some Critical Reflections," in *Collected Essays*, 2:94–97.

The conclusion that can be drawn from these two positions (Augustine as deconstructionist and Augustine as providing an indirect critique) is that Augustine's strategy appears to be twofold. On the one hand, he appears to have intended to show how worshiping the Roman gods makes people unjust because the Roman civil religion is untrue; on the other hand, he wished to preserve some semblance of order by attacking the Roman civil religion indirectly. From the perspective of the argument for Augustine's purposeful excessive rhetoric presented here, it means that Augustine wished to show the truthfulness of Christianity in light of the falsity and general injustice of the Roman civil religion, even though he wished to admit a minimum of justice within the Roman civil religion so as not to undermine completely Roman civil order. This being the case, he appears to have considered Roman civil religion beyond repair, even though he reserves praise for pagan philosophers. Furthermore, he likely saw Christianity fulfilling a modest civil function insofar as only Christianity could adequately and consistently proclaim that God makes the universe and that the lesser pagan gods are false.

Augustine begins his assertion that the Roman civil religion corrupted Romans with a general question:

> First of all, we would ask why their gods took no steps to improve the morals of their worshipers. That the true God should neglect those who did not seek His help, that was but justice; but why did those gods, from whose worship ungrateful men are now complaining that they are prohibited, issue no laws which might have guided their devotees to a virtuous life? Surely it was but just, that such care as men showed to the worship of the gods, the gods on their part should have to the conduct of men. (CD 2.4; see also 2.22)

Augustine claims that if the Roman gods truly cared for Rome they would have promulgated laws that made the Romans just. He observes that the Romans had only the sinful but divinely ordained festivals such as that devoted to Berecynthia, the mother of the gods, whom he compares to an adulteress for shaming the best men of Rome. Such is the justice of the mother of the gods who govern different parts of the Roman Empire. Even the major gods of the Romans and Greeks, Apollo, Neptune, Mars, Venus, and Jupiter, were not capable of preventing injustice, and served as bad models for virtue (CD 3.2). For example, Jupiter and Juno positively aided the Romans and encouraged them to pillage and to steal the wives of the conquered (CD 3.13).[38]

---

38. See also the discussion above of Augustine's description of Jupiter as justifying the Roman lust for domination.

Augustine observes that the virtue teachings of the Greek and Roman philoso-phers and statesmen were sounder than those offered by the civil religion. For example, Cicero opposed obscene theater shows, and Scipio banned obscene depictions of the Romans themselves (CD 2.9, 2.12). Their teachings were ignored, however: "Certainly, all the worshipers of the Roman gods, when once they are possessed by what Persius calls the 'burning poison of lust,' prefer to witness the deeds of Jupiter rather than to hear what Plato taught or Cato censured" (CD 2.7; see also 2.15). The Roman statesmen banned obscene presentations of the Romans themselves even though they assented to the obscene theater shows that were commanded by the gods. This prohibition, however, resulted in a major contradiction:

> The Romans, however, as Scipio boasts . . . , declined having their conduct and good name subjected to the assaults and slanders of the poets, and went so far as to make it a capital crime if anyone should dare to compose such verses. This was a very honorable course to pursue, so far as they themselves were concerned, but in respect of the gods it was proud and irreligious: for they knew that the gods not only tolerated, but relished, being lashed by the injurious expressions of the poets, and yet they themselves would not suffer this same handling. (CD 2.12)

The Romans became impious toward their gods if they tried to be just. Augustine congratulates the Romans for shaming and banning actors involved in the obscene stage shows: "For when I hear that if any Roman citizen chose the stage as his profession, he not only closed to himself every laudable career, but even became an outcast from his own tribe, I cannot but exclaim: What a spirit animated that city, a spirit avid of honor *(laudis)* and genuinely *(germaneque)* Roman!" (CD 2.13).

This practice of stripping actors of citizenship, however, led Rome into the contradiction of barring actors in obscene shows while counting obscene plays among the rites of worshiping the gods. The Greeks, at least, were consistent in their practice of honoring actors. From these considerations, Augustine con-cludes (with some irony) that the Romans themselves knew that their worship of the gods made them unjust, but it took the Christians to point it out: "And the whole of this discussion may be summed up in the following syllogism. The Greeks give us the major premise: If such gods are to be worshiped, then certainly such men may be honored. The Romans add the minor premise: But such men must by no means be honored. The Christians draw the conclusion: Therefore such gods must by no means be worshiped" (CD 2.13). Augustine ar-gues that the Greeks thought that to be consistent, unjust human beings would have to be honored as giving homage to unjust gods; the Romans denied that unjust human beings should be honored but worshiped unjust gods anyway; the Christians conclude from this that unjust gods should not be worshiped if they make human beings unjust. Only Christianity, it appears, provides a rational conclusion to the contradiction in which paganism finds itself.

Augustine observes that this contradiction lasts while it remains within the sphere of civil religion. He points out that pagan philosophers and statesmen recognized the injustice of these plays, and he also provides evidence that they recognized that the pagan gods made them unjust. Turning to Augustine's response to this contradiction, evidence shows that he thought they recognized the contradiction but propagated it either because of their respect for Roman manners (the philosophers) or to secure their own position (the mythologists and priests). As noted above, mythologists, who are learned men who gloried more in the praise of human beings than in the truth, constituted part of Augustine's audience. They were the ones who slandered the Christian religion as weak only to secure their own positions, and who did not necessarily care for Roman virtues. Augustine accuses mythologists of obstinacy (CD 6.pref.) and of keeping the masses patriotic but in error. The priests of Rome also did not care for Roman virtue, as Augustine argues that they claimed the gods taught rules for virtue only to them: "Let them not flaunt against us any doctrines there may have been that were whispered into the ears of a very small group and so transmitted by a kind of mystic cult that should inculcate an honest and chaste life" (CD 2.6). Augustine's accusation that the priests corrupted Rome was not novel, as he cites Cicero ridiculing their manipulative augury rituals (CD 4.30).[39] The mythologists and the Roman priests ignored the historical record of the injustices of early Rome and the sufferings of early Rome (that are just as bad as those suffered under Christianity) because they wished to preserve the lie that governed Rome and from which they benefited (CD 2.3, 4.1, 6.pref.). Such human beings, then, when they portray themselves as protectors of the public order, glory more in the praise received from human beings than in the gods.

In addition to criticizing mythologists, Augustine criticizes some of the Platonists for arrogance. He observes that a few gloried in being called Platonists (CD 8.6). He criticizes Platonists such as Porphyry and Apuleius for seeking to unite the human and divine through prideful magic and theurgy (CD 10.23–28). He calls them impious for refusing to have worshiped the true God and for having considered impure demons as mediators between the divine and human. This criticism is meant to establish the primacy of the Christian religion

---

39. Citing Cicero, De Natura Deorum, 2.70.

as the true religion, for only it, by the Incarnation, provides a perfect mediator between divine and human natures. Philosophy cannot fulfill itself as the love of wisdom because its own pride blinds it to truth, which took human form and died on the cross: "This is despised as a weak and human thing by those who are wise and strong in themselves; yet this is the grace which heals the weak, who do not proudly boast a blessedness of their own, but rather humbly acknowledge their real misery" (*CD* 10.28). The misery of philosophers is their temptation to take their genuine, yet partial, wisdom as a full knowledge of God rather than follow the path of Socrates who acknowledged his ignorance.

Augustine excepted Plato himself from the sorts of criticism he directs toward the Platonists. His criticism of Plato is directed mainly toward his presentation of reincarnation (*CD* 10.30), which, Augustine admits, would resemble the Christian view of life after death had Plato combined his view with that of Porphyry, who thought that a purified soul does not return to the ills of the world after it has returned to the Father (*CD* 22.27). Be that as it may, by praising Plato for his love of God and for avoiding calling Plato vain, Augustine provides an exception to his rhetorical position that philosophy undermines itself at its peak.

Having examined the two poles, so to speak, of the intellectual audience that Augustine addresses, it is necessary to conclude by examining Augustine's assessment of the pagan mind's ability to reform its polity. Augustine understood Varro as a philosopher and historian who was caught in the dilemma of having to attempt to cultivate public virtue while deferring to a corrupt and false Roman civil religion. On the one hand, Varro was a philosopher who wrote to provide benefit or utility *(utilitas)* for human beings. On the other hand, his writings supported the poets who created the civil religion and whose writings delighted human beings (*CD* 6.6). The preceding discussion might suggest that Augustine would view Varro as prideful in the same way as he viewed the mythologists because, like them, Varro defended the false Roman civil religion. However, Augustine understood that the basis for Varro's defense was more subtle. He states that Varro loved wisdom like a philosopher because he understood that God rules the world (even though Varro incorrectly equated God with the soul of the world). Despite his incorrect view about the nature of God as a soul instead of as the maker of souls, Augustine considered Varro correct in his view that God is to be worshiped without the use of images *(simulacra):* "[W]hen he deems that the rites of religion would have been observed more purely without images: who can fail to see how close he has come to the truth?" (*CD* 4.31).

Augustine adds that Varro deferred to the ancient Roman traditions even though Varro himself considered them corrupt and false:

> What says Varro himself, whom we grieve to have found, although not by his own judgment, placing the scenic plays among things divine? When in many passages he is exhorting, like a religious man, to the worship of the gods, does he not in doing so admit that he does not in his own judgment believe those things which he relates that the Roman state has instituted; so that he does not hesitate to affirm that if he were founding a new state, he could enumerate the gods and their names better by the rule of nature *(naturae . . . formula)*? But being born into a nation already ancient, he says that he finds himself bound to accept the traditional names and surnames of the gods, and the histories connected with them, and that his purpose in investigating and publishing these details is to incline the people to worship the gods, and not to despise them. (*CD* 4.31)

Augustine observes that Varro himself did not believe in the Roman gods and elsewhere points out that Varro viewed these gods as human fabrications. He observes, however, that Varro would have preferred to have enumerated the gods "better by the rule of nature."

Augustine continues by pointing out that Varro's weakness and bondage to custom prevented him from saying that the one God is the proper object of worship:

> The same most acute and learned writer *(auctor acutissimus atque doctissimus)* says that in his opinion the only ones who have discovered what God really is are those who have adopted the view that he is the soul which governs the world by a movement that accords with reason. Hence, although he did not yet hold the exact truth (for the true God is not a soul, but the Maker and builder of soul as well), still, if he could have spoken freely against the prejudice of custom *(praeiudicia consuetudinis)*, he would have acknowledged, and taught others, that one god should be the object of our worship, who governs the world by a movement that accords with reason. Then on this point the only question left for discussion would be his statement that God is soul, rather than the Maker of soul. (*CD* 4.31)

Augustine's criticism of Varro is mild in comparison to his criticisms of other defenders of the false civil religion. Varro nearly understood the truth, but he could not speak freely against false custom. Varro was constrained because of his deference toward these customs, but Augustine further hints that the reason for his constraint is rooted in the limitations of the pagan mind and natural reason:

O Marcus Varro, since you are the most acute of all men and beyond doubt
the most learned—though still a man and not a god, and not lifted up by
the spirit of God (*spiritu Dei*) into truth and freedom to see and declare
divine things—you do perceive how necessary it is to separate things divine
from the frivolities and lies of men. But you are afraid to oppose the beliefs
and customs of the people, altogether vicious as they are, where superstition
appears in public rites. (*CD* 6.6)

Varro failed to speak the truth openly because he lacked the spirit of God and
thus the resolve to speak the truth to his fellow Romans. He could not resist
false custom and was compelled to worship the Roman gods instead of the God
of nature who governs the world in accordance with reason: "You desire (*cupis*)
to worship the natural gods; you are compelled (*cogeris*) to worship the civil"
(*CD* 6.6). He is said to have lacked God's grace, which can hardly be said to be
a fault of a pagan.[40]

Augustine's attitude toward Varro's relationship with the false religion is
twofold. On the one hand, Augustine admires Varro's prudence in deferring to
custom. On the other hand, he appears to have wished that Varro had been
able to speak out against the false custom. Varro failed to reform Rome because
he lacked the spirit of God. Augustine's invocation of the spirit of God appears
to reflect his view that Christianity can serve a civic function in positing God
beyond the world and beyond the lesser gods. Christianity appears to surpass
the tension in which the pagan mind finds itself. Pagan philosophers such as
Plato, Cicero, and Varro agreed with or approached the truth of Christianity
that God made the world and is owed thanks. However, they were incapable
of reforming the false religion and thus were incapable of reforming Roman
morals. In this sense, Augustine's deconstruction of paganism and defense of
Christianity in the *City of God* constitute his own reformation of Rome and of
those, seen in the beginning of this chapter, who wonder why the just and unjust
suffer equally. It is in this book, as this chapter has attempted to show, where
Augustine attempts to reform public morals through articulating the worship of
God beyond the gods while preserving the truth discovered by the pagan minds.
This reformation was at once revolutionary and moderate. It was revolutionary
because, as commentators have long shown, the *City of God* was the death knell
for paganism in Rome. It was moderate, however, because Augustine argued for
little more than what the pagans did not already know, as is reflected in his

40. However, see *CD* 10.29, wherein Augustine discusses the Platonic intimation of the Holy
Spirit, and *CD* 11.25, wherein he observes that the pagan philosophers considered God the kindler
of knowledge. See Chapter 6.

curious strategy of criticizing obscure gods and in his general agreement with the pagan philosophers.

Augustine's excessive rhetoric is meant to reform the inordinate desires of his audience. Specifically, he shows how the inordinate love of glory degenerates into the lust for domination while showing his readers how their love of glory can be formed by directing it to its proper end. He identifies different versions of the love of glory: the love of political glory, the piety toward the past and toward the pagan gods, the mythologists' love of glory, and finally the true glory of the philosophers. He shows how each kind of love of glory (except that of the philosophers) degenerates into the lust for domination. His rhetoric of excess is meant to denigrate the objects that such inordinate desires seek as means of self-glorification. This excess is meant to make way for a more substantive political teaching, which will be the focus of the remainder of this study.

## 2

## A  LITTLE  WORLD  OF  ORDER

P OLITICS IS the establishment and maintenance of a little world of
order. The political art requires efforts to form and to negotiate with a
chaos of conflicting longings and desires. Politics provides a shelter or sanctuary
from the disruptive anxieties and fears about the possibility of the senselessness
of mortal life. As we noted with Voegelin above, political society "is as a whole
a little world, a cosmion, illuminated with meaning from within by the human
beings who continuously create and bear it as the mode and condition of
their self-realization." Similarly, Yves Simon argues that "the virtual immortal
life of the community" compensates for the brevity of individual existence
because it provides a field on which a diversity of perfections can be achieved.[1]
According to the Platonic-Aristotelian tradition from which these statements are
drawn, politics is a natural good because political life forms human personhood
and cultivates virtue. Furthermore, classical political philosophy distinguished
between practical virtue and the fully happy life of philosophy, according
to which political life is deficient. Christian revelation is generally seen to
repudiate the classics' teaching regarding political virtue by treating the heavenly
city of God as every human's proper home, and the earthly city as, at best, a
way station for their pilgrimage to their home.

Augustine regarded politics as the natural expression of human beings'
striving to obtain a kind of wholeness, and as building a community as an
expression of their loves. Even though he went to great lengths to point out the
limitations of political life, as was seen in the previous chapter, he acknowledged that politics is the field on which various types of human excellence are

---

1. Simon, *General Theory of Authority*, 18–19.

necessarily cultivated. His criticism of politics is based on his view that political life is the highest practical achievement of human endeavor, but it is not the highest achievement per se, and it cannot satisfy the deepest of human beings' longings for completeness. As observed in the introduction, human beings long naturally for eternal happiness, and Chapter 1 showed that Augustine focused his criticisms on attempts to use political life to secure eternal happiness. Such an attempt is due to pride, but, as we shall see, it is a relatively easy mistake to make because it is tempting for one without spiritual discipline to confuse the sheltering function of political life with that which fulfills one's longing for eternal life; put another way, it is easy to replace analogical thinking about the meaningfulness of politics with a literalist derailment. Later chapters will show further that Augustine recognized that certain pagan philosophers and statesmen could overcome this Caesarean temptation. Augustine's criticism of prideful passions leaves room to affirm that politics can secure a happiness that is not eternal even when he does not always argue this explicitly.

The sheltering function of political society, a sign of its goodness, comes out in Augustine's discussion of Hannibal's destruction of the town of Saguntum. Saguntum's deliberation over whether to break its oath to its protective gods provides a paradigmatic case of Augustine's understanding of political rationality. The following argument also shows that Augustine makes room for the political art as the master educative art in Eden; speculating on the possibility of politics in prelapsarian Eden (before the Fall) enables one to distinguish the nature of the political art from its postlapsarian (after the Fall) condition that is characterized by coercion. Finally, we shall examine how Augustine acknowledges the presence of that prelapsarian *essence* in the actual world of political *practice* by showing that some of his antipolitical statements actually hint at his affirmative essential attitude toward politics. The analysis in this chapter fits with the findings of the last: Augustine is not always explicit in affirming the naturalness of politics. Sometimes he does little more than leave a few scattered clues to enable the reader to put together his political teaching, and sometimes he is a little more explicit.

## THE CITY AS A COSMION

Augustine thought that the founding and maintenance of cities over the course of many generations is a natural good. The city is understood as a little world that understands itself to be in existence for all time, preserved by the bonds of memory from one generation to the next. Augustine's understanding of the desire to constitute this world appears comparable to Aristotle's statement that the common good is "greater and more divine *(theioteron)* than the private good"; in other words, the city participates in imperishability in a way that the private good of individuals does not.[2]

The passage under consideration is found in the context of Augustine's assertion that only Christ is the true Founder of the eternal city of God because he is God. The Romans, Augustine maintained, merely made Romulus into a god in order to bestow eternality onto their city *(CD* 22.6). As a result, citizens of the city of God, unlike citizens of an earthly polity, need not fight for the preservation of the city of God, because Christ preserves that city. Augustine then anticipates a possible objection that his position is antipolitical and would suggest that the defense of the political city is not appropriate and worthy of choice: "I know that Cicero, in the third book of his *De Republica*, if I mistake not, argues that a first-rate power will not engage in war except either for keeping faith or for safety *(nisi aut pro fide aut pro salute)*."[3] Augustine continues to quote Cicero's view that "a city should be so constituted as to be eternal *(aeterna)*" *(CD* 22.6). According to Cicero, a city represents a world constituted by generations of human beings, unlike a human being who lives and dies over a relatively brief period of time. From the citizens' perspective, it is a microcosm of the universe, and as the city goes, so goes the universe. Augustine explains that Cicero's view follows that of the Platonists, who thought that the world would not perish. Augustine goes on to explain that the two ends that a city considers when preserving itself, safety and faith, appear to conflict for the political city.

According to Augustine, this was the case for the lamentable Saguntines who chose to let Hannibal destroy their city instead of breaking faith *(fidem frangere)* with the Romans and the gods. He points out that this deed was applauded by

2. Aristotle, *Nicomachean Ethics* 1.2.1094b7. It should also be noted that in the Greek language, "god" and "divine" are predicates as seen in Euripides' famous saying, "friends to embrace, that is god *(aspazein tous philous theos)*." Hans-Georg Gadamer comments: "This manifests something *beyond* our own feeling and our own existence; something like a common sphere, as Hölderin describes it, is built up there by this moment. Thus, very human, completely human experiences are here pointing to this beyond, one's own self-consciousness as its capacity" ("Articulating Transcendence," 6). This way of speaking of the divine enabled Aristotle to speak of it in the comparative and superlative cases in reference to human being, as when he speaks of mind *(nous)* as the "divinest part *(to theiotaton)*" in human being (*Nicomachean Ethics* 10.7.1177a17). This way of interpreting the Greek symbol divine *(theos)* should show that Aristotle's understanding of the common good differs substantially from the cult of Rome and its heroes criticized by Augustine in the *City of God*, and that ascribing the concept of cosmion to Augustine does not contradict Augustine's criticisms of Roman civil theology.

3. Cicero, *De Re Publica* 3.23.34. The passage is fragmentary, and the speaker appears to be Laelius.

the citizens of the earthly republic: "For certainly, if the Saguntines chose safety, they must break faith; if they kept faith, they must reject safety" (*CD* 22.6; see also 3.20). Augustine implies that citizens of the city of God need not be forced into this dilemma because they are part of the eternal city, founded by Christ, where safety and keeping faith are united. This formulation is perhaps meant to contrast political life, which is necessarily tragic because it forces one to choose between incommensurable goods, and the eternally blessed city of God. This passage, then, reflects Augustine's apparent antipolitical perspective.

The needfulness of preserving the city as a little world provides the background for Augustine's analysis of Saguntum. Augustine does not argue explicitly that it would have been rightful for the Saguntines to have broken their oath, but he does state that it "merits questioning *(merito quaeritur)*" whether they did the right thing in not breaking the oath and being destroyed. He states that the members of the earthly city would applaud the Saguntines' decision to let their city be destroyed, which does not rule out the possibility that members of the city of God may criticize them for that. Does this mean that members of the city of God would urge them to break their oath? This interpretation is not ruled out since Augustine states earlier in the *City of God* that the Saguntines had placed themselves under capricious gods who were in no way interested or capable of preserving their temporal good (*CD* 3.20). Augustine observes that they were besieged by Hannibal who had originally broken his oath with Rome not to attack Saguntum. In fact, he states that the same gods who were mediators of Saguntum's oath to Rome then deceived Saguntum with false oracles. The Saguntines thus faced gods who were neither willing nor able to keep their side of the oath and a besieger who broke his oath with Rome. It was unclear whether there remained any oath for the Saguntines to observe and whether the betrayal of Hannibal had released them from their oath.[4]

These considerations indicate that Augustine's silence concerning the justice of the acts of the Saguntines may mean that he thought it would have been right for them to have broken the letter of their oath. Augustine could not explicitly advocate the breaking of oaths, and he presumably wished to have remained guarded in his treatment of this problem. He did not want to appear to encourage impiety. For example, he elsewhere urges a Roman official, Boniface, to keep faith, even with enemies, in order to maintain peace (*Ep.* 189.6).

---

4. Augustine then compares their situation to the case of Regulus who kept his oath to his gods and to the Carthaginians. However, the two cases are not comparable because Regulus fulfilled his promise of returning after the Romans had broken their faith with the Carthaginians, whereas the Saguntines were faced with one who had broken faith with them and the Romans. Augustine's praise of Regulus is based on Regulus's virtue, and not on Regulus's trust in unreliable gods.

Augustine elsewhere expresses reservations about the rightfulness of maintaining ill-considered oaths. He states it "merits questioning *(merito quaeritur)*" whether God ever commanded Jephthah to sacrifice his daughter, which reflects his view that one should not make imprudent oaths with God (*CD* 1.21; see Chapter 4). Indeed, he uses the exact terminology, saying both this and the Saguntine case merit questioning. Augustine recognized too that a few wise Romans themselves recognized the falsity of some Roman religious practices, such as auspices, because they contradicted the order of nature. He provides the example of the auspice telling the Romans to give greater honor to Mars, Terminus, and Juventas than to Jupiter, the king of the gods, which led to numerous military and national catastrophes:

> The more intelligent and grave Romans have seen these things, but have had little power against the custom of the city *(contra consuetudinem civitatis)*, which was bound to observe the rites of the demons; because even they themselves, although they perceived that these things were vain, yet thought that the religious worship which is due to God should be paid to the nature of things which is established under the rule and government of the one true God, "serving," as said by the Apostle, "the creature more than the Creator, who is blessed for evermore." (*CD* 4.29, quoting Rom. 1:25)

This passage indicates that the "more intelligent and grave" Romans came close to understanding true religious worship *(religio cultus)* in observing the order of nature. Augustine appears to affirm that only respect for Roman convention, and not duty to these lesser gods (demons), stopped them from breaking these oaths.

Augustine generally avoids the deductive mode of moral reasoning that led the Saguntines to their self-destruction through sacrificing their city to honor the gods. Indeed, he criticizes the Saguntines even for their inconsistent adherence to a rule-bound ethic; he points out that they saw themselves faced with only two conflicting principles, maintaining safety and keeping faith, and they were not bound, by their own premises, to choose faith: "But I do not see how they could obey by this mode of disputation, where it is said that no war is to be waged unless either for faith or for safety, but it does not state how to choose, if both principles clash in a single moment of peril, so that one cannot be maintained without the loss of another" (*CD* 22.6). According to Augustine, pressure of events, not logic, led Saguntum to be destroyed. He asks whether there is a way that a city can preserve both faith and its safety, and thus make a plausible claim that it deserves to endure in the world.

Evidence suggests that Augustine's own prudential mode of reasoning points the way out of that conflict while maintaining both faith and safety. His prudential mode of moral reasoning is seen in an analogous case in which he discusses the relationship of the contemplative philosopher to the city. He states that contemplation is superior to political activity but that the philosopher must engage in political affairs when it is necessary: "And therefore holy leisure is longed for by the love of truth; but it is the necessity of love to undertake requisite business. If no one imposes this burden upon us, we are free to sift and contemplate truth; but if it be laid upon us, we are necessitated for love's sake to undertake it" (CD 19.19). Like the pagan philosophers, Augustine saw contemplation as superior to action. The pagan philosophers are sometimes interpreted as always choosing contemplation over action, as if that choice were based on mere deduction from the original premise that contemplation is better than action. The difficulty with such a view is that it assumes contemplation to be in no way dependent on practical activity, as if a philosopher gains nothing from social interaction from other human beings. Augustine avoids this mode of reasoning when he states that the contemplative chooses to serve the city out of the necessity of love. Both words together, *necessity* and *love* (*necessitas* and *caritas*), suggest that the choice to serve the city fulfills the requirements of *caritas*, analogous to the way Aristotle might say that to step outside the normal mode of just action saves the cause of justice. The choice to act is not simply a suspension of *caritas*, nor is it a deduction from a set of absolute rules. Augustine describes necessity in the sense "that it is necessary for something to be as it is, or happen as it does" (CD 5.10). The necessity of love, therefore, moves the philosopher to turn his or her attention to worldly affairs in certain circumstances. Loving and serving God is a free act, so there is no compulsion to return to the city if compulsion means coercing a person contrary to his or her intentions. Further, the dual command to love God and neighbor is unitary insofar as, for Augustine, one cannot love God unless one loves one's neighbor. The love of God and the love of neighbor are both activities of loving God (see DT 8.7.10–8.10.14). This means that the choice to contemplate God or to assist one's neighbor is made from prudent considerations whereby the choice to obtain the latter is done to obtain the former.[5]

These considerations shed light on how Augustine understood the case of the Saguntines, and thus, how a city preserves itself as a little world. The decision

---

5. Augustine indicates that the best of the pagan philosophers seem to have recognized this when they argue that human being is happiest when virtue is combined with bodily goods that make virtue possible (CD 19.3).

to preserve faith and safety falls under the same sort of calculus of deciding to worship and love God through contemplation or political action. Preserving faith and the contemplation of God are nobler pursuits than safety and loving one's neighbor, but not simply so. The decision to preserve safety and to engage in political action is a different mode of honoring and worshiping the gods or God. If this is the case, then Augustine's silence on whether the Saguntines were right to sacrifice their city is significant. It means that they would have been right to have broken the letter of their oath that bound them to Rome and to gods that promised (falsely) temporal goods. They still could have honored the gods (or better gods that promise eternal goods) had they broken the letter of the oath and recognized that their breaking the letter actualized the spirit of the oath. This constitutes, in part, the basis for Augustine's praise of Regulus. Regulus returned to Carthage to face his self-destruction on account of virtue and not because he thought the gods would reward him with temporal success. He did not worship those gods as the Saguntines worshiped them. Augustine's interpretation of the Saguntines points out the possibility that the dilemma either to choose safety or to keep faith is miscast, and Augustine leaves open the possibility that such a choice need not be deduced from absolute rules, but rather that saving the city may be the mode by which a city keeps faith in extreme circumstances such as this one.

This interpretation is strengthened if we consider this case in light of Augustine's view that human happiness depends on the expectation of a stable and peaceful future. For example, among his arguments against certain pagan accounts of cosmic and historical cycles is the view that faith in neighbors is destroyed if one is consciously or unconsciously expecting to abandon one's neighbor: "For who would not be more remiss and lukewarm in his love for a person whom he thinks he shall be forced to abandon, and whose truth and wisdom he shall come to hate; and this too, after he has quite attained to the utmost and most blissful knowledge that he is capable of?" (*CD* 12.21). Even in a Christian dispensation that ensures a stable future without the perpetual turning of cycles, friendship and other human projects, such as politics, are impossible if one consistently expects separation and division. This sentiment is not alien to citizens of modern democracies, who, like busybody pilgrims heading to an immanent heaven, are continuously on the move, and forming and dissolving friendships, which gradually loosens social bonds and contributes to feelings of isolation and loneliness. Communities are based on a faith in the endurance of such projects beyond the anticipations and expectations of the individual participants. Indeed, at one point Augustine consoles distraught Romans by observing that the sack of Rome in 410 A.D. does not mean that Rome has perished, and he suggests that Rome will continue to flourish (*CD* 4.7).

Augustine argues that glory constitutes the response to human beings' longing to attribute this kind of stability to political life (as explicated in Chapter 5). He specifically recognizes the importance of testimonies to the memory of statesmen in providing the glue that holds generations of a regime together. He compares and contrasts the eternal life of the martyrs with that of the Roman heroes, who found their own kind of immortality in testimonies: "But since those Romans were in an earthly city, and had before them, as the end of all the offices undertaken in its behalf, its safety, and a kingdom, not in heaven, but in earth—not in the sphere of eternal life, but in the sphere of demise and succession, where the dead are succeeded by the dying—what else *(quid aliud)* but glory should they love, by which they wished even after death to live in the mouths of their admirers?" (*CD* 5.14). Human beings live in the sphere of demise and succession, and they are formed by the living memories that are handed down from one generation to the next. Historical memory is the glory by which great deeds are transmitted across generations and that constitute the glue that human beings, by their very mortality, use to bind themselves together across the flow of time. Thus, the love of glory cannot be dismissed simply as a product of lust; rather, its root can be found in the love of existence that may or may not be corrupted by inordinate lusts. Similarly, a city, which relies on memory and glory to secure its transmission across generations, cannot be dismissed simply as a product of sin.

It is natural to maintain the city's safety even from a Christian perspective that believes in the finitude of the world. Augustine does not reject Cicero's analogy between the city and the eternity of the world even though he modifies Cicero's view that the world is eternal. However, it is unlikely that there is a *practical* difference, insofar as Augustine's position still enables people to establish and maintain a city as a little world within God's creation and that appears eternal from the human perspective. For instance, Augustine elsewhere affirms the distinction between what is eternal (that is, God) and creatures, such as angels, time, and the world, which exist at all times *(semper)* (*CD* 12.16). Citizens would require that their city, as an analogy of the world, exist sempiternally. The views of both Augustine and Cicero require statesmen and citizens to preserve their cities for all time, and both require the assistance of God or the gods to that end. What is different in Augustine's thought is that God raises and destroys empires but people must act as if cities exist perpetually, because they do not know when God will destroy their city (*CD* 5.1, 5.11; however, see discussion of "divine aid" in Chapter 4). Although Augustine does not explicitly identify political entities as sempiternal, he reasons about their existence in a way that indicates he thought people may properly see them as such. Finding themselves in the middle of things, human beings naturally live their lives as if they move toward a stable end.

## PERFECT COMPLIANCE SCENARIO: EDENIC POLITICS

Turning from the middle of things to their origin, Augustine's affirmation of political life can be seen in his view of Edenic life as the place where a multiplicity of human beings completes the various perfections by interacting with one another and by worshiping God. This continues the discussion of the previous section by showing how the desire for "virtual immortality" translates into seeking the perfection of individual members of the polity. Augustine understood Edenic politics as a perfect compliance scenario. In Eden, had there been no Fall, humankind would have been without sin. This approach permits the analysis of government as a collective action problem because it abstracts out human sinfulness, and enables the examination of political life devoid of coercion.[6] For example, the approach permits one to consider that a governing agency might be needed to coordinate the activities of a group of people who, because of incomplete or partial knowledge, would be incapable of being their own governors. The individuals in the governing agency, by virtue of their position, would have the knowledge of the means of coordinating the actions of people who lack technical knowledge of the workings of the whole unit. Politics is not simply managerial, however, as Augustine's discussion of the arts indicates that he regarded the political art as educative. Although this approach abstracts out human sinfulness, it enables one to focus on the central longing governing politics and thus affirms the naturalness of politics, because this longing itself is natural. Analysis of Augustine's presentation of prelapsarian human beings shows this longing in the human being's desire to seek a unity among the diversity of possible particular perfections.[7]

Augustine's *Literal Meaning of Genesis* shows him, perhaps in a fit of enthusiasm, considering the possibility of an Edenic art of politics when he exclaims:

---

6. This approach is analogous to Augustine's inquiry into the nature of sexuality by arguing that inhabitants of Eden would have procreated, which establishes that procreation is a natural good (CD 14.23–24).

7. See Simon, *General Theory of Authority,* 28–29.

"Of the voluntary working of providence there are other signs: creatures are instructed and learn, fields are cultivated, *societies are governed*, the arts are practiced, and other activities go on both in heavenly society and in this mortal society on earth" (*DGL* 8.9.17).[8] He introduces an ambiguity in his meaning when he adds that "the good are provided for even with the help of the wicked." How can the wicked exist either in Eden or in the heavenly city? Augustine does not intend for the reader to conclude that the wicked exist there. The quotation is situated in a discussion of Gen. 2:15, in which he argues that the art of tilling the soil that Adam learns is done joyfully and not as a punishment for sin. He includes the art of governing societies as part of a more general list of arts that human beings undertake to be in harmony with nature or voluntary providence, as he calls it. Thus, just as the drudgery that characterizes postlapsarian human beings' art of tilling the soil prevents Augustine from concluding that that art originates in sin, so too does he allow for the political art to appear in prelapsarian Eden.

Although Augustine appears to have left behind the categories of voluntary and natural providence by the time he wrote the *City of God*, he does not appear to have changed his mind regarding the place of politics within God's overall providence. His treatment of voluntary and natural providence accords with his view that voluntary action (in other words, acting according to reason) is part of God's providence (*CD* 5.9–11). In the *City of God*, he explicitly identifies nature as the order governing voluntary action, and asserts that it is the nature of a rational and voluntary being to adhere to God: "[T]hose things which have not received everlasting being . . . tend in the divine providence (*divina providentia*) to that end which is embraced in the reason of the government (*ratio gubernandae*) of the universe" (*CD* 12.5).[9] Voluntary and natural providence both fall under the general idea of nature and divine providence; what he previously signified as natural providence (physical motion) is now joined by voluntary providence, and both are considered parts of natural providence (see

---

8. Natural providence, his other category of providence in this text, refers to laws by which bodies move. His distinction between voluntary and natural providence does not reflect a distinction between nonrational beings governed by natural law, and rational beings whose actions merely reflect their sinfulness (see Burnell, "Status of Politics," 22–23). This is seen in his observation that both kinds of providence exist in human beings. Natural providence governs their animalistic functions (that is, coming into being and dying), and voluntary providence governs their "food, [their] clothing, and [their] well being." Augustine then observes that voluntary providence governs their ability to secure the good life: "[B]y voluntary action it is provided that [the soul] acquires knowledge and lives in harmony." This indicates that, as governed by voluntary providence, politics constitutes a natural good that is sought by rational animals exercising their reason.

9. See also Burnell, "Status of Politics," 23.

also *CD* 8.6, 8.10, 11.25). By making this move (which is consistent with his earlier move), Augustine allows for politics to be seen as the proper activity of a rational being seeking its perfection (instead of seeing politics merely as a means to secure material comfort). He makes a similar point in the *Confessions* where he observes that political powers are appointed authority over human beings in a way analogous to God's dominion over human being: "For as among those powers appointed in human society, the greater power *(maior potestas)* is set over the lesser, to command obedience; so is God set over all" *(Conf.* 3.8).

Augustine understood Edenic human being Adam as social, and thus political. He did not distinguish between the political and the social: "[F]or the life of a city *(civitatis)* is certainly *(utique)* a social *(socialis)* life" *(CD* 19.17). Of Adam he states: "And therefore God created only one single man, not, certainly, that he might be a solitary bereft of all society, but that by this means the unity of society and the bond of concord might be more effectually commended to him, men being bound together not only by similarity of nature, but by the affection of kinship" *(CD* 12.22). The text indicates that the principle of community is found already in the first human being, and Augustine calls this principle the means by which the multiplicity of human beings is united.

In another passage that reminds the reader of Aristotle's dictum that man is between the gods and beasts, Augustine emphasizes human beings' social nature and points out that discord stems from corruption (the Fall): "For there is nothing so social by nature, so discordant by sin, as this race" *(CD* 12.28).[10] Later, he states that it is necessary for human beings to actualize themselves in several relationships, which points the way beyond family relations:

> For love was accorded its due importance so that human beings, for whom concord was useful and honorable *(utilis atque honesta)*, might be bound by ties of various relationships. The underlying purpose was that a single human being should not comprise many relationships in his one self but that these connections should be severally distributed among individuals and in this way serve to weld social life more securely by covering in their multiplicity a multiplicity of people. *(CD* 15.16)

Augustine understood human being to actualize himself in social and political relations. An individual possesses a plurality of social roles, and each brings forth different human attributes. Human beings thus profit from engaging in a multiplicity of social roles for the purpose of actualizing their social natures.

---

10. "Nihil enim est quam hoc genus tam discordiosum vitio, tam sociale natura."

Looking ahead momentarily over political bonds, Augustine also points out that human beings' sociableness extends up to religious inclinations. He points out that the word *religio* might be used to describe the worship of God, but also to include relations among neighbors: "We have no right to affirm with confidence that 'religion' is confined to the worship of God, since it seems that this word has been detached from its normal meaning, in which it refers to an attitude of respect in relations between a human being and his neighbor" (*CD* 10.1). Because Augustine saw human beings as social in both the so-called private sphere (that is, marriage, family) and the most expansive so-called public sphere, religion, it appears likely that he would not have disagreed that politics is an intermediate and equally natural step between family and religion. If Augustine understood the growth of the soul to begin with immediate familial relations in order to fulfill its sociable nature, then the soul might require an intermediate, nonfamilial but still particular relation before reaching out into the most fully differentiated community in religion.

Augustine makes this step by thinking that true dominion in Eden extends to political authority.[11] He observes that slavery is not true dominion, and he is generally interpreted as arguing that political authority, unlike family relations, is akin to slavery. Commenting on the Genesis narrative of the sixth day of Creation (1:26), he states that God "did not wish a rational creature, made in His own image, to have dominion *(dominari)* save over irrational creatures: not man over man, but man over the beasts. So it was that the first just men were established as shepherds of flocks, more than as kings of men, so that even so God might indirectly point out *(insinuaret)* what is required by the principle of gradation among his creatures what the guilt of sinners demands" (*CD* 19.15). This statement is often taken to signify Augustine's rejection of political rule as natural, as his having repudiated his position expressed in the quotation taken from the *Confessions* above that political rule is patterned after God's providential rule. However, closer analysis shows that Augustine does not restrict dominion to mean exclusively instrumental relations, such as those of a human being in his dominion over an animal, or in a master-slave relationship. For example, he utilizes the same term, *dominus,* to call God the true lord and governor of the world *(verus dominus gubernatorque)* (*CD* 5.23). This shows that Augustine does not restrict the power of dominion to instrumental rule, but

11. This interpretation differs from the interpretations of Markus (*Saeculum,* 92–93, 197–210) and of O'Donovan ("Augustine's *City of God* XIX," 104). See also the criticisms of the realist position by Burnell ("Status of Politics," 20–21). See also Fortin, "Political Idealism and Christianity," in *Collected Essays,* 2:52 n. 18; and Milbank, *Theology and Social Theory,* 406.

attributes dominion to God as the exemplar of charitable rule. The question remains as to whether human beings can properly imitate that power.

According to Augustine, the first human beings were herders "more than kings *(magis quam reges)."* Burnell demonstrates that Augustine judiciously chose his terms. He does not say they were herders "as opposed to kings" *(pro regibus)* or "rather than kings" *(potius quam reges),* but instead uses the comparative *magis;* he distinguishes kings from shepherds by degree and not by kind.[12] Burnell interprets this passage to mean that God was making a rhetorical point *(ut . . . insinuaret)* and is "not about his preventing something unnatural." This point can be extended because *insinuare* means to express indirectly, rather to merely make a rhetorical point. Augustine uses *insinuare* to explain, for example, the secret ways that the Trinity is expressed and intimated in Scripture *(CD* 11.24). He also contrasts *insinuare* with open declarations *(CD* 13.23). This indicates that when God insinuates or indirectly expresses that man does not domineer over other men, he provides an indirect lesson on the gradation of creatures and does not rule out that human beings can govern other human beings. In this case, this passage shows that political rule is by no means to be domineering and is not analogous to ruling animals (who obey blindly). This being the case, this passage does not rule out the possibility that Augustine affirms the naturalness of politics.

Augustine's indirect way of acknowledging politics in Eden fits with his presentation of the various activities in Eden whose coordination would require political rule. Not all prelapsarian human beings would have been contemplative. Edenic life would have seen both those leading contemplative and those leading active lives. Their activities would have required organization. Adam was needy, and his body required meat and drink to satisfy hunger and thirst *(CD* 13.23, 14.26). Although nature provides a sufficient amount of food through the Tree of Life, Adam's labor and arts in securing his food would have provided the occasion for a common authority that would have had to distribute food (so not everyone would have to remain near the Tree of Life) (see also *CD* 22.22, 22.24). Although Augustine does not explicate this point, one can imagine that his view of Edenic activities allows for a political art necessary to schedule eating times, and to organize other activities.

A common authority would have been needed more when the number of people in Eden increased. Augustine points out that procreation was natural to

12. Burnell, "Status of Politics," 21. Burnell further observes that Augustine makes the same point in his view that "we should have more *(magis)* to do with philosophers than with poets" *(CD* 6.6). This means that philosophers are more reliable guides than poets, whereas poets remain guides of lesser authority.

prelapsarian human beings: "But we, for our part, have no manner of doubt that to increase and multiply and replenish the earth in virtue of the blessing of God, is a gift of marriage as God instituted it from the beginning before man sinned, when He created them male and female—in other words, two sexes manifestly distinct" (CD 14.22). By procreating, human beings participate in a process of distinguishing a multiplicity of beings from the original unity in Adam. As such, the purpose of procreation is not exhausted by the family, but, as seen above, in having a multiplicity of human beings actualize themselves in a multiplicity of relations, some of which lie beyond particular families. Augustine allows room for some sort of political authority being necessary to organize people, because the family was originally intended to serve the higher principle of being part of a greater multiplicity, which would require a different form of organization.

Augustine indicates that human beings in Eden would have been engaged in activities, such as the arts, that would have required political authority for their organization. This is the result of Augustine's understanding of the arts, and of prelapsarian human beings' engagement in contemplation or action or both. The arts, especially the liberal arts, are propaedeutic to the acquisition of wisdom whereby, as Fortin observes, "the rational soul is led to the discovery of those principles from which all science proceeds but which are not themselves the object of any science."[13] The arts discipline the rational soul to see the principles of science and make it ready to see God (although human beings need grace to see God continuously). This understanding of the development of the rational soul indicates that not all prelapsarian human beings would have been contemplative. The role that the arts play in the educational ascent of the rational soul is seen in Augustine's explanation for the art of agriculture in Eden:

> What is a more impressive and wonderful spectacle than this? Where is human reason better able to speak, as it were, to nature than when man sows the seed, plants a tree, transplants a bush, grafts a mallet-shoot, and thus asks, as it were, each root and seed what it can or cannot do, why it can or cannot do it, what is the extent of the intrinsic and invisible power of numbers within it, and what can be attributed to the extrinsic factors applied by human effort? And how can man better understand, than he does in reflecting on these wonders, that "Neither he who plants nor he who waters is anything, but only God, who gives the growth?" For even that part of the work of production which comes from outside comes from a

13. Fortin, "Augustine, the Arts, and Human Progress," in Collected Essays, 3:91.

man whom God has also created and whom He invisibly rules and governs. Now, at this point the mind lifts up its gaze to consider the whole world like a great tree of creation. In it is found a double activity of providence, the natural and the voluntary. (*DGL* 8.8.16–9.17)

Augustine saw the rational soul in movement from production to contemplation. The passage is set within his explanation for the art of agriculture within Eden, and demonstrates that rational souls of Edenic human beings are educated along an intellectual ascent, which means that not all Edenic human beings would be contemplative. Augustine seems to see this even in the case of Adam and Eve, when he states that it is no problem for God to "teach men to speak whom He had made in such a way that they could learn this art from others in case there were others present from whom they might learn" (*DGL* 8.16.35). Adam and Eve themselves knew the arts from God, but they were also made so that humans could learn them from others.[14] Prelapsarian human beings possess different levels of wisdom, which means that some would have been engaged in various arts while others would contemplate and impart their wisdom to others. This would require the political art to organize their activities, and shows the political art as educative.

The relationship between arts and virtue remains after the Fall. Augustine understood the invention of the arts as an expression of human being's genius (while noting that their proper use depends on virtue and not on the arts themselves): "has not the genius of man invented and applied countless astonishing arts, partly the result of necessity, partly the result of exuberant invention, so that this vigor of mind, which is so active in the discovery not merely of superfluous but even of dangerous and destructive things, betokens an inexhaustible wealth in the nature *(natura)* which can invent, learn, or employ such arts?" (*CD* 22.24).[15] The arts are products of human nature (although Augustine also states they are gifts from God [*CD* 7.30]). They exist independently of sin as they arise partly from the necessity of the human being's need

14. Augustine does not reject the hypothesis, articulated by other theologians at the time, that the disobedience of Adam and Eve derived from their impatience to know good and evil (*DGL* 11.41.56). This hypothesis assumes that such wisdom was theirs, but not before they earned it through proper obedience and education from God. Augustine only states that such a hypothesis is not literal but only figurative, and that it "could result in a theory apparently consistent with faith and reason." See also *DGL* 8.13.28–30.

15. See also Augustine, *"The Greatness of the Soul" and "The Teacher,"* 33.72; *DGL* 8.8.15–8.9.18. On the role of the liberal arts, see *DDC* 2.115–16; *DM* 1.3.4, 1.4.6; *Immortality of the Soul,* 4.5; *DVR* 30.54; and *83Q* 78; see also Fortin, "Augustine, the Arts, and Human Progress," in *Collected Essays,* 3:91–95.

to engage in life-sustaining work such as agriculture, which he calls the "most innocent of the arts" (*DGL* 8.8.15–8.9.17),[16] and partly from invention gained by the exercise of intellect. This is also signaled by his referring to virtues as the arts of living *(arte vivendi)* (*CD* 19.3). Since the arts include both virtues and manual arts such as agriculture, this indicates that they would have been present in Eden. Prelapsarian human beings would have been engaged in activities that would have required the coordination of the arts, because the arts would have been required to fulfill their needs and the exercise of their intellects. The collective action problem is one of knowledge, and the multiplicity of the arts would require the existence of an overseeing art or science to coordinate the arts. After the Fall, politics is characterized by coercion to restrain inordinate wills, but the essential collective action problem of organization and education remains.

## POLITICS OUTSIDE OF EDEN

Despite Augustine's antipolitical rhetoric, he distinguishes the usual *practice* of postlapsarian politics from the *essence* of politics. His argument that beauty is found in the weaving together of unity and multiplicity indicates that he believed politics to be a natural good. He compares political order to the beauty and arrangement of the Psalms: "For the rational and moderate harmony of diverse sounds insinuates the compact unity of a well-ordered city" (*CD* 17.14).[17] Whereas the Psalms sing for the city of God, Augustine's "well-ordered city" also includes political cities that represent good order. The order that the city represents is a harmony of its parts, "for each single human being, like one letter in a discourse, is as it were the element of a city or kingdom, however wide is the occupation of land" (*CD* 4.3).[18] Each individual, with his own goodness, is a part that helps to constitute the whole. Augustine chooses to compare the whole to a discourse *(sermon)*. A discourse becomes senseless and incomplete when it lacks its parts, just as a psalm would lack harmony if it lacked the full amplitude of notes and words that it comprises.[19] These comparisons of the city

16. See L. G. Muller, *The "De Haeresibus" of Saint Augustine* (Washington, D.C.: Catholic University of America Press, 1956), 46.

17. "Diversorum enim sonorum rationabilis moderatusque concentus concordi varietate compactam bene ordinatae civitatis insinuat unitatem."

18. "[N]am singulus quisque homo, ut in sermone una littera, ita quasi elementum est civitatis et regni quantalibet terrarum occupatione latissimi."

19. This recalls a statement he makes elsewhere, where he calls individual human beings the elements and seeds *(elementa et semina civitatum)* of cities (*EnP* 9.8).

with music and speech reflect his willingness to consider actual historical cities, full of the virtuous and the reprobate, as capable of bringing the multitude of individual potentials to a kind of perfection.

One can identify the natural good even within the corrupt practices. Augustine compares the sanctuary founded by Romulus and Remus to that founded by Christ (although he does not equate the two): "It is granted that Romulus and Remus, seeking a means of increasing the population of the city they were founding, established a sanctuary *(asylum)* where any man might seek refuge and be free from injury *(noxa liber)*, a wondrous example *(exemplum)* of what followed in honor of Christ" (*CD* 1.34). The foundations of Rome and of the Church are comparable insofar as both constitute sanctuaries that people seek in pursuing freedom from injury. He later states that the sanctuary created by a political founding foreshadows the remission of sins promised by the city of God: "[T]he remission of sins that gathers citizens for the eternal city has something in it of the famous sanctuary of Romulus, which was a sort of shadow *(umbram)* cast ahead. For there the multitude which was to found the city was congregated for the impunity of their crimes" (*CD* 5.17; see also 2.29). Augustine calls both Rome and Jerusalem a shadow *(umbra)* of the city of God (see also *CD* 15.2). He treats remission and sanctuary in the double sense of seeing Rome's inhabitants both as thugs seeking safety from those seeking vengeance on them and as people truly seeking safety to enable them to begin a new life. This double voice is not necessarily equivocation. Rather, it is consistent with the classical view that cities, founded often by violence and for the purpose of preserving life, have their end in the good life. Somewhere in the growth of a city, its citizens discover that their purpose is no longer survival but the good life. Augustine saw this as a general process in the drama of a human being's salvation, stating that humans are born to the earthly city by nature vitiated by sin, but to the heavenly city they are born by grace that heals nature (*CD* 15.1–2). Set within this drama of salvation is the birth and growth of a political city born often in sin, but finding its end not as the heavenly city, but as a foreshadow.[20]

The two passages quoted above indicate that the founding of the political city is a shadow or resemblance of the city of God because it too is a sanctuary for those seeking impunity. This view corroborates the evidence previously presented that Augustine understood the political city as a cosmion, an analogical way of reasoning about political society. Both are proper but distinct

20. Based on Augustine's view that natural things intimate revelation (*CD* 11.28), as examined in Chapter 6.

satisfactions of the human desire for peace.[21] By comparing the two, Augustine rejected the view that the sole purpose of political authority is to punish the wicked. He would have called the political founding a foreshadow of the city of the devil if he thought that its sole purpose was to punish the wicked. However, even the wicked, who seek peace in the political city, receive a "remission" of sorts for their sins.

The founding of Rome was occasioned, of course, by a fratricide. Augustine calls Romulus's fratricide of Remus an archetype, which has led commentators to conclude that Augustine thought politics to be sinful by nature (CD 15.5). Its archetypal status would suggest that all foundings necessarily shed the blood of the innocent, which implies that all cities are giant crimes. Augustine's view is more complicated than this. He points out that Romulus killed Remus because both loved glory and power inordinately and could not share domination. However, his argument remains in the conditional, and he suggests that innocence of the lust for power may be maintained for founders: "Since the goal was to glory in domination, there would of course be less domination if power was limited by having to be shared. Accordingly, in order that all power might accrue to one single person, his fellow was removed; and what innocence (quod innocentia) would have kept smaller and better grew through crime into something larger and inferior" (CD 15.5). Augustine is slightly ambiguous here because, despite calling the fratricide an archetypical founding, he admits the existence of their innocence (however brief), which is odd considering the example and because it is meant to occur after the Fall. Further, his preference for moderate-size political societies elsewhere (discussed below in Chapter 3) suggests that not all of them glory in domination (CD 4.3, 4.15). One could plausibly ask whether Rome would have been more virtuous if it had been founded by one of the pagans, such as Regulus, who sought virtue the right way (vera via). Such virtuous individuals would be the ones that Augustine mentions when he speaks of a good city having concord of command and obedience (CD 19.14, 19.16) according to a pact (Conf. 3.8). The "remission" that was sought in the founding of Rome, impunity for previous crimes, does not necessarily promise the good life.

This understanding is seen elsewhere in Augustine's discussion of the first city that was founded by Cain and named after his firstborn, Enoch (CD 15.17–19). The fratricide of Remus by Romulus is paralleled by that of Abel by Cain. Cain

---

21. Augustine distinguishes between temporal and eternal peace (see CD 19.11, 19.26–27). Generally, peace is the "tranquillity of order (tranquillitas ordinis)" (CD 19.13), which is based upon someone's true enjoyment of his or her true end.

went on to found the first earthly city that "finds its rest in its own temporal peace and felicity *(in eius temporali pace ac felicitate quiescentem)"* (CD 15.17). Enoch means "dedication" *(dedicatio* in Latin), which Augustine interprets to indicate "that this city has its beginning and end on earth, where there is no hope of anything beyond what can be seen in this world" (CD 15.17). The city named after Enoch contrasts with the name of Seth, Abel's son, which means "resurrection." At first glance, Augustine's distinction appears to follow the familiar distinction between the earthly city and the city of God, as Enoch is a descendant of Cain whereas Seth and his son, Enos, are part of the line that carries the city of God. The former appears to be the reprobate, the latter the saved. However, Augustine's understanding of Enoch indicates more than this. Augustine bases his distinction not on the one being vicious and the other virtuous, but on Enoch's city having its beginning and end in time. The earthly city, named "dedication," is a mortal creature, whereas the city of God is eternal. Further, he makes an Aristotelian distinction by referring to that city's "own temporal peace and felicity," as if the basis of the earthly city's peace is itself a good. This passage lacks the kinds of references to perverse sinful peace that characterize his descriptions of the earthly city in other parts of the *City of God.* It is also astonishing that he would go so far as to attribute rest *(quiescentem)* to the city, considering that "our heart cannot be quieted *(inquietum)* till it may find repose in [God]" *(Conf.* 1.1). By attributing to Enoch's city its own kind of rest, Augustine indicates that the city not only is the temporary place from which the pilgrim Enoch is "translated *(translatus)* into heaven" (CD 15.19), but also gives Enoch a home with its own kind of natural peace that allows him to please God.[22]

Augustine uses the difference between eternal and temporal goods to draw a sharp distinction between the peace sought by the city and that attained by the city of God: "It is incorrect, however, to say that the goods that this city covets are not good, since through them even the city itself is better according to its own human kind *(in suo humano genere)*. . . . When, however, the victors [of wars] are those who were champions of the more righteous cause, who can doubt that the victory in that case justifies joyous celebration and that the peace that resulted is desirable? These things are goods and doubtlessly gifts of God" (CD 15.4). Politics is not merely about seeking temporal peace regardless of

---

22. Augustine continues by reflecting on the symbolic significance of the number of generations after Adam and Seth that Enoch was born: "He is also the sixth from Seth, the father of those generations who are distinguished from the progeny of Cain; and it was on the sixth day that man was created and God brought His works to their consummation." See Chapter 6 on the allegorical importance of the number six in Augustine's ethics.

justice. Augustine states here that political goods are of a human kind and then goes on to state that even the most basic of these goods, peace and victory, are gifts of God.[23] Like Aristotle, he calls each item on this list good "according to its own human kind," as if he were treating political things from their own perspective rather than from the perspective of a Christian theologian (see also *CD* 2.21). As we just saw, he speaks of Enoch's city's own kind of felicity in this way. Augustine equates the goods of humankind with the gifts from God in order to illuminate their specifically human way of participating in the order of God. As a result, they are truly good, and their use, as with the arts, depends on the virtue of human beings. Moreover, he considered politics the greatest human kind of good. The death of public human beings, especially virtuous ones, is among the most painful losses that people can bear: "Since, then, the life of mortals is afflicted now more gently, again more harshly, by the death of those very dear to us, and especially of those whose duties are necessary for human society *(maxime quorum sunt humanae societati officia necessaria)*, nevertheless we would rather hear of or behold the death of those whom we love than perceive that they have fallen from faith or virtue, that is, that the soul itself has suffered death" (*CD* 19.8).

The difference between the essence of politics and its corrupt usual practice can be seen in Augustine's distinction between governing for the common good, which reflects the political art in Eden, and arrogant ruling. He distinguishes between the two by noting how some Roman writers, such as Sallust, had obscured the difference between the two kinds of rule by arguing that governing is unjust by nature. Ironically, this is the position that modern commentators commonly attribute to Augustine. Augustine quotes Sallust describing Roman history after the Roman people ejected the kings: "They made the term of command annual, and selected two commanders who were called consuls from taking counsel, not kings or masters from reigning or having dominion" (*CD* 5.12).[24] Augustine objects to Sallust's etymology because he obscures the difference between true and arrogant rulership: "But it would surely seem better to derive kings from the verb which means to rule. As kingdom is derived from king, so is king from the word for ruling. But royal contempt was regarded not as a discipline of a proper ruler, nor that of a benevolent consul, but rather

---

23. This echoes his discussion of virtues and arts as both specifically human and as gifts of God (*CD* 7.30, and above).

24. "[A]nnua imperia binosque imperatores sibi fecerunt, qui consules appellati sunt a consulendo, non reges aut domini a regnando dicti dominando" (quoting Sallust, *"The Conspiracy of Catiline"* 6.7). This passage also appears as a doubtful fragment in Cicero, *De Re Publica* 2.31.53.

as the arrogance of a tyrant" (*CD* 5.12).[25] Augustine's etymological point is also a theoretical point. The republican apologists obscured the two kinds of rule by rooting the noun *king* (*rex*) in the term *to reign* (*regnare*). By rejecting this equation and identifying its root in the term *to rule* (*regere*), Augustine envisages a true rule that is concerned for the common good and free from royal contempt. The various meanings of *regere* denote rule that is concerned with the common good. It means "to keep straight," "prevent from going wrong," "to lead straight," "to conduct," "to direct," "to draw the boundaries," and "to mark out the limits." It is etymologically related to *rectus*, which means "right," "proper," and "appropriate." Furthermore, Augustine elsewhere equates true ruling with correcting: "Thence is He also called King, from 'ruling (*Rex, a regendo*).' For that is no 'ruler that does not correct (*Non autem regit qui non corrigit*).' Hereunto is our King a King of 'right ones (*rectorum*)'" (*EnP* 45.44.15; see also *Conf.* 13.23). This kind of true rulership is seen also in Cicero's statement that God "rules the whole universe (*omnem mundum regit*)." *Regnare*, however, means specifically "to have royal power," "to be lord," "to be king," "to have mastery," and "to dominate." However, its meaning is not always negative, as Augustine elsewhere states: "on this earth the rule of good men (*regnum bonorum*) is a boon conferred not so much on them but on human affairs (*rebus humanis*)" (*CD* 4.3; see also 4.15). *Regere* is the root of all kinds of rule, and not exclusively of royal contempt. Augustine seems to follow Cicero's political thought by calling *regere* the genus and *regnare* one of its species. Cicero states: "And so when the supreme authority is in the hands of one man, we call him king (*regem*), and the status of this republic is kingship (*regnum*)."[26]

Augustine's criticism of the Roman writers also indicates that *consulere* comes closest to the political art as practiced in Eden. It is true rulership because it includes concern for those governed and taking counsel, and true rulership includes consultation with the truth; it involves a kind of statesmanship. As quoted above, he borrows Sallust's observations that the consuls derived their name "from taking counsel (*a consulendo*), not kings or masters from reigning (*a regnando*) or having dominion (*dominando*)" (*CD* 5.12). His usage of *consulere* throughout the *City of God* reflects this double meaning of *consulere* as giving and receiving (from God's truth and from the governed) counsel in official and unofficial capacities for the purpose of achieving civil peace. In this way,

25. "[C]um et reges utique a regendo dicti melius videantur, ut regnum a regibus, reges autem, ut dictum est, a regendo; sed fastus regius non disciplina putata est regentis vel benevolentia consulentis, sed superbia dominantis."
26. See Cicero, *De Re Publica* 6.13.13, 1.26.42.

Augustine's understanding is similar to Cicero's provision that a *populus* must be maintained by a certain amount of consultation *(consilium)* wherein the consulting body (be it monarchic, aristocratic, or popular) must "always owe its beginning to the same cause as that which produced the city itself."[27] This means that consultation must be based upon the common sense of justice prevailing in the society.

*Consul* is the official term that denotes a specific Roman office (*CD* 2.17, 2.18, 2.23, 2.27, 3.16, 3.17, 3.21, 3.24, 5.12, 18.54, 19.16, 22.4).[28] More broadly, it signifies one who governs for the sake of the governed, in the sense that the governor must consult or learn from the governed. For example, Augustine states this principle negatively when he observes that God did not consult the world when he created it because he constitutes his own standard (*CD* 11.23). Human beings, however, do consult, and Augustine speaks approvingly of historical circumstances in which women and the multitude participated in public consultations (*CD* 18.9). The term's special meanings also include taking concern for another, which includes fulfilling the command to love one's neighbor (*CD* 4.5, 5.9, 9.6, 10.5, 11.23, 11.33, 15.7, 15.25, 19.12, 19.14), giving an order (*CD* 2.18, 19.16), true rulership that is concerned for the ruled rather than the ruler (*CD* 2.20, 5.12, 7.4, 14.28), and enabling another to actualize a goal or end (*CD* 9.14). This second general meaning of *consulere*, therefore, indicates that it includes not only concern for the common good or the good of the governed, but also governing that extends to concrete consultation with the governed, where the governed have an input into the way they are governed. Finally, Augustine utilizes the term to mean consultation with the goal or standard by which truth is judged and by which action is performed. He speaks of consultation with reason or truth (*CD* 1.22, 5.26, 7.24, 10.11, 16.6, 21.8, 22.4), God or religion (*CD* 2.17, 18.36, 21.26), and the gods of the pagans in oracular rites (*CD* 2.4, 3.17, 3.22, 4.23, 5.3, 5.4, 18.10, 18.13, 18.53); he also uses the term to speak of acting in service of praise and glory (*CD* 5.14). *Consulere* means counsel and concern for others, and its meaning includes consulting the governed. Governing in the way suggested by the term *consulere* differs from the type of governing that Augustine is usually thought to endorse, which is an authoritarian way of governing that lacks counsel.[29] Augustine instead had in mind the kind of statesmanship in which a statesman

---

27. Ibid, 1.26.42. See also Malcolm Schofield, "Cicero's Definition of *Res Publica*," 77.

28. Consul is related to *episcopatus, overseer,* the term for *bishop* (*CD* 19.19).

29. See Rist, *Augustine: Ancient Thought Baptized,* 210–13. R. Williams more properly suggests translating *consulere* as "spiritual nurture" ("Politics and the Soul," 63).

governs a people within the boundaries of their capabilities and inclinations, seeking their consultation and consent but also informing their choices.

True consulship (if that term may be used to denote true governing) depends on worship of and service to God. Augustine states that princes and those under them serve one another in love: "[B]oth those put in charge and those placed under them serve one another in love, the former by their counsel, the latter by their obedience" (CD 14.28).[30] He defines true consulship as governing for the sake of the governed (and with their consent, as noted above) in an extended discussion of the properly ordered human society whose members properly worship God: "For those who are concerned for others give commands, the husband to his wife, the parents to their children, the masters to their servants; while those who are objects of concern obey" (CD 19.14).[31] This statement is made within the context of a discussion of the family (explicated below), which is the seedbed, as it were, of civic and ultimately of religious virtue. Augustine does not restrict consulere, and thus true dominion by humans, to familial rule. He states that this kind of rule begins with family peace but extends outward, and he articulates the general rule: "For they command not through lust for domination, but by dutiful concern, not with princely pride, but with mercy in providing for others" (CD 19.14).[32] The chapter following this passage includes the above-quoted passage that states that the first human beings were shepherds, thus ruling out instrumental rule over human beings. If one reads these two passages together, one discovers that true authority will take the shape of consulere, which includes political authority.

Augustine has often been seen to treat familial rule as paradigmatic for political rule. This view appears to fit with his statement, discussed above, that human relations are bound together by bonds of kinship (CD 12.22), and with his discussion of consulere in which he appears to treat the paterfamilias as paradigmatic (CD 19.16). The former passage, when read in conjunction with Augustine's other statements of Edenic human activity, indicates that such relations cannot be restricted to the family. The latter passage, despite appearances, actually indicates that Augustine had in mind a more Platonic-Aristotelian understanding of the relationship between the family and the city.

Augustine states that the order of nature (ordo naturalis) prescribes that the rulers of households govern all the members of the household with equal

30. "[I]n hac serviunt invicem in caritate et praepositi consulendo et subditi obtemperando."
31. "Imperant enim qui consulunt, sicut vir uxori, parentes filiis, domini servis. Oboediunt autem quibus consulitur, sicut mulieres maritis, filii parentibus, servi dominis."
32. "Neque enim dominandi cupiditate imperant, sed officio consulendi, nec principandi superbia, sed providendi misericordia."

cherishing (*CD* 19.16).[33] True ruling *(consulere)* that is according to the order of nature appears to find its beginning in the model of the paterfamilias, whose fathers are true *(veri patres)* when they govern for the good of the governed.[34] True ruling entails maintaining domestic peace *(pax domestica)*, the peace found in ordinate concord, which entails promoting the worship of God. Authority, however, is limited by what human society in general permits: "So if any one in the household by disobedience breaks the domestic peace, he is rebuked by a word or a blow or some other kind of just and permitted punishment *(alio genere poenae iusto atque licito)*, to the extent conceded by human society *(quantum societas humana concedit)*" (*CD* 19.16). Family authority may be exercised to execute just punishment that accords with the norms and customs of human society. Augustine limits familial authority to what is permitted by human society in general. This limitation can be understood in two ways. It might mean that familial authority is limited by what is practical according to human society, with an eye on the conventions of a particular society. Such a situation might arise, for example, in contemporary society where a family governed by traditional, hierarchal modes finds itself disagreeing with society's democratic and egalitarian customs. The passage has a more substantial meaning insofar as the justice of familial authority is defined in some way by the nature of the broader human society. In other words, familial authority extends only so far before the natural political order dictates what can be practiced in a family. A second interpretation of this passage might indicate that familial authority is not the exclusive model of authority, but that it is circumscribed by political authority according to the natural order. Augustine envisages this interdependent relationship between familial and political authority, between public and private (as we say today), so that both spheres check one another while retaining their independence. Neither is a complete model for the other. Rather, the choice to follow one would be a prudent one that would attend to the needs of the other while intending the good that nourishes both.

Later in the same passage, Augustine states that familial authority is integrated into political authority because the family itself is an integral part of the political whole:

> Since, then, a human being's home ought to be the beginning or part *(initium sive particula)* of the city, and every beginning ministers to some

33. "[O]mnibus domus suae membris pari dilectione consularent."
34. Rist notes that *familias* extends beyond the biological family to "include the dependent tenants, near-serfs and slaves" (*Augustine: Ancient Thought Baptized*, 210).

end of its own kind and every part to the integrity of the whole of which
it is a part, it follows clearly enough that domestic peace refers *(referatur)*
to civic peace, that is, that the ordered concord concerning command and
obedience among those who dwell together in a household refers to the
ordered concord concerning command and obedience among citizens. Thus
we see that the father of a family ought to draw his precepts from the law
of the city, and so rule his household that it shall be in harmony with the
peace of the city. *(CD* 19.16)

The family is a beginning *(initium)* and a part *(particula)* of the city. *Initium*
is a beginning that issues into something unique with its own integrity. It is
the term Augustine uses to illuminate the uniqueness of human beings, who
were created so there would be a new beginning: "But this beginning *(initium)*
never before existed in that way. Accordingly, in order that there might be this
beginning, a human being, before whom none existed, was created" *(CD* 12.21).
*Initium* is an integral and dynamic part of the whole. Just as the creation of a
human being introduced something new into Creation, so too does the family
constitute the seedbed and source of reform in society. However, God's creation
of human beings was the first part of the story of creation and redemption, and
so one cannot conclude that the family as an *initium* is a beginning and an end
of human society.

Similarly, *particula* literally means particle, and, in classical Latin, it signifies
the primary element of the whole. For example, Cicero speaks in *De Officiis*
of thieves who still cannot cooperate without some small particle or element
*(particula)* of justice, and speaks in *De Re Publica* of not omitting any single
point *(particula)* in a discourse.[35] Augustine uses it here in a similar manner,
and in the same way he understands seeds *(elementa)* and notes, as described
above. Therefore, both *initium* and *particula* refer to integral parts of a greater
whole upon which the whole depends. However, they are only beginnings that,
as their being suggests, find their completion in the whole, as a thief's hint of
justice is completed in true justice and as a single point is completed in a
complete discourse.

Augustine regarded politics as the activity in which citizens act together
to create a little world that is understood, from within, as having tentative
sempiternal existence, and supplies its participants with a kind of wholeness.
Individual participants achieve a kind of wholeness only by interacting with one

35. Cicero, *De Officiis* 2.11.40; *De Re Publica* 1.24.38.

another and by living their lives as if that field is expected to exist sempiternally. The political art, as outlined in the discussion of prelapsarian politics and in Augustine's use of the term *consulere*, assists people to achieve that wholeness by coordination and education. This understanding of politics is not utopianism and does not mean that Augustine neglected the truth of the city of God. To anticipate the argument in Chapter 6, political life has different functions from those found in the Church, and political life consists in perfecting these functions. This chapter has focused only on political life as the field on which these types of longing play. The next chapter focuses more specifically on the types of longings that help to perfect and to destroy that field.

# 3

# A HEADLESS BODY POLITIC?

A UGUSTINE'S apparent ambiguity over whether political life is natural for human beings translates into a kind of schizophrenia when one inquires into the kind of regime that his political thought might support. Either his concentration on the glory of the otherworldly city of God eclipses political goods, such as liberty or political glory, or his theology necessitates an inordinately active political role by the Christian Church. Either his political thought lends itself to a modern realist social-contract construction, where politics is strictly instrumental for other goods, or it lends itself to a Constantinian empire or *sacrum imperium* that requires an excessively high degree of virtue, and requires religious and moral conformity and the suppression of heretics. Insofar as these interpretations agree that politics is not in itself a substantive good for Augustine, they agree that he left the body politic headless, *acephalous* in the words of Sir John Fortescue.[1]

A civilization animated by Christian ends does not need to lose its balance or its head. Augustine's political thought, his understanding of how a people *(populus)* achieves representation in particular, maintains this balance. The balance is achieved by his view that the best kind of *populus* is a kind of political friendship attainable not exclusively by Christian revelation but also by non-Christian political philosophy. Political representation has traditionally been a difficult problem for political theorists in the Christian tradition, who sought an account of politics as a substantive human good. For example, they often borrowed the category of "body politic" from classical political philosophy to explain how a

1. Fortescue, "In Praise of the Laws of England."

polity grows and achieves representation.[2] The difficulty with this approach is that the body politic too often coalesced with the scriptural symbol of the body of Christ. This combination gives the polity a sacral character approaching that of or identical to the Church. This, for instance, was the difficulty of Sir John Fortescue's understanding of representation. He criticized Augustine's understanding of a people or body politic for being headless *(acephalous)*; or, to translate this into contemporary terminology, Augustine saw politics as merely instrumental rather than possessing substantive goods, constituting a proto-Machiavellian immoralism or Hobbesian social-contract theory. Fortescue held this view because he thought Augustine's reformulation of Cicero's definition of a *populus* (*CD* 19.24, provided below) did not necessitate justice or require a monarchy.[3] Fortescue responds by arguing for a monarchy to constitute the head of the body politic, but he also attributed the quality of *corpus mysticum*, the same spiritual substance as the body of Christ, to the realm.[4] This chapter shows that the head of Augustine's *populus* need not be the Church or a monarch, and that the body politic and its head can take a republican form.

It is first necessary to clarify the meaning of political representation. Political theorists today generally think of political representation along Hobbesian lines, viewing institutions and leaders as "re-presenting" the will or interests of the people. This modern way of understanding representation focuses on

2. For example, see the writings collected in Cary J. Nederman and Kate Langdon Forhan, eds., *Medieval Political Theory—A Reader: The Quest for the Body Politic, 1100–1400*.

3. On Augustine's reformulation as not necessitating justice, see John N. Figgis, *The Political Aspects of St. Augustine's "City of God,"* 59; C. H. McIlwain, *The Growth of Political Thought in the West*, 157; and Deane, *Political and Social Ideas*, 118–29. Fortin appears to lean toward this position. He states that Augustine's reformulation "simply calls attention to the unfortunate for habitual cleavage between the 'is' and the 'ought' in the lives of the states" ("Political Idealism and Christianity," in *Collected Essays*, 2:38–39). Most commentators appear to agree that the reformulation does not require a monarchy. A. J. Carlyle observes that his definition was "eccentric" in the mainstream of patristic political thought, and virtually ignored in the earlier Middle Ages (*A History of Medieval Political Theory in the West*, 161–74). Nevertheless, Nicolas of Cusa used it for his conciliarist project: "[E]ven as a republic is a common thing of the people, and a common thing a state, and the state is a multitude of men brought to a kind of bond of concord, as Augustine writes . . . , so he who presides in the pastoral court corresponds to him to whom a republic is entrusted" (*De Concordantia Catholica*, in *Medieval Political Ideas*, ed. Ewart Lewis, 1.6).

4. John of Salisbury similarly argues that priests should constitute the head of the body (*Policraticus*, 5.2). Christian political thought in general is often said to ally itself naturally with monarchy, but this thesis has recently been challenged by Antony Black's analysis of republican themes in Christian political thought. He challenges the conventional thesis (of Quentin Skinner and J. G. A. Pocock, for example) that Christianity necessarily aligns itself with monarchy. Black, focusing on the thought of Saint Cyprian instead of that of Augustine, argues instead that Christianity supports potentially either or both monarchy and republicanism because it supports the fundamental equality of human beings and because Christianity, especially the early Church, was republican in form ("Christianity and Republicanism: From St. Cyprian to Rousseau").

only one element of political representation, according to Augustine's view. This particular element refers to only the external (or elemental, as I shall call it) part of representation. It does not get at the part of representation that symbolizes a society's own self-interpretation and self-realization.

This chapter extends the discussion of politics as a "cosmion" and "virtual immortality" from the previous chapter. Voegelin considers three types of representation, which help to clarify the issue. The first type, elemental, signifies the external existence of a society. It signifies the various agents that hold society together physically. It includes, for example, the laws, the institutions, the mechanics of voting, and geographical districts.[5] Political philosophy cannot stop its analysis with this type of representation, because theory must also examine the question of whether elemental representation actualizes the spirit or idea of a society. Those ideas are what Voegelin calls existential representation, which signifies the idea, spirit, or political culture (as we say today) that animates a society. If the elemental representative does not match the existential reality of a society, then the elemental representative will not last long. This disjunction is seen in well-meaning but often disastrous attempts in American foreign policy to impose liberal democratic constitutions on traditional and illiberal societies.

Transcendent representation is the third type of representation. This type reflects the attempts by a society to interpret itself as representative of something beyond itself. It constitutes its self-interpretation as a just society. This type of representation is more obvious in premodern than modern societies. For example, a look at ancient Chinese, Egyptian, Mesopotamian, Persian, or Native American sources reveals that their societies interpreted themselves as representations of the cosmic order. They sought to harmonize society with the order and rhythms of the cosmos through the way they established rulership or through festivals timed with the seasons.[6] Voegelin calls this kind of transcendent representation "cosmological." Another type of transcendent representation, which he calls "anthropological," is found in the Greek world, as in Plato's view that the polis is "man writ large," where transcendent truth is symbolized as the good for human beings. For Voegelin, following Plato, anthropological truth does not mean the truth for everyone as in Protagoras's dictum that "man is the measure." Rather, anthropological truth signifies the "idea of a man who has found his true nature through finding his true relation to God."[7] Voegelin cites the sayings of Solon, whose laws, which healed fractured

---

5. Voegelin, *New Science of Politics,* 33.
6. Ibid., 54.
7. Ibid., 61–68, citing Plato, *Republic* 368c–d.

Athens, were based on the "unseen measure." Anthropological truth is a type of transcendent representation because it signifies human beings' true relation to God as comprehended by noetic reason. Because it is anthropological, the truth for every individual human being, such representation requires representation of all human beings within that society, and thus consent, according to Voegelin, is a necessary component of such a regime. The society that Aristotle calls "political friendship" reflects this right relationship because it consists of spiritual agreement *(homonoia)* among human beings, and that agreement is possible only when human beings live in agreement with *Nous,* the most divine part of themselves: "[A] city is in accord when men have the same opinion about what is to their interest, and choose the same actions, and do what they have resolved in common."[8] Faction and domination are the result of discord and the failure to live according to the most divine part of human beings.

Christianity introduces new theoretical problems into human beings' relationship to God, and thus representation, because it promises salvation. Voegelin calls this type of transcendent representation "soteriological truth." Politically, the distinction between anthropological and soteriological truth reflects the contrast between the ends of politics and the ends of the Church. The sacerdotal order of the Church, as representative of the city of God, is responsible for soteriological truth, and politics is responsible for anthropological truth. However, as the case of Fortescue shows, Christian political theorists have generally tried to symbolize the transcendent truth of society with soteriological symbols as *corpus mysticum.* The body politic was confused with the body of Christ. Some regimes, medieval and modern, have more successfully articulated transcendent representation within the framework of Christian soteriological truth. For instance, American self-interpretation includes various symbols such as "city on a hill" and other symbols that draw on Christian themes without sacralizing politics. This self-interpretation has led commentators such as George Anastaplo to argue that the Declaration of Independence asserts that the three branches of the U.S. government reflect God's government of the world as legislator, executive, and judge.[9]

Augustine does consider political representation in transcendent terms but regards the transcendent truth of politics as anthropological instead of soteriological, in order to preserve the dignity both of political society and of

---

8. Aristotle, *Nicomachean Ethics* 9.6.1167a20.
9. Anastaplo, *The Constitution of 1787: A Commentary,* 21. On other Christian symbolism, see E. L. Tuveson, *Redeemer Nation;* and Jürgen Gebhardt, *Americanism: Revolutionary Order and Societal Self-Interpretation in the American Republic.*

the Church. This is seen, for instance, in his view that the virtue of pagan peoples was at times superior to that of the Israelites (*CD* 10.13).[10] This chapter shows how Augustine reformulates Cicero's definition of *populus* in terms of anthropological truth. This means, then, that even though the Christian mystery of the Trinity is the perfection of worship and friendship, this perfection does not transform politics in the sense of reorienting it exclusively toward soteriological truth (although such reorientation brings anthropological truth into sharper relief).[11] Augustine understood a republic, being neither a monarchy nor a pure democracy, as including the functions of governors and governed (possibly being traded among different individuals); thus, a republic possesses democratic, aristocratic, and monarchic parts. Although it is true that Augustine did not devote himself to extensive analyses of political regimes, he recognized the phenomenon of representation when he wrote of the one "bearing the person of the public power *(personam gerens publicae potestatis)*" (*CD* 1.21; see Chapter 4). This person is responsible for meting out justice, but he can also be understood to represent the public in his person. Augustine understands *persona* as a mask or signifier: "For all things signified seem somehow to sustain the *persona* of the things that they signify" (*CD* 18.48). An inquiry into Augustine's understanding of political representation, therefore, examines his understanding of what objects of love are personated in the regime.

## THE *POPULUS* AND THE REPUBLIC

### Perfect Justice in the City of God

According to Augustine, perfect politics and justice are found only in the mystical city of God: "True justice, however, exists only in that republic whose founder and ruler is Christ, if it is right to call it a republic, since we cannot deny that it is the people's weal" (*CD* 2.21).[12] Only the city of God possesses true justice, and only it completely actualizes the common good. Augustine defines the city of God as governed by true sacrifice in works of mercy that cannot be

---

10. In general, see Adams, *"Populus" of Augustine and Jerome*, 123–35.

11. On political friendship, compare, for example, with Aristotle, *Nicomachean Ethics* 9.6.1167b3–4.

12. Schofield points out that the term *res publica*, in Cicero and in Latin writers generally, had an elastic range of uses including "public[-spirited] activity," "public affairs/business," "the public interest," "the community," and "the community constituted by the *civitas* or *populus*" ("Cicero's Definition").

performed except through that good of which it is said: " 'For me it is good to cling to God'—it assuredly follows that all this redeemed city, which is to say the congregation and society of the saints, is offered to God as a universal sacrifice through the High Priest who in his passion offered himself for us in the form of a slave that we might be the body of so great a head" (*CD* 10.6, quoting Ps. 73:28). The redeemed city is governed by the perfect sacrifice, which is effected when the High Priest sacrifices himself. Human beings cannot actualize this justice themselves. This does not mean that human beings do not know how to make sacrifices without the message of Christ because both Abraham and the pagan philosophers, for example, recognized that true justice requires the true sacrifice to the Creator God (*CD* 19.22). However, faith in Christ perfects it because he fully actualizes it.

Locating perfect justice in the transcendent city of God enables Augustine to acknowledge that political societies are republics (*CD* 19.22, 19.24–27). Cicero and his Scipio had a natural knowledge of what true justice entails, but Scipio's definition is insufficient because it requires that the paradigmatic just city be earthly:

> For he briefly defines a republic as the weal of the people. And if this definition be true, there never was a Roman republic, for the people's weal was never attained among the Romans. For the people, according to his definition, is community of the multitude associated by a consensus of right and by a community of interests (*Populum enim esse definivit coetum multitudinis iuris consensu et utilitatis communione sociatum*). And what he means by a consensus of right he explicates by disputation, showing that a republic cannot be administered without justice. Where, therefore, there is no true justice (*iustitia vera*) there can be no right. . . . Further, justice is that virtue which distributes everyone his due. Where, then, is the justice of man, when he deserts the true God and yields himself to impure demons? Is this to give everyone his due? Or is he who keeps back a piece of ground from the purchaser, and gives it to a man who has no right to it, unjust, while he who keeps back himself from the God who made him, and serves wicked spirits, is just?[13] (*CD* 19.21)

According to the definition given by Scipio, the city of God, which actualizes perfect justice, is the true republic.

---

13. This passage repeats Scipio's definition of a *populus* as a "coetum multitudinis iuris consensu et utilitatis communione sociatum" (*CD* 2.21); see also his identification of *res publica* with "id est rem populi, rem patriae, rem communem" (*CD* 5.18).

**The *Populus* Exists in between the City of God and the City of Man**

According to Augustine, Scipio's definition of a republic makes it impossible for any earthly republic to be called such, because Scipio's conditions for actualizing it were impossible. To rectify this problem, Augustine reformulates the definition of a *populus* that includes within it perfect (the city of God) and imperfect forms. This is his reformulation of Scipio's definition:

> But if a people is not defined in this mode, but in some other manner, and if we say: "a people is a community of a rational multitude which is associated by a communal concord of the things it loves," then in order to discover the character of any people, we have only to observe what they love. Yet whatever it loves, if only it is a community of rational creatures and not beasts, and is bound together in communal concord as to the objects of love, it is not absurdly called a people; and it will be a superior people in proportion as it is bound together by higher things, inferior in proportion as it is bound together by lower.[14] (*CD* 19.24)

This reformulation reflects Augustine's understanding of political representation in that it corresponds to his view that human beings seek to become like or to imitate the objects they love or prize. Just as one becomes more godlike by imitating Christ, and just as one's soul is dispersed into the flux of the world when one inordinately pursues worldly goods, so too do political societies become more like the objects their people love. Through this reformulation, Augustine theorized about elemental, existential, and transcendent representation more completely than did Cicero's Scipio (or at least Augustine's understanding of him) because Augustine included perfect and imperfect forms in his definition.

Augustine maintained the city of God as the paradigm of the republic, and imperfect cities as reflections of that paradigm. Augustine's reformulation of Scipio's definition reveals three characteristics. First, Augustine specifies a particular kind of reason by speaking of rational beings. We may ask, as is common today, whether such rationality is merely instrumental (or technical) or whether politics fulfills another type of rationality, such as deliberation or counsel that enables one to govern oneself. Augustine appears to favor the latter

---

14. "Si autem populus non isto sed alio definiatur modo, velut si dicatur: 'Populus est coetus multitudinis rationalis rerum quas diligit concordi communione sociatus,' profecto, ut videatur qualis quisque populus sit, illa sunt intuenda quae diligit. Quaecumque tamen diligat, si coetus est multitudinis non pecorum sed rationalium creaturarum et eorum quae diligit concordi communione sociatus est, non absurde populus nuncupatur; tanto utique melior quanto in melioribus, tantoque deterior quanto est in deterioribus concors."

kind of rationality when he states that a good city will cultivate the worship of God, and that such worship enables reason to govern the vices: "For in general a city of the impious, not governed by God, since it is disobedient to the command of God that sacrifice be not offered save to Himself only, whereby in that city the soul should exercise righteous and faithful rule *(recte ac fideliter imperet)* over the body and reason over the vices, has no true justice *(iustitiae veritate)*" *(CD* 19.24). Worship enables the rule of reason over the vices, and it also enables human beings to realize their social nature in loving their neighbor *(CD* 19.5, 19.14). Failure to worship perfectly means that the city lacks "true justice," but it does not mean there is no justice.

Augustine contrasts rational beings with the beasts, who (at least the gregarious ones) seek fellowship:

> For even the most savage beasts . . . preserve their species by a sort of peace: by cohabitation *(coeundo)*, by begetting, bearing, suckling and rearing their young, although most of them are not gregarious, but solitary; not like sheep, deer, doves, starlings, and bees, but like lions, wolves, foxes, eagles, and owls. For what tigress does not gently purr over her cubs, and lay aside her ferocity to fondle them? What kite, solitary as he is when circling over his prey, does not seek a mate, build a nest, hatch the eggs, bring up the young birds, and maintain with the mother of his family as peaceful a domestic society as possible? How much more *(Quanto magis)* is man moved by the laws of his nature, so to speak, to enter upon a fellowship *(societatem)* with all his fellow men *(hominibus . . . omnibus)*, and to maintain peace with them . . . ? *(CD* 19.12)

Augustine contrasts the rationality of rational creatures such as human beings with that of the beasts. He observes that even the most solitary and savage animals seek fellowship of a certain kind. He contrasts these beasts with more gregarious beasts such as sheep and deer, and observes that the latter have a stronger social bond. Gregarious beasts seek fellowship to maintain the species, and some even appear to enjoy each other's company (Augustine observes how ferocious tigresses purr when attending to their young), which indicates that their relations are not merely instrumental. "How much more" does human being seek fellowship with "all his fellow men"? Human relations, due to human nature and rationality, strive for higher goods than do relations among animals, and human relations extend further than the family. If this is the case, then Augustine, in his reformulation of Scipio's definition of a city, indicates that a city is grounded in a kind of rationality that finds fulfillment in communion with others whose purposes are more than merely instrumental.

Turning to the second characteristic of Augustine's reformulation, he uses affective language in his definition by stating that a *populus* is bound in concord, and indicates that he saw a *populus* as a kind of political friendship. *Concors* means literally "with heart," which implies a close solidarity and like-mindedness within a society. Its dictionary meaning includes "of the same mind," "united," and "harmonious." It is the root of *concordia*, which means "mutual agreement," "concurrence of feeling," "friendship," "harmony," and "state of peace and amity between opposing parties." Augustine elsewhere calls peace among human beings an ordinate concord *(ordinata concordia)* (*CD* 19.13), and he approvingly quotes Scipio's comparison of *concordia* of a city with the *harmonia* of musicians: "[W]hat musicians call harmony in singing, is concord in the city" (*CD* 2.21).[15] He speaks of it elsewhere when he points out that the Roman Empire would have been more humane had the nations *(gentes)* entered by agreement or concord *(concorditer)* rather than through compulsion, which indicates that each particular nation, perhaps through some form of federalism, could have helped to constitute the Roman Empire through a common like-mindedness (*CD* 5.17). Further, concord depends on justice, as Augustine equates it with the health *(salus)* of the *populus* (*CD* 19.24).

The meaning of concord is also extended to religiousness. Augustine criticizes the Romans for impiously introducing the discord of civil wars immediately after erecting a temple dedicated to the goddess Concord: "But what was this but to deride the gods, by building a temple to that goddess who, had she been in the city, would not have suffered herself to be torn by such dissensions?" (*CD* 3.25). The goddess Concord was used impiously for human purposes in the same way that the other Roman gods were used. Augustine criticizes the Romans for not taking this worship seriously and thus undermining the grounds for any kind of concord. Having something in concord means a unity of mind or of heart concerning a society object of love.

Augustine also describes a *populus* as an assemblage or, more literally, a coming together *(coetus)*. *Coetus* is a generic term like the Greek *synagoge* or *ekklesia*, but Augustine appears to give it an affective connotation in his definition. Cicero's Scipio uses *coetus* in his definition (*CD* 2.21, 19.21), and Augustine carries this concept from classical political philosophy over into his

15. Citing Cicero, *De Re Publica* 2.42.69. The Latin *harmonia* is not the same as the Greek *homonoia*, the term Aristotle uses to describe political friendship. However, Latin authors appear to have combined the two meanings in *concordia* (see Quintilian, *The "Institutio oratoria" of Quintilian*, trans. H. E. Butler, 4 vols. [London: Heinemann, 1959–1963], 1.10.12; and Cicero, *"De Natura Deorum"* 2.23.61; see also *CD* 2.21, 12.22, 12.23, 14.1, 15.16; and H. G. Liddell and Robert Scott, *An Intermediate Greek-English Lexicon*, 557).

own formulation. Augustine associates his term with begetting *(gignere)* in his description of the fellowship of animals *(CD* 19.12, quoted above). Augustine's choice of *coetus* over one important alternative, *communitas,* is illuminating because it suggests he wished to underline the unitary and affective elements of the definition. *Communitas* would also have worked, as it was a common term in this kind of discourse (see *CD* 5.15, 5.18).[16] Augustine's understanding of *coetus* as affective is seen in an earlier work where he speculates on human beings' natural inclination to seek unity:

> And, what else do friends strive for, but to be one? The more they are one, so much the more they are friends. A people *(populus)* is a city *(civitas),* for whom dissension is a danger. What else is "to dissent *(dissentire)"* but not to think alike *(non unum sentire)*? An army is made up of many soldiers. And is not any multitude *(multitudo)* so much the less easily defeated in proportion as it is the more closely united *(coit)*? In fact, the joining *(coitio)* is itself called a *cuneus* ["troops in wedge-formation"], a co-union, as it were *(quasi couneus).* And what about every kind of love *(amor omnis)*? Does it not wish to become one with what it is loving *(amat)*? *(DO* 2.18.48)

When read in light of Augustine's reformulation of Cicero, this passage shows that human beings are motivated by a natural, affective drive toward unity with one another, which is expressed as a *populus.* The affective aspect of love is also shown in his insistence that *diligo* (used in his reformulation of Cicero in *CD* 19.24) has the same meaning as *amo* (the term used above) *(CD* 14.7).

Augustine's use of affective language to signify political unity is comparable to Aristotle's understanding of political friendship, and reflects his willingness to utilize the categories of classical political philosophy to signify transcendent truth. Specifically, the transcendent truth of political society is what was earlier described as anthropological truth, the proper relationship of human beings toward God as comprehended by natural reason. By using classical categories, Augustine points out that transcendent truth that finds representation in a political society is the transcendent truth of natural philosophy or theology, not the soteriological truth of the Trinity, which is fully present in the city of God. In this sense, Augustine maintains the agreement he had with Cicero earlier in his career on the meaning of friendship as the "agreement *(consensio)* on things human and divine combined with good will and love" *(CA* 3.5.13).[17]

---

16. For example, Cicero speaks of speech extending its benefits with those with whom "we are united by the bonds of community *(communitate iuncti)"* *(De Officiis* 1.44.156). Cicero extends the term's meaning to include community between gods and men (1.43.153).

17. Quoting Cicero, *De Amicitia* 20.

The transcendent truth of political society is anthropological rather than sote-riological.

Augustine confirms this point even on a problem that is often taken as a distinguishing mark between classical and Christian political thought: the relationship between unequals. It is often said that for Aristotle, for example, friendship is impossible between unequals. The Trinitarian teaching of Christianity, on the other hand, shows how all are equal before God. Thus pity or mercy, for the ancients, was considered a vice or at most a quality of a rhetorician rather than a political virtue.[18] Augustine, however, considered this an incorrect view and instead praises Cicero for stating that pity *(misericordia)* is a virtue (*CD* 9.5). This indicates that Augustine believed that politics, in rare cases at its best, provides a foreshadow or intimation of the city of God (see *CD* 2.29, 5.17).

Augustine weaves together affective and military language in calling a *populus* a *coetus*. The affective element indicates that cities are naturally inclined to a unity. However, he compares a people to a wedge-shaped military formation *(cuneus)* that is unified and conjoined *(coitio, couneus)*. *Cuneus* signifies troops in a wedge formation, unified and cutting through enemy lines.[19] *Couneus* translates as counion, *coitio* as joining or coupling. Augustine treats *cuneus* as a pun on *couneus* and *coitio*. The rhetorical emphasis lies with the affective imagery *(coitio* and *couneus)*, but the military reference indicates that such a union with one (that is, friend and citizen) rules out union with others (in other words, noncitizens). A military wedge formation *(cuneus)* separates what it is defined against. This being the case, the fundamental nature of *coetus* and *amor* is toward unity, and the pun here indicates that the divisiveness of this activity vis-à-vis others does not exhaust this activity. Augustine does not equate politics with struggle and war, as Carl Schmitt did, for example, but with peace (*CD* 19.13). This means that a people might generally define itself against outsiders, but it does not necessitate that political love defines itself against that which it is not. Augustine's play on words reminds the reader of the linguistic and conceptual connection in ancient Greek between the *polis* and its war function as a fortress, and, in fact, he may have wished to preserve this connection. Furthermore, his pun also reminds the reader that the political

18. See Seneca, *De Providentia. De Constantia. De Ira. De Clementia,* trans. John W. Basore (Cambridge: Harvard University Press, 1928), 2.4–5; and Aristotle, *Rhetoric,* in *The Complete Works of Aristotle,* ed. Jonathan Barnes, trans. W. Rhys Roberts, 2:2152–269 (Princeton: Princeton University Press, 1984), 2.8.1385b12–1386b7.

19. See Livy, *Ab urbe condita* (The History of Rome), 2.50, 10.29, 22.47; and Virgil, *The Aeneid,* 12.269, 12.575.

is where the unity of political friendship meets multiplicity (of individual characters, of geographical locations, and of particular traditions and customs, for example).

In the third characteristic of Augustine's reformulation of Scipio's definition of *populus*, he indicates that one can judge the quality of a regime by the quality of the object of its love. The city of God is exemplary because it is governed by the love of God (*CD* 2.21, 10.6, 19.23–27). This means that inferior objects of love such as wealth and glory are still republics, but that such republics love inferior objects and are thus less just and less peaceful than the city of God. This enables Augustine to grant that Rome and other nations were indeed republics: "But what I have said about this people [the Romans] and about this republic [Rome] let me be understood to have said and meant about those of the Athenians, those of any other Greeks, of the Egyptians, of that earlier Babylon of the Assyrians and of any other nation whatsoever, when they maintained in their republics an imperial sway, whether small or great *(vel parva vel magna)"* (*CD* 19.24). Augustine's reason for calling these regimes republics is that, unlike Scipio, he did not require true justice *(vera iustitia)* of them. In fact, after having concluded from Scipio's own premises that Rome was not a republic, Augustine argues that a more plausible definition would allow one to see Rome as a republic: "If we follow, however, more plausible definitions *(probabiliores . . . definitiones)*, there was a republic in its own mode *(pro suo modo quodam)*, and it was better administered by the earlier Romans than the later. True justice, however, exists only in that republic [the city of God], since we cannot deny that it was a people's estate *(rem populi)"* (*CD* 2.21). Augustine admits that a definition that allows one to see Rome as a republic is "more plausible" than that of Scipio, or even one that necessitates that only the city of God is just. He also appears to make an Aristotelian distinction by calling Rome a republic according to its own mode, as if he were treating political things from their own perspective rather than from the perspective of a Christian theologian. Since they were called republics, then each one of them cultivated a certain love and fulfilled human nature to some extent.

These considerations of Augustine's definition of a *populus* indicate that justice was never far from his mind when he defines a *populus*, even though his hyperbolic antipolitical rhetoric, in other places of the *City of God*, makes him appear to deny that politics is a natural good. He argues that political representation is not that of the city of God. This being the case, Augustine's political theory includes the three types of representation that I have been discussing: elemental, existential, and transcendent. However, he attempted to articulate the best political society as a political friendship while avoiding the extremes of identifying the substance of the *populus* with the city of God or of restricting it to its elemental representation.

## REPUBLICAN REPRESENTATION OF THE *POPULUS*

According to Augustine, a people best articulates itself through a republican mode. This is best seen in his view that a *populus* precedes the particular constitutional form of a political society. The character of a people depends on the object of its love, and the love determines what form the political society will take (*CD* 19.24). The love itself does not create the people, which means that a political society remains constant even though the objects of its love fluctuate. For example, Augustine would have disagreed with the French and Russian revolutionaries that their revolutions created a new *populus*. The revolutions would have expressed only the change in which the object of love received institutional or elemental representation. Augustine argues that Rome remained a people even when it underwent its internal transformation from republic to decadent empire: "But what this people loved in its early and in subsequent times, and by what moral decline it passed into bloody sedition and then into social and civil warfare, and disrupted and corrupted that very concord, which is, so to speak, the health of the people, history bears witness" (*CD* 19.24). A people remains a people even when concord breaks down, when the body politic becomes unhealthy but is not yet dissolved. Concord is a condition for the health of a people, but the existence of a minimum of concord does not affect the status of Rome as a people, "so long," Augustine concludes, "as there remains some sort of (*qualiscumque*) gathering of rational beings united in fellowship by a communal accord about the objects of its love" (*CD* 19.24).[20] The transformation of Rome and its subsequent civil wars endangered but did not destroy the *populus* of Rome. Augustine does not appear to be thinking of the proverbial peace among thieves (that is, strictly instrumental relations) because he has already ruled this out in his definition of a *populus*, when he points to the presence of rational beings capable of substantive relations as one of the necessary characteristics of a *populus*. Rather, he alludes to the type of concord that remains even in the civil wars that divide citizen against citizen and family

20. This remained true even after the invasion of Rome by Alaric: "The Roman Empire has been shaken rather than transformed, and that happened to it at other periods, before the preaching of Christ's name; and it recovered. There is no need to despair of its recovery at this present time. Who knows what is God's will in this matter?" (*CD* 4.8).

member against family member, which is the most miserable of wars (see *CD* 3.23–24). Augustine identifies this type of concord with the type of peace that even warriors seek when they wage war for the purpose of peace (*CD* 19.12). The *populus* of Rome was a higher entity than the particular claimants to its title in the civil wars, and this entity included all Romans.

The understanding of a *populus* as a political body that remains constant as its specific form changes (until it disintegrates through corruption) is consistent with Cicero's view that a republic is constituted by different parts. Augustine agrees with Scipio's classification of political societies in his first presentation of Scipio's definition of a *populus*. He criticizes Scipio's definition in general for denying the status of Rome as a people, but this criticism leaves Scipio's hierarchy of political societies untouched. Indeed, Augustine's reformulation strengthens the idea latent in Scipio's theory of the transformation of political societies because, according to Scipio's definition (or Augustine's version of it), a *populus* would disappear once it was anything less than perfect:

> Then [Scipio] shows the use of the definition in debate; and from these definitions of his own he gathers that a republic, or "weal of the people," then exists only when it is well and justly governed, whether by a monarch, or an aristocracy, or by the whole people. But when the king *(rex)* is unjust, or, as the Greeks say, a tyrant; or the aristocrats *(optimates)* are unjust (he called their consensus *[consensum]* a faction *[factionem]*) or the people themselves *(ipse populus)* are unjust, and become, as Scipio for want of a better name calls them, themselves the tyrant, then the republic is not only blemished . . . , but by legitimate deduction from those definitions, it altogether ceases to be. For it could not be the people's weal when a tyrant factiously lorded it over the city; neither would the people be any longer a people if it were unjust, since it would no longer answer the definition of a people. (*CD* 2.21)

According to Augustine, Scipio cannot mean this if he wants to uphold his theory of regime transformation, because each deformation would entail the disappearance of the *populus*. Cicero's Scipio actually admits this when he states: "For it is through our own faults, not by any accident, that we retain only the form of the republic, but have long since lost its substance" (*CD* 2.21).[21] Augustine appears generally to have agreed with Scipio's republican understanding of a *populus*, but thought that Scipio's premises could not handle its transformation and endurance through time.

---

21. Quoting Cicero, *De Re Publica* 5.1.

Augustine also does not necessarily restrict the locus of virtue of a political society to any particular group or faction, which challenges the theory mentioned above that Christian political thought necessitates a particular form of political society. He indicates that political society is governed and led by individuals in leadership positions who influence the behavior of the governed. This is a problem of collective action and does not locate virtue exclusively in the monarchy, aristocracy, or common people. The responsibility of social virtue and vice is shared by all parts. For example, Augustine states: "I am sick of recalling the many acts of revolting injustice which have disturbed the city's history; the powerful did their best to subjugate the plebeians, and the plebeians resisted—the leaders of each side motivated more by ambition for victory than by any ideas of equity and good" (CD 2.17). No part of a society, whether patrician or plebeian, has an exclusive claim to virtue, and all may claim vice. He even points out that the parts themselves can be led by tyrants or demagogues who seek their own interest at the expense of their own group and of the polity.

Augustine further sees the virtues and vices of a political society crystallized and modeled in its leaders, although he does not restrict virtue and vice in general to any one class. He observes that the Roman vice of lust for rule existed in its leaders and then spread to the people: "The lust of rule, which with other vices existed among the Romans in more unmitigated intensity than among any other people, after it had taken possession of the more powerful few, subdued to its yoke the rest, worn and wearied" (CD 1.30). Later he blames the intellectuals of Rome for inciting the people's hatred of Christianity in order to make it a scapegoat for the collapse of Rome: "And since there is among them also an unlearned rabble, they are stirred up as by their inexperience that things which have happened unwontedly in their days were not wont to happen in other times gone by" (CD 4.1). According to Augustine, leaders also constitute exemplars of political virtue. He points out that the early glories of Rome were due to great men whose virtue enabled them to conquer multitudes of enemies, and thus that these great men were responsible for the glory of Rome: "And by the wisdom and forethought of these few good men, which first enabled the republic to endure these evils and mitigated them, it waxed greater and greater" (CD 5.12). These same great men made the people of the republic virtuous because, Augustine then points out, the republic was able to withstand the moral degeneration of its leaders. Further evidence that he did not consider the people as simply passive is provided below.

In On the Free Choice of the Will, Augustine speaks of a *populus* in strictly republican terms that encompass democratic, aristocratic, and monarchic forms. He speaks of a *populus* that designates its own rulers, but argues that good rule requires the capability of something like a dictator to save the republic in times of crisis. Augustine and Evodius discuss the "law called supreme reason (lex quae summa ratio nominatur)," which enables one to judge various temporal laws. The supreme law of reason judges it rightful for a virtuous "people (populus) to bring forth (creare) for themselves magistrates to administer their welfare, that is, for the commonwealth (res . . . publica)." Augustine also observes: "[I]t is always just for grave people to institute their officials, but not for irresponsible people (qua semper iustum est gravem populum honores dare, leuem non dare)" (DLA 1.6.15). If they have grown depraved, then the same supreme law of reason judges it rightful, "provided some good man of great ability was found at the time, to strip these people of their power and to subject them to the rule of a few good men, or even to that one good man" (DLA 1.6.14). The "law of supreme reason" necessitates that a virtuous people administer itself through its magistrates in order to represent itself elementally, existentially, and according to transcendent truth. Augustine's statement necessitates that a people should be ruled if the people have become depraved. However, this statement does not necessarily mean that he endorsed democracy where the people are not depraved because his terms for choosing these magistrates do not necessarily entail democratic means. For instance, he does not state who is to institute the magistrates or by what means. However, his statement regarding representation of the people either through magistrates or by some good human being or group of human beings reflects a republican understanding of mixing different parts of a populus.

The verbs Augustine employs for the virtuous people's activity of instituting officials, creare and dare, do not necessarily signify democratic powers. Both terms are general, and Augustine does not use other alternatives such as eligare or deligere.[22] Creare could (but does not necessarily) mean a democratic power, as the term in juridical language meant the election of a magistrate in a popular assembly or the appointment of a magistrate or pontiff. Cicero uses the term to state that the Romans, after the death of Numa Pompilius, created (creavit) Tullus Hostilius king. He also uses the term to signify the election of the consuls, but, in that same passage, he uses the same term to describe the decrees of the Senate.[23] Furthermore, the Roman dictatorship was instituted by a lex de dictatore

---

22. See CD 10.3, where relegare (to "reelect") is said to be related to religion (from religare). Augustine later retracts this common etymology (The Retractions, 1.12.9). He used deligere in his reformulation of Cicero's definition of a populus to describe how a people is characterized by the things it loves or prizes (CD 19.24). The general nature of a populus in the reformulation is consistent with my interpretation of this passage. See Cicero, De Re Publica 1.26.42; see also 1.34.51.

23. Cicero, De Re Publica 2.17.31; De Legibus 3.3.9.

*creando,* and in the later empire, *creatio* became a term signifying appointment to any public office.[24] *Creare* means generally "to beget," "to cause or allow to grow," "to occasion," "to create," "to make," "to bring forth," and finally, "to appoint (a magistrate)" and "to invest (a person) with a specified office." Augustine uses *creare* in the general sense, as when he states that "to create is to make something by bringing forth *(educendo)* something from what is."[25]

Augustine uses *creare* to signify both the work of the Roman dictator as well as the dictator's representative function. He uses the term to speak of Hortensius being made *(crearetur)* dictator, "a measure commonly adopted in times of gravest peril" (*CD* 3.17). Hortensius is said to have recalled *(revocare)* the people *(plebs)* after they had plundered the city. This activity as dictator signifies Augustine's understanding of this institution as one that is endowed with transcendent as well as elemental representation, because Hortensius reasserted moral order by recalling the people. In the same chapter, Augustine guardedly cites the example of the honored Cincinnatus, who had Spurius Maelius slain for aspiring to royal power. Augustine's usage of *creare* to signify the monarchic yet informal function of the dictator in a republic contrasts with the later ideas of Christian theorists such as Fortescue, John of Salisbury, or, indeed, Giles of Rome (the originator of "political Augustinianism"), who reduced transcendent representation to the single office of monarchy. Augustine instead recognizes the informal quality of the dictatorship of Cincinnatus and others who became dictators: "Yet by such extreme poverty these statesmen *(principes)* of the Roman republic not only did not incur the contempt of their fellow-citizens, but were on that very account peculiarly dear to them, and esteemed the more qualified to administer the resources of their country" (*Ep.* 104.6).

Augustine's choice of *creare* to signify the institution of leaders reflects his understanding of the way the *populus* is represented. The meaning of *creare* is consistent with representation, where the representative "re-presents" the original. The association of *creare* with begetting recalls the generative meaning within Augustine's definition of a people as a counion *(coetus).*[26] This indicates

24. See Clinton Rossiter, *Constitutional Dictatorship: Crisis Government in the Modern Democracies,* 15–28. Adolf Berger, "Encyclopedic Dictionary of Roman Law," 417. Augustine's reliance on Roman jurisprudential terminology has been noted by interpreters but never systematically examined. See Carlyle, *Medieval Political Theory,* 168; MacIntyre, *Whose Justice? Which Rationality?* 152–53; Albrecht Dihle, *The Theory of Will in Classical Antiquity,* 135–44.

25. Augustine, "Against the Adversaries of the Law and the Prophets," in *Arianism and Other Heresies,* trans. Roland J. Teske (Hyde Park, N.Y.: New City Press, 1995), i. Quoted by Saint Thomas Aquinas, *Summa Theologiae* 1.45.1.1.

26. Despite their differences over other points, Augustine's understanding of representation as generative compares with that of Fortescue who compared the self-articulation of the body politic

that a people begets, as it were, its representative as part of its self-articulation. Augustine could have used *facere*, which is generally related to *creare* because both terms are used to describe the activity of God's creation and making (*CD* 11.10). However, he may have had a more restricted understanding of the term's political meaning as he would later use it to describe how the Roman people established *(facerent)* the arrogant tyrant Tarquin as their king (*CD* 3.15). Similarly, *dare* is a general term that can mean anything from "to grant" to "to give." Its political meanings are restricted to the juridical language used to describe the action of the magistrate in appointing a tutor or curator for one's private affairs, or the appointment of a judge to a civil trial.[27] These considerations of the meanings of *creare, facere,* and *dare* show that they can both convey democratic meanings (in other words, choosing democratically elected leaders) and, more likely, signify republican terms wherein a monarch or dictator can be instituted through nondemocratic mechanisms that still represent the *populus*. These considerations show that Augustine thought a *populus* requires elemental, existential, and transcendent representation.

The above passages do not necessitate that Augustine considered the governed or the plebs politically passive. For instance, he considered consent a necessary component of a good city. This can be seen in his general observation that it is unjust to break even merely conventional laws and agreements: "So that thing agreed upon *(pactum)* and confirmed *(firmatum)*, either by the custom or law *(consuetudine vel lege)* of a city or nation amongst themselves, may not be violated by the libidinous pleasure of any, whether native or foreigner. For vile is every part that agrees not with its own whole" (*Conf.* 3.8). He also provides the important example of the people of Israel, who participated in the truth to which the laws testify. Augustine argues that they find representation and testify to transcendent truth in the founding of Israel, which he distinguishes from the lack of representation and testimony by the people in the founding of Sparta. He contrasts the public delivery of the Mosaic law with the delivery of the laws of Lycurgus, who purportedly received them privately from Jupiter or Apollo:

> For the people of Israel did not come to believe in Moses in any such way as the Spartans put faith in their Lycurgus—because he was reported to have received from Jupiter or Apollo the laws that he established. No, when the

---

to the way the physical body grows out of the embryo. A *populus* articulates its head out of its people just as a human being grows from an embryonic state ("Praise of England"). As Adams observes, Augustine distinguishes between a *populus* and a *gens* by the greater degree of political articulation that the former has achieved (*"Populus" of Augustine and Jerome,* 42–43).

27. A. Berger, "Encyclopedic Dictionary," 424.

law was delivered to the people by which they were commanded to worship the one God, there were miraculous signs in nature and earthquakes enacted in sight of that same people, in such number as divine providence deemed sufficient; and this showed them that the created world was cooperating with the creator as His instrument, to the end that the delivery of the law might take place. (*CD* 10.13)

Augustine elsewhere states that Lycurgus only pretended to have received authority from Apollo (*CD* 2.16). The Lacedaemonian and Mosaic laws differ in that only the Mosaic law joins the leader together with the people in a common witness to transcendent truth, whereas the Lacedaemonian law does not express the people's communion with transcendent truth.[28] Although this passage raises questions concerning the meaning of God's miraculous signs in nature, it shows that, for Augustine, the plebs constitute a part of the *populus* that represents transcendent truth. When read in the light of the previous passages, this passage indicates that the plebs also play an active role in elemental and existential representation.[29]

This participation is also reflected in Augustine's practices as a bishop. He sought his congregation's consent and testimony when he chose Eraclius as his successor to the bishopric of Hippo. The ceremonial record (dated September 26, 426) records a momentous and emotional event. Augustine appears to have been careful to seek the consent of his congregation, as he notes that he had witnessed the dissension that occurred after a fellow bishop failed to secure the consent of his own congregation. The record shows Augustine asking God to bring agreement to him and all members on the new bishop:

> This, therefore, I desire; this I ask from the Lord our God in prayers, the warmth of which is not abated by the chill of age; this I exhort, admonish, and entreat you also to pray for along with me,—that God may confirm *(confirmet)* that which He has wrought in us by blending and fusing together the minds *(collatis et conflatis mentibus)* of all in the peace of Christ. May He who has sent him to me preserve him! preserve him safe, preserve him blameless, that he gives me joy while I live, he may fill my place when I die. (*Ep.* 213.2)

The record of the union of bishop and people is required for posterity: "The notaries of the church are, as you observe, recording what I say, and recording

---

28. Augustine elsewhere criticizes the Roman civil religion for restricting virtue teachings to the secret society of the priests (*CD* 2.6).

29. He makes the same point regarding the Church's own affairs (*Conf.* 13.23).

what you say; both my address and your acclamations are not allowed to fall to the ground" (*Ep.* 213.2). He continues: "It is my wish, as I was just now saying, that my desire and your desire be confirmed *(confirmatum)*, so far as pertains to men *(quantum ad homines attinet)*, by being placed on an ecclesiastical record; but so far as pertains to the will of the Almighty, let us pray, as I said before, that God would confirm that which He has wrought in us" (*Ep.* 213.3). At this point, the people are recorded as shouting: " 'We give thanks for your decision': then twelve times, 'Agreed! Agreed!' and then six times 'Thee, our father! Eraclius, our bishop!' " This record shows that Augustine understood the role of consent in his own practice as bishop. As bishop, he provided a candidate, and he called on the people through prayer to provide their witness and consent. This episode fits with Christopher Ocker's analysis of Augustine's practices: "The crucial condition of successful leadership was the congregation's ability to recognize the personality of a true bishop and grant him the role, and accordingly, the bishop had to be preoccupied with the maintenance of community support."[30]

This does not mean that Augustine regarded the people as sinless. He criticizes the Roman people for their viciousness and inordinate haste in expelling the Tarquin kings. He states sarcastically: "How justly the people acted, in looking more to the character than the name of a citizen" (*CD* 3.16). Augustine's understanding of the people's or plebs' virtues and vices is explicated below.

Augustine's view of the relations among the different parts of the city indicates he preferred a republican system of trading offices among parts. This is seen in two ways. First, Augustine observes that Rome was made great by virtuous leaders who defeated wealthier neighbors in war (*CD* 5.12). This observation reflects his view that political regimes are spoiled by luxury and idleness *(luxu atque desidia)* that result from inordinate private wealth. The rulers who made Rome virtuous themselves became even more vicious than the people they ruled (see *CD* 1.30), which was a result of their corruption in political office. This indicates that Augustine considered undue reliance on one part of the regime as destructive to the political society. Second, the needfulness of trading offices can be seen where Augustine frequently contrasts a ruler whose lust for rule is so great that he is unable to share rule with others to a virtuous, worshipful ruler who is "not afraid to have partners" (*CD* 5.24). As a result, a good ruler would not mind sharing rule because he sees himself sharing virtue with others.

30. Ocker, "Augustine, Episcopal Interests, and the Papacy in Late Roman Africa," 191.

## HIERARCHY OF CITIES AND FORMS

Turning now to the question of which cities correspond to the quality of various objects of love, we are reminded that the best regime is the mystical city of God. All earthly cities and the objects of their love fall short of the city of God. The incarnation of the city of God in the world has two characteristics. First, Augustine emphasizes that the two mystical cities, the city of God and the earthly city, are commingled until their final separation at the end of time (*CD* 19.26). Both the Church and political cities are filled with the virtuous and the reprobate. Second, even the Church, which represents the city of God in its earthly pilgrimage, achieves a peace that is only fleeting and less certain than that found in the mystical city of God: "Our very justice, too, though true, thanks to the true final good to which it is subordinated, is nevertheless in this life only such as consists rather in the remission of sins *(remissione peccatorum)* than in the perfection of virtues" (*CD* 19.27). The peace of the best practical city must necessarily be inferior even to the remission of sins (and the institutional apparatus that executes the remission [such as priestly functions), but, as will be shown presently, achieves some sort of civic virtue rooted in nature (*CD* 19.13).

If we follow Augustine's reformulation of Cicero, it follows that the best practical regime is that whose objects of love are the best practically obtainable short of the sacramental order of the Church. Despite this, these objects must be some sort of shadow or imperfect imitation of the objects loved by the Church, because the object of love of the Church, the representative of the city of God, is architectonic. This means that politics must find some way not to interfere with the Church, and perhaps it must prepare human beings for the sacramental life, insofar as the ends of politics intimate but do not eclipse the ends of the Church. This issue will be explored in greater detail in Chapter 6.

What are the highest political objects of love, and what does the best practical city for Augustine look like? This topic can be touched upon only briefly in this chapter. A fuller consideration of the relationship between politics and religion, and of Augustine's position on the coercion of heretics, will be taken up in Chapters 6 and 7. Analysis here is restricted to the type of desires, public expressions of worship in particular, that Augustine sees as requiring political expression. Augustine has been historically interpreted, by the tradition of "political Augustinianism," for example, as requiring some close association between political regimes and the Christian Church. More recent interpretations have postulated a kind of neutral or pluralistic liberalism. R. A. Markus, for example, bases this interpretation on the grounds of Augustine's "neutral" political order.[31] This opinion, however, depends on the idea of Augustine's view of religion as a private matter. This position leads Markus to argue that Augustine removes religious considerations from politics because there cannot be a state based on Christianity or any other religion; rather, Christians are to use political offices to act in a Christian way. Instead of allying the state with Christianity and having Christian principles inform its laws, Markus argues that Augustine's political thought emphasizes personal virtue. Although this view has the advantage of showing why Augustine does not advocate a Christian state (as did his colleague Eusebius), it raises the difficulty of explaining how a state official relates to a state's laws and the degree to which a state is expected to support Christian principles. It also poses the problem of explaining the activities of one who represents a state: are his or her actions representative of the state or of Christianity?

Augustine states that a nation is truly blessed if it is ruled by people who combine the science of ruling people and true piety: "But if those who are endowed with true piety (vera pietate) and live good lives know the science of ruling peoples (scientiam regendi populus), there is no greater blessing for mankind than for them, by the mercy of God, to have power" (CD 5.19). The best and happiest city is one that is governed by true piety and by the science of ruling. True piety needs, then, to be expressed in some way. Consistent with the argument presented here, Augustine refers to those with true piety and the science of ruling in the plural, which means that a good city may be governed by one, a few, or many. This means that the best practical regime is not necessarily a monarchy or a democracy. True piety and worship constitute the foundation of virtue: "For in serving God the soul rightly commands the body, and in that very soul the reason that is subject to God as master rightly commands the lusts and the other vices" (CD 19.21; see also 19.25). A city that is governed by true piety will cultivate a degree of virtue. As always, Augustine was a political moderate, as indicated above in his statement that human peace remains a struggle with the sins. He elsewhere explains that human law must not attempt to remove all vices, such as prostitution, because removing them only makes vices find other and more unsettling ways of expressing themselves: "Remove prostitutes from human affairs, and you will unsettle everything because of lusts" (DO 2.4.12; see also Ep. 153.6.26). The inability of a city to perfect virtue is also reflected

31. Markus, Saeculum, 151. This has recently been criticized by Michael J. White, "Pluralism and Secularism in the Political Order: St. Augustine and Theoretical Liberalism."

in Augustine's view that a city cannot be governed completely by nature and by the wisdom of philosophy. Philosophy cannot rule because cities generally discount truth and prefer to live in confusion like Babylon (*CD* 18.51). The conflicting opinions of the philosophers also make it impossible for the city to adopt authoritatively any one philosophic doctrine.

Augustine's so-called mirror of princes expresses how the truly pious and wise governor of the best practical regime will act (*CD* 5.24). This passage has received intense scrutiny by scholars and princes alike. Augustine provides a list of virtues and actions that are required of such a ruler. Most of these virtues and actions would be considered "private" rather than public; for example, he advocates humility and self-restraint. He mentions two political virtues worthy of consideration, however. First, he states that such a humble and moderate ruler should "make his power a servant to the divine Majesty, to spread the worship of god as far as possible" (*CD* 5.24; see also 4.3).[32] This passage shows that Augustine does not restrict religion to the private lives of state officials. Rather, the power (*potestatem*) must serve the majesty of God by spreading worship (*Dei cultam*) as far as possible (*maxime dilantandum*). Power can signify one's political and legal function (but the term has a broader meaning; see *CD* 2.21), which indicates that piety and *cultus* are not to be understood as having an exclusively private function. Augustine does not in this passage clarify how far such worship must be spread. As will be shown below, he prefers a small, moderate city to an empire, so this passage would have to be read in light of his preference for small cities. A governor's desire to expand his rule would also be checked by Augustine's standard that a governor should rule over his or her base desires rather than over nations (*CD* 5.24).

The love of God and of neighbor constitutes a foundational virtue for the best practical city, and is expressed as a civic sense of gratitude. This passage does not specify how such worship would express itself politically. However, Augustine understood *cultus Dei* primarily as a virtue, and thus the laws can only approximate this goal and would also have to respect the freedom of humans to be persuaded of the truth. The political expression of the love of God and of neighbor will be analyzed in greater detail in the final two chapters. It is necessary here, however, to indicate how the best practical regime and its characteristic dominant love relate to inferior regimes and their characteristic dominant loves. The best practical city, in which *cultus Dei* is expressed, first and foremost cultivates the virtues of love of God and of neighbor. For Augustine, the glorification of virtuous human beings is the best way to achieve

---

32. "[S]i suam potestatem ad Dei cultum maxime dilatandum maiestati eius famulam faciunt."

this, because such human beings serve as a proximate good. Thus, the best practical city makes room for the ordinate love of glory. For Augustine, *cultus* as an architectonic virtue includes the glorification of good human beings: "For we are said to 'cultivate *(colere)*' men too, when we give them constant honorable mention or honors by actual presence *(quo honorifica vel recordatione vel praesentia frequentamus)"* (CD 10.1). As shown below in Chapter 5, the love of glory, the preeminent political love, can serve virtue when exercised ordinately. For Augustine, the truth of God is best expressed not simply by recitation of creeds and church attendance, but also and perfectly by virtuous action. Virtuous acts, such as dying for one's friend or country, shine out and attract the clear understanding and praise of those who can see them. Thus, Augustine urges his readers to use their virtue to testify to God and to let others "become what you are" (CD 5.15). The best practical city will be the one that engages in the cultivation of virtuous human beings and in their glorification as testaments to he who made them, and the city does this in communal displays of gratitude. A contemporary example might be seen in the American cult of the Founders, from which one party's primary identity is either the "party of Jefferson" or the "party of Lincoln." The parties do not necessarily identify with the specific legislation enacted by these leaders, but they believe themselves to be animated by the spirit of those leaders. One can also point to the growing cult of various civil rights heroes such as Martin Luther King Jr. The key element in this type of *cultus* is that it assumes that virtue exists prior to the application of rules. Americans and their parties may well reject some of the ideas of the Founders, but they perceive themselves as personating and representing their spirit, and their actions as participating in a kind of liturgy whose substance lies in the spirit that is consistent with yet transcends the letter of the laws.

Augustine notes that the glorification of virtuous human beings forms a society when he reflects on the cognates of *cultus*. Its verbal form, *colere*, also means "to cultivate," as in to cultivate a field or cultivate a virtuous human being. Always one to seek the truth behind popular meanings, he points out that *colere* is the root of colonists *(coloni)* and inhabitants *(incolae)*. His interpretation of their etymology indicates that the activity of *cultus* and *colere* is performed by and for the purpose of cultivating *coloni* and *incolae*. Augustine observes, of course, that worshiping God differs from cultivating fields or virtues, but his reflections indicate that this activity is necessarily communal. This is consistent with his view that glorification is a communal activity and that the life of the saints is communal. The best practical city, therefore, is governed by the love of virtue that is cultivated by the glorification of virtuous human beings who embody the aspirations of that city. This reflects Augustine's view that virtue, based on the love of God and neighbor, is the good that human beings can share most in. Virtue is accompanied by glory, which is the means by which virtue is known and praised. The glory that accompanies virtue constitutes the dominant love of the second best city (described below; see also Chapter 5), which is a corruption of the best practical city because it loves glory inordinately.

The other political virtues of the good ruler in the "mirror of princes" are ruling *(regere)* and protecting *(tueor)*. Augustine states that the punishment of criminals should (in addition to attempting to reform the criminal) be undertaken "as required by considerations of ruling and protecting the republic *(pro necessitate regendae tuendaeque re publicae)"* (CD 5.24). *Regere* is the generic term for ruling that was analyzed in the last chapter; it means guiding one to virtue. *Tueor* has a similar meaning: "to view," "to keep safe," "to observe," "to preserve," and "to have oversight." It was an important Roman legal term that signified guardianship and, as the word suggests, tutorship.[33] Its meaning as the function of an overseer and tutor coincides with Augustine's definition given elsewhere of a good ruler as one who oversees or superintends *(superintendere, episkopein)* (CD 19.19). Augustine's "mirror of princes," therefore, emphasizes the personal virtue of the good governor, but also notes that these virtues improve the virtues of the citizens whose glorification of the virtuous constitutes their mode of dwelling together.

Augustine has a second-best city that is governed by a second-best love. Worship, the best love, therefore, permits glory, the second-best object of love, and its cultivation as long as glory is sought for sake of virtue and not virtue for glory's sake. Augustine, despite his severe criticism of Roman politics, saw in it an intimation of the best city (especially in the case of early Rome) because its love of glory and honor (although inordinate) brought forth great virtue (see CD 5.12–13). He criticizes Rome not for loving glory and honor, but for loving them inordinately, and because Romans bestowed their greatest honors onto false gods and transformed their heroes into gods. For example, he criticizes Rome's inordinate love of glory in that it neglected an important way of loving glory. He criticizes the Romans for glorying in having a virtuous citizen such as Regulus, yet fearing "to have such a city" (CD 1.15). In a sense, the Romans did not love glory enough because they feared having to pay the price for the kind of glory that Regulus received. Furthermore, Augustine reminds his Christian readers not to dismiss Roman virtue too easily, because the Roman love of glory inspired tremendous love of the common good and selflessness that Christians can imitate and transcend (since the glory of God is their greatest

33. A. Berger, "Encyclopedic Dictionary," 747–50.

love) (*CD* 5.15, 5.18–19). To be sure, Augustine uses grim irony in praising the Romans' splendid vices, but he also stresses that even Christians would find it extraordinarily difficult to surpass their achievements and sacrifices. Augustine proposes that the love of glory is superior to the love of wealth; he observes that it was good that the Romans' love of glory suppressed their baser lusts for wealth, for example (*CD* 5.13, 5.15). Even the love of freedom serves the love of glory. Love of glory, then, appears to be the second-best political love after worship because it cultivated the common good well, but not as effectively as the regime that cultivates true piety.

The love of wealth is the third-best political love. Augustine observes that the Romans' love of glory and of the public good suppressed their avarice (*CD* 5.13, 5.15). He notes (quoting Sallust) that prosperity was the origin of Rome's moral degeneration after the collapse of Carthage (noting that Sallust admits these vices dominated Rome from its beginning): " 'On the other hand, after the destruction of Carthage, discord, avarice, ambition, and other vices commonly arising from prosperity *(secundis rebus)*, particularly increased' " (*CD* 2.18).[34] Augustine tends to equate the inordinate love of wealth with luxury and servility. For example, he writes in the *Confessions* about the irony that "the idling *(nugae)* of men is called business *(negotia)*; the idling of boys, though exactly like, is punished by those same men" (1.9). The inferiority of business (as a species of the active life in general) to contemplation is brought out further when Augustine, in what could be considered his farewell address to his congregation when he retired, warns his congregation not to envy *(invidere)* his leisure *(otium)*, in which he could devote his time to the study of Scripture, because he, as bishop, had already devoted too much time on business affairs by serving them *(negotium)* (*Ep.* 213.6). That *negotium* is the negation of *otium* would have been noticed by Augustine, the former rhetorician. Despite having the perspective on business of one who always preferred the life of contemplation to action, he does not appear to have objected to an ordinate love of wealth, as he speaks of business affairs *(negotiatio)* as themselves useful whose goodness depends on their use (*EnP* 71.16–17). He objected to inordinate love of wealth because it and its luxuries enable the wealthy to dominate the poor. He describes the position of the wealthy in their own voice: "It interests us more that one should constantly increase one's wealth *(divitias)* to support one's daily extravagance, and to enable the more powerful individual to make weaker men his subjects. Let

---

34. Quoting Sallust, *The Histories* 1.16.

the poor court the rich to fill their bellies and to enjoy under their patronage an undisturbed idleness; let the rich misuse the poor as clients and to minister to their pride" (*CD* 2.20). This comment is situated in Augustine's discussion of the abuse of the poor by the wealthy, in which, through the voice of the same wealthy person, he criticizes what we today would call the "secular" state:

> Let provinces be subordinate to governors not as directors of morals but as lords of their possessions and providers of their pleasures; and let them not honour them in sincerity but fear them in servility. Let the laws penalize the damage a man does to his neighbor's vineyard rather than the damage he does to his own life. Nor should a man be led into court unless he harms another's property, home, health, or is a nuisance or impediment to someone against his consent. Otherwise, let each one do what he will with his own either in the company of his own people or of anyone else who is willing. (*CD* 2.20)

Augustine seems to argue here that the domination of the rich over the poor, and the strong over the weak, is characteristic of a city in which laws primarily protect one's person and property without regard to forming one's virtue, where the city thinks of morality in terms of an agreement among consenting agents, and where those agents act in any way they please in private. Augustine argues that such a coordination of private vices engenders the kind of public vices that rampaged Rome because it reflected a morality that favors the strong.

Augustine's attitude toward democracy is complex. On the one hand, he favored a virtuous people's ability to choose and elect its own leaders, as shown above. On the other hand, his assessment of the typically democratic loves for freedom and equality resembles that of Plato, and he treats them as dimensions of earthly love in need of correction. He thought these objects of love may be easily replaced by licentiousness and moral confusion. That he considered freedom and equality proper objects of love indicates that he considered democratic loves good, but easily corruptible without being mixed by nondemocratic loves. For example, he affirms the love of freedom understood as independence from external attack and tyranny. He praises the Roman ability to secure independence (*CD* 5.12) and the Roman people's ability to eject the Tarquin kings (even though he notes they were more motivated by their own lust for domination) (*CD* 3.15–16). He often points to the unjust treatment of the plebeians as evidence of the injustice of Rome (*CD* 2.17, 5.17 [where he advocates feeding those without their own land from the public treasury]; see also 3.24).[35] He points out that in the consulship period of the Roman republic, the plebs were oppressed by the oligarchic vice of charging high interest. Again, he quotes Sallust, his authority on Roman moral degeneracy: "'From that time on the patricians treated the plebs as slaves, ordered them executed and flogged as the kings had done, drove them from their land, or behaved like tyrants to the rest who were landless. The plebs, crushed by this savage treatment and particularly by high rates of interest, and bearing a double burden of taxation and military service in constant wars, withdrew under arms to the Sacred Hill'" (CD 3.17).[36] Augustine cites unjust oligarchic vices as the source of oppression of the plebeians, and opposes the domineering kind of rule that rejects political friendship.

The unrestrained love of freedom is lawlessness and licentiousness, which make people susceptible to lawlessness and blind obedience to their leaders. Augustine notes, for example, that leaders are often motivated more by the love of contention than by justice (CD 2.17). He also observes on occasion that Roman intellectuals set the mobs after Christians (CD 4.1, 4.6). He observes that though they suffered injustices, their love of freedom led to lawlessness. Observing that civil war is more lamentable than war among nations, he states that the Social War of 90 B.C. (led by Tiberius Gracchus, a tribune of the plebs) was caused by the unjust treatment of the plebs by the patricians: "First on the list of civil disorders came the sedition stirred up by the agrarian laws of the Gracchi, for they wanted to divide among the populace the land that the nobles wrongly possessed (perperam possidebat). But to dare to attack an ancient wrong was a very perilous business, or rather, it was utterly fatal, as the event showed. . . . Not by laws and orderly processes, but by armed mobs in conflict, were noble and ignoble done to death" (CD 3.24).[37] The desire to arrange for a more equal distribution of wealth and land was taken over by the mob's lawlessness.[38] This lawlessness is reflected in Augustine's occasional characterization of the vulgus as unlearned people (ineruditus) (CD 2.3) whom

35. Plebs would be considered part of the populus (see CD 2.21, where he identifies the populus both with the entire public and with what would otherwise be called plebs). Augustine also uses plebs to signify the Israelites and the Christian laity as the people of God (CD 16.24, 17.3, 17.5, 17.16, 22.30). He also speaks of the rich among the plebs of God (CD 17.16, quoting Ps. 45:10–17).

36. Quoting Sallust, The Histories 1.11.

37. Augustine notes that this war was occasioned by the Romans' animals becoming wild, rejecting their domestication under human rule, and wandering at large (CD 3.23). One is reminded of Plato's criticism of democrats whose love of equality is extended to animals who then roam the streets alongside human beings (Republic 563c).

38. Lawlessness distinguishes a populus from a mob (turba): "Grant a point of unity, and a populus exists; take that unity away, and it is a mob. For what is a mob except a confused multitude (multitudo turbata)?" (Serm. 103, quoted in Adams, "Populus" of Augustine and Jerome, 35).

the demagogues inflame and set against the Christians (*CD* 4.1, 4.6). The *vulgi* are characterized also as unphilosophical because they think that happiness consists in pleasure (*CD* 14.2), and as being carnal and inexperienced *(imperitus)* readers of Scripture (*CD* 14.17). He also signifies, with irony, Christians as *vulgus* in his criticism of those who call themselves Platonists, and whose pride prevents them from becoming Christians: "They fear that, if they share one designation with the common mass *(vulgus)*, it will detract for the wearers of the Greek cloak *(palliatorum)* from the prestige of their fewness, for they are puffed up in inverse proportion to their number" (*CD* 13.16). Augustine's criticism of the Platonists for their snobbery reminds the reader that though the plebs have characteristic vices, all parts of the *populus* have vices, and thus no part has an exclusive claim to rule. The poverty of the plebeians certainly does not prevent members from ruling. Augustine observes that effective dictators such as Cincinnatus were impoverished; his virtue enabled him to be dictator. As a result, plebeians who are depraved would be able to have an active political role, according to Augustine's observation of how a good *populus* institutes its magistrates.

Augustine's criticism of the lawlessness of the mob compares with his description of the confusion of the paradigmatic earthly city. He speaks of Babylon, whose name is "confusion," in similar terms and even blames its confusion on its love of a false equality and its indifference toward the good life:

> Has [Babylon] not rather held in its bosom in random confusion, without any verdict, all these [philosophic] controversies between men whose difference is not a matter of fields, houses, or any financial accounting but of the issues of life that determine whether we are to be wretched or blessed? To be sure, some of their statements were true. Those that were false, however, had equal privilege, so that it is not for nothing that such a city has received the symbolic name of "Babylon." (*CD* 18.41; see also 16.4, 16.10, 16.11, 16.17, 18.51)

Even though Babylon was ruled by King Nimrod (*CD* 16.4) and Augustine (following the prophet Isaiah) figuratively calls the devil the prince *(princeps)* of Babylon (*CD* 11.15), his criticism of its lawlessness and confusion relates to them more as democratic vices than as characteristics of a society where a solitary tyrant rules and imposes his own unified vision of the good life on his people.

The love of equality plays another role in Augustine's political thought. On the one hand, he recognizes differences in virtue and acknowledges that these differences ought to be recognized politically. I have just attempted to demonstrate that Augustine characterizes the love of equality and chance as the vices of Babylon. On the other hand, his Christianity emphasizes that virtue ultimately originates in God and that everyone is equal on account of that common origin. This aspect of equality would emphasize the necessity of looking to the poor and uneducated in a republic as a crucial source of morality. As noted above, Augustine criticizes the sort of pride that hates equality with others. Equality before God enables him to acknowledge that people who lack the highest intellectual virtues can still testify to moral and spiritual truth. This ability to testify to truth leads him to exclaim that one of the great attributes of the Christian religion is that it was spread by uneducated human beings:

> It is incredible that a very few men, of mean birth and the lowest rank, and no education *(ignobiles, infimos, paucissimos, inperiotos)*, should have been able so effectually to persuade the world, and even its learned men, of so incredible a thing. . . . But if [skeptics] do not believe that these miracles were wrought by Christ's apostles to gain credence to their preaching *(praedicantibus)* of His resurrection and ascension, this one grand miracle suffices for us, that the whole world has believed without any miracles. (*CD* 22.5; see also 16.2)

Such people were "untrained in the liberal arts and untaught in the learning of the pagans, not skilled in grammar, not armed in dialectic, not puffed up with rhetoric" (*CD* 22.5). Their lack of education, mean birth, and low rank made them plebs. The ability to testify to moral and spiritual truth puts everyone on a more equal footing with regard to the ability to live an upright moral life. The virtues of such uneducated human beings are not restricted to obedience and moderation, as they are in Plato's *Republic*, for example.[39] Furthermore, Augustine's affirmation of their ability to testify to truth challenges the contemporary divide in modern democracies between the intellectual and scientistic elites and those who lack such education, and who are generally dismissed by the former as "redneck." Augustine indicates, rather, that such human beings are capable of testifying to truth through their virtuous actions, and thus to persuade others of that truth. Their ability to persuade, however, depends on moderating their characteristic tendencies toward lawlessness.

The worst love belongs to the worst regime: tyranny. The worst love is the lust for domination, which characterizes the earthly city *(civitas terrena)*. Scholars disagree over the identification of the earthly city—whether it merely signifies

---

39. For example, see Plato, *Republic* 431c–433.

the lust for domination or can be identified with any historical city such as Rome, for example. The analysis in Chapter 1 showed how the earthly city is a mystical symbol for the lust for domination, and the subsequent analysis there distinguished the earthly city from the political city that experiences a multiplicity of desires. Augustine isolates the lust for domination from the other types of love in his description of the emperor Nero, whose love of luxury and contempt for the praises of others (evidence of shamelessness) led him to the greatest of evil:

> But he who disregards glory and yet is eager for rule outstrips wild beasts in vicious cruelty or in luxurious living. There have been Romans of this type, who, though they had lost interest in their reputation, still were not free from lust for domination. History publishes the names of many such men, but it was the emperor Nero who first mounted to the summit and citadel, so to speak, of this vice. So far did he who in his luxury that it might seem needless to fear any manly act from him, yet so cruel was he that, except for knowing him, we might suppose that he was exempt from weakness. (CD 5.19)

Augustine observes that this citadel of vice was shameless and contemptuous of human praise (and of human relations in general). The lust for domination expresses itself in imperial policies, as the history of Rome testifies. Augustine notes, for instance, that Rome would have remained of moderate size were it not for the lust for domination.

Augustine generally, although not always, associates empire with the lust for domination. For instance, he asks:

> Is it wise or prudent to wish to glory in the breadth and magnitude *(latitudine ac magnitudine velle gloriari)* of an empire when you cannot show that the men whose empire it is are happy? For the Romans always lived in dark fear and cruel lust, surrounded by the disasters of war and the shedding of blood which, whether that of fellow citizens or enemies, was human nonetheless. The joy of such men may be compared to the fragile splendor of glass: they are horribly afraid lest it be suddenly shattered. (CD 4.3)

Empires such as that of Rome glory in themselves and in the subjugation of others. Both the conqueror and the conquered are unhappy. Like Plato's tyrant, an empire lives in constant fear for its security. The tyrannical earthly city, therefore, is the city and empire that glories in itself and in its domination over others, just as the human being dominated by the lust for domination glories in himself in dominion over others. Unwilling to share in the good, the human being, like the monster Cacus in his corresponding city, finds himself bereft of company and of friends (*CD* 19.12, discussed in Chapter 4).

This hierarchy of political objects of love and regimes is based on a descending ability of cities and their objects of love to cultivate the common good. The best practical city cultivates virtue, participation, and a civic sense of gratitude; the city of glory bestows glory on a few; the city of wealth divides the wealthy few from the many poor; the city of freedom and equality isolates individuals from each other in their lawlessness; and the tyrannical desire, the lust for domination, is alone in its refusal to share.

## OPTIMAL SIZE

Augustine preferred small cities to large empires because small cities preserve moderation and are less prone to engendering the lust for rule. He does acknowledge that it is "beneficial *(utile)*, then, that good human beings should rule far and wide and long, worshiping the true God and serving Him with true rites *(sacris)* and good morals" (*CD* 4.3). He appears to admit that a large city is acceptable if it glories in virtue rather than in itself. However, he likely considered its actuality unlikely, as he emphasizes the benefits of moderate-size cities.

Two passages demonstrate Augustine's preference for moderate-size cities. He compares the virtues and vices of a good and bad city to those of a good and bad man. The good man is of middling circumstances, neither too rich nor too poor, and contented with a "small and compact estate, most dear to his own family, enjoying the sweetest peace with his kindred, neighbors and friends, in piety religious, benign in mind, healthy in body, in life frugal, in manners chaste, in conscience secure" (*CD* 4.3). The bad man, on the other hand, is "anxious with fears, pining with discontent, burning with covetousness, never secure, always uneasy, panting from the perpetual striving of his enemies, adding to his patrimony indeed by these miseries to an immense degree, and by these additions also heaping up most bitter cares" (*CD* 4.3). The good man finds satisfaction in his moderation and his enjoyable relations with friends and family, whereas the bad man's covetousness leads to an endless quest for acquisition that leads him to a state of insecurity. This means that a compact and moderate city will be good whereas an imperial one will be feverish.[40]

---

40. He repeats this claim in his discussion of Romulus and Remus: "Therefore, in order that the sole power should be wielded by one person, the partner was eliminated; and what would

Augustine argues that empires are built despite the intentions of good men and because of the intentions of bad men. He argues that without the necessity of waging war to defend (and then conquer) hostile neighbors, kingdoms "[w]ould certainly have been small if the peace and justice of neighbors had not by any wrong provoked the carrying on of war against them; and human affairs being thus more happy, all kingdoms would have been small, rejoicing in neighborly concord *(concordi vicinitate laetantia)*; and thus there would have been very many kingdoms of nations *(regna plurima gentium)* in the world, as there are very many houses of citizens in a city" (*CD* 4.15). Had there been no wars of defense and imperialism, the world would have been filled with a plurality of kingdoms of nations. This means that there would not have been a world empire, which was created by expansionary wars. Augustine also leaves room for some form of "thick" federation of nations *(gentes)* that would enjoy *(laetari)* each other in neighborly concord, which he compares to the relations of neighbors within a healthy city. Kingdoms of nations would find their primary identification with their fellow nations within a broader concord based upon common love of virtue and piety or *cultus*. Augustine does not specify how close this concord among nations would be, but indicates that such a federation would grant each part far greater autonomy than that found in the empire.[41]

The foregoing commentary showed that Augustine accounts for elemental, existential, and transcendent political representation. He provides an account of politics that does not reduce politics to mere instrumentality, but sees it as a natural human good necessary for humans to flourish. His understanding of the basis of politics and of political representation does not lead either to a value-neutral rule of procedure or to a sacred empire. Augustine manages to articulate a theory of politics that can acknowledge a good city in a multiplicity of cultures. The next two chapters examine the specific virtues required to maintain this type of politics, and in emergency situations to save the cause of justice itself.

---

have been kept smaller and better by innocence grew through crime into something bigger and worse" (*CD* 15.5).

41. Augustine hints that the Roman Empire became more humane when it granted Roman citizenship to conquered peoples, and it would have been better if it had not conquered but welcomed those peoples into Rome by concord *(concorditer)*. This indicates that the Roman Empire could have maintained a relatively thick bond of community among its nations without each nation having to give up its particular existence (*CD* 5.17).

## *ORDO AMORIS* AND
## POLITICAL PRUDENCE

P EOPLE HOPE and pray that their polity will enjoy peace, security, and at least a modicum of neighborly flourishing. They are willing to suffer and bear large amounts of corruption and injustice in the body politic until a time comes when measures are required to save the polity, and perhaps even the cause of justice in the world. Unfortunately, people in such dark times generally are least likely and least suited to save their polity; thus hoping for such action is like hoping for nature to act outside its usual course that would allow a corrupt body politic to decompose and die. Saving the cause of justice in the world and preserving political life requires unusually austere virtue. The devil tempted Christ with a kingdom over the world. Can one preserve political life without losing one's soul by proclaiming oneself Caesar? Augustine is usually seen to think that one cannot preserve one's virtue, or at least that one can keep one's soul only if one follows the absolute rules of engagement as set by Scripture and by the Church. Taking extreme actions in extreme circumstances is forbidden because forbearance and submission purify the soul. This chapter shows that, Augustine, though not denying the virtue of forbearance, thought that one can know the right and good, and act upon it, through right-by-nature, and that moral and political reasoning is not restricted to the application of universal rules to all circumstances. His treatment of political reasoning is considered where following the letter of the law would have disastrous consequences in rare extreme circumstances (lying, adultery, and tyrannicide and rebellion). What appear as exceptions to the absolute rule (based either on natural law or on God's commandment) actually fulfill the law's purpose. Thus, Augustine thought that God's absolute commandments forbidding actions are inverted ways of expressing what human beings naturally desire when they ordinately love God and neighbor. Augustine is never explicit about this, although he provides clues that allow the reader to collect together and interpret discussions about disparate but related topics, such as knowledge of miracles and special divine providence, and understand the totality of their interconnections as his final view. Thus, he forces the reader to practice forbearance by taking a circuitous route that enables him to understand fully Augustine's account of how one can know and obtain the just when it appears that doing so breaks the letter of the law. To repeat a point made in Chapter 1, he told Firmus, his literary agent, that the *City of God* was to be read repeatedly (*Ep.* 231A).

For Augustine, the quality or order of love *(ordo amoris)* determines virtue: "For though it be good, it may be loved with an evil as well as with a good love: it is loved rightly when it is loved ordinately; evilly, when inordinately" (*CD* 15.22). As will be shown, ordinate love is not "love and do what you will *(ama et fac quod vis)*," as Augustine's ethics is sometimes interpreted. Prudence allows one to choose good instead of evil, and to direct one's appetites to the good (*CD* 19.4; see also 4.21; *DLA* 1.13.27; *DT* 12.12.17, 12.14.21, 14.8.11, 14.9.12). Virtue consists in ordinate desire, in knowing and loving rightly. Political virtue does not require perfect virtue, derived from seeing God directly, but rather on "inferior righteousness," by which one's ordinate love prevents one from sinning:

> Forasmuch, however, as an inferior righteousness *(iustitia minor)* may be said to be competent in this life, whereby the just man lives by faith although absent from the Lord, and, therefore, walking by faith and not yet by sight, it may be without absurdity said, no doubt, in respect of it, that it is free from sin; for it ought not to be attributed to it as a fault, that it is not as yet sufficient for so great a love to God as is due to the final, complete, and perfect condition thereof. It is one thing to fail at present in attaining to the fulness of love, and another thing to be swayed by no lust. . . . Only let us see to it that we so constitute the soul of man in this corruptible body, that, although it has not yet swallowed up and consumed the motions of earthly lust in that super-eminent perfection of the love of God, it nevertheless, in that inferior righteousness . . . gives no consent to the aforesaid lust for the purpose of effecting any unlawful thing.[1]

Such "inferior righteousness" is not saintly or perfect virtue, but it is still justice because it rejects sin and is anchored by the love of God. This affirmation of justice in worldly activity compares with Augustine's observations that political

---

1. Augustine, "On the Spirit and the Letter," in *Anti-Pelagian Writings*, 36.65.

and other worldly goods are good in their own way, as seen in the first two chapters. As will be seen, Augustine acknowledges that the rare statesman can avoid the Caesarian temptation of consenting to the unlawful lusts in political activity, and, indeed, in performing acts otherwise regarded as unjust. All can be tempted to become Caesar, and most will succumb to such temptation, which helps to explain why Augustine's rhetoric is so antipolitical. However, Augustine's theory of virtue allows for a few to reject the temptation. As his language of "inferior righteousness" or minor justice *(iustitia minor)* indicates, Augustine's political rationality does not allow expediency to guide action.[2]

Even though it is "inferior righteousness," Augustine's understanding of judgment necessitates that he requires a higher achievement of righteousness than a natural-law ethic and certainly higher than an ethic based on expediency. He argues that wisdom and ordinate love help to determine one's capacity to judge:

> So far as freedom of judgment is concerned, then, the reason of a considerate human being is far different from the necessity of one who is in need, or the desire of the pleasure-seeker. For reason considers what value a thing has in itself, as part of the order of nature, whereas necessity considers how to obtain what will meet its need. Reason considers what appears to be true according to the light of the mind, whereas pleasure looks for whatever agreeable thing will gratify the body's senses. (*CD* 11.16; see also *DT* 3.3.8, 12.2.2, 13.13.17)

Practical wisdom exercised through an understanding of right-by-nature does not provide a more easygoing ethic than natural law ethics. On the contrary, it requires the disciplining of the mind and the desires to be directed to their proper objects so one will know and desire to use and enjoy one's proper objects in the right way. Augustine observes that, since the human mind is mutable, judgment improves as one's mind is exercised: "The judgment of the more talented *(ingeniosior)* will be better than that of the slow-witted *(tardior)*; that of the skilled *(peritior)* than that of the unskilled *(inperitior)*; that of the more experienced *(exercitatior)* than that of the less exercised *(minus exercitatus)*; and, as the same person grows more proficient, so does his judgment become better than it was formerly" (*CD* 8.6). Augustine elsewhere links this wisdom and experience to his teaching of practical rationality when he points out that something that appears wicked according to convention and natural law may

---

2. See Fortin, review of *Augustine and the Limits of Politics*, by Jean Bethke Elshtain, 367.

not be wicked if the person performing the act is guided by right desire: "[W]hat is generally speaking wicked in other people is the sign of something great in one who is divine or a prophet" (*DDC* 3.44).[3] Citing biblical examples, Augustine argues that some people can act in ways that are otherwise wicked, but that such people are virtuous on account of their right desire and wisdom. Although the previous quotation is taken from his early *On Christian Teaching,* his treatment of biblical examples in his later *City of God* reflects the same view.

Such virtue enables one to perceive the principles underlying the multiplicity of various manifestations of justice in the world. Augustine states that his carnal ways of thinking prevented him from understanding how the universally valid end of loving God and neighbor could find expression in a diversity of laws and customs: "Nor did I know that true and inward righteousness which judges not according to custom but according to the most righteous law of Almighty God. By that law, mores of different places and times are shaped as is best for those places and times; itself in the mean time being the same always and everywhere; not another thing in another place, nor otherwise upon another occasion" (*Conf.* 3.7; see also *Ep.* 138.4).[4] The just is constant and changes according to circumstance, and Augustine thought that knowledge of that depends on intellectual and moral virtue.

One of the difficulties in handling such knowledge is that Augustine had to explain God's special revelations and particular providence to his readers. How can the love of God and neighbor be constant if God demands different ways of expressing them? Not only their manifestations but also their very principles appear to change. According to the guiding interpretive principle, explicated in the examples below, Augustine regarded special revelations and particular providence as explicable in terms of natural causation. That is, God's revelations do not contradict the political and moral precepts that would derive from a kind of natural theology, such as the one Augustine saw in the Platonists, even though such a theology would not necessarily on its own obtain the same kind of insight that is gained by God's revelation. Frederick Crosson explains how Augustine relates the miraculous events in his own life in terms of natural causation:

> No event in the *Confessions* is brought about by a situation inexplicable in
> terms of natural causes. Nature is a self-enclosed whole, not independent

---

3. "Ita quod in aliis personis plerumque flagitium est in divina vel prophetica persona magnae cuiusdam rei signum est."

4. "Et non noveram iustitiam veram interiorem non ex consuetudine iudicantem, sed ex lege rectissima dei omnipotentis, qua formarentur mores regionum et dierum pro regionibus et diebus, cum ipsa ubique ac semper esset, non alibi alia nec alias aliter."

in its being from God but a whole whose course is adequately explainable in terms of immanent natural causes. Even the telling of the extraordinary event of hearing in a child's voice in the garden, the overtone of a divine command never questions that the voice comes from children playing next door.[5]

According to this view, divine agency, such as God's mysterious command to Abraham to sacrifice Isaac (which Augustine treats as an exception to the injunction against killing, as seen below), does not suspend or overturn the order of nature. For Augustine, the insights that direct such action derive from a wisdom of the whole on which the hierarchy of human ends depends. Thus, action based on knowledge of right-by-nature is, for Augustine as for Aristotle, a way of translating the right, which is eternal, into the realm of changing circumstance.

We now turn to three examples of moral and political reasoning in which Augustine theorizes in terms consistent with right-by-nature: lying, adultery, and rebellion. He is generally considered to prohibit all three, but evidence shows that "inferior righteousness" permits them under certain conditions.

## MORAL REASONING IN EXTREME CIRCUMSTANCES

### Lying

Augustine's general rejection of speaking falsehoods is based on the biblical injunction.[6] He justifies prudent action in extreme circumstances by arguing that such action appears as lying but in fact effects the principle of loving God and neighbor and attempting to educate one's neighbor to do the same.

Several texts support this argument. The main texts are *On Lying* (written 395 A.D.) and the later *Against Lying* (written 419 A.D.).[7] The former is a general treatise, whereas the latter is a response to Spanish priests who wished to infiltrate the heretical Priscillianists in order to convert them to orthodoxy. Augustine argues in the later treatise that lying in all cases, especially in matters of faith, is prohibited because it prevents people, such as the Priscillianists, from taking Christianity seriously. The prohibition against lying is made clear,

---

5. Crosson, "Structure and Meaning," 32.

6. See Rist, *Augustine: Ancient Thought Baptized*, 192–93; Kenneth W. Kemp and Thomas Sullivan, "Speaking Falsely and Telling Lies," 152; Fortin, "Problem of Goodness," 186; Sissela Bok, *Lying*, 31–38, 43–44; and Paul J. Griffiths, "The Gift and the Lie: Augustine on Lying."

7. Both works are translated in Augustine, *Treatises on Various Subjects*.

as would be expected for a treatise intended to diffuse a potentially dangerous situation in which priests thought they could lie to promote Christianity. This greater clarity in the latter text is often taken to represent Augustine's mature view. However, Augustine's own view on the matter is that the earlier *On Lying* is "obscure, prolix, and troublesome *(obscurus et anfractuosus et omnio molestus)*."[8] In *The Retractions,* he states that he prefers his later *Against Lying* because it is an overt attack on lying, meant to correct the Spanish priests, whereas *On Lying* is more theoretical. This indicates he distinguished the two works in terms of style and subtlety, not in content. One of the terms he uses to describe *On Lying* is *anfractuosus,* a term he also uses to describe the twists and turns of dramatic dialogues, such as those he wrote.[9] He also characterizes the work as an *exercitatio mentis,* a spiritual exercise meant to train one for intellectual and moral virtue.[10] His view that *On Lying* is theoretical and prolix does not mean that it was immature, but, rather, indicates that its character is more that of a subtle philosophic dialogue than a direct, dogmatic work.

This subtlety is signaled at the beginning of *On Lying:*

> I shall treat this question so carefully as to seem to be seeking truth myself along with my questioners. Whether I shall succeed in this quest the treatise itself will indicate sufficiently to the attentive reader, even though I assert nothing rashly. The problem is involved; because of certain profound and intricate issues, its solution often eludes the comprehension of the one probing it, so that what has been ascertained at one moment escapes one, at another moment reappears and is once more apprehended. In the end, however, it will, like a carefully laid snare, seize upon our mind. If there is error in this presentation, I think that, since truth frees one from all error and lack of truth enmeshes one in all error, it is better to err by an excessive regard for truth and by an equally emphatic rejection of falsehood.[11]

This passage indicates that nothing is asserted rashly, or even directly, in this treatise, and that Augustine's ideas will be clear only to the attentive reader,

---

8. Augustine, *The Retractions,* 1.26.

9. See Augustine, *Greatness of the Soul,* 31.63. Similarly, he elsewhere characterizes his *City of God* as prolix *(prolixus),* which provides him the excuse to focus on the apologetic purposes of the work rather than on the science of number and "appearing to parade *(iactare)* our little smattering of science *(scientiolam)* with more levity *(leviter)* than utility *(utiliter)*" (CD 11.31).

10. Augustine, *The Retractions,* 1.26. On the meaning of *exercitatio mentis* as a spiritual exercise, see Lewis Ayres, "The Christological Context of Augustine's *De Trinitate* XIII: Toward Relocating Books VIII–XV," 114–16; and Robert J. O'Connell, S.J., *St. Augustine's "Confessions": The Odyssey of Soul,* 15–16.

11. Augustine, *On Lying,* 1.1.

for whom the truth will "seize upon our mind." Inattentive readers will fail to come to this conclusion, and for them, the nature of lying will have to be presented with error "by an excessive regard for truth and by an equally emphatic rejection of falsehood."[12] Augustine's discussion leans toward expressing the truth as if it were lawlike in order that, if he should err, he should err toward expressing what is generally true. In other words, he prescribes the usual required practice, as the general prohibition against lying demands. If we attend to the styles of writing that were common in Augustine's time, we find that this view is consistent with Roman legal practice where the term *obscurus*, used by Augustine to describe this treatise, referred to obscure expressions of will that are to be interpreted in a way "which seems more likely or which mostly is being practised."[13]

His analysis of lying indicates that the final purpose of telling a falsehood is a more important consideration than the performance of the act itself:

> He lies, moreover, who holds one opinion in his mind and who gives expression to another through words or any other outward manifestation. For this reason the heart of a liar is said to be double, that is, twofold in its thinking: one part consisting of that knowledge which he knows or thinks to be true, yet does not so express it; the other part consisting of that knowledge which he knows or thinks to be false, yet expresses as true. As a result, it happens that a person who is lying may tell what is untrue, if he thinks that things are as he says, even though, in actuality, what he says may not be true. Likewise, it happens that a person who is actually lying may say what is true, if he believes that what he says is false, yet offers it as true, even if the actual truth be just what he says.[14]

Lying consists of the double heart *(duplex cor)* where the speaker represents the truth with the false. The concept of double heart leads him to state: "For, a person is to be judged as lying or not lying according to the intention of his own mind, not according to the truth or falsity of the matter itself. . . . In reality, the fault of the person who tells a lie consists in his desire to deceive in expressing his thought *(in enuntiando animo suo fallendi cupiditas)*." Lying is sinful because it damages the conformity of the inner and external human being, of inner thought and intention and external deed. Lying is prohibited,

12. He elsewhere contrasts the subtlety of philosophic writing and apologetic writing, which follows a fixed rule (see *CD* 10.23, 15.7).

13. A. Berger, "Encyclopedic Dictionary," 605.

14. Augustine, *On Lying*, 3.3.

therefore, because it damages one's soul, and, as Paul J. Griffiths perceptively notes, lying "is an action that incoherently repudiates the central conditions of its own possibility, which is God's gift."[15]

Augustine provides some exceptions to this general prohibition that actually fulfill the obligation to love God and neighbor. In considering the example of hiding an innocent human being from persecution, he cites as exemplary the actions of Bishop Firmus of Thagaste who suffered tortures to protect a persecuted man. Firmus stated that he would neither lie nor betray the man. He suffered physical torments until the impressed emperor granted pardon for the man whom Firmus was protecting. In cases where one refuses to betray and lie, Augustine argues: "Whatever you suffer for this act of fidelity and kindness, then, is not only judged as unmerited but even as praiseworthy, with the exception of those pains which are said to be suffered not courageously but basely and shamefully." Augustine praises Firmus's fortitude and righteousness. However, he considers the more likely possibility of how a more timid person, placed in similar circumstances, would react. Augustine does not state that a more timid person sins because he cannot undergo similar torments. Instead, he states that Firmus understood the principle of Scriptures "better *(melius)* and fulfilled their commands more courageously *(fortiter)*."[16] He does not state categorically that the timid person does not understand Scripture or does not fulfill its commands. He wrote in the comparative case, which leaves room for telling falsehoods in certain extreme circumstances where truth telling would cause one to suffer shamefully and basely.

Augustine also admits that speaking falsely can fulfill the obligations of neighborly love. He states that it is actually unjust not to lie to protect another in cases where someone wishes to commit an injustice against another. He provides the case of lying to prevent rape, but does not limit the principle to that case:

> [W]e should deter, even by our sins, those assaults which are perpetrated upon a human being so that he is defiled, and whatever is done for this purpose, namely, to prevent uncleanness, should not be called sin. For, that is not a sin which happens in such a way that one would be justly blamed if

15. Ibid., 3.3. Elsewhere, Augustine states: "For, a lie is a false signification told with a desire to deceive. But, that is not a false signification where, even though one thing is signified by another, that which is signified is nevertheless true if rightly understood" (*Against Lying*, 12.26). Griffiths, "The Gift and the Lie," 27.

16. Augustine, *On Lying*, 13.23–24.

it were not done. . . . There would be no sin if action were taken to avoid the defilement. Therefore, whoever has lied in order to avoid such situations does not sin.[17]

Lying is not only permissible in certain circumstances, but also required because not lying would involve implication in the sins of another. This also means that lying is necessary in a case where one is faced with someone of such vicious or deranged disposition that that person is incapable of acting virtuously. Such situations are rare, and, as we shall see, Augustine places the duty of bringing such a person to virtue on the shoulders of the one who must lie.

Augustine argues elsewhere that, when faced with someone who is incapable of hearing the truth, one must first attempt to remove what hinders that person from appreciating truth and virtue: "The first thing to do, then, is to remove the hindrances which bring about his failure to be receptive. For certainly if it is his degenerate condition (sordes) that renders him unreceptive, he must be made clean either by word or by deed as far as that is possible for us."[18] In using the phrase "as far as that is possible for us," Augustine indicates that sometimes it is not possible for us to do this, and that it might be necessary to lie to avoid being implicated in another's sin. Lying in this instance would entail uttering a falsehood about the particular situation, but one that communicates the universal truth about God, which the auditor may be incapable or unwilling to receive.

Augustine applies this idea elsewhere when he discusses the Platonic example of lying in order not to return a sword to a friend who has gone mad:

> As a matter of fact, where one does not have a double heart (duplex cor), there cannot be said to be a lie. As if, for example, a sword be entrusted to anyone, and he promises to return it, when he who entrusted it to him shall demand it: if he chance to require his sword when in a fit of madness, it is clear it must not be returned then, lest he kill either himself or others, until soundness of mind be restored to him. Here then is no duplicity (Hic ideo non habet duplex cor), because he, to whom the sword was entrusted, when he promised that he would return it at the other's demand, did not imagine that he could require it when in a fit of madness. But even the Lord

17. "[I]lla vero quae ita committuntur in hominem, ut eum faciant immundum, etiam peccatis nostris evitare debeamus; ac per hoc nec peccata dicenda sint, quae propterea fiunt ut illa immunditia devitetur. Quidquid enim ita fit, ut nisi fieret, juste reprehenderetur, non est peccatum. . . . Nullum enim peccatum esset, quidquid propter illa evitanda factum esset. Propter haec igitur evitanda quisquis mentitus fuerit, non peccat" (ibid., 9.15).

18. Augustine, Lord's Sermon on the Mount, 2.20.69.

concealed the truth, when He said to the disciples, not yet strong enough, "I have many things to say unto you, but ye cannot bear them now." (*EnP* 5.7, quoting John 16:22)

Lying requires there to be a double heart, but this example indicates that one does not have a double heart if one utters a falsehood to someone incapable of using well the truth; thus, lying is permissible if it communicates justice.

This principle is illustrated differently in Augustine's explanation of the lying spirit that God sent to King Ahab (*83Q* 53.2, commenting on 1 Kings 22:20–23). This example is used to show how God utilizes base things to effect his providence, and Augustine argues that the lying spirit misled King Ahab about his military victory but not about the truth about God, which the king rejected. Ahab intended to attack Ramothgilead, and he ordered his court prophets to provide good news about his chance of success. After the sycophant court prophets assured him of victory, the prophet Micaiah provided good news of which the meaning did not straightforwardly refer to King Ahab's intended project: "Go, and prosper; for the Lord shall deliver it into the hand of the king" (1 Kings 22:15). Yahweh sent a lying spirit to speak through the sycophant prophets to lure Ahab to his destruction. Micaiah did not prophesy success in battle, but then prophesied to one of the court prophets: "Behold, thou shalt see in that day when thou shalt go into an inner chamber to hide thyself" (1 Kings 22:25). Ahab threw Micaiah into prison and then proceeded to be killed in battle, thus fulfilling Yahweh's purpose. Augustine observes: "Thus, if anyone merits being deceived, not only does God not deceive by that person by himself. . . . Rather, God deceives either through the man who has not yet divested himself of such desires or through the angel who, because of his perverseness of will, has been appointed to the lowest station in nature, either in punishment for his sins or for the exercise and cleansing of those who are reborn through God's power" (*83Q* 53.2). Augustine observes that God does not lie. He sent the lying spirit because King Ahab was incapable or unwilling to hear the truth, and, as Micaiah's comment reflects, the lie lay originally in the court prophets and in the king.

Augustine indicates that lying is necessary to hide from one's attackers, and that one may send those attackers to a third party if that third party will suffer lesser injuries and, most important, if that third party consents:

If anyone who can be concealed by a lie is sought for violation, who dares to say that such a lie should not be uttered? But, if he can be hidden only by such a lie as may injure the reputation of another by the false charge of that uncleanness for the endurance of which the first person is being sought—as if one should say to the seeker, naming a certain chaste man unblemished by crimes of this sort: "Go to him. He will manage so that you may get your pleasures more easily, for he knows and loves these things," even though the wicked person should be thus turned away from the one whom he was seeking—I am inclined to think that the reputation of one person must not be injured by a lie even to prevent the body of another from being violated. In general, a lie must not be told for the sake of another person when by that lie a third person may be injured, even though a slighter injury may come upon him than would happen to the second party if the lie were not told; one man's bread may not be taken from him against his wishes, even though he is comparatively strong, so that a weaker person may be nourished, nor may an innocent person be scourged against his wishes so that another may not die. If the man in question is willing, however, let such an action be taken, because he is not wronged who so accedes.[19]

This passage demonstrates that uttering falsehoods is additionally permissible when a stronger third party consents to bear the burden of being attacked. This actualizes the principle of serving other human beings, and so shows how uttering falsehoods can fulfill the love of God and neighbor. It also points to the principle that the third party must consent to the deed.

These passages show that Augustine's injunction against lying points to a higher principle of promoting and actualizing justice in the world. Lying is generally prohibited because it prevents people from knowing how to live virtuously and provides bad examples for others to imitate.[20] However, he indicates that there are extreme circumstances where truth telling is sinful and uttering falsehoods actually serves justice.

### Adultery

Turning now to another seemingly exceptionless rule, we find that Augustine condones adultery in extreme circumstances when it preserves marital fidelity. He provides an unusual example of a man who faced the punishment of death because he could not pay the pound of gold he owed to the imperial treasury in Antioch.[21] A wealthy man offered to pay his debt on the condition that he have intercourse with the debtor's beautiful wife. The act was completed

19. Augustine, On Lying, 9.16.
20. This rule governs Augustine's criticism of pagan civil theology, which lies about the gods. See CD 4.27, 6.6, 6.10.
21. Augustine, Lord's Sermon on the Mount, 1.16.50. See Fortin, "Problem of Goodness," 184–86.

with the debtor's permission and without lust on the part of the wife, and the imperial officials were so ashamed of themselves for letting the laws put the couple into this position that they compensated the couple with an amount far exceeding the debt. Augustine is faced with a situation where the prohibition of adultery might cause an innocent man's death. He observes that this is a horrific, extreme example, but he argues that the debtor and his wife did a just deed on three grounds. First, they followed the Pauline marriage principle that the bodies of the man and wife belong to each other (1 Cor. 7:4), and that she had received her husband's consent. Second, she performed the act without lust, thereby maintaining the purity of her love for her husband. Third, it was a heroic act in that the wife performed an action for her husband that would otherwise have been prohibited by moral rules that command her to preserve her fidelity.[22] Augustine guardedly states: "I dispute nothing of this story. Let each one pass judgment as he wishes." Despite this caution, Augustine provides strong evidence that one should not view this as adultery. He states that "human sense *(sensus humanus)* is not ready to cast out *(respuit)* what happened." This in itself is insufficient because man's moral sense may be faulty, and not casting out differs from affirming an activity as rightful. The gospel forbids fornication, which Augustine has previously defined in the case of adultery as "every carnal and lustful concupiscence" but which he admits does not fit this particular case.[23] The prohibition against adultery is part of the wider prohibition of fornication (which also includes worshiping idols). It follows, then, that no adultery occurs when there is no fornication. The action of the woman was meant to preserve marriage and, as a result, establishes the rightful.

### The Possibility of Tyrannicide and Rebellion

Homicide and, more specifically, tyrannicide are the sins with the greatest political import. The general prohibition against them can be suspended only by agents of the polity who must punish criminals, and by those described in Scripture who have received a special revelation from God. For everyone else, Augustine bases his general rejection on Paul's command: "Let every soul be subject to the higher authorities, for there is no authority except from God" (Rom. 13:1). Everyone must submit to political authorities; doing

22. This compares with Augustine's argument that Abraham did not sin by impregnating Hagar, Sarah's handmaiden: "[I]n using Hagar he had guarded the chastity of Sarah his wife, and had gratified her will and not his own" (*CD* 16.25).
23. Augustine, *Lord's Sermon on the Mount,* 1.12.36.

so only halfheartedly because one wishes to avoid the authorities' anger is insufficient, for that would be deceitful. Rather, one must go further and submit to political authorities out of love. This does not mean that Christians should be involved and implicated in political evils, however. One may resist, and gain glory, only by martyrdom: "[W]hether the authority approves your good deed or persecutes you, 'You will have praise of him,' either when you win it by your allegiance to God, or when you earn the crown of martyrdom by persecution."[24] Rather than advocating political withdrawal or perpetuating political evil, Augustine saw great merit in the ability of martyrdom to effect political reform: "[B]y confessing, embracing, and proclaiming [their faith], and for its sake enduring all things with faith and fortitude, and by dying with godly assurance, they shamed the laws by which it was forbidden, and caused them to be changed" (CD 8.19). Martyrdom is an effective mode of political reform and appears as the only mode that Augustine affirms. This section shows, however, that Augustine's way of treating exceptions to the general rule indicates that martyrdom is not the only weapon in his arsenal of political reform. Although submission and martyrdom are general responses to political rule, he allows for rebellion in circumstances when even one's oppressor cannot be so shamed.[25]

The first part of this discussion considers the conditions under which Augustine thought it just to have a rebellion, by showing how he thought its leader can hold public authority but not necessarily public office, and what conditions need to be met. Because Augustine bases exceptions to rebellion and killing on what appear to be an appeal to divine intervention and a suspension of otherwise absolute rules, the second part examines more closely how he understood that one can have knowledge of special revelation and particular providence in a way that does not offend natural reason.

Augustine lists two exceptions to the general prohibition of homicide: (1) when sanctioned by a general law and (2) in special cases sanctioned by God's command:

---

24. Augustine, *Augustine on the Romans: Propositions from the Epistle to the Romans and Unfinished Commentary on the Epistle to the Romans,* 72.1–74.3.

25. See Burnell, "Problem of Service." He argues that Augustine's affirmation of the justice of rebellion can be seen in his treatment of Rome's expulsion of the Tarquins (CD 3.15–16), his allowance for resistance against the revolt led by Spartacus (CD 4.5, 4.15), just war (CD 19.7), and his treatment of Virgil's monster, Cacus, as a political analogy (CD 19.12). This section shows that Augustine's justification involves fulfilling the moral principle rather than in suspending it, and it extends Burnell's discussion of the Cacus example to show that rebellion can be rightful to secure social and political goods in addition to material goods.

> But the divine authority itself has made certain exceptions to the rule that
> it is not lawful to kill men. These exceptions, however, include only those
> whom God commands to be slain, either by a general law, or by an express
> command applying to a particular person at a particular time. Moreover, he
> who is commanded to perform this ministry does not himself slay. Rather,
> he is like a sword which is the instrument of its user. And so those who,
> by God's authority, have waged wars, or who, bearing the public power in
> their own person, have punished the wicked with death according to His
> laws, that is, by His most just authority: these have in no way acted against
> that commandment which says, "Thou shalt not kill."[26] (*CD* 1.21)

His rhetoric appears to suggest that exceptions are restricted to those executing positive law and those biblical examples inspired by God. The rhetoric is guarded in part because Augustine faced civil disorder during the collapse of the Roman Empire. One of the causes of disorder were the Circumcellions, a group of Donatists who claimed special dispensation to kill on behalf of God in order to rid the world of the wicked. Augustine himself narrowly escaped a Donatist assassination attempt. As a result, his rhetoric makes him appear to say that the only nonlegal exceptions to killing are allotted to those beneficiaries of direct revelation listed in Scripture and recognized by the Church's authority, such as Abraham, Jephthah, and Samson (whom he lists immediately after the passage quoted above). If rightful exceptions consist only in scriptural examples and those recognized by the Church, must politics necessarily be subservient to the Church?

Augustine's language is guarded, but his choice of words indicates that the person carrying the public power (*personam gerens publicae potestatis*) refers primarily to the authority of a virtuous human being and secondarily to an officeholder.[27] Because Augustine appears generally to speak of political power as something wielded by actual officeholders, evidence must be pieced together from various sources to show that the power he mentions in the above passage

---

26. "Quasdam vero exceptiones eadem ipsa divina fecit auctoritas, ut non liceat hominem occidi. Sed his exceptis, quos Deus occidi iubet sive data lege sive ad personam pro tempore expressa iussione (non autem ipse occidit, qui ministerium debet iubenti, sicut adminiculum gladius utenti; et ideo nequaquam contra hoc praeceptum fecerunt, quo dictum est. *Non occides*, qui Deo auctore bella gesserunt aut personam gerentes publicae potestatis secundum eius leges, hoc est, iustissimae rationis imperium, scleratos morete punierunt)."

27. Augustine's usage contrasts with that of John of Salisbury who signified the prince as the *gerens personam publicam* (*Policraticus*, 4.2). John equates the term with an officeholder, whereas Augustine leaves informal power open as a possibility. It also signifies an officeholder in the writings of Louis the Pious (814–840) and in the Synods of Worms and Paris (829) (see Voegelin, *The Middles Ages to Aquinas*, vol. 2 of *History of Political Ideas*, 62, 86).

may include individuals without official power. The distinction between the worth of the individual and his office was actually close to Augustine's own experience, as it formed the basis for the Roman understanding of political power and understanding of the office of dictator, which relied on the virtue of someone hitherto without political office who temporarily had to set aside the laws in order to save the republic.[28] Augustine's distinction between virtue and officeholder is seen in the fact that he actually treats politics in personalist terms; he refers to each human being, rather than the city's institutions and physical attributes, as the primary element or seed of a city (*CD* 4.3; *EnP* 9.8). The dictator's power *(imperium)* was conferred upon citizens, almost always private citizens, by the constitutional form of *lex curiata*, and the most common and most general function he had was to be the *dictatura rei gerundae causa*, literally, "the dictatorship for getting things done." For instance, early in Augustine's career he explicitly regarded such a power as just: "would it not also be right, provided some honest man of great ability was found at the time, to strip these [corrupt] people of the power to elect public officials and to subject them to the rule of a few good men, or even to that of one man?" (*DLA* 1.6.14). Augustine's recognition of this power is seen in his observation that Cincinnatus was entrusted with Rome's security because of his extreme poverty (*Ep.* 104; *CD* 3.17, 5.18). In the case of Hortensius, he notes that instituting a dictator was a "measure commonly adopted in times of gravest peril" (*CD* 3.17). Thus a Roman, upon reading the above passage, would have heard the *gerens publicae potestatis* as "the bearer of the public power." He would have understood it as the power conferred to a virtuous human being who would be called in on a particular occasion to save the republic.

Indeed, Augustine's term *persona* plays a central role in his theory of virtue; one's personhood is realized only when one is fully conscious of oneself as the image of God. The term *persona* means, literally, "sound through," and derives from the masks used in Etruscan religious rites, possibly related to the worship of Persephone.[29] In legal terminology, it signifies the fundamental category of a

28. Lendon, *Empire of Honour*, 16. See Livy, *Ab urbe condita*, 2.18. Augustine used Livy as a source of Roman history (James J. O'Donnell, "Augustine's Classical Readings," 160; see also Hagendahl, *Latin Classics*, 1:195–206). In general, see Rossiter, *Constitutional Dictatorship*, 15–28.

29. Mary T. Clark, "Augustine on Person: Divine and Human," 100–107. For example, Augustine points out that Adam and Eve, each of whom carried their own persons *(personam suam quisque portabat)*, were fully self-conscious of themselves as images of God (*DT* 12.12.18). See also Augustine, "Reply to Faustus the Manichaean," in *Writings against the Manichaeans and against the Donatists*, 23.8.

bearer of rights.[30] Augustine uses it and its verbal form to signify proclamation and related activities: "For all things signified seem somehow to sustain the *persona* of the things that they signify" (*CD* 18.48).[31] He continues: "[T]hus it is said by the Apostle, 'The rock was Christ,' since the rock of which this was said at any rate *(utique)* signified Christ" (ibid.). *Persona* as the primary signifier is also the meaning of the title given by a later editor to a chapter on the prophecies of Hannah, who is said to personify the Church *(persona gerens ecclesiam)* (*CD* 17.4). The language of *persona* as *gerens* is identical to Augustine's description above of a *persona gerens publicae potestatis* (*CD* 1.21). Cicero, also distinguishing between virtue and office, used *persona* similarly. Cicero signifies this representative power when he proclaims in his speech against consuls Lucius Piso and Lucius Philippus: "O immortal gods! what a task it is to sustain the person of a leader in the republic!"[32] In his speech against Marcus Lucullus and Publius Servilius, from whose clutches and jaws *(manibus ac faucibus)* he states that he himself snatched *(eripui)* the republic, Cicero argues that they would have faltered before the solemn pronouncements of the "men who by their dignity upheld the persona of the Roman people."[33] This way of speaking of *persona* was reflected in Roman understandings of the emperor. As Charles Cochrane observes, the emperor "emerged as the supreme embodiment of Roman virtue, speaking and acting not merely *for* but also *as* the sovereign people whom he professed to 'represent.'"[34] Cicero understood the human being "bearing the public persona" to earn his role by his dignity or virtue and by his ability to represent the public good. Therefore, he did not restrict the powers of the *persona* to the office of the emperor, as his reference to himself saving Rome indicates.[35]

30. Gaius, *The "Institutes" Gaius,* ed. Francis de Zulueta, 2 vols. (Oxford: Clarendon Press, 1946–1953), 1.8–9; Justinian, *Justinian's "Institutes,"* 1.3. Barry Nicholas, *An Introduction to Roman Law,* 60. See also A. Berger, "Encyclopedic Dictionary," 628–29.

31. "Quoniam omnia significantia videntur quodam modo earum rerum quas significant sustinere personas." The term *persona* is carried over from the theater where it signifies the actors' masks (*CD* 6.7). He uses it also to signify proclaiming, to signify the Word of God through various prophets or testimonies (*CD* 2.2, 2.28, 17.4, 20.20, 21.14, 22.8): Virgil poetically sketching the person of Christ (*CD* 10.27); the voice of nature proclaiming its truth (*CD* 18.2); what books generally report (*CD* 18.8); what pagan sacrilegious songs resound (*CD* 6.6); and dramatic voice, as when he speaks of Cicero speaking in another's person (*CD* 5.9; see also *CD* 11.15, 17.12, 17.18).

32. "O di immortales! quam magnum est personam in re publica tueri principis!" (Cicero, *Philippics* 8.29). He also calls them "first men of the city *(principes civitatis)*" (8.28).

33. "[Q]ui sua dignitate personam populi Romani" (Cicero, *De Domo Sua,* in *Pro Archia. Post Reditum in Senatu. Post Reditum Ad Quirites. De Domo Sua. De Haruspicum Responsis. Pro Cn. Plancio,* trans. N. H. Watts [Cambridge: Harvard University Press, 1923], 52.133).

34. Cochrane, *Christianity and Classical Culture,* 127.

35. Cicero makes a similar statement in *De Officiis* concerning the human being dedicated to the public good, although he does not use the term *persona*: "But those whom nature has endowed

This meaning of *persona*, which includes but transcends its legal meaning, is consistent with Augustine's usage of *potestas*, which is included in his definition of the *persona gerens publicae potestatis*. *Potestas* was a Roman republican legal term with a broad meaning covering the person who holds either physical ability *(facultas)* or right *(ius)* or both. According to Berger, "it generally indicates the power of a magistrate whether he is vested with *imperium* or not." Since *imperium* was the official power of the higher magistrates under the republic and of the emperor under the empire, this means that one could have *potestas* to act in the public good without necessarily holding office. *Publica* is a general term that is not reducible to legalistic structure. As a Roman jurisprudential term, *publicus* meant "in the interest of the Roman people," which, as we have seen, extended to the work of the dictator, and opposes that which is *privatus*. Augustine uses *publicus* in a wider sense when he speaks of God's public law *(leges publicae)*, which opposes an individual's private law *(leges privatum)* that constitutes rebellion against God (83Q 79.1; see also *CD* 1.17). Further, Augustine's metaphor of the hand that holds the sword, and his reference to criminals in the passage under consideration, invokes the Roman legal concept of the *ius gladii*, the power to punish criminals, which the emperor alone held (though he could delegate it).[36] Augustine shifts this to include also people without offices when he states that this power is given to the person *(ad personam)* commanded by a law or by God (*CD* 1.21).

These considerations indicate that the *persona gerens publicae potestatis* includes but is not restricted to bearers of political offices. Augustine's understanding of the component words signifies a more general meaning than the specifically legal, and indicates that Augustine would also include a virtuous individual acting as a dictator.

Having established that the one who serves as the sword for another may include someone who is not a political officeholder, we turn to consider the grounds of rebellion. Rebellion is just when rulers force the citizens to commit unjust or impious deeds, or when they fail to provide for their citizens' material well-being: "As for this mortal life, which ends after a few days' course, what

---

with the capacity of administering affairs *(rerum gerendarum)* should put aside all hesitation, enter the race for public office and take a hand in directing the republic *(gerenda res publica)*" (1.21.72; see also 1.25.85). Cicero presents Scipio in *De Re Publica* as the model statesman whose virtue makes his soul the source of justice in the polity (see Walter Nicgorski, "Cicero's Focus: From the Best Regime to the Model Statesman," 242–43).

36. A. Berger, "Encyclopedic Dictionary," 640 *(potestas)*, 494 *(imperium)*, 661 *(publicus)*, 529 *(ius gladii)* (see also *Ep.* 153.6.16).

does it matter under whose rule a man lives, being so soon to die, provided that the rulers do not force him to commit impious and unjust acts *(si illi qui imperant ad impia et iniqua non cogant)?"* (*CD* 5.17). This passage is often cited as an example of Augustine's political passivism and otherworldliness because it seems to diminish the importance of mortal life.[37] However, it only compares mortal life to the infinite good of immortal life, and does not deny that mortal and political life possess their own goods. Furthermore, as Burnell observes, the passage is written in the subjunctive, which indicates that Augustine treats this problem as hypothetical. Contrary to advocating passivism to tyranny, Augustine leaves grounds for resistance against unjust rulers who force impious and unjust acts. An examination of related texts specifies what kind of acts entail, and necessitate, rebellion.

Augustine's violent language in this passage contrasts with his admonitions, referred to above, that Christians should welcome martyrdom when persecuted:

> [T]he heavenly city . . . knew only one God to be worshiped and believed with faithful piety that He is to be served with that service which in Greek is called *latreia*, and should be rendered only to God. Because of this, it has come to pass that the heavenly city could not have common laws of religion *(religionis leges . . . communes)* with the earthly city, and on this point must dissent and become a tiresome burden *(dissentire haberet necesse atque oneri esse)* to those who thought differently, and must undergo their anger and hatred and persecutions, except that at length it repelled the hostile intent of its adversaries with fear of its own numbers and with evidence of the ever-present divine aid *(nisi cum animos adverantium aliquando terrore suae multitudinis et semper divino adiutorio propulsaret).* (*CD* 19.17)

This violent language contrasts with the message of the passage, in which Augustine calls for the oppressed to suffer persecutions by a tyrant who forces them to worship falsely, up to the point where their numbers and "evidence of divine aid" (explained below) "repel" the tyrant. This passage is consistent with the one seen above where Augustine advocates martyrdom to shame tyrants into changing laws (*CD* 8.19), since their being repelled may take the form of feelings of shame at seeing a major part of his population rejecting his rule.[38] However, this passage comes closer to allowing rebellion than either *CD* 8.19 or his *Propositions from the Epistle to the Romans*, where Augustine claims that

---

37. For example, see Markus, *Saeculum*, 70–71. For the opposite view, see Burnell, "Status of Politics," 20.

38. As seen in Chapter 3, Nero lacked all shame (*CD* 5.19).

martyrs will be praised by their oppressors. In the passage under consideration here, martyrs do not actively rebel, but their martyrdom can make it exceedingly difficult for a tyrant to govern a country. But is this merely to beg the question? Is Augustine using martyrdom merely to provoke the tyrant to create more martyrs (as the Donatists tried to provoke Roman authorities to do to them)? Do martyrdoms not further provoke violent resistance by non-Christians not bound by scriptural injunctions? Augustine does not appear to consider these questions, but his argument for martyrdom *seems* to create the conditions in which rebellion constitutes a threat to political rule. If he is indeed making this argument, and this is doubtful, then he would have martyrs treat non-Christians instrumentally by having them do their political bidding.

Augustine elsewhere allows more explicitly for rebellion. He treats Cacus, the monster in Virgil's *Aeneid* as a political analogy (*CD* 19.12).[39] That this is an analogy of the drama of a rebelling body politic can be seen from the many political terms Augustine uses to describe Cacus's lonely existence in his kingdom *(regnum)*, his cave. The analogy exemplifies a community in *stasis,* as images of rebellion and civil war abound in the passage. Cacus's internal strife symbolizes revolution by a population lacking material necessities for living, and as the result of destroyed political goods such as comity and friendship. Augustine introduces Cacus (whose name is derived from the Greek "evil [*kakos*]") to show that even the most savage and unsociable being strives for its own peace: "[A]ll that he desired was peace unmolested by any man's violence or fear of it. In a word, he longed to be at peace with his own body; and so far as he succeeded in this, all was well with him." However, his "mortality" rebelled against its ruler, "and in order to pacify with all possible speed his mortal nature when it rebelled against him through its impoverishment, and incited hunger to wage rebellion and sedition that aimed to sever and eject his soul from his body, he ravished, slew and devoured" (*CD* 19.12).[40] The organizing principle, reason, was ejected by the body's parts. Augustine adds:

> And yet, cruel and savage though he was, he was providing by his cruelty and savagery for the peace of his life and safety; so if he had been willing to keep the peace with other men as he was content to keep it in his cave and with himself, he would not be called bad or a monster or a semi-man. Or if the ugliness of his body and his belching of murky flames frightened off human

39. Virgil, *The Aeneid* 8.190–305. See Burnell, "Problem of Service," 186–88.

40. "[E]t ut suam mortalitatem adversum se ex indigentia rebellantem ac seditionem famis ad dissociandam atque excludendam de corpore animam concitantem quanta posset festinatione pacaret, rapiebat necabat vorabat."

companions, perhaps it was not through lust for harm but through the necessity of keeping alive *(sed vivendi necessitate)* that he was fierce. (ibid.)

Burnell argues that "the whole sequence of events . . . originates in necessities involved in staying alive *(vivendi necessitate)*."[41] Rebellion is justified and necessary when the people are prevented from securing their mortal needs. As the extreme nature of the example indicates, they would have to be facing massive oppression and flagrant injustices.

Cacus's mortal problems were actually the result of his being unsociable: "[I]f he had been willing to keep the peace with other men as he was content to keep it in his cave and with himself, he would not be called bad or a monster or a semi-man." Augustine introduces Cacus as having "no wife to exchange fond words with him, no little children to play with, none to command when they were bigger, no friends to give him the enjoyment of conversation *(conloquio)* . . . although he gave to none, but took what he chose from anyone he chose whenever he could" *(CD* 19.12). Rebellion of the parts against Cacus's body politic was symptomatic of his deeper rebellion against his social nature that, at the very least, would have helped him to satisfy his mortal needs more efficiently. His lusts, savagery, and desires preceded the hunger of his mortality. This example indicates that Augustine thought rebellion justified and necessary when a tyrant destroys political and social life in such a way that civil friendships and associations are seriously prevented from developing. His description of Cacus also reflects historical examples of revolution where the desperate citizenry finally rebel when they become deprived of their mortal needs after having long suffered the destruction of political life by their rulers.

Just rebellion requires "fear of [a people's] own numbers and . . . evidence of the ever-present divine aid" *(CD* 19.17). The first condition indicates that resistance must be sufficiently widespread and must possess the means to constitute a threat. This means that in addition to a just cause, rebellion must have sufficiently widespread support to have an effective claim to represent the common good. Large numbers would constitute a threat to a tyrant's grip on power. The paradigmatic case of large numbers of people with divine aid resisting a tyrant is Israel's situation in Egypt. The "Egyptians marveled at the great increase of that people, and feared it *(terrerent)*" despite the Egyptians' policy of killing every male child *(CD* 16.43; Exod. 1.7). The Israelites fled Egypt rather than rebel, but they nevertheless terrified the Egyptian powers. As with the discussion of martyrdom above, there is little difference between threatening

41. Burnell, "Problem of Service," 187.

the authority of political power and actively rebelling against it. Conversely, Augustine's requirement for large numbers indicates that escape from tyranny and then martyrdom are required when small numbers are involved.

## EXCEPTIONS BASED ON DIVINE DISPENSATION?

Discussion so far has focused on the conditions in which Augustine affirms the justice of rebellion and maintains that the leader of a rebellion may be the "bearer of the public person." Turning to the grounds for that authority, Augustine states: "These exceptions, however, include only those whom God commands to be slain, either by a general law, or by an express command applying to a particular person at a particular time" (CD 1.21). Later in the same chapter he states that the basis for the general law and the specific command is the same: "[w]ith these exceptions, then, which are justified either by a just law that applies generally, or by a special command from God Himself, the fountain of justice" (CD 1.21).[42] How does knowledge of the general rule found in the eternal law relate to the knowledge of the exception? Can Augustine avoid giving license to false prophets who claim special but unverifiable special dispensations to justify their breaking of natural laws? These questions go right to the heart of Augustine's understanding of nature and grace, and reason and revelation. This section focuses on the political dimensions of this understanding, whereas Chapter 6 provides a more sustained account of his understanding of the love of God and of neighbor.

Augustine regarded the authority of special exceptions as consistent with what natural reason can discover, as shown in his unusual examples of such exceptions: Abraham, Jephthah, and Samson, who all ostensibly received their authority because of special revelation. Augustine thought that nature itself does not always act according to its general course, and that natural reason can neither confirm nor deny that exceptional events are due to chance or are part of a greater plan. Thus, practical wisdom of right-by-nature does not require that one need be a prophet or have perfect knowledge of God's miracles. Rather, practical wisdom is analogous to scientific knowledge, which cannot rule out the possibility that prodigies such as monstrous births and eclipses are part of a greater plan and are not necessarily due to chance. By analogy, God's

---

42. "[H]is igitur exceptis, quos vel lex iusta generaliter vel ipse fons iustitiae Deus specialiter occidi iubet." *Iubere* in Roman legal terminology is applied to the right of magistrates to issue orders (A. Berger, "Encyclopedic Dictionary," 517).

apparent suspension of the natural law in the cases of Abraham, Jephthah, and Samson cannot be ruled out as intentional exceptions to the usual course of nature. A digression to explain Augustine's general understanding of the way scientific understanding perceives miracles and revelations is necessary before considering the special knowledge required to make an exception to the general prohibition against killing.

For Augustine, natural causes, prodigies, and miracles are all part of God's unchanging plan:

> There is, however, no impropriety in saying that God does a thing contrary to nature, when it is contrary to what we know of nature. For we give the name nature to the usual common course of nature; and whatever God does contrary to this, we call a prodigy, or a miracle. But against the supreme law of nature, which is beyond the knowledge both of the ungodly and of weak believers, God never acts, anymore than He acts against Himself. As regards spiritual and rational beings, to which class the human soul belongs, the more they partake of this unchangeable law and light, the more clearly they see what is possible, and what impossible; and again, the greater their distance from it, the less their perception of the future, and the more frequent their surprise at strange occurrences.[43]

He argues that miracles and prodigies contravene only what is generally known as the natural order. Miracles and prodigies are not due to chance nor do they reflect a change in God's mind:

> [B]ut where and when he performs them depends on an unchangeable plan that rests in the keeping of him alone in whose ordered design all the days to come have already been made *(facta sunt)*. For though he creates the movement in time of things temporal, he himself does not move in time; and his view of things that are to be done is no different from his view of things already done. Nor does he harken in one way to those who are calling upon him and in another way perceive those who will call upon him later. . . . [A]nd his commands are executed in time, though they are seen in one view by his eternal law *(aeterna eius lege)*.[44] (*CD* 10.12; see also 21.5–8, 22.2)

Creation is governed by God's providence, and, accordingly, no event within it contradicts the eternal law.

---

43. Augustine, "Reply to Faustus the Manichaean," 26.3. See also *CD* 21.5–8.
44. See also Augustine, "Reply to Faustus the Manichaean," 24, 26.

Augustine treats nature and the miraculous as almost equivalent. Indeed, he calls creation the greatest miracle of all:

> For we cannot listen to those who maintain that the invisible God works no visible miracles, since even in their view he himself made *(fecit)* the universe, which they surely must admit is visible. Now any marvelous thing that is wrought in this universe is assuredly less than this whole universe, that is, heaven and earth and all things that in them are, which God assuredly made. But the means by which he made it are as hidden and incomprehensible *(occultus . . . et inconprehensibilis)* to man as he is himself who made it. (*CD* 10.12)

By arguing that creation is itself a miracle, Augustine argues that the greatest manifestation of the miraculous is not the unfamiliar or unintelligible (the particular oddities of prodigies, for example), but the immediate and intelligible. He argues that even the union of body and soul, which human beings experience daily, is more miraculous than the translation of bodies to heavenly bodies: "If we consult sober reason *(sobria ratione)*, however, we surely find that the more miraculous *(mirabilioris)* of the two divine works is the interweaving, as it were, rather than the coupling of earthly things with heavenly, which, though different, are nonetheless both corporeal" (*CD* 22.4). Similarly, he regards human individuality as miraculous: "But the consideration of their dissimilarity is more miraculous *(mirabilior)*, since a common nature seems more properly to require similarity" (*CD* 21.8).

Lesser miracles, such as those performed by Moses, are necessary to refocus people's minds back to the structure of the universe when that structure has become forgotten. Augustine emphasizes the quality of the mind that is so refocused when he calls it wise:

> Although, therefore, the wonders of the visible order of nature are held in low regard *(viluerint)* because they are always before us *(assiduitate)*, yet, when we view them wisely, we see that they are greater than the least familiar and rarest miracles. For man himself is a greater miracle than any miracle performed by man. God, then, Who made the visible heaven and earth, does not disdain to perform visible miracles in heaven or earth. He does this in order to inspire the soul *(excitet animam)*, hitherto given up to things visible, to worship Him, the invisible. (*CD* 10.12)

The purpose of miracles is to quicken the soul *(excitet animam)* to recognize the invisible causes behind the visible, which are obscured to those "given up to visible things." Augustine argues that creation itself is miraculous and a gift, and that human sinfulness and casual familiarity with the world makes human beings oblivious to its order.

How can Augustine argue that there are miracles such as the virgin birth and Sarah's motherhood while simultaneously arguing that natural causation is itself miraculous, without undermining the view that such miracles are due to God's direct intervention in history? He does so by speaking of God's providence in two ways. On the one hand, he characterizes God as the legislator of creation, in order to emphasize the eternal law and God's immutable will. On the other hand, he characterizes God as judge of creation, so as to emphasize that God can act in ways that appear to contradict God's eternal law. The latter characterization is based on Augustine's view that nature itself contains exceptions that natural reason cannot deny that are governed by a rational plan (or put inversely: natural reason cannot conclude with certainty that they occur by chance). As we shall see, Augustine's characterization of exceptions to the general prohibition against killing, as based on special commands from God, is analogous to the way he understands the exceptions that nature herself produces.

Augustine treats God as a legislator of creation when he argues that God is immutable and that his creation follows his eternal plan. This is the God of natural or eternal law (*CD* 22.2). For example, he speaks of God's supernal court in which resides the "immutable Truth which reigns as the eternal law *(imcommutabilis Veritas, tamquam lex aeterna)*" (*CD* 16.6).[45]

Augustine characterizes God as judge when he wants to portray God's characteristic prudence in guiding creation, and to signify how God maintains his continual providence over creation. He compares God's providence to an emperor's rule over a republic: "For nothing happens in a visible and sensible manner throughout the most immense and boundless republic *(republica)* of all creation that is not commanded or permitted by that inner, invisible, and intelligible court of the supreme emperor *(summi Imperatoris)*, in accordance with the ineffable justice of His rewards and punishments, and of His graces and retributions" (*DT* 3.4.9; see also *CD* 2.19, 10.7, 16.6). God is also said to govern *(gubarnare)* creation through his providence (*CD* 5.21). Augustine usually relies on this idea to explain God's miracles in Scripture: "[A]nd the ark would be piloted when afloat by divine providence rather than by human prudence so as to avoid shipwreck anywhere" (*CD* 15.27).[46] God governs the

45. For a more sustained examination of Augustine's view of the natural and eternal law, see Chroust, "Philosophical Theory of Law."

46. "[M]agisque divina providentia quam humana prudentia natantem gubernet ne incurrat ubiqcumque naufragium."

ark/Church according to his final purpose, even though the means of doing so vary in different periods of time. The methods of governing vary in proportion to the kind of souls being governed; unusual methods of governing, such as visible miracles, would be employed when souls have become corrupted (*83Q* 27; see also *DGL* 5.22.43). Although this usage signifies miracles and revelation, it uses *gubernare*, a traditional concept from Roman law and classical political philosophy, to signify God as the steersman of providence.[47]

Augustine also characterizes God's governance in terms of judgment in relation to natural causation. For instance, we saw above that Augustine thought that the opinion that miracles and prodigies occur contrary to nature is based on human ignorance of the eternal law, and that a greater philosophic wisdom could recognize them as consistent with nature. This assessment of reason is based on his view that nature acts along its usual course, but can produce exceptions to that course.

Augustine's understanding of God as judge clarifies what was characterized above as the miraculousness of nature or the naturalness of miracles. Augustine did not think it strange for prodigies, monstrous births, portents, signs, hermaphrodites, and other "unnatural" events to occur (*CD* 16.8, 21.5–8). He believed that such occurrences are part of God's plan, but also argued that natural reason cannot simply dismiss them as being due to chance. Natural reason can understand natural causation, but nature itself reveals only parts of itself at a time: "For as mothers are pregnant with unborn offspring, so the world itself is pregnant with the causes of unborn things, which are not created in it except from that highest essence *(summa essentia)*" (*DT* 3.9.16). Not every cause and not every form have become manifest. For instance, in a Darwinian-sounding statement, Augustine describes how "some things arise as others pass away, the less succumb to the greater, and the things that are overcome are transformed into the qualities of those that overcome *(qualitates superantium superata vertuntur)*; and this is the appointed order of transitory things" (*CD* 12.4). This is seen again in his reference to Genesis, when he discusses creation at the beginning and in the present: "From [certain hidden seeds], at the Creator's demand, the water brought forth the first swimming things and the winged fowl, and the earth brought forth the first buds according to their kinds *(prima sui generis)*, and the first animals according to their kinds *(prima sui generis)*" (*DT* 3.8.13). He warns skeptics not to dismiss miracles too quickly because

---

47. A. Berger, "Encyclopedic Dictionary," 484; Cicero, *De Re Publica* 1.34.51, 2.9.15, 3.35.47; *De Officiis* 1.25.87; *De Finibus Bonorum et Malorum* 4.27.76. See also *CD* 5.23, 5.26; *83Q* 27. The term originally derives from the Greek *kubernitikos*.

they themselves cannot explain prodigies and other "unnatural" occurrences (*CD* 16.8, 22.5–8). They cannot so easily dismiss miracles when their own scientists and historians record alterations in natural properties: "A portent, therefore, is an occurrence contrary not to nature, but to nature as we know it" (*CD* 21.8).

Just because something contradicts "nature as we know it" does not mean it is unknowable, as Augustine observes in the quotation above, asserting that one's knowledge of occurrences outside the normal course of nature depends on one's intellectual and moral virtue. Such knowledge of nature, though it looks like prophecy (defined as knowing the causes and signs *[causae vel signae]* of things that exist in the present [*Conf.* 11.18; *DT* 4.17.22]), is not perfect knowledge of God's general and particular providence. Augustine merely points out it is possible to understand how nature acts outside its usual course, and that natural reason cannot deny that such occurrences are due to chance. By analogy, he affirms that one can have wisdom to establish the just outside the normal course of action based on natural or eternal law. Such wisdom imitates the prudence of God as judge of creation, who at times acts outside the normal course of nature. Such wisdom still finds miracles mysterious and not completely intelligible because it still lacks perfect knowledge of God's particular providence. However, in facing such miracles, it can understand them in terms of a natural causation acting outside the normal course of nature. As seen above in Crosson's observation of Augustine's *Confessions,* nature is a self-enclosed whole understood not in its independence from God, but as a whole whose course is explainable in terms of immanent natural causes. If we relate this discussion to the source of the general prohibition against killing and to the exceptions that appear to be inspired by special revelation, we find that natural reason cannot deny the miraculous nature of miracles anymore than it can deny that the physical manifestations are intelligible to a wisdom that understands occurrences that become manifest outside nature's usual track.

Although God is the helmsman for the city of God's pilgrimage in this world, his providence also governs the variable courses that nations take. Augustine utilizes Roman jurisprudential language to describe God's providence over the rise and decline of nations in addition to speaking of the providential laws *(providentiae legibus)* they follow (*CD* 5.11). God preserves the rational purpose behind the letter of the natural law when it appears to a human being that the natural law has been broken. Augustine states that human beings can recognize evidence that human sins and mistakes cannot stop the benefits and justice that providence bestows on human beings even when their sins make them unworthy recipients: "These things being so, we do not attribute the power of giving kingdoms and empires to any save to the true God, who gives happiness on earth both to the pious and impious, as it may please Him, to whom nothing is pleasing unjustly *(sicut ei placet cui nihil iniuste placet)"* (*CD* 5.21). Augustine goes on to discuss how God bestowed rule to the Persians, Assyrians, Israelites, and Romans "according to His pleasure": "Manifestly, these things are ruled and governed by the one God according as He pleases; and if His motives are hid, are they therefore unjust?" (*CD* 5.21).[48] Translators usually translate *sicut ei placet* as "according to His pleasure" and *ut placet* as "as he pleases," but modern English does not do justice to the term *placere,* suggesting as it does that God's "pleasure" is whimsical, pernicious, or voluntaristic. The modern English translation implies a God of arbitrary will, which contradicts Augustine's meaning. *Placere* is a Roman legal term well known to Augustine's readers. For example, Ulpian states that "what the emperor has decided *(quod principi placuit)* has the force of law."[49] It is also the jurist's opinion in deciding a particular case that falls outside the general scope of the law. As Berger points out, *"Mihi placet"* meant "In my opinion."[50] *Placere* signifies judgment, which is reflected in Augustine's view that it is appropriate to regard the city of God as a republic: "True justice, however, exists only in that republic whose founder and ruler is Christ, if it is right to call it a republic *(si et ipsam rem publicam placet dicere),* since we cannot deny that it is the people's weal" (*CD* 2.21). The Latin meaning is reflected in the archaic English still used in parliamentary tradition, as when the Speaker of the House of Commons asks if a proposed motion accords with the "pleasure of the House," and in the case of Royal Assent, sometimes called the "Signification of the Queen's Pleasure."[51] Augustine's usage of this language does not imply that God's will is arbitrary; rather, he invokes the language of judgment and of Roman jurisprudential concepts that refer to the jurist's activity of determining the meaning of the law when its letter insufficiently covers a particular circumstance.

God, by his mercy, can provide a nation with someone with true piety and the science of ruling people: "But if those who are endowed with true piety *(vera pietate)* and live good lives know the science of ruling peoples *(scientiam*

48. "Haec plane Deus unus et verus regit et gubernat ut placet; et si occultis causis, numquid iniustis?"

49. Gaius and Ulpian, *The Commentaries of Gaius and Rules of Ulpian,* ed. Bryan Walker, 3rd ed. (Cambridge: Cambridge University Press, 1885), 1.4.1pr. See also Justinian, *Institutes,* 1.2.

50. A. Berger, "Encyclopedic Dictionary," 632; see also 410. Cicero treats it synonymously with judiciousness (*De Finibus Bonorum et Malorum* 1.8.29).

51. See *The Constitution Act,* 1867 (Consolidated Statutes of Canada, Ottawa, Supply and Services, 1985), s. 57.

*regendi populos),* nothing is more blessed *(nihil est felicius)* for mankind than for them, by the mercy *(miserante)* of God, to have power" *(CD* 5.19). Like the philosopher-king for whom the classical right-by-nature theorists prayed, such a ruler would be exceedingly rare. Augustine explains that if such a ruler were to appear, he would consult with the immutable Truth, which is another way of characterizing God's providential rule: "Could there have been any other cause of all those visible and invisible actions, except that invisible and unchangeable will of God, acting through the just soul *(per animam iustiam)* of that man as the seat of its Wisdom, and making use of all . . . ?" *(DT* 3.3.8). He adds:

> What we have, therefore, proposed by way of illustration about one wise man, although he still bears a mortal body and sees only in part, may be extended to any house in which there is a society of such men, or to any city *(civitate),* or even to the whole world, provided that the government and direction of human affairs *(principatus, et regimen rerum humanarum)* are in the hands of wise men who are devoutly and perfectly submissive to God. *(DT* 3.4.9)

Augustine adds that since human beings have not generally reached that state, they should instead "think of that higher and heavenly country itself" (see also *CD* 22.22). He describes the wise human being as part of a chain of causation wherein each link is described by its characteristic prudence, which he calls subtlety: "as grosser *(crassiora)* and lower *(inferiora)* bodies are directed in a certain order by subtler *(subtiliora)* and stronger *(potentiora)* bodies, so all bodies are directed by the spirit of life" *(DT* 3.4.9). *Subtiliora* is the key word in this passage. As in English, it signifies quickness, prudence, and the ability to make fine distinctions; Augustine uses the term to signify the distinctive virtues of philosophers *(CA* 3.3.6, 3.14.30, 3.17.37, 3.19.42, 3.20.43). Such a human being would rule others who are motivated by causes less just than that of true piety, such as the desire for a reward for their "carnal desires or to avoid carnal inconveniences *(incommoda carnalia)*" *(DT* 3.3.8). Augustine's characterization of such rulers and effective causes as "subtle" can be explained in terms of eternal or natural law, if one regards these causes as subtle in their ability to effect a cause within the normal course of nature. However, we have already seen that Augustine treats lying and adultery as examples of establishing the just outside the normal course of nature. Further, he observes that such a ruler often must act contrary to the normal course of nature, although he remains part of the chain of natural causation. Even so, Augustine never permits the performance of an evil act so that some good may come of it; such an act would transgress even the limits that God places on his own actions.

The paradigmatic case of Augustine's view of God as acting outside the normal course of nature is his explanation for why God allows evil to exist in creation. Evil is, of course, a corruption of nature. The *City of God* addresses the question of why God permits the just to suffer evil. Thus, in a sense, the entire work is an inquiry into why God allows acts to occur outside the normal course of nature. The short explanation for the existence of evil in creation is that evil is a consequence and punishment for original sin, and human beings suffer it as an opportunity to have their souls purified. Careful to avoid being misinterpreted, Augustine also argues that evil adds to the beauty of creation. For instance, understood in theological terms, the Fall and the subsequent suffering point to the Resurrection, in which human beings find their greatest freedom: "[T]he first free will consisted in [Adam's] being able not to sin, and the last will consist in his being not able to sin" (CD 22.30). God brings good out of evil: "Good things prevail over bad, however: so much so that, although evil things are permitted to exist in order to demonstrate how the justice and perfect foresight of the Creator can make good use even of them" (CD 14.11; see also 11.18). In more naturalistic terms, Augustine compares the struggle of good and evil to the antitheses of a poem: "Just as the opposition of contraries bestows beauty upon language, then, so is the beauty of this world enhanced by the opposition of contraries, composed, as it were, by an eloquence not of words, but of things" (CD 11.18). This beauty, however, is repulsive. Augustine does not give license to human beings to be evil, and he does not pull any punches when it comes to listing the evils we experience: floods, earthquakes, poisons, injuries, hunger that leads to cannibalism, tyrants, persecutions, wars, and so on (see CD 22.22–23). At one point, he even observes the bizarre beauty of a violent cockfight (DO 1.8.25–26, 2.4.12). Pain, death, and destruction are part of the "appointed order of transitory things":

> We take no delight in the beauty of this order, because, being ourselves only parts of it, woven into it by virtue of our mortal condition, we cannot perceive *(sentire)* that those particular aspects which offend us are blended aptly and fittingly enough into the whole. This is why, in those circumstances where we are less able to contemplate the fitness for ourselves *(contemplari minus idonei)*, we are most rightly instructed to have faith in the Creator's providence, lest, in the temerity of human rashness, we dare to find any fault with the work of so great a Maker. (CD 12.4)

Augustine's explanation for evil in the world is difficult for us to accept because our own dark times have produced so many examples of unjust suffering, which seem to constitute weighty evidence that his view is horribly mistaken and even the result of a moral blindness.

However, this subtly phrased quotation crystallizes Augustine's right-by-nature dim knowledge of the purpose of suffering, while showing that natural reason cannot adequately understand it, and indicates the reason Augustine refused to permit an ends-justify-the-means moral calculus. He states that there are some circumstances in which human beings are less able to contemplate the fitness of creation. "Some circumstances" and "less able" indicate that there are instances in which the fitness of creation can be discerned. These would probably include occasions when human beings observe an individual, a part of creation, improving as a result of corporal punishment, for example. Another example would be the ability of natural reason to discern generally that being is good, which is seen in Augustine's argument that the Platonists regarded being and good as synonymous (*CD* 8.6, 8.8, 11.21; see Chapter 6). However, the Platonists, by their general knowledge of the goodness of being, cannot perfectly understand why the just and unjust suffer alike. It is surely better to suffer injustice than to commit injustice, but Augustine repeatedly argues that the pagan philosophers inadequately responded to individual suffering, as exemplified by Cicero's inadequately explained lamentations over the death of his daughter (*CD* 19.4; see Chapter 6). Thus, human beings, whose perspective is that of a part, are sorely tempted to "dare to find any fault with the work of so great a Maker." However, their natural reason can tell them that creation is good even though it cannot perfectly explain the presence of evil. For Augustine, evil's existence in the world is evidence of God allowing acts to occur outside the normal course of nature. Human reason can have imperfect knowledge of God's acting outside the general course, but it remains always imperfect.

The imperfect understanding that natural reason has of God's action outside of nature's general course helps to explain why Augustine chooses to signify the authority of exceptions to the prohibition against killing, based both on the general law and on the specific command to an individual. He uses Abraham, Jephthah, and Samson to illustrate his point. It is first worth noting Augustine's unusual choice of exceptions. They do not obviously offer themselves as more appropriate candidates than David and Moses. For example, he approvingly mentions Moses who killed an Egyptian while defending an Israelite (*CD* 16.43). Moses appears as a more straightforward example of an exception than the others. Why did he choose them? Perhaps Augustine wished to emphasize how problematic it is to understand exceptions to homicide when using ambiguous examples.

The discussion of Abraham, Jephthah, and Samson is set within a wider discussion concerning the rightfulness of killing, and suicide especially, and the wisdom that purports to justify suicide (*CD* 1.20–26). Augustine observes that the Church honors certain saints who committed suicide, but he points out that one should not question whether they really were commanded to do so by God because one cannot see into the conscience of another, and because their example has become part of Church tradition:

> [T]heir martyrdom is celebrated with veneration by great numbers in the Catholic church. Of these women I do not venture any casual judgment. For I do not know if the Divine Authority has, by some trustworthy testimonies, persuaded the church so to honour their memories; and it may be that this is so. For what if they did this thing not because they were deceived by human frailty, but by divine command, and so were not in error, but obedient? (*CD* 1.26)

He treats this question subtly because the Church may or may not have been persuaded to choose to honor these women by divine authority. But that raises the question: if not by divine authority, then by whom? Just by raising the question, Augustine raises the possibility that the Church may have been misled in honoring them while suspending judgment about whether the women were indeed commanded. He had political reasons to be guarded in treating the Church's honor of those who committed suicide because some, including the Circumcellions, commonly practiced suicide as a way of obtaining eternal glory (*Ep.* 185.3.13). He leaves only the wisdom of the saints and the propriety of the Church in honoring them as an open question.[52]

With the question left open as to whether God specially commanded these martyrs to commit suicide, we can turn to Augustine's treatment of Abraham, his first example of one whom God apparently commands to kill. Augustine appears to speak in two voices here. The first voice, the most obvious one, presents an Abraham who received special revelation from God to sacrifice Isaac. Later in the *City of God*, Augustine states: "Of course Abraham could never reasonably believe (*numquam sane crederet*) that God delighted in human sacrifices; yet when the divine commandment thundered (*divino intonante prae-cepto*), it was to be obeyed, not disputed" (*CD* 16.32). Abraham by his natural reason understood that human sacrifice was not a requirement for worship. Yet, God "thundered" for him to do it.

---

52. Augustine rarely, if ever, questions Church tradition. The most that can be said about it is that he allows for the Church to suffer corruption and to require internal reformation (see Chapter 7).

God's "thunder" is a corporeal signification of divine communication.[53] For example, the voice of God is said to thunder when he speaks in his law, commanding the corporeally minded Hebrews to sacrifice to him alone (*CD* 19.23). As seen in Chapter 1, Augustine follows biblical practice by utilizing corporeal images to teach the corporeally minded. His way of presenting God's communication to Abraham is ambiguous, inasmuch as he denies that God commands by corporeal visions (*CD* 11.2; see also 16.6). This is supported by statements made elsewhere concerning the relationship between intellectual vision and corporeal and spiritual visions. For example, Augustine uses corporeal images to describe the vision at Ostia that he and his mother experienced; he characterizes it as a meditative experience wherein the soul transcends the noise of the contingent to listen silently to the Word of God. The Word of God itself, unlike Augustine's description, transcends all "dreams and imaginary revelations *(somnia et imaginariae revelationes),*" and it is "not pronounced by any tongue of flesh, nor by the voice of the angels, nor by the sound of thunder *(sonitum nubis),* nor in the enigma of similitude" (*Conf.* 9.10). He also states that one's intellectual vision judges one's spiritual vision whereby one sees according to images. Intellectual vision sees things in themselves, and cannot be deceived because it shares in likeness to the intelligible. Intellectual vision apprehends or "intellects" the intelligible; it is a union of like and like. Dreams and prophecies must be consistent with natural reason (*DGL* 12.10.21, 12.26.53; see also 12.14.28, 12.25.52; *DT* 4.17.23, 4.20.27–28; *CD* 10.13).

An examination of Augustine's treatment of Abraham in other passages of the *City of God* indicates that Augustine did not think that Abraham understood the general requirements of loving God exclusively according to corporeal images, which allowed him to trust in the special revelations he received. Augustine treats Abraham as a founder of a new religious order. He states that the name Abraham means "father of many nations *(pater multarum gentium),*" whereas his earlier name, Abram, means "eminent father *(pater excelsus)*" (*CD* 16.28). God's promise to make Abraham the father of many nations was stated with the "greatest of evidence *(cui evidentissime dictum est)*" (*CD* 16.28). Augustine notes that Abraham and Sarah were too old to have children according to the normal course of nature. Abraham begot a child with Sarah's handmaiden, Hagar, on the right-by-nature basis that they did so without lust and with Sarah's consent (*CD* 16.25; see the Adultery section above). Augustine uses the unlikelihood of their procreating as an opportunity to explain the relationship between nature

---

53. In the Latin Vulgate, published after Augustine's time, God actually speaks to him *(dixit ad eum)* (Gen. 22:1–2).

and grace, between acts caused by necessity and those caused by God's free gift: "For although it is God who also operates the natural processes of procreation, still, when God's work is manifested where nature is already decayed and failing, then His grace is the more clearly recognized. And since this was to take place not merely by generation, but by regeneration, therefore circumcision was instituted at this time. . . . For what else does circumcision signify but the renewal of nature by the stripping of the old?" (*CD* 16.26).[54] Rather than treating nature and grace as two different orders, Augustine shows God's grace working through nature. Regeneration is signified by Isaac's generation, which itself is contrary to nature's normal course. Augustine observes that "novelty *(novitatem)* resounds through the story; and the new covenant is presented, in a veiled manner, in the old" (*CD* 16.26).

Augustine expresses indecision over whether the descendants God promises to Abraham in his third promise descend from Abraham "not after the flesh but after the spirit" (*CD* 16.21). God compares Abraham's progeny to grains of sand, which are innumerable to human beings but numerable to God. These innumerable grains of sand, souls, are in Israel and "in all the nations throughout the whole world," which intimates the city of God. Taken in a spiritual sense, the grains of sand signify individual souls scattered about inside and outside the nation of Israel, whose expressions of worship take the form of the virtuous life. Later, Augustine argues that God's promise is spiritual when God compares Abraham's descendants to the stars of heaven: "Here, I think, the promise is rather that his descendants are to be exalted in heavenly bliss. . . . One might perhaps argue that the comparison is a sound one, inasmuch as the stars too are innumerable, since we must believe that not all of them are visible to us. For the keener *(acutius)* the sight of one who looks at them, the more stars he sees; and it may be supposed that some stars are hidden from the view of even the keenest eyes, quite apart from those stars which are said to rise and set in another part of the world" (*CD* 16.23). Just as some have acute vision to see more stars than others, Abraham's acute understanding allowed him to understand the spiritual meaning of God's revelation. This is not to say that he could have understood the heavenly felicity of his progeny on his own. Rather,

---

54. "Quamvis enim et naturalem procreationis excursum Deus operetur; ubi tamen evidens opus Dei est vitiata et cessante natura, ibi evidentius intelligitur gratia. Et quia hoc non per generationem, sed per regenerationem futurum erat, ideo nunc imperata est circumcisio. . . . Quid enim aliud circumcisio significat quam naturam exuta vetustate renovatam?" Abraham could still beget children in his old age, and did so after Sarah died. Augustine observes that people lived much longer in the early times so that "a hundred years did not bring a man to the decrepitude of old age" (*CD* 16.28).

Augustine's observations indicate that he thought Abraham could understood the spiritual meaning of God's revelations as the worship of God, or *latreia* (see, for example, *CD* 10.3). He could not have gained the wisdom he derived from God's revelation about Israel or the Resurrection on his own, but it would have been intelligible for someone with natural knowledge of *latreia*.

Augustine observes that God tested Abraham in order that Abraham's obedience be put "to the proof or to be shown *(obedientia probaretur)*, and be brought to the attention of later ages, rather than of God" (*CD* 16.32). He states explicitly that such proof was not required for God because God already knew Abraham's wisdom. He also states explicitly that such proof or exhibition (another meaning of *probaretur*) was meant for later ages. However, he does not state explicitly that such proof was required for Abraham's self-knowledge. Augustine adds: "And in general *(Et plerumque)* there is no other way for the human mind to arrive at self-knowledge except by the trial of its strength in answering, not merely by words, but by performance, the questions set by temptation" (ibid.). The key to this passage is "[a]nd in general *(Et plerumque)*"; Augustine treats Abraham as someone who hardly experiences things "in general." He emphasizes the unique character of Abraham's experience, and uses the term *plerumque*, which, like *interdum* (which means "sometimes"), was used by jurists to "limit a general classical rule and to leave a way open for exceptions."[55] Abraham can actually be understood to fall under both the general and the unique, depending on whether one views him (and he views himself) from the perspective of grace, natural law, or right-by-nature. Abraham's faith was tested insofar as he responded to God's miracles and command to sacrifice Isaac, which seems to suspend the natural law. He falls under the general lot of human beings by having his faith tested in this way. However, he was unique among human beings by being able to understand that his test was in some distant way related to the general requirements of *latreia*, of offering up one's first fruits. He had already received the spiritual meaning of his revelation, and would have understood that Isaac signified his first fruits. To be sure, he did not perfectly understand God's revelation. He likely would have asked himself why on earth God would force him to revert to a kind of expression of worship that he himself was taught to overcome.[56] Augustine states: "Abraham, of course, could never

---

55. A. Berger, "Encyclopedic Dictionary," 512.
56. The prohibition of human sacrifice is stated in Jer. 7:31: "And they go on building the high place of Tophteh, which is in the valley of the son of Hinnom, to burn their sons and daughters in the fire—which I did not command, nor did it come to my mind" (see also Ezek. 20:25–31).

have reasonably *(sane)* believed that God takes pleasure in human victims. Still, when the divine command thunders, we must obey without disputing its orders" *(CD* 16.32). Abraham followed orders, but, according to Augustine's reasoning, he could do so because he could understand the sacrifice as an expression of the kind of *latreia* that he already comprehended. As with his faith in God's promise that he would inherit the land, he likely would have asked:

> "Lord God, whereby shall I know *(secundum quid sciam)* that I shall inherit it?" . . . For he did not say, "How shall I know *(Unde sciam)?*" as if he did not yet believe. He said, "Whereby shall I know?"—that is, he sought some sign whereby he might know how what he believed already would come to pass. In the same way, there was no lack of faith on the part of the Virgin Mary when she said, "How shall this be *(Quo modo fiet istud)*, seeing that I know not a man?" She was certain that it would come to pass, but she asked in what way it was to come to pass. *(CD* 16.24)

Abraham, like Mary, could understand that natural reason cannot deny various prodigies and miracles. Their characteristic prudence, however, could not tell them precisely how they occur even though it could assure them that natural causation had not been offended.

The case of Abraham, for Augustine, is not an example of what Kierkegaard thought of as the teleological suspension of the ethical, because nothing was suspended. Abraham experienced an epiphany as if the entire cosmos served as an experience of grace. Similarly, Crosson, referring to the *Confessions*, explains that Augustine understood revelations to use the cosmos to disclose the divine:

> If an event of the world can be a disclosure of the divine, and if at the same time God cannot appear within that event, within the whole, then it can only be that the whole of the cosmos, coming to be and passing away in time, is His speaking to us. Contrary to the only way in which Cicero could conceive of it, the epiphany of the divine is not just an event within the whole, it is the whole itself as epiphany. The vehicle of God's presence is the created world, the world experienced as telling of God. The illumination of the moment of epiphany, occurring in a particular locus of space and time,

---

Human sacrifices were made on mountaintops. I have not been able to find evidence that Augustine knew about such sacrifices in the ancient Near East. However, from the historical knowledge we possess today, it appears that Abraham intended his act to resemble this ritual as he took Isaac up Mount Moriah (a play on the Hebrew word *to see*, translated in the later Latin Vulgate as *terra Visionis* [Gen. 22:2]). The gods to which such sacrifices are made are the ones who thunder (such as Jove), which Augustine might be alluding to when he states that God "thundered."

radiates outward, suffusing and transmuting the meaning of the whole of finite beings.[57]

Crosson's analysis indicates that human existence is interspersed with epiphanies whereby God's plan is expressed through natural causes, as the whole itself appearing. The covenant is not a suspension of the ethical or the natural; rather, it is an epiphany in which the whole presents itself as a creation of the divine and from which flow the renewal and "circumcision" of human beings' experience of the natural. Thus, the characteristic wisdom gained from this experience is not a specific divine command (as Augustine's guarded language might suggest), but the divine command is accepted in terms of the insight gained by one's characteristic wisdom.

The example of Abraham shows that an exception may be made to the general prohibition against killing, by virtue of one's wisdom that still imperfectly understands miracles. If Abraham is an exception, then Jephthah makes for a dubious exception at best. Jephthah may not be a good example of an exception because he is traditionally seen as illustrating the consequences of making rash promises. For example, Augustine's teacher, Saint Ambrose, thought the incident was "something that teaches us not to promise rashly to do something wrong."[58] Jephthah's wisdom is not exclusively divine, for Augustine says it "merits questioning *(et merito quaeritur)*" whether he was commanded at all. Jephthah promised God a sacrifice of the first thing that he met as he returned victorious from battle, and it turned out that Jephthah had to sacrifice his daughter to keep his promise (Judg. 11:29–40). Scripture speaks of Jephthah keeping his promise, but it does not say that he killed his daughter. Instead of constituting an exception to the Israelite prohibition of human sacrifice, Jephthah is said to have fulfilled his vow by keeping her a virgin, as was the Israelite tradition. For the Israelite who sought salvation through generation, keeping his daughter a virgin was equivalent to human sacrifice. Augustine apparently passes over this example without further comment here or elsewhere. Jephthah's sacrifice of his daughter might be better understood as the fulfillment of the natural obligation to keep one's oath, an act of worship, which in this case was made unsolicited. Jephthah, in that sense, is comparable to Abraham in relation to Isaac except that Augustine does indicate that Jephthah

---

57. Crosson, "Structure and Meaning," 34. He observes that Augustine also asserts that God's voice from the clouds at Jesus' baptism must have been the voice of a creature (38 n. 16, citing *Conf.* 11.6).

58. Ambrose, Bishop of Milan, *On Virginity,* 2.6.

understood *latreia* spiritually. The example stands more as a warning against making (and keeping) imprudent vows.[59]

The exception of Samson is not straightforwardly based on the grounds of special dispensation that appear to contradict natural understanding (see *CD* 1.26). Samson prayed to God to kill his persecutors and himself. Augustine states later that he and other saints received their command from divine authority and did not deceive themselves: "This is the case with Samson. When God commands any act, and intimates without obscurity that He has commanded it, who will call obedience criminal? Who will accuse so pious a submission?" (*CD* 1.26).[60] To regard Samson's orders as ambiguous is impious. Yet, Augustine himself makes the reader suspect this when comparing Augustine's account of God's command to Samson with his account of how God communicates with human beings. Prophetic visions must be consistent with intellectual vision, meaning that prophecies must be consistent with natural virtue; this makes Augustine's insistence on the unambiguous nature of Samson's vision perplexing.[61]

An examination of these exceptions, especially that of Abraham, puts us into a better position to understand what Augustine means when he states the justice of rebellion depends in part on "ever-present divine aid" or God's providence. We have seen how natural reason can neither confirm nor deny the intelligibility of events occurring outside the general course of nature, which provides Augustine the grounds to call them miracles. Miracles are not fully intelligible even to the wisest, since they lack perfect understanding of God's particular providence. As seen above, Augustine observes: "Manifestly, these things are ruled and governed by the one God according as He pleases; and if His motives are hid, are they therefore unjust?" This imperfect knowledge extends to political affairs. For Augustine, political affairs, like the rest of creation, fall under God's providence: "[I]t can never be believed that He would have left the kingdoms of men, their dominions and servitudes, outside of the laws

59. Augustine generally disparages oaths and vows because by their habit one can lapse into false and careless swearing: "[L]et one who realizes that swearing is to be accounted not among the better things but the necessary ones, refrain, as much as possible, from resorting to it; necessity alone should be the exception, when he sees persons reluctant to believe something which they would do well to believe" (*Lord's Sermon on the Mount*, 1.17.51).

60. "[S]icut de Samsone aliud nobis fas non est credere. Cum autem Deus iubet seque iubere sine ullis ambagibus intimat, quis oboedientiam in crimen vocet? Quis obsequium pietatis accuset?"

61. According to Jerome's Vulgate, which appeared after Augustine's time, Samson was not commanded to destroy himself, but, rather, he prayed to God to remember him and to help him gain revenge over the Philistines (Judg. 16:28).

of His providence" (*CD* 5.11).[62] God's purpose for kingdoms and the course of nations is imperfectly known because the providential order is imperfectly known. Unlike modern ideologues, for example, Augustine did not claim to know the end of history.

What are we to make of "divine aid"? If we apply the relationship between nature and grace explicated above to "divine aid" and the course of nations, we find that Augustine can speak quite comfortably about divine aid in terms of natural causation. Two principles govern Augustine's understanding of the maintenance and disintegration of nations. First, all nations actualize their highest virtue, and this also constitutes their downfall because their highest virtue is necessarily incomplete. Second, their shortcomings illuminate how their societies are maintained in ways beyond their abilities and intentions. The first principle is seen when Augustine states in several passages that God granted rule to the Romans as a reward for their courage, their highest virtue (see, for example, *CD* 5.15, 5.18–19). The virtue of a few was indeed impressive and real. These few, as well as the prideful Romans, received their empire as reward for their virtues, and Augustine quotes Matt. 6:2 ("they have received their reward") to acknowledge its justice (*CD* 5.15). However, he does so with some irony, in order to indicate that the dissolution of the empire and the horrible wars caused by the more dominant inordinate love of glory were also part of their reward. The insufficiency of virtue and the corruption caused by vice contributed to the empire's disintegration. Even though Augustine quotes Matthew to provide his interpretation with a supernatural and biblical explanation, the disintegration of societies can be understood as part of natural justice, because the virtues that a particular society idealizes and attains are insufficient for securing that society's permanence. The Roman love of glory was inordinate, and this caused the collapse of Rome.

Despite this, Augustine also indicates that societies are preserved even when they neglect virtue in general and the virtues specific to the regime for a period of time. He points out that neither the Assyrian nor the Persian empires worshiped the Roman gods, whom the Romans considered necessary for empire. The Assyrians and Persians received goods, such as harvests, for which they failed to ask, "though [the Persians] did not worship the goddess Segetia [the goddess of harvests], who gave the other blessings of the earth, though they did not worship the many gods which the Romans supposed to preside, each one over some particular thing, or even many of them over one thing" (*CD* 5.21). This

---

62. "[N]ullo modo est credendus regna hominum eorumque dominationes et servitutes a suae providentiae legibus alienas esse voluisse."

passage is significant, not because the Persians failed to worship the Roman gods, but because nations cannot possibly ensure blessings by asking for all of them or by attempting to control the natural processes by which they receive them. As observed above, virtue is an insufficient guarantor of a regime. Augustine criticizes the Romans for attempting to secure every particular good by worshiping each particular god. He argues not only that this is impossible, but also that nations receive those blessings even when they fail to observe all the expected rituals. Nations are preserved even when they fail to fulfill the requirements of *latreia*, although they cannot impede its practice too long, as shown above. Natural reason can neither conclude nor deny with confidence that either chance or providence maintains a nation's existence. Divine aid, therefore, is present even when it is not asked for or noticed by most of the people most of the time.

This brings us into a better position to appreciate Augustine's natural understanding of divine aid as a condition for rightful rebellion. Divine aid is not always noticed, but is present when one can understand and act upon the ways in which a society disintegrates and is preserved (though in different forms). Each society attempts to guide itself by its specific virtue, including the mystical city of God governed by the love of God and of neighbor. As seen in Chapter 1, most Romans were dominated by the inordinate love of glory, which undermined other virtues and led to the degeneration of Rome. The Roman Empire was not governed by ordinate loving, and this caused its downfall. By definition, only the mystical city of God, the virtue of which is perfect, can exist eternally because only it is governed by the whole of virtue. Augustine discusses the way divine governance aids societies despite their understandings and intentions, in order to indicate that human goods that are hitherto ignored or unrecognized will reassert themselves in a variety of ways. If a society ignores the other virtues for a long enough time, and ignores the injustices and other problems that this ignorance creates, then the regime disintegrates because the conditions for rebellion are created. This was true of Rome, as Augustine never fails to point out; it was corrupted long before Alaric marched his troops into town.

Divine aid includes miraculous occurrences such as the massive increase of Israel's population under the Pharaohs. This can be interpreted in the context of natural law, according to which God's laws keep a society in existence as long as that society conforms to those laws. It can also be interpreted according to right-by-nature: "But if those who are endowed with true piety (*vera pietate*) and live good lives know the science of ruling peoples (*scientiam regendi populos*), there is no greater blessing for mankind than for them, by the mercy of God, to have power" (*CD* 5.19). For Augustine as for the classical right-by-nature thinkers, the best a society can do is pray for someone to come from its midst and rule it well according to characteristic prudence. This is especially to be prayed for in dark times, because of their inherent danger and because they inhibit one's ability to recognize such a miracle.

Augustine usually speaks as if human activities such as political life follow absolute rules. Derivations from the normal course appear to be due exclusively to God's intervention in history. We have seen that Augustine allows for a prudence that can understand derivations from nature's usual course as both consistent with that course and remaining obedient to God's revelations. He opposes false prophets by emphasizing the eternal law, and by arguing that deviations from the normal course must remain consistent with natural law. Consistent with theories of classical right-by-nature, Augustine thought it would be exceedingly rare for someone with wisdom, *latreia*, and, of course, moderation to have political power. The next chapter examines how he tries to restrain the ambitions of such false prophets and others while teaching them to cultivate a moderately improved political life.

# 5

## GLORY AS A PROPER END OF POLITICS

*The veterans who serve in the wars, and move in the midst of wounds for so many years, enter upon the military service from their youth, and quit it in old age: and to obtain a few days of repose in their old age, when age itself begins to weigh down those whom the wars do not break down, how great hardships do they endure; what marches, what frosts, what burning suns; what privations, what wounds, and what dangers! And while suffering all these things, they fix their thoughts on nothing but those few days of repose in old age, at which they know not whether they will ever arrive. Thus it is, the "steps of the good man are ordered by the Lord, and he delights in His way."*

—Augustine, *Exposition on the Book of Psalms*

S TATESMEN like to be remembered, and they enjoy glory. For them, glory and honor are the materials of politics. As Aristotle states: "A consideration of the prominent types of life shows that people of superior refinement and of active disposition identify happiness with honor; for this is, roughly speaking, the end of political life."[1] The love of glory motivates them to distinguish themselves as monuments to virtue and in public service, although an inordinate love of glory undermines the public good. Societies too are bound together by their glories, although an inordinate love of glory sends them off on imperial

---

1. Aristotle, *Nicomachean Ethics* 1.5.1095b24.

campaigns. Modern democracies avoid the language of glory because of its aristocratic roots and connotations. The love of glory is said to cause unjust treatment of those not glorified, the poor and marginalized in particular. As a result, modern societies see glory and honor as obsolete. Modern democracies instead have replaced the concept of glory with the "dignity" of the individual and the "politics of recognition."[2]

For good reason, Augustine is usually seen to disparage political glory. For example, he states: "However, men who do not obtain the gift of the Holy Spirit and bridle their baser passions by pious faith and by love of intelligible beauty, at any rate live better because of their desire for human praise and glory *(melius saltem cupiditate humanae laudis et gloriae)*. While these men are not saints, to be sure, they are less vile *(minus turpes sunt)*" *(CD* 5.13). Passages like this, in which Augustine reluctantly admits that the love of glory can lead people to be "less vile," suggest that such love has nothing to do with real virtue, but merely restrains baser passions even though doing so may inspire noble deeds.[3] However, his account preserves an element of glory that modern notions of "dignity" and "recognition" lack, to the detriment of a flourishing political life. If honor and glory are as important to politics as Aristotle said they are, then this lack constitutes a troubling deficiency in our society. Augustine shares (as does Aristotle) the modern concern that the inordinate love of glory causes injustice. What Augustine preserves, however, is a way to understand glory for those who are not completely responsible for their own glory, and, by doing so, transforms the terms upon which glory is conferred. The strategy of his teaching on glory extends his general rhetorical strategy, explored in Chapter 1, according to which he evacuates certain words of their meaning, at least in part, and then resuscitates them and redeems them within his own conceptual framework. He sides with Aristotle in arguing that glory is best shared, but differs with him in arguing that it is shared even when one has distinguished oneself. Whereas modern authors root "dignity" and "recognition" in the depths of the self, Augustine roots them both inside and outside those depths, as it were. He understands glory as the result of one's praiseworthy qualities and the quality that Penelope Johnson has compared to the archaic notion of *mana*: "a warrior gains *mana* from the defeat of his enemies while the generative power of the

2. Peter Berger, "On the Obsolescence of the Concept of Honor"; Charles Taylor, *Multiculturalism and the "Politics of Recognition."* The concept of recognition, of course, derives from Hegel's account of the master-slave dialectic. For an alternative account of it and its importance for modern politics, see Barry Cooper, *The End of History: An Essay on Modern Hegelianism.*

3. Louis J. Swift, "Defining *Gloria* in Augustine's *City of God*" and "Pagan and Christian Heroes in Augustine's *City of God.*" See also Milbank, *Theology and Social Theory,* 352, 389–91.

soil and the inherent quality of merchandise to earn money all seem magical in a primitive society. In later Latin, *virtus* came to mean valor, merit, and the generalized energy necessary to achieve glory."[4] Augustine's understanding of glory, of course, transcends those qualities listed by Johnson, but her point is that Augustine's understanding of glory constitutes his translation of the archaic "miraculous and magic" power whose origins transcend the individual. As we shall see, Augustine's understanding of political glory is more conducive to community without the classical liability of marginalizing some members of the community.

For Augustine, political actions have unexpected effects. Sometimes the outcome is the opposite of one's intention. Sometimes the outcome forces one to recognize that the order of events has little to do with human agency. To whom is glory due in this case? Augustine argues that politics is guided ultimately by God's providence (this statement should be read in light of the discussion of nature and grace in the previous chapter as well as the next one).[5] This response, however, must also fit into an account of human agency and free will: how are human beings to be understood as free yet as parts within a whole? Augustine argues that political glory is part of the greater glory of God (which does not contradict what can be known by natural reason). This chapter focuses on how Augustine considered political glory to be a part of this greater glory. Augustine's understanding of political glory is more sufficient than modern accounts because he shows how political glory can be preserved without reducing it to social class (as moderns fear), while maintaining the basis of glory in a view of politics where the conditions for glory (for example, achievement and virtue) are fleeting.

## TRUE *GLORIA* AND POLITICAL GLORY

Augustine illuminates the limitations of political glory in light of the glory of the city of God by arguing that the glory the pagans sought is found and perfected in the city of God. He agrees with the pagans on the definition of true glory as that which can be found by loving virtue first and praise secondarily. True glory consists of virtue and of having that virtue recognized, but only the city of

---

4. Johnson, "*Virtus:* Transition from Classical Latin to the *De Civitate Dei*," 233.
5. This notion has not been rejected completely by moderns. Taylor, for example, argues that the religious grounds for judging political societies cannot be ruled out, although his grounds differ from those of Augustine (*Multiculturalism*, 72–73).

God can perfectly fulfill the necessary requirement of having a wise judge, God, sufficiently competent to judge one's virtue correctly. However, both agree that virtue, if it is to be glorious, must be recognized also by human beings, and thus that true glory has both a social and a political element.

Glory and praise are central concepts in Augustine's thought. For instance, the *City of God* opens with the words, "Most glorious *(Gloriosissimam)* is the city of God" *(CD* 1.pref). As seen in Chapter 1, the term *gloria* derives from *clara*, meaning clear or shining. Glory is clear knowledge together with praise *(clara cum laude notitia)*.[6] Glory is the combination of love and knowledge, and praise is the means of expressing it. This combination is seen in Augustine's description of the difficulty of praising God: "And again, they shall praise the Lord that seek after him: for, they that seek shall find; and finding they shall praise him" *(Conf.* 1.1). Human beings cannot fully praise God because they cannot fully know God. Despite this, they are described as desirous of praising God *(laudare te vult homo) (Conf.* 1.1). Praises are described as thanks given primarily to God, whether as prayer or as virtuous conduct in general *(Serm.* 18, 193).[7]

Perfect honor and glory are found in the city of God: "True glory will be there, where no one will be praised by mistake or by flattery, and true honor will be denied to no one who is worthy, and conferred on no one who is unworthy. Neither will anyone who is unworthy aspire to it, for no one except the worthy will be allowed to dwell there" *(CD* 22.30). Later, Augustine distinguishes varying degrees of glory for the city's members: "But who is qualified to imagine, much less declare, what will be the degrees of honor and glory proportioned to the merits of each one? However, there is no doubt that there will be such degrees." It is true for Augustine that human happiness is union with God and that this union glorifies one who acts justly in the world even though the world vilifies him. However, Augustine also insists that human life is social, which means that, at least from the perspective of a human being, glory requires both God and other human beings.

God is not the only object of glorification. Human beings praise qualities of the soul, and it is appropriate to be ordinately delighted by such praises. For example, Augustine defines glory in this way: "Glory is the widespread and praiseworthy reputation of a person. Rank is the distinguished authority that a person has—an authority worthy of veneration, honor, and reverence" *(83Q* 31.3).[8] Praise is the normal accompaniment of a good life and good works: "If

---

6. Augustine, "Answer to Maximinus the Arian," 2.13.2.

7. *Lord's Sermon on the Mount,* 2.4.15.

8. Augustine presents this as Cicero's position as developed in *De Inventione,* in *De Inventione. De Optimo Genere Oratorum. Topica,* trans. H. M. Hubbell (Cambridge: Harvard University Press,

praise both is and ought to be the normal accompaniment of a good life and good works, we ought no more to abandon that accompaniment than goodness of life itself" (*Conf.* 10.37). Furthermore, he states that though the earthly city glorifies itself exclusively, the city of God finds its greatest (*maxima*) glory in God (*CD* 14.28). His use of the comparative case means that lesser glory can be found elsewhere, perhaps in political glory. However, just as our praise of God is necessarily imperfect, so too is the praise bestowed for human virtue, because others' praise for oneself rarely reflects one's knowledge of oneself: "For in a sense I am not being praised, when my own opinion of myself is not praised—when, that is, things are praised in me which do not please me at all, or praised more though they please me less" (*Conf.* 10.37).[9] Glory, therefore, is perfect only when bestowed by a perfectly knowledgeable judge who can know the virtue and motivations of individuals. As we shall see, both Augustine and the classical political philosophers agree on this formal requirement, but Augustine argues that only Christianity can provide that judge.

Augustine's rhetorical strategy obscures his substantial agreement with the pagan philosophers' definition of glory. His rhetoric suggests that he thought the pagans were incapable of loving virtue more than glory. This is seen in his definition of the Roman understanding of glory and in his alternative Christian definition:

> [T]he glory with the desire of which the Romans burned is the judgment of men thinking well of men (*iudicium hominum bene de hominibus opinantium*). And therefore virtue is better, which is content with no human judgment save that of one's own conscience. Whence the Apostle says, "For this is our glory, the testimony of our conscience." And in another place he says, "But let everyone prove his own work, and then he shall have glory in himself, and not in another." That glory, honor, and power, therefore, which they desired for themselves, and to which the good sought to attain by good arts, should not be sought after by virtue, but virtue by them. (*CD* 5.12, quoting 2 Cor. 1:12 and Gal. 6:4)

Two themes are apparent in this comparison. First, Christianity surpasses the Roman view because for Christians, virtue is the goal of glory and not vice-versa. Second, despite this, Christian glory includes human praise because the Christian too wants to have his good actions seen not so he may be praised, but

---

1993), 2.53.159–55.167. In his *Retractions* (1.25), Augustine repeats this attribution, and again does not express disagreement with it.

9. See also Aristotle, *Nicomachean Ethics* 8.8.1159a22.

for the sake of those who view it. The difference between the Roman cultural concept, as presented here, and the Christian concept is that the Christian seeks human praise in order to elevate other human beings to love God and virtue, whereas the Roman appears to seek virtue in order to receive human praise.

Leaving aside momentarily whether this view presents accurately Augustine's final word on the Roman understanding of glory, it is apparent that he emphasizes the public nature of Christian glory, thus suggesting that human praise is a necessary, though insufficient, element of true glory. He advises Christians to steer a middle course between disparaging praise and actively seeking it. This middle course is found in seeking the glory of God and sharing it with one's neighbors. Augustine notes that the Apostles preached and were martyred and so won great glory in the Church of Christ. He then warns against seeking glory at the expense of virtue: "Take heed that you do not place your righteousness before men to be seen of them, or otherwise you shall not have a reward from your Father who is in heaven" (CD 5.14; Matt. 6:1). As seen above, he next articulates the public purpose of glory:

> But again, in case they should take this in the wrong sense and be afraid to please men and so, concealing their goodness, should be of less help to others, he showed them with what object they ought to attract attention: "Let your works so shine *(Luceant)* before men that they may see your good deeds and glorify *(glorificent)* your father who is in heaven." Your purpose, therefore, is not to be seen of men, that is, a desire that they should turn and notice you *(vos converti velitis)*, for of yourselves you are nothing. Rather, "it is that they may glorify your father who is in heaven," and that they may turn to him and become what you are *(conversi fiant quod estis)*. (CD 5.14, quoting Matt. 5:16; see also DT 8.6.9; Conf. 13.25)

Glorifying God, therefore, involves being virtuous and educating others to "become what you are." One's personal glory consists not in imprinting one's will or oneself on another, but in acting as a transparent lens, as it were, by which one can understand and love the truth of God, and, conversely, through which the truth of God shines out onto others.[10] True *gloria*, therefore, consists in acting virtuously before God and human beings. For Augustine as for Romans,

10. This does not mean, however, that there cannot be a multiplicity of such lenses or that one lens must be the final and most perfect lens (or representation) of truth of the city of God on earth. As seen in Chapter 3, Augustine's preference for republican regimes forbids a cult of leadership or an exclusive identification of virtue with one particular class. Further, the next chapter shows that Augustine's account of worship does not restrict the practice of virtue to the sacerdotal order of the Church.

glory is a public good. Augustine's view differs from that of most Romans in that they found their judge in the good opinion of men, whereas Augustine significantly added God, the judge of right action, to that definition.

Similarly, Augustine affirms human beings' capacity to judge according to natural reason. For example, he observes that human beings judge temporal things (such as actions) according to eternal standards (*DT* 12.2.2). Judgment depends on the ability to evaluate whether a part functions well within the whole. This capacity depends on one being "spiritual" in the image of God, and on being able to distinguish between spiritual and corporeal (*Conf.* 13.23). This requirement for good judges for glory compares with Cicero's view.

Augustine's definition of Roman political glory, of men thinking well of other men, recalls but actually modifies Cicero's own understanding of glory. For example, in *Philippics*, Cicero himself defines glory as the "praise accorded to right actions and the good reputation that is attested not only by the multitude but by all the best people." Augustine omits mention of right action in his definition of Roman glory but incorporates it into his own definition. Similarly, in *De Officiis*, Cicero summarizes his now lost treatise on glory, and he states that true glory depends on "the affection, the confidence, and the mingled admiration and esteem of the people," which depends on justice: "[T]rue and philosophic greatness of spirit regards the moral goodness to which Nature most aspires as consisting in deeds, not in fame, and prefers to be first in reality rather than in name. And we must approve this view; for he who depends upon the caprice of the ignorant rabble *(qui ex errore imperitae multitudinis pendet)* cannot be numbered among the great."[11] Cicero, then, argues that virtue is to be preferred to human praise but that the virtuous human being is to seek praise because virtue and glory are public goods. Augustine omits mention of right action from his allusion to Cicero. For Cicero, the virtuous human being finds his or her glory in virtue and in receiving praise from a competent judge, who cannot be capricious. True glory, therefore, consists in virtue and in receiving praise from a reliable or virtuous judge. Whether Cicero found that reliable judge remains open to debate, but Augustine's reference to biblical passages indicates that he thought Cicero failed to find a reliable judge for true glory.

Augustine does not explicitly display his substantial agreement with Cicero on true glory, probably because his rhetorical strategy is to illuminate the glory of the city of God (*CD* 1.pref.) at the expense of all political cities, and to persuade the Romans of the superiority of God's judgment to theirs. As a result, it

---

11. Cicero, *Philippics* 1.12.29; *De Officiis* 2.32, 1.65.

would have undermined his rhetorical strategy to show explicitly his agreement with non-Christian philosophers.

However, both Cicero and Augustine agree that true glory (however each defines it) first depends on virtue or right action, and, second, on human praise. Both Augustine's quotations of biblical texts and Cicero's definitions indicate that true glory is constituted by two necessary (but insufficient if taken singly) conditions: virtue and praise by a competent judge. Cicero failed to provide the true judge, and the force of Augustine's rhetoric suggests that failure to do so meant that the Romans loved human praise more than virtue. However, Augustine's allusion to the few who practiced virtue the true way *(vera via)*, Regulus for example, means that a few actually loved virtue more than human praise even though they may have sought human praise for their virtue, because the common good is furthered when people praise virtue.[12] In the next section, we shall examine in specific detail how Augustine teaches individuals, specifically the political actors, to practice virtue and to achieve glory.

## BOOK 5 OF THE *CITY OF GOD* AS AN EDUCATION IN STATESMANSHIP

A consideration of Augustine's discussion of glory in book 5 of the *City of God* shows that the teaching is meant as a kind of spiritual exercise intended to bring the reader into a state of spiritual freedom that recognizes one's participation within a greater whole. Augustine considered his preservation of political glory within a framework of divine providence superior to the pagan approach that (according to Augustine) had to deny spiritual freedom to believe in God and vice-versa.

Book 5 can seem like an odd book, and interpreters generally overlook its internal consistency. It is the final book of the first set of books dealing with the theme of whether the pagan gods ensured Rome's political success. The book begins with a discussion of fate and free will, and ends with a discussion of the emperors Constantine and Theodosius; Peter Brown has called them "some of the most shoddy passages of the *City of God*" because they fail to conform to historical reality. Brown admits, however, that they do conform to Augustine's

---

12. For Augustine's references to pagans acting truly virtuously *(vera via)*, see *CD* 5.12, 5.15, 5.19. He singles out Regulus as the noblest example of the Romans who practiced virtue for the common good (*CD* 1.24). See below for our own examination of Regulus as evidence for Augustine's view that he exemplifies true virtue.

political ideas.[13] The book's contents appear disjointed because Augustine fails to clarify explicitly the relationship among fate, providence, free will, heroism, and statesmanship.

Four themes are evident in book 5 once it is read as a protreptic argument meant to educate statesmen about the workings of divine providence in history: (1) the refutation of fate (chaps. 1–11), (2) the limitations of Roman political psychology (chaps. 12–17), (3) the articulation of divine providence (chaps. 21–23), and (4) an account of Christian statesmanship (chaps. 24–26).[14] This construction demonstrates that Augustine thought his first argument against the Ciceronian concept of fate was insufficient and that a longer, more complex method was required to show the mystery of divine providence. His subsequent analysis of Roman political psychology was intended to educate future statesmen whose desires and longings are paradigmatic, yet deficient, for the Christian. Book 5 teaches the statesman to understand the fragility of his or her own glory, to show how one's glory is not exclusively one's own, but must reflect God's glory.[15]

The protreptic nature of book 5 is first reflected in Augustine's intended audience. The entire *City of God* is directed specifically toward Roman aristocrats who were uncertain as to whether Christianity undermined political virtue, and whether Christian humility undermined their own nobility. As Colin Starnes argues, Augustine's audience is figured in two people, who each correspond to the two divisions of the treatise: Augustine's friend Marcellinus and Volusianus, proconsul of Africa: "Marcellinus is satisfied throughout the first part (Books I–X) where Augustine shows the Christian response to the charge, and Volusianus in the second (Books XI–XXII) where Augustine shows that Christianity provides a world order to replace that of Rome." Although the division of Augustine's argument into two parts is insufficient, Starnes points out the advantage of understanding the political element of the *City of God* as represented in these two figures. Van Oort echoes this observation and adds that the *City of God* has catechetical and apologetic purposes.[16]

---

13. Brown, "Political Society," 319. Markus echoes this sentiment (*Saeculum*, 57 n. 1).

14. This truncates the division of the book set out by Deferrari and Keeler, but better illuminates the thematic consistency than theirs, which treats chaps. 14 and 19–20 as necessary corrections to Augustine's previous statements praising Roman glory. See Roy J. Deferrari and M. Jerome Keeler, O.S.B., "St. Augustine's *City of God*: Its Plan and Development," 119, 128.

15. Viewing the *City of God* as protreptic is consistent with the argument of Johannes Van Oort, who shows that it is a catechetical work intended to teach Christian virtues to beginners (*Jerusalem and Babylon*, 195).

16. Starnes, "Augustine's Audience in the First Ten Books of the *City of God* and the Logic of His Argument," 389. See also *CD* 1.pref.; *Ep.* 132; and Van Oort, *Jerusalem and Babylon*, 195.

We see that his argument is protreptic and directed toward the Roman aristocrats when, already in book 2, Augustine claims—rather startlingly—that Roman aristocrats must awaken their natural virtues to see the glory of the city of God. As seen in Chapter 1, Augustine exhorts them to "[a]wake more fully *(evigila plenius):* the majesty of God cannot be propitiated by that which defiles the dignity of man" *(CD* 2.29). Augustine states that only the Christian religion can satisfy the Romans' already present love of glory. What needs awakening? "Desire these things, then, O praiseworthy inborn Roman quality *(o indoles Romana laudabilis)*—O offspring of Reguli, Scaevolae, Scipios, Fabricii."[17] In directing these aristocrats to awaken their inborn qualities more fully, Augustine is telling them that their potential requires greater actualization. By this, Augustine refers not to a biological or genetic quality, but to acquired virtue symbolized by the archaic *mana* (noted by Johnson). His rhetoric, which combines both persuasion and inspiration, is meant to educate these pagans. This is not perfect Christian glory, but Augustine signals to his readers that this notion is consistent with Christian glory.

Conversely, we can look ahead and see that one can understand Christian glory in terms of its needing to transcend the austere goals of political glory. Augustine's utilization of examples *(exempla)* provides the *City of God* with a protreptic character for his Christian audience: "[E]xamples are set before us *(nobis proposita necessariae commonitionis exempla)*, containing necessary admonition, in order that we may be stung with shame if we shall see that we have not held fast those virtues for the sake of the most glorious city of God, which are, in whatever way, resembled by those virtues *(virtutes quarum istae utcumque sunt similes)* which they held fast for the sake of glory of a terrestrial city" *(CD* 5.18). This passage shows Augustine's attempt to form and guide the Christian love of eternal life so that his Christian audience understands the virtue practiced by the Romans, and so that their piety does not degenerate into an arrogant attitude toward the Romans because of the superiority of the Christian goal of virtue. This passage and the passage cited previously indicate that Augustine sought to awaken and perfect the love of glory among political actors while balancing the Christian enthusiasm for eternal life with concrete particular political examples, in order to show the natural particular place of the political within people's lives.

17. Burnell comments on this passage: "It would be difficult to find a word more redolent of nature than *indoles*—and he immediately makes that explicit: *si quid in te laudabile naturaliter eminet. Laudabilis,* moreover, shows the opposite of moral neutrality. . . . So *indoles Romana laudabiles* means what was naturally, morally good in a politically constituted culture acting politically" ("Status of Politics," 17–18).

Chapters 1–11 consist of Augustine's refutation of the pagan conception of fate. This continues his discussion of fate and providence from book 4, but the discussion in book 5 takes on a political meaning when he draws out the implications of his interpretation of Cicero's discussion of fate. Augustine challenges Cicero by arguing that divine foreknowledge is consistent with human freedom, which constitutes the basis for human responsibility of action. Cicero reaches an aporia because he concludes that either God has foreknowledge and human beings have no free will or human beings have free will and God does not exist (*CD* 5.9). For Augustine, this view means that either human beings are completely responsible for the motivations and results of their actions or God is completely responsible for human beings' motivations and the results of their actions. Instead, Augustine argues that Christians "faithfully and sincerely confess" that God has foreknowledge, which helps them believe well, and that the will is free, which helps them live well: "Consequently, it is not in vain that laws are enacted, and that reproaches, exhortations, praises, and vituperations had recourse to *(leges obiurgationes exhortationes laudes et vituperationes)*" (*CD* 5.10). Glory and praise, along with good laws, depend on human beings having free will. This matter is not exclusively a matter of faith, but, as we shall see, Augustine could not have been happy that his demonstration of the will's freedom sufficed because he felt compelled to return to the topic of divine providence in chapter 21 after his extensive treatment of Roman political psychology.

For Augustine, Cicero's position on fate leads to the conclusion either that one is wholly glorified because one's freedom exists without God or that one cannot receive any glory because everything that happens is due to fate. Augustine's reformulation of Cicero's categories into free will and divine providence indicates that one may receive glory and still have faith in a providential God. God is responsible for establishing the circumstances and conditions in which one's virtue is tested and practiced. One is glorified by the virtuous response to a providential order because one is free to act virtuously or viciously in whichever particular circumstances one finds oneself.

However, there is something unpersuasive about Augustine's argument that Cicero's position was impious and that Christians confess their belief in God's providence. He was already writing for a skeptical audience, and reliance on revelation would be insufficient to convince his readers of the truth of divine providence. His argument could be seen as persuasive if all he needs to do is to show how Cicero's position leads to an aporia. This solution, however, does not necessarily involve faith in God's providence. A pagan has no more reason to believe in God's providence than he does in taking one of Cicero's positions of either becoming an atheist or rejecting free will but believing in God. The pagan, however, finds either of Cicero's positions alone unsatisfying because each position lacks the experience he feels in the other. How, then, can one articulate a position that accounts for the experience the pagan (and Christian for that matter) has of freedom and of being in a situation or context beyond his or her control? Augustine's solution in this chapter of book 5 is to respond that one requires faith in divine providence. However, he appears to assert it and then, inexplicably, turns to other unrelated topics such as glory. His discussion of glory is intended to address indirectly this aforementioned experience of spiritual freedom and one's participation within the whole. He does this by enabling glory to shine out in an individual's free responses to unforeseen circumstances caused by what Augustine symbolizes as providence. In doing this, he casts the glorious individual as one who glorifies himself and truth (and therefore God) by acting rightly.

## ROMAN POLITICAL PSYCHOLOGY

Augustine's analysis of Roman psychology, and his subsequent attempt to articulate a form of ordinate love of glory, constitutes the spiritual exercise that leads the reader into a state of spiritual freedom, which also affirms one's participation within the whole. Augustine does this by showing that glory can be loved ordinately when one first strips oneself of the love of glory and other earthly attachments, in order to love virtue exclusively. This constitutes spiritual freedom. Only then can one readmit the love of glory into one's soul and have it serve his good and the common good. That this process is common to both potential statesmen and struggling Christians enables Augustine to argue that both see a model of virtue in the other.

Chapters 12–20 consist of Augustine's analysis of the two motivations of Roman politics: the loves of liberty and of glory (CD 5.12, 5.18). These chapters explore the ways these loves motivated the Romans to perform the tremendous political and heroic deeds that created the world's greatest empire but also caused its own downfall. He demonstrates how the Roman inordinate reliance on human praise caused a variety of injustices and how that reliance has failed to instill the perfect virtue that the Romans themselves sought. He argues that the city of God fulfills human beings' need for glory because it supplies a competent judge. However, he admits that the Romans could, on occasion, practice true virtue. Augustine provides enough clues to indicate that certain Romans were quite capable of acting virtuously despite public opinion and without the need for Christian revelation. Such individuals, Regulus for example, may indeed have practiced true virtue.

Augustine understood most Romans to be caught between desiring true virtue and having to rely inordinately on human praise. Reference was made previously to Augustine's use of Cicero's definition of glory, which is based upon the opinions of virtuous human beings. Before examining the deformations that this tension or fault line caused, it is first necessary to consider the virtues that the Romans displayed and that Augustine admired.

The loves of liberty (*libertas*) and of glory or human praise (*laus humanis*) (*CD* 5.18) promoted exemplary self-sacrifice and concern for the common good. Augustine indicates that the love of liberty is a necessary but insufficient element of the love of glory, which was the goal of the Romans: "In short, since they held it shameful (*ingloriam*) for their native land to be in servitude, and glorious (*gloriosum*) for it to rule and command, their first passion to which they devoted all their energy was to maintain their liberty (*libertam*); the second to win dominion (*dominam*)" (*CD* 5.12). He later states: "There are those two things, namely, liberty and the desire of human praise, which compelled the Romans to admirable deeds" (*CD* 5.18). The political passion for liberty necessarily precedes the more substantial love of glory because it eliminates their condition of shame or ingloriousness (*ingloriam*). In other words, liberty from external threats does not constitute sufficient glory but is only the negation of shame. True political glory consists in something more.

The first passage is significant because it indicates Augustine's qualified admiration for not only the love of liberty that inspires any nation to repel a foreign enemy, but also that which inspired the establishment of the Roman republic and the expulsion of the tyrannical Tarquin kings. The love of liberty is insufficient by itself, as Augustine here indicates, because in this case it served the desire for domination, which the Romans identified with glory. However, understanding the love of liberty as the love that seeks to remove Rome from shame (*ingloriam*) does not necessitate that glory consists in the desire to dominate. Augustine observes this elsewhere when he distinguishes the love of glory from the love of domination (*CD* 5.19). The love of liberty may erupt into the love of domination, but it may also include other loves such as the desires for self-government and for the kind of justice that God will grant for the practice of virtue (see *CD* 5.15). However, the love of liberty must serve a higher end than that of self-glorification.

The love of glory is a crucial political virtue for Augustine. Roman heroes longed to be remembered for their achievements. By itself, this longing degenerated into the lust for domination. Being remembered, however, has the effect of tying together future generations of citizens who, by remembering heroic and often paradigmatic deeds, participate within the collective memory of their society. As shown in Chapter 2, Augustine argues that the love of glory ties a community together and thus ensures (or at least attempts to ensure) its continuance across generations of mortals. Over the yawning gap of forgetfulness and the "sphere of demise and succession where the dead are succeeded by the dying," a society has nothing besides glory to tie one generation to the next: "[W]hat else but glory should they love (*quid aliud amarent quam gloriam*), by which they wished even after death to live in the mouths of their admirers?" (*CD* 5.14). Glory is the means by which a city, and not only Rome, strives for continuance and immortality, and by which its heroes utilize the city to ensure their own glory. The heroes' great deeds for the common good are not completely motivated by selflessness because they can obtain their immortality through the city, by being remembered, memorialized, and by living "in the mouths of their admirers." Glory or praise can be expressed in public rituals and festivals—one thinks of Memorial Day, Remembrance Day, and Independence Day—meant to glorify these human beings and their contributions to the common good. Citizens participate in these rituals and thus reenact the formative events and virtues of their society. Reenactments do not simply mimic in a servile or hollow manner because such mimicry actually undermines virtue, and undermines the dignity of the citizens who are *elementae* and *particulae* of their society and fully participate in the song that their society performs.

Augustine was aware of the glorifying effect of festivals. Although he severely criticizes Roman festivals for their perversity in serving the worship of false gods, he does not dispute that some form of public festival, with political purposes, is necessary and good for a healthy body politic. For instance, R. A. Markus finds it significant that Augustine, in *On Christian Teaching*, included secular festivals "among those human institutions which could serve the laudable ends of securing greater cohesion among men."[18] Consistent with the interpretative strategy offered here, Markus notes that Augustine's complex discussion of theaters, actors, dancers, mimes, and pantomimes notably places them not among demonic institutions, but among simply useless institutions. Markus suggests that Augustine silently hints in the passage under consideration that other festivals such as circuses and hippodromes are actually "useful and neces-sary" by cultivating social harmony. Since Augustine appears to deny that such festivals are idolatrous, it is likely that his categories of useful festivals would

18. Markus, *The End of Ancient Christianity*, 121, referring to *DDC* 2.96–101 and *CD* 19.6.

also include respectful homage to virtuous leaders. Thus, the idea of citizens acting in the light of heroes is consistent with Augustine's statement, quoted above, that people "may turn to Him and become what you are" (CD 5.14). Becoming "what you are" occurs in public festivals that commemorate heroes.

Despite Augustine's severe criticism of and sarcasm toward the Roman inordinate love of glory, he indicates that the love of glory can serve the common good. The love of glory dominated the Roman soul to the extent that it suppressed all other loves including good and bad loves: "Glory they most ardently loved: for it they wished to live, for it they did not hesitate to die. Every other desire was repressed by the strength of their passion for that one thing" (CD 5.12). He praises the love of glory for suppressing more private and luxurious loves such as for wealth and for luxury: "So also these despised their own private affairs for the sake of the republic, and for its treasury resisted avarice, consulted for the good of their country with a spirit of freedom" (CD 5.15). Earlier, he had stated that God had rewarded their austerity with political success: "And, in order that it might overcome the grievous evils which existed among other nations, He purposely granted it to such men as, for the sake of honor, and praise, and glory, consulted well for their country, in whose glory they sought their own, and whose safety they did not hesitate to prefer to their own, suppressing the desire of wealth and many other vices for this one vice, namely, the love of praise" (CD 5.13). These passages indicate an ordering of political loves. Glory suppresses lesser, private loves such as that of wealth and "many other vices," which indicates that Augustine thought the love of glory to contribute to the common good more satisfactorily and consistently than does the love of wealth.[19] This is understandable because glory, unlike wealth, can be better shared with others and has the power to inspire deeds for the common good. Glory can be given to multiple individuals, and having to share that glory does not entail as much of a loss as does sharing wealth. The ability to share glory depends on Augustine's understanding of glory, analyzed above, as a by-product of virtue. Glory understood this way consists in seeing the glorious individual not as the source of his or her light, but as a lens according to which he or she serves as a witness to truth in community with others. This part of the love of glory to serve the common good indicates that a regime dominated by it, though not as just as the city of God, is a good regime. In fact, Augustine distinguishes the quality of it from regimes governed by inferior desires such as those of wealth or freedom. If one follows up his statement in book 19 that the quality

19. See Cicero, De Officiis 2.88, where he argues for the superiority of the love of glory to that of wealth.

of a regime depends on the quality of its object of love, then this hierarchy of objects of love is comparable to that outlined by Plato in the *Republic*, as argued in Chapter 3.

Despite the ambitions of the Romans and their illusions of grandeur, the love of glory inspires obedience: "[N]evertheless they who desire the true glory even of human praise *(tamen qui veram licet humanarum laudum gloriam concupiscunt)* strive not to displease those who judge well of them. For there are many good moral qualities, of which many are competent judges, although they are not possessed by many; and by those good moral qualities those men press on to glory, honor, and domination, of whom Sallust says, 'But they press on by the true way *(vera via)*' " (*CD* 5.19). The love of glory can inspire great acts of virtue, including obedience, because the individual seeks praise from and wishes to avoid giving offense to those who would judge. This is imperfect because even the most virtuous and prudent can fail to understand the motivations of another, but it indicates that Augustine saw in the lovers of glory the ability to attain a high degree of virtue if they were obedient to their judges—indeed, if they could find the appropriate judge.

The inability to find perfect judges, or to find the best ruler, is the greatest difficulty of political rule, and is a source of the degeneration of the love of glory into vice. Augustine observes that the Roman love of liberty was subordinate to their love of glory (*CD* 5.12, 18), and this love did not necessarily have to be subordinate to the love of domination if removing oneself from the state of shame *(ingloriam)* required one to dominate others. Augustine thought the love of liberty and glory can be formed if a proper judge can be found for the Romans to obey: "There is assuredly a difference between the desire of human glory and the desire of domination; for, though he who has an overweening delight in human glory will be also very prone to aspire earnestly after domination, nevertheless they who desire the true glory even of human praise strive not to displease those who judge well of them *(bene iudicantibus)*" (*CD* 5.19). There can exist competent judges who bestow just praise on individuals, but few possess such qualities. Augustine stresses, however, that glory can be bestowed as long as the judges hold sufficient virtue, and the quality of ordinately seeking glory was open to the Romans themselves; Augustine quotes Sallust as follows: "But they press on by the true way *(vera via)*" (*CD* 5.19; see also 5.12, 5.15).

However, because the judgment of the true judge, God, is not as easily discerned as the glory that people bestow, political glory tends to degenerate into the quest for human praise. This tendency drives Augustine's presentation of Caesar and Cato (*CD* 5.12). Caesar's preference of praise over virtue is clear because he sought "a great empire, an army, and a new war, that he might have a sphere where his genius and virtue might shine forth. Thus it was ever the prayer of men of heroic character that Bellona would excite miserable nations to war, and lash them into agitation with her bloody scourge" (*CD* 5.12). Whereas Caesar was known for his self-aggrandizement, Cato is cited in book 5 as the Roman whose virtue was nearer *(propinquior)* to the idea of true virtue, and of whom Sallust observes: "The less he sought glory, the more it followed him." However, he too is criticized for preferring praise to virtue because he pursued honors instead of being content to have the state confer honor upon him, and avoided humiliation by committing suicide (*CD* 1.23).

Augustine confronts directly the way political glory foreshadows Christian virtue when he cites Romans who practiced virtue by the true way *(vera via)* as examples for Christians to follow: "What great thing, therefore, is it for that eternal and celestial city to despise all the charms of this world, however pleasant, if for the sake of this terrestrial city Brutus could even put to death his son—a sacrifice which the heavenly city compels no one to make? But certainly it is more difficult to put to death one's sons, than to do what is required to be done for the heavenly country" (*CD* 5.18; see also 1.24). In this chapter Augustine brings this foreshadowing to the forefront by providing examples of Roman heroes who sacrificed even more than a Christian must in order to gain glory. The text here is significant because it shows the skeptical potential statesman that the glory of the city may demand greater self-sacrifice and renunciation of the world than even Christian humility and charity require. Augustine blends his ridicule of Roman virtue with a warning for the Christian that his or her humility and charity may not be as difficult as the sacrifices made by the Romans: "[O]ught they not to understand that they should not vaunt themselves, because they do that to obtain the society of angels, when those men [Romans] did well-nigh the same thing *(paene tale aliquid)* to preserve the glory of the Romans?" (*CD* 5.18).

Augustine provides examples of those who were willing to sacrifice their possessions, lives, and even glory in order to cultivate the common good and to worship their gods. For example, Brutus and Torquatus slew their sons for insubordination; Curius obeyed the oracle of the gods who demanded that the Romans destroy the best thing they possessed; Marcus Pulvillus obeyed the gods by continuing to dedicate a temple even when he received (unknown to him) false news about the death of his son; and Lucius Valerius and Cincinnatus loved the public good so much that they returned to poverty after their tenure in public office (*CD* 5.18).

Augustine reserves his greatest praise for Regulus who underwent torture to preserve the oath that he had made to the gods who are supposed to ensure temporal success (*CD* 1.15). Regulus was the Roman general who had been captured by the Carthaginians and who promised them that he would ensure a prisoner exchange with the Romans. He swore an oath to the gods that he would return to face death if he betrayed the Carthaginians. However, when Regulus returned to Rome, he advised the Senate against the prisoner exchange because it was not to their advantage. Instead of remaining safe in Rome, Regulus voluntarily returned to Carthage and suffered a horrible death.

Augustine describes Regulus as the most noble example the Romans had: "So that I am not concerned meantime to discuss *(disputo)* what kind of virtue Regulus possessed: enough, that by his most noble example *(isto nobilissimo exemplo)* they are forced to admit that the gods are to be worshiped not for the sake of bodily comforts *(corporis bona)* or external advantages *(earum rerum quae extrinsecus homini accidunt)*; for he preferred to lose all such things rather than offend the gods by whom he had sworn" (*CD* 1.15). Augustine is convinced that Regulus acted virtuously, out of the true way *(vera via)*, because he kept his oath to the gods despite knowing that keeping his oath meant death, and that the purpose of worship is not to secure bodily advantages or external advantages. He refuses to discuss or dispute the virtues of Regulus beyond stating this. It is impossible to know Regulus's true motivations, but he acted virtuously according to Augustine's own standard.

The lesson that Augustine directs to the Christian is that the Christian must recognize that even the virtuous political actor understands the transitoriness and contingency of his own achievement, and that the political actor is capable of acting according to virtue even if human glory is not forthcoming or is not a sufficient consolation for virtue. Augustine provides these examples as a protreptic for Christians so they recognize the standards given by nature that they must transcend and so they avoid becoming arrogant toward the earthly. The examples of statesmen disclose the standard of natural virtue that those claiming supernatural virtue (to borrow anachronistically from later medieval language) must transcend. These examples also serve the education of the political actors, or statesmen, because they teach them to recognize that their ambitious desire for happiness and glory, which require tremendous sacrifice to achieve, remains transitory and contingent. In effect, Augustine argues that an ambitious politician must strip himself of the love of glory and be capable of loving virtue exclusively. Only then can he readmit the love of glory back into his soul and have it serve the common good. The politician then finds his counterpart in the Christian who strips his soul of his love for the glory of eternal life in order to focus exclusively on loving God, and only then readmits the love of the glory of eternal life back into his soul from the perspective of one who loves God before loving the prospect of obtaining eternal life.

He concludes his discussion on praise and glory by stating, as we saw in the last chapter, that the happiest state of affairs would be that in which a true lover of God and neighbor, presumably one who has meditated on these pages, rules: "But there could be nothing more fortunate for human affairs *(nihil est felicius rebus humanis)* than that by the mercy of God, they who are endowed with true piety of life *(qui vera pietate praedidti bene vivunt)*, if they have the skill for ruling people *(si habent scientiam regendi populos)*, should also have the power. But such men, however great the virtues they possess in this life attribute it solely to the grace of God that He has bestowed it on them—willing, believing, seeking" *(CD* 5.19). The coincidence of true piety, the science of ruling, and political power brings about the happiest of affairs, although the difficulties surrounding political glory indicate that this coincidence is unlikely to occur.

This combination, observed in the previous chapter, is unlikely and, if indeed it occurs, is due to God's providence. Referring the reader to the discussion of fate in chapters 1–11, Augustine reminds him that this coincidence is due to God's providence:

> Wherefore, though I have, according to my ability, shown for what reason God, who alone is true and just, helped forward the Romans, who were good according to a certain standard of an earthly state, to the acquisition of so great an empire, there may be, nevertheless, a more hidden cause *(alia causa essa latentior)*, known better to God than to us, depending on the diversity of the merits of the human race *(propter diversa merita generis humani)*. *(CD* 5.19)

With terms such as "a more hidden cause" that depends "on the diversity of the merits of the human race," Augustine attributes to virtue and political success an element of mystery and incompleteness combined with an inner divine order.

These chapters bring together Augustine's thoughts on divine providence and political glory. From his extended discussion of glory we have learned that political virtue is radically incomplete, that it degenerates without being secured in virtue, but that it also cultivates virtues that resemble true virtue and promotes a degree of peace in the world. Augustine concludes from this that political virtues foreshadow perfect virtue. In chapters 21–23, he combines this argument with his understanding of divine providence, in order to demonstrate how human agency is to be glorified properly even though a large aspect of human affairs lies beyond human control. He states that the pious human being recognizes his deficiencies in attaining virtue, and:

Seeing that these things are so, let us not ascribe the power of granting kingdoms and empires to any except the true God. . . . Well then, the one true God, who never fails either in judgment or help for mankind, gave empire to the Romans at the time he chose, and as much as he chose. He gave it to the Assyrians, then also to the Persians, who worshiped only two gods, one good, the other bad, as their books relate. I will say no more of the Hebrew people, of whom I have already said as much as seemed necessary. They worshiped only one God, even at the time when they had a great kingdom. He it is, therefore, who granted crops *(segetes)* to the Persians without the worship of the goddess of the harvest (Segetia), and the other gifts of the earth without the worship of so many gods, such as the Romans assigned each to his function, or sometimes several to one function. And he also granted them empire, though they did not worship the gods through whom the Romans supposed that they had held their rule. (*CD* 5.21)

This passage is quoted in its entirety so as to provide the reader with an understanding of the surface teaching and the two deeper meanings within Augustine's argument.

As for the surface teaching, Augustine argues against the Roman conception of fate and virtue by asserting that, just as God is responsible for one's virtue, so too is he responsible for the seemingly random rise and fall of regimes, and for determining which apparently random figure will be permitted to rule. In this sense, it appears that Augustine ends up agreeing with the Stoic conception of fate that treats human agency as a material instead of a voluntary or efficient cause. In fact, it almost seems that divine providence controls human life even more than does fate, in the sense at least that the Romans believed that sacrifice would ensure temporal reward. This passage shows Augustine arguing that the Assyrians, Persians, Romans, and even Jews rose and fell regardless of the god(s) they worshiped and that their fortunes depended on powers far beyond anything they could muster.

One might think that Augustine replaces freedom-denying fate with an equally freedom-denying divine providence. However, this interpretation is insufficient for two reasons implied in the text quoted above. First, Augustine has already shown how individual virtue and glory have contributed to the common good, and that this virtue was in a sense the Romans' own. Some of the Romans were able to practice virtue by the light of nature. Second, Augustine's category of divine providence indicates that human beings cannot be glorified for being completely responsible for the success of their particular regimes, because there remains a strong element that lies outside human control. As such, providence can harm human fortunes as much as it can help them, as shown in Augustine's remarks about the Persians, who grew crops despite not worshiping the crop god. However, human beings are properly glorified for their appropriate responses to providence, to those events and circumstances that require them to act virtuously. Augustine teaches the reader that the glory proper to human beings is their virtue, and that this glory is completed if providence brings about circumstances favorable for that virtue being recognized and shared by others.

Having brought the potential statesman into the position of understanding the relationship between himself and his glory, and divine providence, and having taught him that he cannot be happy if he places his hope in happiness when he desires human praise primarily and virtue only secondarily, Augustine concludes this book with a description of the personal virtues of the good statesman.

The list of virtues of the good statesman is divided into two groups, and highlights his personal virtues (CD 5.24). The first group is related to his rulership, and Augustine presents it in terms of preserving a mean between extremes. Augustine, for example, argues that the likelihood of ruling justly increases when the statesman remembers that the advisors who praise him are mere men, and thus fallible, and their praises may be just at times and unjust at other times. He argues further that the statesman will take care not to use either pardons or punishments excessively, so as not to promote among the people either laxity or hatred toward him. Augustine then says that the good statesman's luxury must be as restrained as it otherwise would have been unrestrained.

The second group of virtues is related to the statesman's faith: he will love, fear, and worship God; he will love the city of God "in which they are not afraid to have partners," so that he recognizes his fundamental equality with his subjects; and he will use his majesty for the furthest possible extension of God's worship.

Augustine concentrates on these personal virtues because, as he has pointed out in the previous chapter and in his discussions of Constantine and Theodosius, the fortunes and political glory of the statesman are fragile and subject to contingency. For example, he describes Constantine's great political successes, which included founding a city to preserve his name for posterity and having his sons (named Constantius, Constantine, and Constans) succeed him, but Augustine is silent about his personal virtue except to say that he worshiped the true God instead of demons. Augustine suggests that Constantine's glory is anomalous, and is quick to point out the disparity between faith and success or lack of success among his other successors. He emphasizes the humility and virtues of Theodosius, mentioning both the penance he paid for his massacre of the Thessalonians and his able war making. Despite Theodosius's greater virtue, Augustine testifies less to his memory than to that of Constantine: "These and other similar good works, which it would be long to tell, he carried with him from this world of time, where the greatest human eminence and loftiness (*culminis et sublimitatis*) are but vapor" (CD 5.26). Augustine concentrates on Theodosius's virtue rather than on his glory, but does not denigrate glory completely. The fact that he has set Theodosius's memory down in the *City of God* is evidence that his deeds are not forgotten, and that Augustine has glorified him.

Augustine considered the ordinate love of glory an appropriate political love. Glorification consists in one providing a model for virtue for others who, by imitating, glorify the leader as one who testifies to truth. The leader is so defined as a leader on account of his or her virtue, not exclusively by social or political position. Augustine considers Roman heroes to have testified to truth in a way from which Christians can draw. He also thought that the Christian love of God moderates inordinate love of glory. Book 5 of the *City of God* educates both politicians and Christians by showing that glory depends on virtue where one acts virtuously for the sake of virtue and where glory is loved secondarily. This love of glory as secondary to virtue constitutes Augustine's grounds for glorifying Regulus, who practiced natural virtue. He was able to purge the love of glory from his soul only to readmit it as subordinate to the love of virtue; his virtue made him glorious. He was also glorified by good judges such as the thankful Romans and Augustine himself, who remembered him. This view of Regulus enables Augustine to consider political glory as a natural good and one worthy of pursuit in a world where one of the conditions of glory, the judgment of good judges, is unreliable and fleeting. We turn now to consider how people of diverse faiths can participate in a common political glory that intimates true glory.

# 6

# LOVE OF GOD AND NEIGHBOR
# BY FOLLOWING THE FOOTPRINTS

*He begins to leave who begins to love. Many are the leaving who know it not, for the feet of those leaving are affections of the heart: and yet, they are leaving Babylon.*

—Augustine, *Expositions on the Book of Psalms*

*We were not pioneers ourselves, but we journeyed over old trails that were new to us, and with hearts open. Who shall distinguish?*

—J. Monroe Thorington, *The Glittering Mountains of Canada*

ORDINATE loving is actualized through the love of God and of neighbor. This chapter shows first how Augustine envisaged the virtuous human being who embodies natural virtue and is thus the best judge of right and wrong, and who can love his neighbor on a basis intelligible to natural reason. The second part of the chapter shows how Augustine envisaged the proper relationship between political and ecclesiastical authority as understood by the virtuous human being. The first part can be understood as analyzing the "prophetic" aspect of love of God and neighbor, and the second part as analyzing the institutional side that stands before the judgment of the prophetic perspective.

The love of God and of neighbor forms the other virtues, and thus constitutes the root of Augustine's right-by-nature theory of virtue and politics: "For our good, that is the great subject of dispute among philosophers, is nothing but to cling *(cohaerere)* to him, the sole being by whose incorporeal embrace the intellectual soul *(anima intellectualis)* is, if we put it so, impregnated and made to give birth to true virtues" *(CD* 10.3). This chapter shows that Augustine's view that the love of God and of neighbor as the architectonic virtue is consistent with his right-by-nature view of politics. Similarly, virtue depends on the extent to which one has shed inordinate worldly desires: "But since the mind, itself, though naturally capable of reason and intelligence *(ratio et intellegentia naturaliter)*, is disabled by besotting and inveterate vices not merely from delighting and abiding in, but even from tolerating His unchangeable light, until it has been gradually healed, and renewed, and made capable of such felicity, it had, in the first place, to be impregnated with faith, and so purified" *(CD* 11.2; see also *CD* 8.6, 11.16; *DT* 3.3.8, 12.2.2, 13.13.17; *Conf.* 3.7). As observed in the previous chapter, ordinate loving does indeed involve dying to the worldly pleasures, as Augustine signifies this process in his writings. However, ordinate loving does not require regarding worldly goods as evil, but simply as inferior goods. This chapter, therefore, explicates the relationship of his political and moral thought and what could be regarded as his view of natural theology. This argument does not deny the importance of grace for Augustine, nor his well-known statements that one must have faith before one can know God, or that he would not believe the gospel except for the authority of the Catholic Church, as he states in his anti-Manichaean writings.[1] The argument is instead based upon Augustine's paradoxical view that the mind cannot understand anything that it does not already know in some implicit way *(DT* books 9–10), and that some prephilosophic experience, common to everyone, is necessary to understand initially what the phrase "faith in God" would mean (see *DT* 10.7.10, 14.8.11).[2] Even so, as was pointed out in the Preface, this study considers the "results" of Augustine's meditations, and considers only how those meditations bear on political life, and how

---

1. See Augustine, "De Utilitate Credendi" (On the advantage of believing), in *Writings of Saint Augustine,* trans. Robert Catesby Taliaterro, Fathers of the Church, vol. 2 (New York: Cima Publishing, 1947), 31. Eugene Teselle denies that the latter statement can even be taken as Catholic dogma. Rather, such statements "are procedural arguments in a legal context, what we today call 'pre-trial arguments' and the ancients called 'prescriptions.' Their purpose is to limit the scope of debate even before considering the content of what is said on each side: either the Manichaeans have no right to base their claims upon the gospel, since it has been transmitted through the Church; or, if they are correct, I can believe no one; but in fact I have come to believe through the Church, to which I am held by many bonds, and that is where I continue to look" *(Living in Two Cities: Augustinian Trajectories in Political Thought,* 6). By recognizing the legal context of such statements, Teselle's observation reminds the reader to consider the polemical circumstances of some of Augustine's statements.

2. See also Augustine, "On the Teacher," in *Greatness of the Soul,* and the discussion of Platonic philosophic experience below.

he presented those results in his political writings, especially the apologetic *City of God*. Thus, though this study has drawn from the debates of moral theologians on Augustine's understanding of God and neighbor, the focus of this chapter differs from theirs, and refers to them only as much as the subject material permits.

An individual who becomes fully self-conscious as the image of God is not the same as one who by faith understands himself as the image of the Trinitarian God. Augustine allows for what would later, in the scholastic tradition, be called "natural virtue," although without the problems associated with what is generally known as naturalism, that is, thinking of natural virtue as self-sufficient and as providing perfect blessedness (see *CD* 11.25, 12.5, and below). This claim needs also to be qualified by the fact that Augustine did not distinguish the "natural" from the "supernatural," as is seen in later medieval theology. All that is meant here by "natural" virtue is Augustine's recognition that Christians and non-Christians can practice virtue based on a standard beyond mere self-interest, and without directly invoking the Christian God (although Augustine would say that God acts indirectly), and that it does not necessarily degenerate into *libido dominandi*, or what, throughout this study, has been called the "Caesarian temptation." Augustine affirms the natural virtue of the classical philosophers and comes to similar conclusions about wisdom and friendship in his reflections on the love of God and of neighbor. His understanding of human beings' sociality is inconsistent with the interpretation that sees love of neighbor negated by the love of God, which requires that particular relations be subsumed as mere occasions for the universal love of God and neighbor that ultimately renders love of neighbor meaningless.[3] The discussion of his account of wisdom and friendship in this chapter rounds out discussion of practical reasoning and the naturalness of politics in the previous chapters. In keeping with the earlier chapters, this chapter shows that Augustine's account of natural wisdom entails the ability to understand the interconnections of creation and the ability to provide (or at least the ability and willingness to assent to) a scientific account of politics and creation in general. The best statesman is not necessarily a philosopher, but must be able to assent to it in commonsense terms when it is presented to him. Similarly, the best statesman actualizes his moral virtues by perfecting (as humanly possible) his will. Augustine affirms that the love of neighbor is not instrumental to the love of God.

The discussion of the formation of the soul as the image of God is accompanied by a consideration of the good regime's relationship with ecclesiastical

---

3. For example, see Arendt, *Love and Saint Augustine*, 97.

institutions. The good regime, a cosmion, secures a temporal kind of happiness yet is fully aware of its inability to secure eternal happiness, which, according to Augustine, is demanded by the nature of happiness itself. The two orders cannot simply be distinguished by the one being responsible for temporal goods, and the other for eternal goods. Insofar as citizens in their cities appropriately strive to become something beyond themselves, politics can be seen as embodying a religious element (broadly defined; see CD 10.1 and below). This is not the religiosity of a strict theocratic code. Rather, politics, like the life of the Church, consists of knowing and praising greatness, that is, both are concerned with their particular kinds of glory. Seen in this light, Augustine thought that politics is partly religious just as religion is partly political. Thus, the two orders overlap even though what distinguishes them is definitive and irresolvable. The first part will show how Augustine saw the soul could achieve a natural understanding and love of God and of neighbor. The human ability to do this constitutes the focal point on which political and sacerdotal orders meet to supplement their respective virtues and ends, and check their respective vices. The Church checks the political order by reminding it that it cannot establish perfect, universal justice, and the city checks the ecclesiastical order by reminding it that it cannot wield political power on the basis of revelation alone. Rightful actions by either side must accord with natural understanding.

## THE "PROPHETIC SIDE" OF ORDINATE LOVING

### The Virtue of *Latreia*

Augustine's view that one loves God through loving neighbors is reflected in his search for a proper Latin term for the service that is owed to God *(latreia)*, as opposed to the service owed to others, including masters and neighbors (CD 10.1–3). He understood *latreia* as the activity (or exercise or expression) of the virtue of loving God and neighbor, which is also justice, and asserts that it can be exercised individually and publicly.

Early in the City of God, Augustine defines *latreia* as the true piety that leads to membership in the city that serves the one true God (CD 5.15). Elsewhere, he states that *latreia* includes the "worship, priestly offices, the tabernacle or temple, the altars, sacrifices, ceremonies, feast days and whatever else *(quidquid)* belongs to the service due to God that is properly called *latreia*" (CD 7.32). However, he treats *latreia* explicitly as virtue in terms of ordinate loving. He explains that the temples and priestly offices are signs of the love of God:

To him we owe the service which is called in Greek *latreia*, whether this service is embodied in certain sacraments or is within our very selves *(in nobis ipsis)*. For all of us together are his temple and all of us singly his temples, since he deigns to dwell both in the united heart of all and in each one separately. . . . When we lift our hearts to him, our hearts are his altar; with his only begotten Son as our priest we seek his favor. We sacrifice bleeding victims to him when we fight in defence of his truth even unto blood; we offer him the sweetest incense when in his sight we burn with pious and holy love, when we vow, and pay the vow, to devote to him his gifts bestowed on us and to devote ourselves with them; when we dedicate and consecrate to him a memorial of his benefits in solemn feasts on appointed days, lest, as time unrolls its scroll, a thankless forgetfulness should creep in; when we offer him on the altar of our hearts a sacrifice of humility and praise kindled by the fire of our love. *(CD* 10.3)

All the external parts of worship such as altars, temples, and incense culminate in the virtue of the soul by which one loves God and neighbor.

Augustine's attempt to isolate a term for the worship of God distinct from other forms of piety or reverence reflects his view that God is loved through loving one's neighbor. It reflects his view that the love of God is expressed through various other kinds of love (for example, for neighbor or for city), and it reflects the difficulty of separating out the love of God that is exclusive from these other types of love. He characteristically moves through choices of various terms but then sets them aside, explaining that they fall short of expressing the love of God. This method is analogous to his negative theological method of inquiry into the nature of God, which first considers and then rejects worldly things as God.[4]

In the ancient world, *latreia* meant, in a general sense, one's service to another, usually a master, and extended to one's service to the gods. It was taken up in the New Testament to signify true worship. Augustine states that *latreia* is the term used in Scripture to signify service *(servitus)*. He also equates its meaning with liturgy *(leitourgia)*, which means, literally, "work" or "service" *(ergon)* for the people *(leitos) (EnP* 136.135.3).[5] Thus, he understood *latreia*

---

4. For example, he states: "God . . . is better known by knowing what He is not" *(DO* 2.16.44). Elsewhere he states: "For it is a part of no small knowledge if we aspire from this depth to that height, namely, if before we can know what God is, we can already know what He is not" *(DT* 8.2.3). See also *Conf.* 10.16, 10.19.

5. *Latreia* and its cognates (for example, the verbal *latreuo*) appear most frequently in Luke and the letters of Paul (Horst Balz and Gerhart Schneider, eds., *Exegetical Dictionary of the New Testament,* 344–48).

as a public virtue.[6] He first identifies the proper object of worship: "For this is the worship which is due *(debitus)* to the Divinity *(divinitati)*, or, to speak more expressly *(expressius* [literally, "more pressed out" or "more pointedly"]), to Deity *(deitati)"* (*CD* 10.1). Augustine notes that Christian apologists coined *deitas* as a translation of the Greek *theotes* (*CD* 7.1).[7] As apologists, they would have coined this term to distinguish and defend the *deitas* that transcends the pagan gods. Augustine makes the same move when he distinguishes the general category of things divine, signified by *divinitas*, from the specific and more pointed *deitas*, denoting what the pagan philosophers knew. However, Augustine later distinguishes between the popular and philosophic meanings of divinity, stating that "those things are called simple that are fundamentally and truly divine *(divina)*, because in them quality and substance are the same; and they are themselves divine *(divina)* or wise *(sapientia)* or happy *(beata)* without being so by participation in something not themselves" (*CD* 11.10). *Divinitas* and *deitas* both signify God for Augustine. *Divinitas* as a philosophical term signifies the same thing as *deitas*. However, Roman polytheistic civil theology had difficulty distinguishing lesser divinities from the one head of the gods. Thus, Christian apologists used *deitas*. *Deitas* is identical with the *deus* intimated in the worship of lesser divinities: "[A]ll users of the Latin language . . . think of a supremely excellent and immortal being. Now although he alone is thought of as the god of gods *(deorum deus)*, he is also thought of by those who imagine, invoke, and worship other gods, whether in heaven and earth, in so far as their thinking strives to reach a being than which there is nothing better or more sublime *(melius atque sublimus)"* (*DDC* 1.14–15). Elsewhere, he notes his agreement with Cicero's philosophical definition of *deus* (*CD* 22.20). If we consider Augustine's usage of *deitas* against this background, it follows that he uses it to focus the pagan popular mind on what pagan philosophers had already discovered. If this is the case, then Augustine's apologetic strategy is one directed not merely to replacing the pagan gods with his imperial god, but also to urging the Romans to acknowledge what their philosophers had already discovered (although, for apologetic purposes, Roman opinion of their philosophers was of only secondary interest for Augustine).

---

6. Black points out that *leitourgia*, in the Greek city-states, was the service rendered by wealthy citizens. He observes generally of Christian practice in the early Church: "Service (*leitourgia*, liturgy) of God was conceptually related to service of human beings and especially of fellow believers. These were elements of a new republicanism, built around Roman and even Ciceronian values. Here, too, as for the elder Brutus, ties of blood must be sacrificed for the greater good" ("Christianity and Republicanism," 648; see also Liddell and Scott, *Intermediate Greek-English Lexicon*, 468).

7. *Deitas* does not appear in the *Oxford Latin Dictionary*. Alexander Souter suggests it was coined by Pseudo-Cyprian, *de aleatoribus*, para. 7 (*A Glossary of Later Latin to 600* A.D., 93).

Augustine next observes that Latin lacks any single term to signify the worship of God *(cultus Dei)*. He states that Latin lacks an equivalent to the scriptural *latreia*. Even the usual Latin term, *cultus*, is insufficient:

> [I]n that case it would not seem to be due exclusively to God *(non soli Deo)*; we frequently "cultivate" men also, either their memory or in person *(quos honorifica vel recordatione vel praesentia frequentamus)*. Also, we say that we "cultivate" not only those things to which we subject ourselves in religious humility, but also certain things which are subject to ourselves. From it, too, we derive the words "cultivators of the field," "settlers," and "inhabitants *(agricolae et coloni et incolae)*." And the gods are called *coelicolae*, for no other reason than that they cultivate *(colant)* heaven, not by worshiping *(venerando)* but by dwelling *(inhabitando)* in it, as if they were a kind of celestial settler *(caeli quosdam colonos)* . . . in the sense in which the great master of the Latin language says, "There was an ancient city inhabited by Tyrian colonists." . . . So it is perfectly true that *cultus* in its truest sense *(verissimum)* is due to none save God, but as *cultus* is used also in connection with other objects, it is for that reason impossible in Latin to convey in one word the meaning of worship due to God.[8] *(CD* 10.1)

*Cultus* in the philosophical sense would be a proper translation of *latreia*. However, common meanings include the glorification of human beings, and Augustine attempts to show that those meanings share in, but do not exhaust, the meaning of *cultus*. His statement here is nuanced because, on the one hand, he distinguishes the worldly activities associated with *cultus* from its philosophic meaning, worship of God, but, on the other hand, he does not deny the truthfulness of popular meanings, even though they could be expressed with other terms such as *colonus* and *incola*, for example. The experience he wishes to isolate for his entire audience, by using a word to translate *latreia*, will not deny the reality of these lesser forms of worship.

As briefly shown in Chapter 5, *latreia* includes other experiences associated with *cultus*, such as honoring the memory and presence of great human beings and dwelling together. For instance, whereas sacrifice is due only to God, *cultus* and veneration are due to worthy human beings (a practice often mistaken for true sacrifice): "There are indeed many kinds of worship that have been appropriated from the service of God to be conferred upon men for their honor, an abuse that may come either from carrying humility too far or from

---

8. Quoting Virgil, *The Aeneid* 1.12. See also *DT* 14.1.1, where, noticing the impossibility of translating *theosebia* with one word, he observes that "it is better to use two words, so that it should rather be called worship of God *(cultus Dei)*."

the pestilential practice of flattery. Yet those who received such tribute were still considered only men. They are spoken of as men worthy of worship and reverence *(colendi et venerandi)*, or even, if we chose to bestow still more honor, by adoration *(adorandi)"* (*CD* 10.4). Augustine acknowledges the rightfulness of venerating virtuous human beings, but he distinguishes this from true sacrifice. His willingness to accept a politics that involves the *cultus* or glorification of virtuous human beings is further seen in his criticism of the Romans, who rightly glory in Regulus, their hero, but refuse to glorify the city of God: "What, then, are we to make of men who glory in having such a citizen, yet fear to have such a city?" (*CD* 1.15). The Romans were right to glory in Regulus but wrong not to glory in the city with virtues that correspond to his, the city of God. Regulus stands as a paradigm that Rome should have glorified but failed to do so.

Augustine also considers religion *(religio)* as a possible translation for *latreia*. He states that it would be insolently misleading *(insolenter auferri)* if he were to restrict its meaning to the worship of God. The most learned *(doctissimi)* and ignorant alike use it to signify "human relations, affinities, and necessary ties of every sort *(humanis atque adfinitatibus et quibusque necessitudinibus)"* (*CD* 10.1). He rejects *religio* as a translation of *latreia* in order to preserve the necessary lower relations that the term signifies. It includes the love of God, as noted when he quotes Cicero stating that *religio* is derived from electing *(eligentes)* or, rather, reelecting *(religentes)* God in order to love God (*CD* 10.3).[9] However, *religio* includes other relations. Augustine rejects piety *(pietas)* on the similar grounds that this term includes the duties *(officii)* conducted toward parents even though it is also customarily meant to include works of mercy.

*Servitus* is the general translation of *latreia*, but Augustine concludes that this too is insufficient because it includes service rendered to another human being. He ends up having to use two words, *cultus Dei*, to translate the experience: "This we say is owed to that God alone who is the true God and makes gods of his worshipers *(facitque suos cultores deos)"* (*CD* 10.1). With this statement, Augustine has included under the worship of God alone all the other necessary experiences signified by *pietas, religio,* and *cultus*. Not only is service rendered to God alone, but also God's worshipers are transformed into his co-dwellers in the sky (equivalent to the *caelicolae*), who deserve the honor conveyed to virtuous human beings.[10] Augustine's method of isolating a Latin translation in

9. See Cicero, *De Natura Deorum* 2.28.72. Both Cicero and Augustine thought *religio* derives from *relegere* instead of from *religare* (to bind).

10. On deification through worship of God and his general agreement with Plato's view, see *CD* 9.23. See also *CD* 11.1 (where he states that God and gods are the objects of worship in the city

a single word for the Greek *latreia* discloses how he considered the love of God inseparable from the love of neighbor, because the other acts such as *pietas*, *cultus*, and *servitus* participate in the love of God.

## Candidates for the City of God Outside the Sacramental Order of the Church

People outside Israel and the Church could love God and neighbor. A consideration of this issue clarifies the extent to which one can love God and neighbor according to one's own capabilities. It is indicated in Augustine's observations of the Israelites: "[I]t is in that people, and in the saints, and, in a shadowy *(adumbrata)* and mysterious sense, in all mankind, that the pilgrim City of God is embodied" (*CD* 16.3). However, we shall first consider the possibility of pagans practicing this virtue.

Plato and various Platonists loved God and understood God as the maker of creation. Augustine's treatment of them indicates that their intellect and love have the same object. He discusses the Platonists because they love wisdom, which Augustine equates with the love of God: "[W]e must confer with the philosophers, whose very name, when interpreted in Latin, proclaims their love of wisdom. Furthermore, if God, the maker of all things, is wisdom, as divine authority and truth have shown, the true philosopher *(verus philosophus)* is one who loves God" (*CD* 8.1). Augustine considers the Platonists the philosophers closest to the Christian faith: "[I]f the Platonists, or those who think with them, knowing God, glorified Him as God and gave thanks *(glorificarent et gratias agerent)*, if they did not become vain in their own thoughts, if they did not originate or yield to the popular errors, they would certainly acknowledge that neither could the blessed immortals retain, nor we miserable mortals reach, a happy condition without worshiping the one God of gods, who is both theirs and ours" (*CD* 10.3; see also 4.29, 8.3–12, 10.1–3, 10.23, 10.29, 11.25, 19.22–23; *DT* 1.6.13, 4.20.27–28, 14.1.1). Plato himself receives special mention as Socrates' best disciple, and whom later great philosophers, the Platonists, follow (*CD* 8.4, 8.11, 9.10; see also *DVR* 1.1–4.7).

Augustine thought that Plato understood God to be incorporeal and to be the maker of the world. He acknowledges that Plato "did not doubt that to practice philosophy is to love God" (*CD* 8.8). He compares Plato's understanding of God to the Mosaic wisdom concerning God as "I am he who is" (*CD* 8.11), which

---

of God); *Serm.* 166.4.4, 192.1.1; *EnP* 49.1.2; and *Homilies on the Gospel of John*, 48.9. He also states that "in Holy Scripture, men are called gods more explicitly than are those immortal and blessed beings with whom it is promised that we shall be equal in the resurrection" (*CD* 9.23).

Plato and the later Platonists understood, according to the Pauline dictum, "through created things" (Rom. 1:19–20):

> But from whatever source Plato learned these things, whether from books of ancient writers who came before him or, as is more likely, to quote the Apostle: "Because that which is known of God is plain among them, for God has showed it to them. For His invisible attributes from the creation of the world as well as His eternal power and godhead are clearly seen and understood through created things," in either case I think I have sufficiently demonstrated that I had good reason to select the Platonic philosophers in order to debate with them a point of natural theology *(de naturii theologia)*. (CD 8.12)

He acknowledges that Platonic wisdom can know God as the maker of creation.

Augustine further acknowledges that Platonic wisdom can know that creation is good. In his discussion about the ways in which the traces of the Trinity in nature prompt the human mind to seek wisdom, he asserts: "Nor is there any author more excellent than God, nor any art more effective than God's word, any cause better than that something good should be created by a good God *(a Deo bono)*. Plato too gives this as the proper reason, beyond all reasons, for the world's creation, namely that good works might be created by a good God" (CD 11.21). This means that, for Augustine, the mind can know that being and good are identical. Plato and the Platonists can know this because they know God as immutable and simple (CD 8.6) and as the highest good *(summum bonum)* that is sought for its own sake (CD 8.8). Knowing the simplicity of God lets Plato (and thus, natural reason) understand that Being is identical with the Good and wisdom. This makes possible the virtuous life because Plato can know that all action is done for the Good; it enables him to argue that the philosopher is the lover of God.

Plato's speculations even bear the mark of the Trinity, since he divides philosophy into its three parts (natural, logic, and ethics): "Plato is said to have been the first to discover and promulgate this distribution, and he saw that God alone could be the author of nature, the bestower of intelligence *(intelligentiae dator)*, and the kindler *(inspirator)* of love *(amoris)* by which life becomes good and blessed" (CD 11.25; see also *Conf.* 7.9). Plato's understanding of God implicitly hints at the Trinity insofar as both Plato and Christianity affirm God as the first cause of existence, as the cause of intelligence and intelligibility, and the mover of all things to God through love. Augustine does not conclude that natural reason could know that God is triune, however.

The second function of God that Augustine argues Plato knew, the kindler or inspirer of love, compares with what Augustine elsewhere calls preceding grace, which he distinguishes from sanctifying or subsequent grace.[11] This function shows that, for Augustine, natural wisdom can understand that it is moved to seek that which it seeks. This will be explicated further in the subsection on the image of God. Elsewhere, he states that philosophers themselves understand that philosophy is prompted by grace: "Still, you acknowledge the existence of grace, since you say that it has been granted *(dicis esse concessum)* to only a few to attain to God by the strength of their intelligence. For you do not say: 'A few decided to attain' or 'A few chose'; no, when you say: 'It has been granted,' you are undoubtedly bearing witness to the grace of God, and not to any self-sufficiency of man" *(CD* 10.29).[12] This passage suggests that Augustine understood natural intelligence to be a gift (see also *DT* 4.20.27–28). Augustine argues that the grace or the natural inclination that moves human beings to philosophy is an intimation of the Holy Spirit. For instance, he compares the experience of the Holy Spirit to what, he notes, Plato calls the intermediate: "You proclaim the Father and His Son, whom you call the intellect or the mind of the Father, and an intermediate *(medium)* by whom we suppose you mean the Holy Spirit *(Spiritum sanctum)"* *(CD* 10.29). This side of the Holy Spirit does not reduce grace to nature because it is part of prevenient grace. Augustine remained adamant that the natural theology of the Platonists is incomplete. For instance, as far as the question of being turned to philosophy by nature is concerned, Augustine points out: "No man in those books hears [Christ] calling *(vocantem):* Come to me all that labour" *(Conf.* 7.21). The grace experienced by the philosophers is not as complete as the redemptive grace offered by Christ; however, they can understand it.

The experience of the intermediate and the Holy Spirit is made intelligible by the observation of nature, as Augustine observes when he compares the spirit of the creator God to the water and air that Plato saw to bind together creation:

> [I]n the *Timaeus,* his treatise on the formation of the universe, Plato says that God in this operation first united earth and fire. But it is clear that he assigns to fire the region of heaven. So this opinion bears a certain resemblance to

11. Augustine notes: "But subsequent grace *(subsequens gratia)* indeed assists man's good purpose, but the purpose would not exist if grace did not precede *(nisi praecederet gratia).* The desire of man, also which is called good, although in beginning to exist it is aided by grace, yet does not begin without grace, but is inspired *(inspiratur)* by Him" ("Against Two Letters of the Pelagians," in *Anti-Pelagian Writings,* 2.10.21–22; see also "On Nature and Grace," in ibid., 35.31).

12. See also *CD* 22.22, citing Cicero, *Academica* 1.2.7.

the statement: "In the beginning God created the heaven and the earth." Next Plato speaks of the two elements, water and air, which by their intermediate position *(interpositis)* form a bond *(copularentur)* between the two extremes. This prompts *(unde putatur)* the thought that he so understood the scriptural words: "The spirit of God moved over the waters." I mean that he did not note accurately what term Scripture usually employs for the Spirit of God and, because air too is called spirit, it may be thought that he supposed that the four elements are mentioned in this text. *(CD* 8.11)

Nature serves as the occasion for human beings' experience of the Holy Spirit. Both natural reason and Scripture agree on the governing principle of creation, and on what moves human beings to turn to God.

For Plato, the love of God and of neighbor informs virtue: "Plato defined the ultimate good as living in conformity with virtue, that he held this possible only for the man who comes to know God and to copy him, and that he believed happiness to be due to this cause alone. For this reason he has no doubt that philosophy is the love of God, whose nature is incorporeal" *(CD* 8.8). For Plato, according to Augustine, virtue consists of knowing and imitating God. Virtue is also the way to secure the goodwill of the gods: "[T]he right way [of securing the goodwill of gods] is through resembling them in goodwill *(sed per bonae voluntatis similitudinem)*, which enables us to be with them, to live with them, and to worship with them the God they worship, even if we cannot see them with the eyes of the flesh" *(CD* 8.25).

One of the differences between the Platonic love of God and that of Augustine is that Plato and the Platonists worshiped a multiplicity of gods and demons. This was due partly to their respect for pagan traditions, and partly to their view that God is purely contemplative and remains pure by having no concern for human beings *(CD* 9.1, 10.30). As a result, they undermine friendship if they strive to imitate the solitary, contemplative God. Contrary to the Christian view of grace, they doubted that God bends down to mingle with mere humans. Thus, their worship of demons had a philosophical reason: good and evil demons serve as mediators between God and man *(CD* 8.20). Augustine's full response to this problem lies outside the scope of this study because it touches on the epistemological and theological problems of the communicability of divine wisdom and its embodiment, which, for Augustine, can be perfectly achieved by only the mediator of the God-man, Jesus Christ *(CD* 9.17).

However, two points can be observed. Augustine argues that it is absurd for the Platonists to argue simultaneously that God does not communicate with human beings while evil demons carry God's messages to tell the city to perform obscene theatrical performances. If they actually believed this (and Augustine indicates that they may not have since, he notes, they and Plato himself veiled their speech [CD 8.4]), then Plato would not have banished the poets from his city:

> [God] has no communication with a man [Plato] who by means of philo-sophical writings seeks to expel poets from a well regulated city, but He has with a demon who demands from the chiefs and pontiffs of the state the stage representation of the ribald compositions of the poets. He has no communication with a man who forbids writers of fiction to attribute crimes to the gods, but He has with a demon who takes delight in fictitious crimes of the gods. (CD 8.20; see also DDC 2.144)

Their position is insufficient because a good God (and there are no evil gods according to Plato [CD 8.13]) would not command people to sin. Furthermore, Plato would have been disobedient to the gods by banishing the poets or trying to cultivate civic virtue. Augustine questions the necessity of having such mediators, good or evil, indicating that it is unclear why a mediator is necessary when a good god cannot be deceived by a good mediator. A god that cannot be deceived by a mediator, according to Augustine, already knows the truth and thus would not need a mediator (CD 8.21).

The Platonists themselves admit that God communicates with human be-ings:

> But Apuleius also says that the knowledge of this God which wise men have, when by the power of their mind they have removed themselves as far as they can from the body, is like the briefest flicker of lightning illuminating the deepest darkness. If then we are to suppose that the truly supreme God, who is above all things, does visit, occasionally though it be and like a flash of white light though it be, that darts at lightning speed, yet he does draw near to the minds of wise men with a kind of intelligible and ineffable presence (intelligibili et ineffabili quadam praesentia) when they have withdrawn from the body as far as was permitted, and if we are to suppose that he cannot be contaminated by them, what is the point of placing those gods far away in a lofty abode in order to avoid contamination with men? (CD 9.16)

Augustine interprets the Platonic language of illumination to mean that the Platonists thought that God communicates with human beings (see CD 10.2, discussed below). This is a figurative way of expressing the experience of re-ceiving the gift of wisdom, which the philosophers themselves acknowledge. Augustine denies that truth is literally perceived as light when he observes that truth is perceived immediately by the intellect (see CD 11.2, 16.6). The idea of

God's communication with human beings is suggested elsewhere, when he says of the Platonists: "I found it stated, differently and in a variety of ways, that the Son being in the form of the Father thought it not robbery to be equal with God, because by nature He was God" (*Conf.* 7.9).[13] This and the previous passages show that human beings know God because intelligibility is an attribute of divinity, and this attribute is expressed as "intelligible and ineffable presence" and as what, according to Augustine, the Platonists symbolized by "the Son being in the form of the Father."

In addition to the testimony of pagans, Scripture itself testifies to members of the mystical city of God outside the sacerdotal order. Augustine explicitly states that various individuals stood apart from the official history of the city of God: "[I]n those days what gods but those did the world worship, except for the one Hebrew nation and certain individuals outside of it, wherever any were found worthy of divine grace by the utterly mysterious and righteous judgment of God?" He reiterates this later:

> Nor do I think that the Jews dare to maintain that no one has belonged to God who was not an Israelite, from the time when Israel began his line after his elder brother was rejected. To be sure, there was no other people especially [or literally] (*proprie*) called the people of God; nevertheless, they cannot deny that among other peoples too there have been certain human beings who belonged not by earthly but by heavenly fellowship to the company of true Israelites who are citizens of the country that is above.[14] (*CD* 18.47)

This means that members of the city of God can exist outside of the official body that "especially" or "literally" represents the city of God.

Augustine lists Job as a member of the city of God. Job "was neither a native-born Israelite nor a proselyte, a stranger received among the people of Israel. He traced his descent from the race of Edom, was born in the land of Edom

---

13. See Augustine's comment on Porphyry's "three gods," which he regards as an intimation (*umbracula*) of the Trinity (*CD* 10.29). See R. D. Crouse, "'In Aenigmate Trinitas' (*Confessions*, XIII,5,6): The Conversion of Philosophy in Augustine's *Confessions*," 58–60.

14. See also *CD* 16.3 and *Ep.* 102.15: "[N]or were there ever wanting men who believed in Him, from Adam to Moses, and among the people of Israel itself, which was by a special mysterious appointment a prophetic nation, and among other nations before He came in the flesh. For seeing that in the sacred Hebrew books some are mentioned, even from Abraham's time, not belonging to his natural posterity nor to the people of Israel, and not proselytes added to that people, who were nevertheless partakers of this holy sacrament, why may we not believe that in other nations also, here and there, some more were found, although we do not record their names in these authoritative records?"

and died there" (*CD* 18.47). From this Augustine concludes: "And I do not doubt that it was divinely provided by this one example that we should know that there could be also scattered among other peoples human beings who lived as followers of God and found favour with Him, being members of the spiritual Jerusalem." Melchizedek is also a member of the city of God. He is the Canaanite priest-king who blessed Abraham with bread and wine (Gen. 14) and to whose priesthood Jesus Christ belongs (*CD* 16.22, 17.5, 17.7). Melchizedek is not distinguished by his family and blood, as are the Aaronic line of priests, but, rather, "each human being is chosen in accordance with the merit that the divine grace has bestowed on him" (*CD* 20.21). With Melchizedek, whose origin is unknown, "then first appeared the sacrifice which is now offered to God by Christians in the whole wide world" (*CD* 16.22).

Augustine also mentions an Erythraean sibyl who cryptically prophesied Christ. One of her writings contained the passage that had the initial letters of the lines so arranged that their words could be read (in Greek): *Iesous Chreistos Theou Uios Soter,* "Jesus Christ the Son of God the Saviour." The letters make the word *ichthys,* meaning fish. Though cryptic, this prophesy and her condemnation of false gods provide sufficient evidence for Augustine to suggest her as a member of the city of God: "Moreover, this . . . Sibyl is far from admitting anywhere in her whole poem, of which this is only a very small part, any reference to the worship of false or fabricated gods; on the contrary, she even inveighs so strongly against them and against their worshipers that she seems dignified to be counted *(deputanda)* among the number who belong to the city of God" (*CD* 18.23). Augustine's praise of the Sibyl is distinguished from his criticisms of the poets *(poetae)* or *theologi,* such as Orpheus, who "if . . . among their many vain falsehoods sang at all of the one true God, they certainly did not serve Him truly when they worshiped along with Him others who are not gods, and offered to these the service that is due to the one God alone" (*CD* 18.14).

Augustine goes so far as to include members of the city of God within Babylon, the city normally associated with the city of man. He notes that Nineveh was founded in the Assyrian kingdom, was named after Ninus (*CD* 16.3), and was founded by Assur, the son of Shem, Noah's son, whose line represented the city of God. Augustine states that "[h]ence it is clear that men of Shem's line later occupied the kingdom [Babylon] of that mighty one [Nimrod, the giant] and went forth from it to found other cities, the first of which was named Nineveh after Ninus." Yet, later in the city's history, the sinful people of Nineveh were judged by God, repented, and were saved. Augustine quotes from Matt. 12:41: "The men of Nineveh shall rise in the judgment with this generation and shall condemn it, because they repented at the preaching of Jonah" (*CD* 20.5;

see also *CD* 21.18, 21.24, *Ep.* 162.1.2). This statement indicates that one can find inhabitants of the city of God outside its institutional representative, and even in the "official" city of man, Babylon. As Augustine observes elsewhere, "Wherefore, even though there is no explicit statement that there was any godly race of men at the same time when Babylon was founded by the wicked, this obscurity is not so great as to frustrate, but only to exercise, the ingenuity of any who investigate the question" (*CD* 16.11). It shows, as Van Oort observes, that "Augustine can, in an apologetic form, demonstrate universality, already present before the coming of Christ, of the Christian doctrine of salvation."[15]

Augustine argues that the city of God exists outside Israel because he does not consider the genealogical account of the city of God that he and Scripture present as exclusively historical. He explains the reason that Scripture does not list all members of the city of God after the Flood:

> From the blessing of the two sons of Noah [Japheth and Shem], down to Abraham, or for more than a thousand years, there is, as I have said no mention of any just human beings who duly worshiped God. I cannot bring myself to believe that none such existed, but if all were recorded the tale would be too long, and would exemplify diligent historical research rather than prophetic providence. Consequently, the writer of these sacred Scriptures, or rather the spirit of God working through him, deals not only with the narrative of past events but also with the forecast of things to come, though only in so far as they concern the city of God, for whatever is here said of those also who are not citizens of that city is said to the end that the city may gain profit or distinction by contrast with its opposite. (*CD* 16.2; see also 15.8, 15.15, 16.1, 18.1)

The purpose of Scripture as analogical rather than strictly historical leads Augustine to believe that members of the city of God would have existed outside the biblical narrative. The purpose of the scriptural narrative is to display the sharpest distinction between virtue and vice so that virtue can shine out in its clearest form.

## The Soul as the Image of God

Augustine understood the soul as the image of God, which provides the basis for his view that virtue depends on wisdom and ordinate loving: "We too as a matter of fact recognize in ourselves an image of God. . . . Yet it is nearer

---

15. Van Oort, *Jerusalem and Babylon*, 99.

to Him in the scale of nature than any other thing created by him, although it still requires to be reformed and perfected in order to be nearest to Him in its likeness to Him *(adhuc reformatione perficiendam ut sit etiam similitudine proxima)"* (*CD* 11.26; see also *DT* 4.18.24).[16] The acquisition of virtue requires the exercise of the soul:

> God himself, therefore, gave a mind *(mentem)* to the human soul *(animae humanae)*. In the infant, reason and intelligence *(ratio et intelligentia)* somehow slumber, as if non-existent, but are ready to be exercised *(excitanda)* and developed *(exerenda)* with the increase of age, so as to become capable of knowing *(scientiae)* and learning *(doctrinae)*, and competent to perceive truth and love the good *(et habilis perceptioni vertitatis et amoris boni)*. Thanks to these capacities it may imbibe wisdom and be endowed with the virtues so as to struggle with prudence, fortitude, temperance, and justice against errors and other inborn vices, and conquer them by desiring nothing except that supreme, immutable Good *(nisi boni . . . summi)*. (*CD* 22.24)

For Augustine, the exercise of the soul in the life of virtue teaches us to love the good. Loving the good entails not only right desire but also the intellectual virtues of wisdom, knowledge, and prudence.

According to Augustine, the soul is the image of God because it reflects the Trinity. Although only Scripture reveals God as triune, Augustine also thought we can understand ourselves as the image of God (although not as triune) through "natural" reason. This presupposes that, for him, "nature" is a category. "Natural" reason is generally considered more of a Scholastic term than one used by Augustine because, as noted above, he does not utilize the categories of "natural" and "supernatural" since he regarded all of God's action as "natural."[17] Be that as it may, he equates *natura* with the Greek *physis*, which constitutes the first division of philosophy for Plato (*CD* 8.6, 8.10). Natural philosophy examines the first principle of things, which God revealed through created

---

16. A fuller account of Augustine's formulation of how the soul becomes and becomes conscious of itself as the image of God would require a detailed study of his discussion of this process in *On the Trinity*. My purpose here is simply to outline how Augustine considers the soul's formation as the image of God through the love of neighbor and through the intellectual virtues. See Lewis Ayres, "Between Athens and Jerusalem: Prolegomena to Anthropology in *De Trinitate*" and "The Discipline of Self-Knowledge in Augustine's *De Trinitate* Book X"; see also the Introduction for citations to Williams, Crosson, and Milbank (n. 3). Their work is significant because it challenges the traditional view that Augustine offers an individualistic account of the Trinity. Rather, his view of the Trinity indicates that human beings are social.

17. This is not to say that Scholastics disagreed with Augustine's formulation. For instance, Saint Thomas Aquinas cites Augustine to argue that nature is a form of grace (*Summa Theologiae* 1–2.109.1).

things. Furthermore, Augustine speaks of natural aptitude *(natura ingenius)*, which is studied by natural philosophy *(CD* 11.25), and speaks of natural objects that "when they are where they should be according to the order of their nature, they tend to their own being *(suum esse custodiunt)* according to the measure in which they received it" *(CD* 12.5). This is not to say that nature is self-sufficient and that one who knows and loves God according to nature is self-sufficient and not needy. Rather, for Augustine, understanding the nature of something and acting according to nature is to acknowledge that created things glorify their maker, that is, it is the nature of a thing to glorify that which made it *(CD* 12.4). The natural end of a human being is, therefore, to glorify, to know and give praise (as Augustine defined glory) to its maker. This is the natural end of the intellect and the will. One can then speak of natural reason as a capacity that can fulfill its purpose by its own capability, even though it is created and God indirectly brings it to completion.

According to Augustine, the soul is the image of God because we exist, we know that we exist, and we delight in our being and in our knowledge *(CD* 11.26–28). These three acts intimate the Trinity, but they also provide the basis for a natural understanding and intimate the characteristics of the fully self-conscious image of God. They provide this basis by giving us unmistakable and immediate certainty of our being, our certain knowledge that we exist, and our love of both. Augustine argues that these three acts are certain; one cannot be mistaken about one's existence because one still exists and knows by being mistaken (and by hating being mistaken), and because even the miserable seek self-preservation *(CD* 11.26). The three acts form the possibility of natural virtue because their incompleteness forces human beings to question their being, and because the certainty of these three intimates the goal of that questioning. Reflecting on them means that human beings cannot deny that they are needy and dependent beings who require others to assist them in bringing themselves to completion: "If . . . our natural being *(natura nostra)* originated in ourselves, it follows that we should have generated our own wisdom too and should not take pains to acquire it by instruction *(doctrina)*, that is, by learning it from some other source. Our love *(amor)* too, proceeding from ourselves and returning to ourselves, would not only be sufficient to provide a happy life but would have not need of any other enjoyment" *(CD* 11.25). The inclination of human beings to seek instruction and to love indicates that they acknowledge that their being does not originate in them, and leads them to seek the highest cause of their being. Since they are dependent beings, they must love and learn from others and, ultimately, God to fulfill their being. This completion is also intimated in the immediate perception of their being, their knowledge of their being, and their delight in both. This leads Augustine to argue that it is necessary for human beings to ask for the assistance of others and, ultimately he would say, of God.

Human beings' initial move after perception of their being, their knowledge, and their love is to seek the reasons for them, because the mind itself is predisposed to ask them:

> But because it was fitting that three great highest truths regarding the creature be intimated to us *(Quia vero tria quaedam maxime scienda de creatura nobis oportuit intimari)*, namely who made it, by what means, and why, Scripture says: "God said, 'Let there be light'; and there was light. And God saw that the light was good." So if we ask: "Who made it?" the answer is: "It was God." If we ask: "By what means?" the answer is: "God said, 'Let it be'; and it was." If we ask: "Why?" the answer is: "Because it is good." (*CD* 11.21)

Human beings ask, "whence comes it *(unde sit)*?" "whence comes its wisdom *(unde sit sapiens)*?" and "whence comes happiness (*undi sit felix*)?" (*CD* 11.24). Although Scripture makes a threefold response that God made it, that God gives it light, and that happiness consists in enjoying God (thus turning the impersonal question into the personal "who *[quis]* made it?"), the mind naturally asks these questions based on its perception of its own being. These three questions disclose the three divisions of philosophy that Augustine credits Plato with discovering: natural philosophy, rational philosophy or logic, and ethics or morals (*CD* 11.25, 8.6–8). The first science inquires into natural causation, the second inquires into the method or form of science *(scientiae formam)*, and the third inquires into the good life and proper use *(propter usum)* (*CD* 11.25). This threefold division intimates the Trinity, although it does not discover the nature of the Trinity: natural philosophy intimates God the Father as Maker; logic intimates the Son as Logos; and ethics intimates the Holy Spirit who reveals that God made creation by his word so it might be good. Thus, Augustine states that human beings made in the image of God can detect God's "footprints *(vestigia)*" in creation: "[T]herefore, let us gather up *(colligamus)*, as it were, the footprints that he left, deeply impressed in one place, more lightly in another, since they could not so much as exist, or be contained in any shape, or follow and observe any law, had they not been made by Him who supremely is, and is supremely good and supremely wise" (*CD* 11.28).

Augustine's view that the Trinity is intimated in creation constitutes part of the basis for a natural understanding of the soul as the image of God, although the soul cannot understand God as triune: "But if the divine goodness is nothing else than the divine holiness, then certainly it is a diligent use of reason *(diligentia rationis)*, not presumptuous audacity, that makes us see in the work of God, in the secret manner of speaking *(secreto . . . loquendi modo)* by which our mind's intention is exercised *(exerceatur)*, how the trinity is insinuated *(insinuata)* to our intelligence when it is written who made each creature, how did he make it, and why did he make it?" *(CD* 11.24). He comments on God's statement that creation is good: "And if we are right in understanding that this goodness is the Holy Spirit, then the whole Trinity is intimated *(intimatur)* to us in the works *(operibus)* of creation" *(CD* 11.24). The intellect can recognize creation as good: "[T]here cannot exist a nature in which there is no good" *(CD* 19.13). As noted above, this is also seen in Augustine's acknowledgment that Plato was a lover of God because he loved wisdom *(CD* 8.8) and could recognize that God's simplicity necessitates that he is also good.

Augustine uses the terms *insinuare* and *intimare* to signify God's indirect way of communicating the Trinity through creation *(CD* 11.24, quoted above). God insinuates the Trinity to exercise the intellect so that it can become the self-conscious image of God. As seen above, *insinuare* signifies indirect communication or hinting something in order to arouse interest and investigation. Elsewhere, Augustine contrasts God's open declarations with his insinuation when he explains the use of bodily images to signify incorporeal beings *(CD* 13.23–24, 15.25). He also states that the lineages of Cain and Abel represent or insinuate the two cities of God and of man *(CD* 15.15, 15.20). As shown in Chapter 2, Augustine uses the term to signify the way God used the art of shepherding to teach human beings that they are lords over the animal kingdom but that human government differs in kind *(CD* 19.15). His use of this term signifies the way that nature both stimulates inquiry and signifies truth. Insinuation is superior to open declarations because insinuation exercises the mind so the mind can seek its perfection.

Augustine's way of phrasing this stimulation and exercise indicates that God intends human beings to become the image of God through the exercise of reason and will, and not exclusively through obedience. Augustine explains that God prefers to insinuate rather than to declare openly because open declarations do not necessitate the exercise of the intellect. This indicates that an inquiry into the reasons something is insinuated is the most appropriate response. If we relate this to politics, it means that political and ecclesiastical authority best perform their functions when they encourage people who inquire into the reasons for things. This indicates the need for open and deliberative political processes in which the common good is approached indirectly, that is, through forms in which citizens act freely and rationally.

Augustine's reflections on the soul as the image of God show that it seeks its natural perfection by reflecting upon its nature as the image of God and by loving and knowing God, not yet as triune (which requires Scripture), but as the source of its being, the source of its wisdom, and the source of the good life. This perfection is not that due to redemptive or subsequent grace, but, rather, that attainable by preceding grace. The self-conscious intellect understands creation to the point at which one understands that the things of the world did not make themselves, but that they proclaim: "[W]e are not God, but He made us" (*Conf.* 10.6) and "He is to be praised when we contemplate all the natures which he has made" (*CD* 12.5). To be sure, this "natural" wisdom is not perfect happiness, which is not attainable by human effort alone; similarly, this praise and contemplation approach blessedness, but are not blessedness itself. Although Augustine affirms the greatness of philosophy, he cautions that, at its highest achievement, it can be tempted to think that it is perfect happiness: "Such is the salvation which, in the world to come, will also itself be our final happiness. Yet these philosophers will not believe in this happiness because they do not see it. Thus, they endeavor to contrive an entirely false happiness, by means of a virtue which is as false as it is proud" (*CD* 19.4). Augustine's understanding of "natural" wisdom is that held by those such as Plato, whom Augustine praises for seeing that philosophy aims at the happy life even though it cannot obtain it eternally (*CD* 8.8). I turn now to show how Augustine fills in the space between the three things of which human beings are certain, and the perfection of the human being. He thought that knowing God through creation, and loving God through loving one's neighbor, exercises the soul to become virtuous.

### The Virtuous Human Being as Partaker in Creation

Augustine considered the intellectually and morally virtuous human being as the analogue of the providential God. Because knowledge is only one part of action, it will be shown that Augustine also understood the virtuous human being's action as the effective cause of creation. This enables us to comprehend his understanding of statesmanship better. This section examines Augustine's presentation of the intellect as the image of God in his account of creation in book 11 of *City of God*. It shows how Augustine attempted to harmonize the activity of the intellect and its cognition of the world with the vision of God.[18]

---

18. The argument is based on the view that *scientia* for Augustine is the knowledge of the interconnections of creation, and is as such equivalent to Aristotle's *episteme*. For instance, Crosson

One is just (and wise) when one understands and praises God through his creation. Augustine states that human beings know justice by viewing the just human being, just as human beings know mathematical figures by their physical representations: "For there is a great difference between knowing a thing in the design in conformity to which it was made, and knowing it in itself—e.g., the straightness of lines and correctness of figures is known in one way when mentally conceived, in another way when described on paper; and justice is known in one way in the unchangeable truth *(in veritate incommutabili)*, in another in the soul of a just human being *(in anima iusti)*" (*CD* 11.29). The soul of the just human being reflects perfect justice just as a mathematical figure reflects the mathematical object itself. Elsewhere, Augustine observes that such a just human being attempts to act according to what he contemplates: "He does this so that his mind may engage to some degree in contemplation, and so that he may in some degree act according to such contemplation, thereby displaying that ordered agreement of thought and action which, as we have said, constitutes the peace of the rational soul" (*CD* 19.14). The prudent human being attempts to act according to the truth discovered by contemplation. Augustine's analogy between the mathematical figure and the soul of the just human being may seem misleading, however, because it appears to overlook the distinction that mathematical figures are constant, whereas the soul of the just human being and its actions are variable. Mathematical figures and fires are identical in Athens and Persia, but just human beings differ from place to place and time to time.

Augustine's apparent oversight is corrected, however, by his subsequent description of God's creation, which also includes his creation through the souls of human beings. Augustine uses his allegorical description of creation to illustrate how one can understand justice through the soul of the just human being. Augustine presents this argument in the form of a description of the creation account in Genesis, which is also an allegory of the unfolding of human knowledge of God (*CD* 11.7, 11.9, 11.30–31; *Conf.* 11–13; *DGL*).[19] The six days

states of Augustine's *On the Teacher*: "The firmness of *scientam*, which is the terminus of inquiry, rests upon the fact that the judgment arrived at is not isolated. It is very important to stress that for Augustine *scientiam* does not come about simply by some inner light illuminating an intelligible object. That would be a simplistic picture, and a misleading one. Rather, his conception of firmly grounded knowledge, like that of Aristotle's *episteme*, requires that the interconnections of judgments be seen, that the entailments and reasons become visible. And for that, discursive ratiocination is required, which the dialogue exemplifies" ("Show and Tell," 59). Crosson observes that Augustine's understanding of *scientia* is based on his understanding of *cogito* as collecting together different parts to provide a synthetic account of the whole (*Conf.* 10.11).

19. He elsewhere describes the mind's ascent to self-knowledge in God as a process of the mind's "unfolding *(evolvere)*" (*DT* 9.4.5).

of creation are an allegory for the perfection of creation. Creation took six days because six is a perfect number composed of its own parts (the sum of one, two, and three is six) and is thus complete because it fully reflects how God "has ordered all things in number, and measure, and weight" (CD 11.30, quoting Wisd. of Sol. 11:21). His description of the mind's understanding of the six days of creation is an allegory for the mind's increasing understanding of the perfection of creation, and also as an allegory for the constitution of the soul as the image of God.

Augustine states that one cannot fully know specific parts of creation without knowing the whole: "We must note that the knowledge of creatures when contemplated by themselves (in se ipsa) is more colorless (decoloratior), so to speak, in comparison with their brilliance when seen in the realm of God's wisdom, and, as it were, in the design according to which they were made" (CD 11.7). Within the context of the Genesis story, knowledge of creatures is called "decolored" or shadowy because one cannot fully know them without knowing the whole, God and creation, in which they reside. Augustine uses the allegory of knowledge of God as day (or, rather, dawn) to describe the process of education:

> [N]ight in its course becomes morning again when the creature returns to praise and love of the Creator. And when the creature does this in knowledge of itself (in cognitione sui ipsius), that is one day; but when it does so in knowledge (in cognitione) of the firmament which, lying between the lower and the upper waters, was called heaven, it is the second day. When it does so with the knowledge (in cognitione) of the earth, the sea, and all things that come to life from the earth and are bound to earth by their roots, it is the third day; when it does so with knowledge (in cognitione) of the greater and lesser luminaries and all the stars, it is the fourth day; when it does so in knowledge (in cognitione) of all living things that swim in the waters and of all that fly, it is the fifth day; and when it does so in knowledge (in cognitione) of every beast of the earth and of man himself (atque ipsius hominis), it is the sixth day. (CD 11.7)

The soul that grows as the image of God becomes more illuminated, and it views creation in this light. Augustine uses Platonic illumination imagery to signify the constitution of the intellect as the image of God (see CD 10.2). This passage indicates that one knows oneself or recognizes oneself as part of the whole, and as distinct from other parts of creation, when one has collected together (the literal meaning of cogitatio [Conf. 10.11]) knowledge of creation. Wisdom depends on the dialectic collecting-together of the parts of the whole, God's footprints, which culminates in the knowledge that God created them.

Wisdom is the knowledge that each part of creation is not its own cause and that each part of creation is a sign of God that proclaims: "We are not God, and He made us" (*Conf.* 10.6). Augustine describes this meditation in intellectual and moral terms: "It is a great and very unusual thing for man, after he has contemplated all creation, corporeal and incorporeal, and found it to be subject to change, to pass beyond it by concentrated thought *(intentione mentis)* and so to arrive at the unchangeable substance *(incommutabilem . . . substantiam)* of God, and there to learn from God Himself that all nature that is not identical with Himself *(quae non est quod ipse)* has been made by none other than He" (*CD* 11.2). This passage describes the process of coming to understand that creation depends on the ground of being. At this point, the activity of the intellect and the will is praise and adoration: "Yet, when these works are referred to the praise and adoration *(Creatoris laudem venerationemque referuntur)* of the Creator Himself, it is as if morning dawned in the minds of those who contemplate them" (*CD* 11.29).

The soul is fully conscious of being made in the image of God when it arrives "at the unchangeable substance" (*CD* 11.2). Wisdom of this kind is important for political theory today because, as articulated by premoderns in the Socratic tradition, it has come under scrutiny as the source of the enframing and objectifying type of metaphysics that has generated modern technology.[20] Its primary danger resides in its tendency to justify coercive, technological regimes, a category into which twentieth-century totalitarian regimes fall, because it convinces people that their perfect wisdom can create a perfect society. Heidegger, for instance, argues that metaphysics, which leads to technology, must be supplemented or replaced by a kind of listening or "letting be" (*Gelassenheit,* a term Heidegger borrowed from the medieval German mystic Meister Eckhardt) by which Being is allowed to appear.[21] This Augustinian

20. Most notably by Martin Heidegger. See his analysis of the Aristotelian and Platonic treatments of causation, *telos,* and revealing ("Question Concerning Technology," 290–95). He instead characterizes thinking as *Holzwege,* likening it to wandering through the forest in directions yet untrodden.

21. Heidegger identifies the poetic as that which "brings the true into the splendor of . . . that which shines forth most purely" (ibid., 316; see also, "Letter on Humanism," in *Basic Writings,* ed. David Farrell Krell). Leslie Paul Thiele compares Heidegger's understanding of freedom or "letting-be" with Augustine's understanding of freedom in being unable to sin (which, for Augustine, would occur only in beatific vision [*CD* 22.30]) ("Heidegger on Freedom: Political Not Metaphysical," 284). George Parkin Grant, from a Platonic-Christian perspective, also observes the need for this listening and silencing of oneself as the means to transcend technological rationality (see *Technology and Justice,* 48–49). Like Augustine but unlike Heidegger, however, he sharply distinguishes between poetic splendor and sanctity. Augustine's metaphysics, often interpreted as dualistic, is often seen as a stumbling block to scholars seeking to affirm the "world" as the home or goal for human beings

notion of wisdom and love of God is also important today because criticisms of "monotheism" echo Heidegger's critique of premodern rationality by arguing that having one god beyond the others necessarily leads to dogmatism and fails to reflect the ambiguities of Being found in a polytheism.

Although space prevents anything more than an outline of this problem, Augustine's description of the understanding and love of the world and of God in a key passage in his *Confessions* provides evidence that he foresaw the difficulty of reducing wisdom to art and to "objective knowledge" while recognizing the necessity of being able to give an account of creation based on the activity of *cogitatio.* This spiritual experience of dying to the ambitions of the world (as it is often presented) would then avoid the tendency to impose a coercive regime (see Chapter 7 on Augustine's own strategy for dealing with heretics).

The relationship between the knowledge of creation and experiencing God is presented in Augustine's description of the Vision at Ostia shared by him and his mother: "[W]e relinquished there the first fruits of our spirits *(religatas primitias spiritus)*" *(Conf.* 9.10). The "first fruits" consist of the dedication of their love to God, just as he elsewhere speaks of tendering one's first fruits to philosophy *(CA* 3.4.7). The image of "first fruits" invokes ideas of sacrifice such as that offered by Abraham and reflects Augustine's view, explicated below, that external rituals such as sacrifice are signs of the activity of the virtuous soul *(CD* 10.3). He emphasizes the necessity of silencing one's self in order to "hear" the Word of God:

> If to any man the tumult of the flesh grew silent *(sileat)* . . . and the very soul *(anima)* grew silent to herself and by not thinking of itself mounted beyond itself *(et transeat se non se cogitando):* if all dreams and imagined visions grew silent, and every tongue and every sign and whatsoever is transient—for indeed if any man could hear them, he should hear them saying with one voice: We did not make ourselves, but He made us who abides forever: but if, having uttered this and so set us to listening to Him who made them, they all grew silent, and in their silence He alone spoke to us, not by them but by Himself: so that we should hear His word, not by any tongue of flesh nor the voice of an angel nor the sound of thunder nor in the darkness of a parable, but that we should hear Himself whom in all these things we love, should hear Himself and not them. *(Conf.* 9.10; see also the priority he places on hearing in *Conf.* 10.27)

---

for whom modernity has transformed the world into an alien, hostile place. On this question, a fruitful interpretation is offered by John Milbank who, with some irony, goes so far as to attribute "hints . . . of a monistic ontology underlying his apparent dualism" to Augustine, which anticipate the Heideggerian critique ("Sacred Triads," 465, 473 n. 59).

This is a description of meditation in which the soul focuses its attention on God, who is beyond one's self-assertions or attempts to model the truth of God on worldly objects (see also *Conf.* 7.1; *DT* 10.7.10).[22] The soul simultaneously lets slip away the things of the world while knowing the structure of creation, in order to focus its attention on the God that made the world. This description of "hearing" God's word, like Augustine's famous description of his conversion after hearing the voice of a child, cannot be reduced to vulgar claims that God uses dreams or audible signs to command human beings to perform unnatural and otherwise vicious deeds. Rather, such hearing and listening reflects the general narrative of the *Confessions*, in which Augustine states that God uses creation to bring human beings to him according to their own understanding. The experience of the divine is necessarily consistent with understanding of creation, and does not derail into mystical ecstasy.

Such wisdom forms the basis of the action of the just human being who is the analogue of the providential God. As seen above, the just human being wishes to harmonize his action with his contemplation. Augustine indicates elsewhere that the being of human beings is that of the days of creation. For instance, he states: "We ourselves shall become *(nos ipsi erimus)* the seventh day, when we have been filled up and made new by His blessing and sanctification" (*CD* 22.30). Human beings do not merely know and do not merely participate in the seventh day: analogously, they become it. He makes a similar point when he states that, on the seventh day of creation, "God's rest signifies the rest of those who rest in God," and God's creation signifies the activity of his rational creatures (*CD* 11.8). Perhaps concerned that readers might think that God has human properties, Augustine argues that Scripture signifies God's actions indirectly, by signifying his actions by their effects:

> as when a letter is said to be joyful because it makes those who read it joyful. Most appropriately, therefore, when prophetic authority tells us that God rested, it signifies by this that those rest who are in Him, and whom He causes to rest. And the prophecy also promises the men to whom it speaks, and for whose sake it was written, that they themselves, after those good works which God performs in them and through them *(in eis et per eos)*, shall have eternal rest in Him if they have first drawn near to Him in this life by faith. (*CD* 11.8)

---

22. See also T. J. van Bavel, O.S.A., "God in between Affirmation and Negation according to Augustine," 84–85. For evidence of a negative theology in Augustine, see Vladimir Lossky, "Les éléments de 'Théologie négative.' "

The narrative of the six days of creation, therefore, symbolizes God's creation, human beings' cognition of creation, and the "good works which God performs in them and by them." As God's greatest creation, human beings take in all parts of creation, which is indicated by Augustine with reference to Adam's creation on the sixth day, and his view that human beings can possess a kind of "first-day" knowledge of creation. Furthermore, by stating that God performs good works "through them," Augustine indicates that human beings are effective agents of his creation, as seen in the discussion of the just human being in Chapter 4 (see *DT* 3.3.8; *CD* 1.21). To be sure, the action of human beings differs from that of God because human beings constitute an effective cause, not the formal or final cause of creation. Human action is bounded by God's action, which appears variable to human beings but follows his constant eternal plan (*CD* 12.18). Prudent human activity compares with that of God's creation, however, insofar as both may appear variable according to varying circumstance; however, they are both in accord with the single purpose of cultivating the love of God and of neighbor, as Chapter 4 showed.

### Love of Neighbor

The question that remains is whether this fully self-reflective image of God, this *lex animata,* can love his or her neighbor. One of the difficulties in interpreting Augustine's political thought has been in determining how his "otherworldliness" harmonizes with the command to love one's neighbor. As observed above, Hannah Arendt concluded that one's neighbor is nothing more than an occasion for one's love. Claiming that only God is to be enjoyed *(fruor),* Augustine thought that the things of the world, which include neighbors, are to be used *(utor).* Neighbors can at best be used only instrumentally for one's pilgrimage to the celestial city of God.[23] This section challenges this interpretation by showing that Augustine considered proper use as noninstrumental and that the love of neighbor is consistent with the classical understanding of friendship where friends are seen as another self.

For Augustine, the two commandments to love God and one's neighbor entail bringing one's neighbor and being brought by one's neighbor to virtue:

---

23. See Oliver O'Donovan, "*Usus* and *Fruitio* in Augustine, *De Doctrina Christiana* I," 396–97. On the other hand, Milbank points out that "[i]n the *Civitas Dei,* where 'fruition' evidently includes a social dimension, it is much clearer that nothing is merely used, but, being used rightly, is also enjoyed" (*Theology and Social Theory,* 421; see also Elshtain, *Limits of Politics,* 101–5).

To love this good with all our hearts, with all our souls, and with all our strength, is what we are enjoined to do. Toward this good it is our due to be led by those who love us and our duty to lead those whom we love. In this way those two commandments are fulfilled on which depend all the law and the prophets: "You shall love the Lord your God with all your heart, and with all your soul, and with all your mind" and "You shall love your neighbor as yourself." . . . So when the man who now knows how to love himself is commanded to love his neighbor as himself, what does this mean but that, as far as he can, he is to commend his neighbor to love God. This is the worship of God *(Dei cultus)*, this is the true religion *(vera religio)*, this is genuine piety *(recta pietas)*, this is the service *(servitus)* due to God. (*CD* 10.3)

Augustine here equates the true religion with the cultivation of one's own love of God and with the cultivation of the love of God in one's neighbor. This is understood as a characteristic of human nature, which, as seen in Adam, is made to live together with other humans and in a multiplicity of relationships (*CD* 15.16; see Chapter 2).

The social nature of human beings is reflected in the soul as constituted as the image of God: "We have yet to speak of the love wherewith they are loved, to determine whether this love itself is loved. And doubtless it is; and this is the proof. Because in men who are justly loved, it is rather love itself that is loved; for he is not justly called a good man who knows what is good, but who loves it. Is it not then obvious that we love in ourselves the very love wherewith we love whatever love we love?" (*CD* 11.28). At first glance, this passage appears to support the view that Augustine reduces relations with one's neighbors to mere use. The human being appears merely as the accidental container and only an occasion for love. This first interpretation, however, is insufficient. Augustine states in this passage that the lover experiences a communion of love with his or her beloved in the love that they share. They share and are constituted by the love that is present to both of them, because loving someone or something entails becoming like the object of that love (see *DVR* 39.72; *DO* 2.18.48). They do not share this love as a kind of third object, like two people share a bench in the park, for example. Rather, they share this love as something that constitutes each; Augustine states that human beings love the love in another that also constitutes themselves. The way that this love is shared and experienced is seen more clearly in his description of how one with ordinate love "uses" his or her neighbor.

Augustine's understanding of the love of neighbor can be illuminated by examining his understanding of how individuals use and enjoy things in general. The evidence is drawn from his systematic account in *On Christian Teaching*. O'Donovan has argued that Augustine dropped using the pair of *usus-fruitio* after this treatise, and turned in later writings to love of neighbor as enjoyment, because he could not articulate a way of signifying love of neighbor in terms of *usus*.[24] Be that as it may, Augustine still had to deal with the problem of reconciling the love of God and of neighbor, and of avoiding having to treat neighbors instrumentally. By returning to *On Christian Teaching*, one can see how Augustine could articulate the love of neighbor in terms of noninstrumental *usus* by showing that he thought virtuous human beings can imitate God's use of human beings. Augustine bases this imitation not on the unattainable goal of foregoing one's advantage (for God loves without regard to his advantage), but on the priority human beings place on the good of another (as God "uses" human beings for their good).

*Usus* and *fruitio* are two basic categories used by Augustine to describe the relationship of human beings and things: "To enjoy something is to cling *(inhaerere)* to it in love for its own sake *(propter se ipsam)*. To use something is to refer *(referre)* whatever it may be to the purpose of obtaining *(obtinere)* what you love—if indeed it is something that ought to be loved. (The improper use of something should be termed abuse)" (*DDC* 1.8). In his subsequent discussion, he emphasizes that only God is to be enjoyed for his own sake, and neighbors, therefore, can be only used (although he strives to reconcile the "use" of neighbors with loving them). He describes our pilgrimage through life as a journey where God is our destination. Enjoying a neighbor would be equivalent to distracting us and preventing us from reaching our destination.

Before turning to the problem of how Augustine strives to reconcile use with loving one's neighbor, it is necessary to consider his choice of terms to define *usus* and *fruitio*. One enjoys something for one's own sake by clinging *(inhaerere)* to it. *Inhaerere*, like *cohaerere*, means clinging or cleaving, and Augustine generally reserves the term for the love of God, because it signifies the condition of utter dependency on the object of one's clinging (*CD* 8.10, 10.3, 10.5, 10.6). This is reflected in his statement that "you enjoy the one by whom you are made happy" (*DDC* 1.79). Thus, it is better to cling to the unchangeable truth than to malleable earthly goods (*CD* 1.10) and demons (*CD* 6.4); similarly, Augustine signifies the obsequious courtiers of Theodosius as those who cling (*CD* 5.26). This being the case, he confesses to God: "You glue *(agglutinas)* [friendship] between souls that cleave *(haerentes)* together through that charity which is shed in our hearts by the Holy Spirit" (*Conf.* 4.4). However, in this passage Augustine

24. O'Donovan, "*Usus* and *Fruitio*," 363, 397.

is careful to clarify that the Holy Spirit constitutes the transcendent bond that glues friends together. He emphasizes the transcendent element of friendship because he saw that friends are tempted to love each other as one loves God, as if one's friend will not die (*Conf.* 4.5, 4.8), as another self on account of whom, when he dies, one feels literally that oneself has died (*Conf.* 4.6). This constitutes inordinate love. As with the English "to cling," Augustine's Latin terminology signifies that clinging to earthly goods, including friends, is unseemly.

Augustine defines *usus* as the relationship between an individual and the object he wishes to obtain, which suggests an instrumental relationship, but, upon further examination, one that can be seen in terms not instrumental. For instance, *usus* is the term he uses to signify what has been translated into contemporary idiom as ethics and "practice" (*CD* 11.25; *DT* 10.11.17). This implies that the meaning of *usus* is closer to the old English notion of "usage" or "practice." *Obtinere* means obtaining one's goal, and Augustine speaks of how Romulus obtained his rule (*CD* 3.13) and how the apostles share things in common to obtain the company of angels (*CD* 5.18; see also 3.28, 5.19, 8.8, 10.32, 11.11, 11.25, 13.18, 14.3, 15.16). He also uses *obtinere* to signify how something comes into practice or usage; for example, he describes how the term *usus* itself is commonly used: "However, in the current expression which has obtained the sanction of custom *(obtinuit consuetudo)*, we both use fruits and enjoy practices *(fructibus utimur et usibus fruimur)*. For we quite properly [or literally] *(proprie)* speak of the fruits of the field, even though these are temporal things of which we all make use" (*CD* 11.25). Something that has been obtained is understood as something that receives usage. *Obtinere* in this sense reflects the Roman legal usage in which *obtinuit* refers to the reception of a legal principle into custom via jurists, judicial practice, and common usage.[25] It is synonymous with *placuit*, which was a phrase used by jurists to mean "in my opinion" (see Chapter 4). This meaning of *obtinere* indicates that it and *usus* are not merely instrumental because these customs, as Augustine's reference to language indicates, dictate practices in which people participate.

Augustine's comment that we both use fruits and enjoy practices (or uses) indicates that his strict distinction between the two in *On Christian Teaching* is not as strict as it might at first appear. He appears willing to speak of them either as distinct or as overlapping. His use of the double voice has puzzled scholars.[26] Closer examination of his understanding of *usus* and love of neighbor, however,

25. A. Berger, "Encyclopedic Dictionary," 606.

26. For instance, O'Donovan notes: "But why Augustine should prefer this loose mode of speech to the strict one we are left to guess" (*"Usus and Fruitio,"* 389).

shows that he intends his readers to understand that human beings are to model their "use" of neighbors on God's use of human beings and creation, which Augustine understands as caring. Before turning to this, however, it is worth noting that in the above quotation from the *City of God*, Augustine states that it is proper *(proprie)* for Latin speakers, even in common usage, to speak of enjoying in terms of using. In *On Christian Teaching*, he notes that mixing *usus* and *fruitio* like this is to speak in a loose (O'Donovan's translation) or transferred sense *(abusive)* rather than in a literal or proper *(proprie)* sense. In this treatise, Augustine appears to stress that the philosophical and proper way to understand these two terms is to distinguish between them, whereas the loose or transferred sense is to conflate them. This is not quite the case, however, as Augustine elsewhere points out that even common ways of speaking can be sophisticated, because those ways also use tropes such as the transferred or catachrestic way of speaking (*DDC* 3.89). Augustine uses the common grammarian example of the use of slightly inappropriate metaphors to signify similar objects, as when one refers to a swimming pool as a *piscina* even though it is not made for or does not contain fish. These tropes signify truths that cannot be communicated directly: "A knowledge of them is necessary for the resolution of ambiguities in scripture because when a meaning based on the literal interpretation of words is absurd we must investigate whether the passage that we cannot understand is perhaps being expressed by means of one or other of the tropes. This is how most hidden meanings have been discovered" (*DDC* 3.91). Augustine's understanding of a term with a transferred *(abusive)* meaning indicates that his mixture of *usus* and *fruitio* is not merely loose. Further examination indicates that, even though their strict distinction serves the philosophical purpose of distinguishing things that are enjoyed for their own sake and things that must be loved for the sake of God, the distinction also serves a rhetorical purpose. This in turn indicates that combining the two actually serves a higher philosophic purpose, despite Augustine's "loose" talk. Augustine admits of a philosophic way of understanding *usus* and *fruitio* as mixed.

Augustine combined his definitions of *usus* and *fruitio* because, he states, our use of our neighbor is to be modeled on God's use of us. In introducing this idea, he acknowledges an uncertainty in speaking of the dual love of God and neighbor in terms of *usus* and *fruitio* (*DDC* 1.73). He rejects the argument that God loves human beings by enjoying them, since that would mean that "He stands in need of our goodness" (*DDC* 1.74). Augustine rejects this idea on the ground that God is ontologically prior to human beings, just as a light is ontologically prior to that which it illuminates. According to Augustine, God does not need human beings (*CD* 10.5). This statement recalls his definition of enjoyment as an act of clinging (*inhaerere*). Human beings cling to God for their being, but God does not need human beings. Augustine thus concludes:

> So God does not enjoy us, but uses us (If he neither enjoys nor uses us, then I fail to see how he can love us at all). But he does not use us in the way that we use things; for we relate the things which we use to the aim of enjoying God's goodness, whereas God relates His use of us to his own goodness. We exist because he is good, and we are good to the extent that we exist. Moreover, because he is also just, we are not evil with impunity; if we are evil, to that extent we exist less. (*DDC* 1.74–75)

God's use of human beings consists in his being the cause of their being and goodness. God cannot be said to need human beings because his being is prior to that of human beings. Thus, from God's perspective, he uses human beings by creating and sustaining them through his superabundant mercy.

God's use of human beings is exercised solely out of God's goodness, which happens to be to human beings' advantage, and this leads Augustine to argue that the love of neighbor is analogous:

> So the kind of use attributed to God, that by which he uses us, is related not to his own advantage but solely to His goodness. If we pity someone or take thought for someone, we do so for that person's advantage, and we concentrate on that; but somehow (*quomodo*) there also results an advantage to us, since God does not let the compassion we show to the needy go unrewarded. This reward is the supreme reward—that we may thoroughly enjoy Him and that all of us who enjoy Him may enjoy one another in Him. (*DDC* 1.76)

Human beings model their love for each other on God's love for them. They love each other as themselves by concentrating on the advantage of others, in the same way that God loves human beings on account of his goodness rather than for his benefit. To be sure, human beings' love for one another differs, inasmuch as they, unlike God, are needy. However, Augustine indicates here that the love of neighbor is analogous to God's love for human beings by referring primarily to the concern for another's good before one's own. Only then does there "somehow (*quomodo*)" result an advantage to oneself. The *quomodo* in this statement is important because it signifies that an individual with ordinate love will experience his own benefit secondarily, perhaps as something that creeps in and surprises him unexpectedly, as the fruits of one's labor surprise one when one concentrates on the task at hand.

Augustine's way of modeling the use and love of neighbor on the use and love that God has for human beings can be seen as a middle position between strictly instrumental relations, on the one hand (where one always attends to one's own advantage), and inordinate love of one's neighbor (where one loves one's neighbor more than oneself and where one clings exclusively to one's neighbor), on the other hand. Ordinate love of one's neighbor, or proper use of one's neighbor, entails loving one's neighbor as oneself. This is achieved by modeling one's love for one's neighbor on God's love for and use of human beings. This analogy, therefore, enables Augustine to combine his meanings of *usus* and *fruitio*, when he states that "all of us who enjoy him may enjoy one another in him" (*DDC* 1.76; *CD* 19.13). Thus, he states that "the idea of enjoying someone or something is very close to that of using someone or something together with love" (*DDC* 1.79).

Certainly, Augustine emphasizes that human life is a journey that uses and engages in a transient love of things of this world. His emphasis on a strict distinction between *usus* and *fruitio* makes sense, however, because the philosophical sense of combining them requires that human beings become godlike, which tempts them to forget about their journey. Such people are few and far between; Augustine observes that one who can distinguish proper from improper *usus* and *fruitio* must be virtuous. Like the Aristotelian mature human being who is the measure of right and wrong, "[t]he person who lives a just and holy life is one who is a sound judge of these things. He is also a person who has ordered his love, so that he does not love what it is wrong to love, or fail to love what should be loved, or love too much what should be loved less, or love two things equally if one of them should be loved either less or more than the other, or love things either more or less if they should be loved equally" (*DDC* 1.59). The virtuous human being, then, is one who best judges what and how much to love.

How is such a human being to love his or her neighbor? In keeping with the commandment, all people are to be loved equally. Augustine is aware of classical and political objections to this view. The injunction to love others equally appears to undermine friendship and other particular loves, because it seems inconsistent with friendship to treat a longtime friend as one would treat an enemy or a stranger. Augustine's way of reconciling universal love with particular loves is treated more fully in the next section. A comment is in order, however, on how he saw the way human beings relate to one another when they are virtuous. Even though perfected love treats all people equally, one cannot do good to all people equally:

[S]o you should take particular thought for those who by the chance of place or time or anything else are, as if by lot *(quasi quadam sorte)*, in particularly close contact with you. Suppose that you had plenty of something which had to be given to someone in need of it but could not be given to two people, and you met two people, neither of whom had a greater need or a closer relationship to you than the other: you could do nothing more just than to choose by lot the person whom you should give what could not be given to both. Analogously, since you cannot take thought for all men, you must settle by lot in favor of the one who happens to be more closely associated *(adhaerere)* with you in temporal matters. *(DDC* 1.61–62)

According to this statement, human beings do not choose their neighbors or friends (or enemies for that matter). One loves one's neighbor by loving those in proximity, which defines them as neighbors *(proximi)* *(DDC* 1.68); their proximity is determined by lot, as it were. Augustine describes the basis of friendship this way to underscore the extent to which the identities of our friends and compatriots are due to causes beyond our control. For instance, one individual would be unlikely to form a friendship with another had they not attended the same university at the same time, or met by chance in a particular social situation. The randomness of one's choice of friends is seen when one considers the multiplicity of factors that can prevent individuals from meeting were they to make different choices at numerous points in their lives.

Particular love is preserved by defining one's neighbor who, by lot as it were, shares our particular time and place. Universal love is preserved by defining one's neighbor as one who, like oneself, deserves mercy *(DDC* 1.68). Augustine characterizes particular love when he argues that those in one's temporal and spatial proximity should be the primary recipients of one's mercy. People, therefore, do not become friends or compatriots by nature. Augustine's perspective compares with that of Plato and his noble lie that acknowledges citizenship as conventional. Augustine and Plato differ, however, in that Augustine requires everyone, including people dominated by base loves, to strive to love everyone equally. One who loves all others equally will do so because he or she has gained (or learned through Scripture) the perspective of God, as it were, which enables him to love human beings as himself—as beings whose end is to enjoy God and not to save as mere occasions of one's love on one's pilgrimage.

Augustine affirmed a right-by-nature understanding of love of neighbor, which is similar to the understanding that natural reason can have *(scientia)*. Certainly, he sounds different from Cicero who, in *De Finibus*, defines friendship as loving a friend for himself *(propter ipsum)*. However, closer inspection shows that their understandings of friendship are consistent with one another. Cicero himself, in *De Amicitia*, states that friendship is desirable, not because it is useful (an instrumental good), but rather because "its entire fruit *(fructus)* is in the love itself." Similarly, Cicero argues that one must love one's friend as oneself because that friend is, as it were, another self (Cicero's understanding of friendship appears to demand inordinate love, to require one to love a friend "as if he would never die" (see *Conf.* 4.5, 4.8), when he states that "since nature is unchangeable *(mutari non)*, therefore true friendships are sempiternal *(sempiternae)*."[27] Augustine appears to transfer Cicero's definition of friendship as loving another for himself exclusively to loving and enjoying God for his sake. Augustine further appears to argue that friends can be loved only ordinately, that is, as mortal beings but as beings we never wish to lose, when we believe that "he alone loses no one that is dear to him, if all are dear in God, who is never lost" (*Conf.* 4.9).

Cicero requires that friendship be a reflection of nature and that it strive to imitate nature's eternal being. This imitation, however, closely resembles Augustine's understanding that love of neighbor consists in imitating the love of God for human beings. Despite the appearance of inordinate love, Cicero's philosophical understanding of friendship would require that imitating nature includes acknowledging that friends are mortal and must be loved as such. His definition of friendship as sempiternal repeats his, and Augustine's, view that a city exists sempiternally (*CD* 22.6; see also Chapter 2). Friendship, like the city, is a kind of analogical or "virtual immortality" (Simon's term) or "cosmion" (Voegelin's term) in which humans achieve their natural perfections. Even so, friendship is "virtual" and an imperfect (at best) imitation that necessarily ends with death. Augustine notes that friendship, as a temporal good, contains an element of the tragic. He acknowledges that the classical philosophers knew this, citing Cicero's lamentations over the death of his daughter (*CD* 19.4). He notes that Cicero expressed these lamentations to the best of his abilities, but asks: "But what did 'the best of his ability' amount to?" Augustine notes of philosophers in general that they are tempted to believe themselves perfectly happy in this life, which, as in the case of the Stoics, usually means that they deny themselves affections such as enjoyment and grief. Such a denial is not evident in Cicero, as his lamentations indicate, and further, such a denial actually undermines friendship because it prevents anyone from enjoying friends and grieving over their deaths:

27. Cicero, *De Finibus Bonorum et Malorum* 2.24.78; *De Amicitia* 9.31, 21.80, 9.32.

Anyone who forbids such grief must forbid, if he can, all friendly conversation: he must prohibit or extinguish affection; he must with ruthless
disregard sever ties of all human companionship, or else stipulate that such
companionship must merely be made use of, without giving rise to any
delight of soul. But if this can in no way be done, how can the death of
one whose life has been sweet to us not bring us bitterness? For this is why
the grief of a heart which is not inhuman is like a kind of wound or ulcer,
healed by the application to it of our loving words of consolation. And
though healing takes place all the more quickly and easily when the soul is
well conditioned, we must not suppose that there is nothing at all to heal
in such a case. (CD 19.8)

This passage suggests three possible responses to the tragedy of friendship.
The first is to deny oneself friendship, which Augustine dismisses though
noting that it must be the position of one who thinks perfect happiness is
achievable in this life. The second is to acknowledge the tragedy of friendship
and to lament it, but not to seek adequate consolation for it. This appears
to be the position of classical philosophy, including that of Cicero who faced
the tragic human condition without succumbing to the problems of the first
position; his is the position of the classical philosopher who does not think
the love of wisdom simply overrides the love of neighbor. The final option is
to seek consolation, as Augustine does by having faith in God. For Augustine,
Christianity offers a resolution to the aporia of friendship as understood by
the classical philosophers. Friendship indeed is sempiternal and even eternal
when it is in God. His understanding of friendship and love of neighbor as
enjoyment in God, then, does not contradict the classical understanding, but
rather completes it by fulfilling its own requirement that it be sempiternal or
eternal. Augustine and Cicero do not disagree on the meaning of friendship,
but, rather, on how it is effected.

Augustine's other discussions of classical understandings and practices of
friendship can be seen in the light of this discussion. He acknowledges that
Plato loved his neighbors by writing dialogues to improve their morals (as seen
above). Pagan virtue is also seen in Augustine's recognition that Regulus could
sacrifice himself for his city and for virtue (see Chapter 5), which fulfills the
command to love God and one's neighbor.

The purpose of this section on the "prophetic" element of the love of God
and of neighbor has been to illuminate Augustine's view of the soul as the image
of God that is formed by loving God and loving one's neighbor. He thought
that one loves God by loving a multiplicity of neighbors. The intellect can know
God (though not as triune) through understanding creation. Augustine argued

that Platonic wisdom recognizes that being is the object of intellection and that the good is the object of love of the will. This means that the love of God and of neighbor depends on wisdom and ordinate loving. The existence of members of the city of God outside the sacramental order shows the extent to which Augustine considered this type of virtue "natural." Virtue, as ordinate loving, may be practiced outside the sacerdotal order. This has important political implications because it provides a natural ground, a midway point as it were, between the ends of politics and the ends of the Church where the footprints of God can be tracked. We turn now to consider how this "prophetic" aspect of the love of God becomes manifest in political practice.

## THE POLITICO-ECCLESIASTICAL PART OF ORDINATE LOVING

Previous chapters showed that Augustine considered virtue and political friendship as the ends of politics. This section expands on that discussion by focusing on the interdependent relationship between political and ecclesiastical ends. "Church" is used in its broad sense of *ecclesia*, which represents the worldwide communion of Christians, and that hoped for by those in Eastern, Roman, and Protestant communions. Whatever its form, it represents the city of God most explicitly, but it remains a mixture of virtuous and reprobate. That said, the "Church," and the current Churches, will always remain an institution led by fallible human beings with varying degrees of political prudence whose decisions in leading the Church(es) will both benefit and damage political life. Although interdependent, political society and *ecclesia* are permanently separate. The powers that reflect those ends also reflect the interdependent relationship of those ends. The Church administers the sacraments that fulfill the human being's natural longing for eternal happiness. The city, however, cannot fulfill this longing because its end is composed of temporal goods (such as material security and wealth) and goods that intimate the eternal (such as friendship and justice). This profound inability of the city to secure eternal happiness prevents one from seeking eternal happiness through political or ideological means. Nevertheless, the city possesses its own means to cultivate virtue and to prepare citizens to receive the sacraments. The argument of this section finds that the naturalness of politics necessitates an interdependent relationship between the city and the Church.[28] *Interdependent* here is used to

28. See E. A. Goerner, *Peter and Caesar.*

mean that each side's virtues supplement the other, and that each side checks the other at crucial interstices. This interpretation challenges the traditional view of Augustine's understanding—that he viewed political power as generally serving ecclesiastical power (if the two have anything to do with each other at all). However, Augustine states that governors are to "make their power a servant to the divine majesty, to spread the worship of God *(Dei cultum)* far and wide" (*CD* 5.24). Similarly, Augustine appears to restrict his praise of Constantine and Theodosius to the extent to which they practiced Christian piety. He praises Theodosius, for example, for submitting to the authority of Ambrose when he punished the Thessalonians after promising Ambrose he would treat their crimes leniently (*CD* 5.26). Yet, as shown below, Augustine also hints in this passage at an interdependent relationship between city and Church. Further, it was shown above that Augustine believed it is appropriate to adore and venerate virtuous human beings to testify to truth, indicating that politics has a religious dimension. Augustine does not think that politics directly serves the interests of the Church in securing human salvation. Instead, politics should cultivate the virtues that prepare human beings to love God and neighbor more fully. In this sense, politics serves a natural good. This natural good is manifest in various ways according to natural intelligence, just as the mind sees nature as the "footprints" of God as discussed above.

### *Exempla* of Virtue

Previous chapters showed that Augustine maintained that the Church and the political city serve as models of virtue for each other. This does not mean that he thought supernatural virtue or grace is deficient. Rather, because the cities of God and of man exist intermingled in the Church and in the political city, both need each other to be reminded of their respective insufficiencies in their pilgrim's existence. For instance, Augustine reminds Christians not to disdain political virtue: "[E]xamples are set before, containing necessary admonition, in order that we may be stung with shame if we shall see that we have not held fast those virtues for the sake of the most glorious city of God, which are, in whatever way, resembled by those virtues which they held fast for the sake of glory of a terrestrial city" (*CD* 5.18). In the same chapter he points out that the political city often demands greater sacrifices for its good than does the city of God. Similarly, he urges Romans to "awake more fully" their own virtues and see how they are completed in the city of God (*CD* 2.29). Augustine indicates that the political city and the Church should consider each other as models of virtue, because each will have an imperfect self-understanding in their pilgrimage through life, and each provides a model of virtue to supplement the other's shortcomings.

### The Function of the Church

This general understanding of the two orders as *exempla* for each other means that Augustine did not think the Church has absolute authority over the city. Rather, the Church and the city share a relationship of interdependence. This can be seen if we consider their respective functions. The Church is the place where human beings from all nations and backgrounds are invited to receive the sacraments. The sacraments are signs of the promise of eternal happiness, which only God can bestow. This function is necessary because human means, politics in particular, fall well short of securing eternal happiness. Further, this longing for eternal happiness is itself natural for Augustine, and so redemptive grace is understood as fulfilling the natural desire that nature requires but cannot complete by itself.

The Church, as the most explicit representation of the city of God, is the place where people, regardless of nationality, seek perfect happiness:

> While this heavenly city, therefore, goes its way as a stranger on earth, it summons citizens from all peoples, and gathers an alien society of all languages, caring naught what difference may be in mores, laws and institutions *(moribus legibus institutibusque)* by which earthly peace is gained or maintained, abolished and destroying nothing of the sort, nay rather preserving and following them (for however different they may be among different nations, they aim at one and the same end, earthly peace), provided that there is no hindrance to the religion that teaches the obligation to worship one most high and true God. (*CD* 19.17)

This passage indicates that the Church is the place where all nations—Greek, Jewish, Roman, and now American, Canadian, Indian, Chinese, African, and others—find their perfections through loving God. Ecclesiastical ends surpass political ends because the Church administers the sacraments for loving God, and its universality teaches human beings that their final end transcends their political end.

The worldwide communion that was foretold by the prophets and intimated by Israel is that which most explicitly represents the city of God. As such, its power to proclaim the gospel and to administer the sacrament must be free from absolute political and lay control. This would include the ability to excommunicate and even discipline political leaders, although this power is subject to restraint by the laity within each polity (as shown below). As is evident in the case of Israel, which most explicitly represents the city of God, the Christian Church(es) does not exhaust the representation of the city of God, as seen above. Augustine also allows for what is called "baptism of desire," according to which one's longing for God constitutes one's baptism (see below). Because institutional expression of the city of God does not exhaust its being, Augustine allows for different expressions of *latreia* in various contexts that do not undermine political association. The ability to express *latreia* differently means that a group (or groups) that cuts itself off from another group does not cut itself off from political association. Chapter 7 shows that this was one of the reasons Augustine took so long to assent to the use of political power to coerce the Donatist heretics. They had cut themselves off from Catholic communion about a hundred years before Augustine advocated coercion, and he advocated coercion to preserve the peace in a disintegrating empire rather than to impose orthodoxy.

Immediately following this statement on the use the heavenly city makes of the earthly city, Augustine gives the impression that the Church dominates the city and that they do not enjoy an interdependent relationship:

> Even the heavenly city, therefore, in this its pilgrimage makes use *(utitur)* of the earthly peace, and guards and seeks the merging of human wills in regard to the things that are useful for man's mortal nature, so far as sound piety and religion permit, and makes the earthly peace refer *(refert)* to the heavenly peace, which is so truly peace that it must be deemed and called the true *(vera)* peace, at least of a rational creature, being as it is, the best ordered and most harmonious fellowship in the enjoyment of God and of one another in God. (*CD* 19.17)

This passage appears to suggest that the Church, which represents the heavenly city, "makes use" of the political city, which secures earthly peace, in order to lead human beings to the true peace. This interpretation, however, misses a deeper meaning. It has already been shown that Augustine admits to the "intermingling" of the cities of God and of man, and that each representative is to consider the other as an *exemplum* of virtue. The previous discussion of *usus* also indicates that proper use is not merely instrumental. Furthermore, the previously quoted passage indicates that the Church will respect the particular ways in which each nation preserves civil peace, as long as worship is not hindered. This provides room for cities to cultivate these particular ways of virtue. Their ability to cultivate their own particular paths to virtue is rooted in Augustine's distinction between the prophetic and the institutional parts of virtue as ordinate loving.

Augustine's understanding of the relationship between the two orders can be seen in his nuanced and brief praise of Theodosius's penance, which was commanded by Ambrose after he punished the Thessalonians for their "abominable and grave" crime. Augustine apparently praises Theodosius for submitting to the judgment of God through his bishop, Ambrose. The episode of emperor bowing before bishop appears as a wonderful example of worldly authority submitting to that of the Church. However, according to historians, the episode offers a more complicated picture, which Augustine recognized.[29] Theodosius had to repent before Ambrose for ordering the massacre of many Thessalonians for their uprising. Theodosius was known for having a short temper, and his penance was meant as punishment for his rash deeds, as Ambrose told him that execution of all of his future commands would have to wait thirty days so that he would have time to reconsider them. Theodoret also reports that Ambrose accused Rufinus, Theodosius's advisor, of ordering the massacre. Rufinus was known in antiquity for his ambition for imperial power, and some, like Augustine's student Orosius, accused him of treacherously orchestrating the barbarian invasion of Alaric and others. Most ancient historians viewed Rufinus as ambitious, cruel, and capable of manipulating Theodosius. Theodosius did not completely live up to Augustine's vision of a virtuous ruler who would not be excessively moved by the honors and speeches of courtiers (CD 5.24).

Augustine praises Theodosius for his religious humility and for repenting for having exacted vengeance against the Thessalonians. However, his praise is sufficiently ambiguous to make the reader wonder whether Theodosius's own political purposes were being served more than Augustine explicitly acknowledges:

> For, at the intercession of the bishops (episcopis intercedentibus), he had promised to treat their offence leniently; but he was then compelled (compulsus est) to take vengeance on the people by the tumult of certain persons close to him (tumultu quorumdam, qui ei cohaerebant). Then, however, coerced by the discipline of the church (ecclesiastica coercitus disciplina), he did

29. Ancient sources include Theodoret, Ecclesiastical History: A History of the Church in Five Books from A.D. 322 to the Death of Theodore of Mopsuestia A.D. 427, trans. Edward Walford (London: Samuel Bagster, 1843), 5.17–18; Sozomen, The Ecclesiastical History of Sozomen, Comprising a History of the Church, from A.D. 323 to A.D. 425, trans. Chester D. Hartranft, Nicene and Post-Nicene Fathers, vol. 2 (Grand Rapids, Mich.: Wm. B. Eerdmans Publishing, 1957), 7.25; and Orosius, Historiarum adversus paganos libri septum (The seven books of history against the pagans), trans. Roy J. Deferrari (Washington, D.C.: Catholic University of America Press, 1964), 7.37. See also Theodor Mommsen, A History of Rome under the Emperors, 494–95; and Stephen Williams and Gerard Friell, Theodosius: The Empire at Bay, 128.

penance with such humility that the people, as they prayed for him, were more ready to weep when they saw the imperial majesty thus brought low than they were to fear it when it was angered by sin. (*CD* 5.26)

Few historical episodes better display the greater power of the Church over political power than this one apparently did. As Augustine observes, Theodosius's penance enabled people to venerate the power of God through his ministers rather than through imperial power. Augustine's language suggests that political authority serves ecclesiastical authority. For instance, he calls Ambrose and his fellow bishops' act an *intercessio*, which, in Roman legal terminology, was a veto by a higher magistrate against an official act, and was never permitted against an act of a dictator.[30] In general, it was invoked to protect the interests of the plebs against the abuses by magistrates, which fits this case in that Augustine observes that the people who witnessed Theodosius's penance learned to fear God more than the emperor. One wonders, though, whether it was Theodosius himself from whom the Roman people needed to be protected. Augustine points out that this episode was occasioned by Theodosius being compelled to take vengeance by the "tumult of certain persons close to him." Such persons would likely have been his courtiers, such as Rufinus. Further, if Theodosius were truly compelled, then it is unclear why he would have to repent, since acting by compulsion is not sinful. If Theodoret is correct in stating that Ambrose accused Rufinus of ordering the massacre, then he would have been the sinful one requiring penance. No purpose appears to have been served by Theodosius's submission, except for him to take responsibility for misuse of imperial power. His submission and penance, therefore, served political purposes (including those of the Church and perhaps his own) instead of the exclusive purpose of saving his soul.

Augustine's silence on Rufinus's sin suggests another issue raised in this passage. Although not explicitly stated, it is consistent with Augustine's description of this episode to see him arguing that the episode constituted an attempt to correct, on the part of the Church and of Theodosius himself, a power imbalance between Theodosius and his overbearing courtiers. Both the Church and Theodosius would have benefited politically from Theodosius's repentance. The Church benefited by securing a stronger relationship against the emperor, and the emperor benefited by using Church power to secure his

---

30. A. Berger, "Encylopaedic Dictionary," 506. Similarly, Augustine speaks of the saints interceding for human beings. The saints do not "veto" God's decision, but, rather, save human beings from their own decisions (*CD* 21.27).

position against the courtiers, by appealing to the favor of the people. Both the Church and Theodosius secured their political power, and Theodosius secured his power through an additional alliance with the people against his courtiers. Furthermore, although Augustine does not mention it, the episode likely would have benefited Theodosius, who was attempting to prevent the Western empire from disintegrating. Instead of reflecting a relationship of subservience, this example, rather, reflects an interdependent relationship whereby Theodosius's act benefited both the Church and himself as emperor.

The limitation of ecclesiastical authority is seen in another passage in which Augustine distinguishes the offices of priest and bishop from those who are priests and bishops by God's grace. He provides a way for the "prophetic" side of love of God and neighbor to balance the "institutional" side:

> And after the words, "Over them the second death has no power," there is added: "but they shall be priests of God and of Christ (*sacerdotes Dei et Christi*) and shall reign (*regnabunt*) with him for a thousand years" (Rev. 20:6). And this surely is said not only of bishops and presbyters (*episcopis et presbyteris*), who are now literally (*proprie*) called in the church by the mystical name priests; but just as we call all Christians "christs (*christos*)," because of the ritual anointing (*mysticum chrisma*), so we call all Christians "priests" (*sacerdotes*) because they are members of one holy priest (*sacerdotis*). Of them the apostle Peter says: "A holy people, a royal priesthood." Certainly the Apocalypse hints, though briefly and only in passing, that Christ is God, by saying: "Priests of God and Christ," that is, of the Father and the Son, although it was thanks to his taking the form of a servant and as the Son of Man that Christ was made a priest forever after the order of Melchizedek. (*CD* 20.10, quoting 1 Pet. 2:9)

Augustine distinguishes between those who hold the office of priest and those who are priests by virtue of their being members of the body of Christ. Recalling the previous discussion of the difference between literal and figurative meanings of Scripture, the former are literal priests and the latter are figurative priests. The latter are virtuous as members of the body of Christ, although not necessarily as members of this or that congregation. For instance, Augustine elsewhere admits of a baptism of desire whereby one's desire, not one's participation in ritual, constitutes baptism: "For all those who perish for their confession of Christ (*pro Christi confessione*), even though they have not experienced the cleansing water of regeneration, are just as effectively delivered from their sins as they would be if they were washed by the holy font of baptism" (*CD* 13.7). A similar contrast between offices and those who informally represent the public good was seen in

Chapter 4 in the discussion of rebellion. This example differs from the previous example because here the contrast is between subsequent or supernatural grace and its institutional expression, whereas the just rebel in Chapter 4 receives his authority through right-by-nature.

This example has two implications for Augustine's political thought, however. First, the Church must find a way to be restrained in its own sphere of competence. It must find a way to balance its authority with the "prophetic" voice of subsequent grace. It must be open to those whose witness to truth can remind it to restrain itself. Second, such a habit of institutional moderation also means that the Church must be open to those voices of love of God and of neighbor by nature, which restrain it from inordinate political intrusions. Whereas natural virtue is not identical with supernatural virtue, we have seen that the latter does not undermine the former, and thus they would have the same political authority in balancing ecclesiastical authority in political matters. On political matters, the voices of both natural and supernatural virtue would restrain the Church on the grounds of natural virtue. Within the sphere of the Church's competence, ecclesiastical authority would be restrained by supernatural virtue (which, as we have seen, does not contradict natural virtue).

These passages, and Augustine's understanding of *exempla,* indicate that the Church's power to "make use" of earthly peace is circumscribed by the fact that there may be real priests in the city who may or may not be members of the Church, but who are capable of reminding Church leaders of the virtues they must practice. This passage further provides a defense against false claims of personal witness, in that he reminds the reader that the true priests will not be fully known until the final judgment. Their virtue may be glimpsed by those whose understanding of virtue enable them to distinguish true from false prophets. In the meantime, the Church members must obey divine command so that they can learn virtue (see *CD* 15.6). Augustine's strategy of internal Church reform is shown in the next chapter.

The possibility of the existence of actual "priests" outside the sacerdotal order circumscribes the Church's ability to assert itself as the sole authority for virtue, especially on the basis of revelation. This is not to say that politicians or the laity can have authoritative control over the proclamation of gospel or the administration of sacraments. Rather, the existence of priests on account of their virtue enables the laity to give or withhold assent to the Church's political actions. Thus, the relationship between laymen and churchmen is far more balanced and reciprocal when political actions by churchmen are at issue than it is in the traditional interpretation of Augustine's understanding of the two powers. The interdependent relationship requires one power to be responsible for human beings' temporal end, the other to be responsible for human beings' eternal end, with the latter not trumping the former. Augustine's admission that real priests can exist outside the official priesthood and outside of the sacerdotal order, and that political virtues are true virtues, indicates that politics can cultivate people's virtues in its own particular way without undo interference from the Church. However, because the end of the city is to cultivate a degree of "natural" virtue, the city cannot impede, but, rather, must attempt to nurture, the ends of the Church, insofar as the city understands the love of God and of neighbor by nature.

## The Function of the City

The purpose of politics is to bring citizens to their particular kinds of perfection. The discussion in this study has so far indicated that a city cultivates a kind of natural virtue. Chapter 3 showed that the city practices the love of neighbor by committing itself to becoming a kind of political friendship whereby citizens reach a kind of perfection. Augustine stresses that governing entails a concern with and the nurture *(consulere)* of citizens' well-being. The perfection of the city falls well short of the perfection offered through the body of Christ, but it is not merely "inferior" or "subordinate" to the virtue cultivated by the Church. Rather, the virtues of political life complement those of the Church. For instance, it was noted above that Augustine reminds Christians that political life often demands more of them and tests their virtue more than does the city of God. Combined with the argument in previous chapters, this view helps us to see how the virtue cultivated by the city intimates the infused virtues. A consideration of how the love for all human beings required by the Church relates to particular political loves helps to clarify the elements that act as a "bridge" between city and Church but also keeps them separate.

Augustine treats human relations as a set of expanding concentric circles emanating from the individual. Family relations are closest, then the city, the entire world, and finally the universe (CD 19.3, 19.14, 19.17). God commands human beings to love their neighbors as much possible; this includes loving all human beings: "Therefore, he will be at peace, so far as in him lies, with all men in that human peace, or ordinate concord, of which the pattern is this: first, to do harm to no one, and second, to help everyone that he can" (CD 19.14). The Golden Rule commands loving everyone equally regardless of particular familial, national, or ethnic relationship. This constitutes the kind of universal love cultivated by the Church. As shown above, however, Augustine does not think that this undermines particular familial or political relationships: "In the first place, then *(Primitus ergo)*, he has the care of his own household, inasmuch as the order of nature or of human society provides him with a readier and easier access to them for seeking help. Wherefore the Apostle says: 'Whoever does not provide for his own, and especially for those of his household, he denies the faith, and is worse than an infidel'" (CD 19.14, quoting 1 Tim. 5:8). Augustine indicates that the love of neighbor is practiced most fully with those neighbors who are in the immediate vicinity, such as family, friends, and fellow citizens. Although he illustrates this idea with the example of the family, he indicates with his "[i]n the first place," and his subsequent discussion of the relationship between the family and the city, that he includes political relationships in this discussion.

Augustine's invocation of Paul shows how the love of neighbor is actualized in these close ties and how these ties test our love the most. It is in our relationships with family, friends, and fellow citizens that we face the constant, day-to-day difficulties of securing justice and civil peace. These relationships test our patience with the various demands of the members of our community. Such demands include those of fellow citizens whose political views and programs we dispute, the poor who plead for help at inconvenient times, friends who fail us but who deserve our forgiveness, and family members whose needs divert our attention from other pursuits. These relationships also constitute human beings as images of God because they teach them how to love and how to know the good. This idea of loving God through one's neighbor was seen above in the discussion of *latreia* and its constituent parts. Augustine, therefore, would reject the claim that the love of neighbor undermines particular relationships, because it is through engaging in those particular relationships, not strictly in our concern for those in faraway places ("telescopic philanthropy," as Charles Dickens once called it), that our love is tested. Therefore, the city's way of teaching the love of neighbor cultivates the charity and forgiveness that is required for the Church (see CD 15.6).

The ability of cities to cultivate virtue in particular and local settings is greater than that of the Church, whose universal vision of virtue may blind it to particular expressions of virtue. Thus, it would be consistent for Augustine to allow the laity in a particular city to limit the political influence of the Church by ensuring that it respects its political order. For example, a constitutional democracy can reasonably demand that the Church respect the separation of church and state, by ensuring that it follows the electoral laws and respects the liberal idea of self-government. The idea of self-government is supported by Augustine's view that the truth of God is insinuated into nature, and that human beings' intellects and wills are better exercised when they inquire into these truths, rather than when these truths are directly proclaimed to them. Thus, Augustine's ideas rule out the possibility for the Church, in a relatively healthy society, to direct its members to act unconstitutionally.[31] This being the case, Augustine leaves room for Church members to resist tyranny, in which case the Church's representative in a particular country, if he or she has sufficient justice, prudence, temperance, and fortitude, could serve as a possible leader of resistance. Thus, it is just for the Church to resist and even to rebel: "[I]t has come to pass that the heavenly city could not have common laws of religion with the earthly city, and on this point must dissent and become a tiresome burden to those who thought differently, and must undergo their anger and hatred and persecutions except at length it repelled the hostile intent of its adversaries with fear of its own numbers and with evidence of ever-present divine aid" (CD 19.17). As shown in Chapter 4, rebellion is rightful if it can also practically fulfill stringent requirements, and Augustine thought that the Church can assert its exemplary virtue when the city becomes tyrannical.

The ability of the city to teach virtue to the Church is consistent with Augustine's insistence that civil peace is inferior to eternal peace. The inability of human beings to secure peace by their own efforts, and the perpetual threat of people falling into sin, prevents earthly institutions such as families and cities from being perfect. More often than not, cities are made miserable by litigation and the constant threat of war and sedition: "If then, the home, our common refuge amid the ills of this human life, is not safe, what of the city? The larger it is, the more does its forum teem with civil and criminal lawsuits, even though its calm be not disturbed by the turbulence, or more often the bloodshed, of sedition and civil wars. Cities are indeed free at times from such events, but never from the threat of them" (CD 19.5). The Church's ability to provide an account of eternal happiness and perfect virtue counters the city's inability to overcome its perpetual litigation, sedition, and war (not that the Church itself does not suffer from those ills).

The Church's ability to provide a context for all people from all backgrounds to find perfection and eternal happiness also balances the city's own tendency to consider itself universal. The Church can heal dissension by teaching a vision of peace next to which civil peace and the objects of political ambition pale. For instance, Augustine exercises this kind of pastoral care in his own teaching

---

31. These principles would prevent churches from directing their congregations to vote as a bloc. Such a tactic might follow the letter of the constitution, but it undermines the spirit of constitutional self-government. It can also provoke an antireligious backlash, which undermines the mission of the Church.

in the *City of God*, by constantly reminding readers of the miseries of temporal and political life. The city degenerates by confusing its ends with eternal ends, as was the case with Rome, which gloried in dominating others. Augustine uses the example of Babylon and the Tower of Babel to show that the city that forgets ordinate loving attempts to dominate others (*CD* 16.4). Its neglect of the love of God and of neighbor leads to injustice and domination, because it resorts to its own devices, such as the common language of the Tower of Babel, to glory in itself. Augustine interprets God's action in destroying the Tower of Babel and dispersing the people to show that particular nations, languages, and other human things are parts of the greater whole. The attempt to transform one of these parts into the whole reflects the lust for domination: "What sort of penalty was meted out in this case? Since an emperor's dominion *(dominatio imperantis)* resides in his tongue, it was in that member that he suffered the penalty for his pride" (*CD* 16.4). Similarly, the teachings of the Church remind the city of its own internal dissensions and the deficiency of its own desire to glory in itself.

Instead of postulating a model by which the city serves the Church, Augustine argues that each sphere constitutes a model of virtue for the other. The virtues cultivated by the city supplement those cultivated by the Church. The Church preserves its freedom to proclaim the gospel, but political authorities cultivate civic virtue, which in extreme circumstances might include suppressing heretics who undermine civic peace. Contrary to most views, Augustine did not justify coercion of heretics to enforce orthodoxy, but believed that coercion is the only way to preserve civic peace in an emergency situation, where it appears that a group's beliefs will lead inexorably to violence (see Chapter 7). Conversely, the city cultivates civic virtues and can reasonably limit the Church's incursions into its sphere. It can do so by demanding that its incursions be justified by natural reason. The city's freedom is limited by the Church's ability to excommunicate leaders (and entire populations), and by the ability of the Church's national organization to form the center of resistance in a city dominated by a tyranny. To be sure, no institutional arrangement can prevent the complete dissolution of either Church or city. When that occurs, the only recourse is the prayer and the hope that righteous people will again come forth to rebuild from amid the ashes. Between those times, however, the two orders are responsible for their own ends, and relate to one another in the sphere of action in ways intelligible to natural reason.

Augustine understood the relationship between the love of God and of neighbor and political rule. The foregoing analysis was based on an account of the "prophetic" aspect of the love of God and of neighbor, which shows that the soul can be constituted as the image of God by encountering a multiplicity of relationships, and through the exercise of the intellect to understand creation. Thus, one learns to love God through the love of neighbor, and one learns to know God through creation. This means that the love of God is accompanied by intellectual virtue. It also means that loving God does not give one license to commit injustices. One cannot merely "love and do what you will" because the will must be guided to the good by the intellect. Furthermore, loving God means that one enjoys one's neighbor in God, and one does not instrumentally "use" one's neighbor; by loving one's neighbor, one is at once partially constituted by him or her, which indirectly constitutes one as the image of God.

Politically, the love and knowledge of God through the world require that the city and the Church consider each other as models for virtue. They check each other's vices and supplement each other's virtues. They do this by sharing the kind of wisdom outlined in the first part of this chapter. This, of course, is an unlikely condition and one that would be "most fortunate," as Augustine states (CD 5.19). He doubted the practicality of a city governed by philosophy (CD 18.41) but sympathized with Varro and other "more intelligent and grave Romans" who wished to guide Rome by nature rather than according to its corrupt ancient traditions (CD 4.29, 4.31). Such an arrangement would be rare, though. However, speculation on this cosmion is not fruitless, because it enables people to understand the best practical regime, and thus make practical judgments about other regimes, and frame constitutions and laws based on those judgments. In this interdependent relationship, the state cannot dominate the Church (as is necessary in the system of sovereign states), nor can the Church dominate the city (as was practiced at times in medieval Europe).

Augustine's paradigm both elevates and moderates politics. It acknowledges that politics is a substantive good, but it stresses that only the sacraments offer hope for eternal happiness. Some modest observations can be offered to show us what aspects of political and ecclesiastical life need to be emphasized and de-emphasized in order to secure a more harmonious balance. The ability to achieve such a balance, it must be noted, is contingent on a multiplicity of factors, and its endurance is fragile at best. Furthermore, such observations must always remain general and open to modification, since acting upon principle in politics begets unknown consequences that may require the abandonment of those principles.

Previous chapters showed that Augustine thought that political life is a positive good. If we apply his view to contemporary politics, it would require the sovereign state to cultivate fewer instrumental relations among people. Smaller civic units bound in loose and fluid federations might constitute an alternative that cultivates political friendships. Augustine appears to have hoped for something like this in the Roman Empire. As the world seems to be moving toward a dualistic system of internationalism (that is, of the market, of international law, and of transnational organizations) and localism (that is, state and provincial rights and assertions of ethnic autonomy), it would seem logical to cultivate a system in which the longings expressed by the universal city of God can be in a position to restrain internationalist ambitions from building another Tower of Babel, and in which particular associations can envisage their particular political friendships and ties as if they were chosen "by the lot," as it were.

According to Augustine's reasoning, it is a mistake to embrace fully or to denounce completely the Enlightenment and liberalism, the philosophy and ideology that begat the sovereign state system. One cannot denounce them since liberalism's commitment to public, rational debate reminds the Church that God's truth is insinuated into nature and that cities share in truth. Open public debate at its best indirectly leads to truth, just as Augustine thought that God's insinuations and footprints encourage human beings to become more virtuous. Similarly, this, as well as the liberal concept of equality, reminds the Church of Augustine's view that there is a distinction between priestly offices and those whose priestly virtue makes them living testaments to truth. The Church must remember that its institutional authority needs to be balanced by the authority of the "prophetic" soul. Finally, the Church must remember that the restraint that natural reason places on its political incursions also restrains the Church's misuse of power. Historically, this power has tended to try either to dominate politics or to escape it. Natural reason, as understood by Augustine, enables a political role for the Church that nevertheless limits its ability to transform politics from the perspective of revelation alone.

The next chapter takes up the test case of this paradigm by examining Augustine's own justification for the coercion of heretics. It shows that what appears to be a case of Augustine's invocation of political power to enforce orthodoxy (which contradicts this paradigm) is in fact the restoration of civil peace.

# 7

## THE COERCION OF HERETICS

IT IS NECESSARY to examine Augustine's arguments for the coercion of heretics because these arguments appear to undermine his general understanding of love of God and of neighbor as virtue. This understanding allows expressions of love that differ from those of the Catholic Church. It is notable that Augustine even made an argument to justify coercion instead of assuming that it should be used simply as a matter of course. However, the mode and premises of Augustine's argument do raise concerns. His justification of having heretics "compelled to enter" appears to undermine this view and instead appears to constitute an imposition of orthodoxy. This chapter provides evidence that Augustine's justification of coercion does not undermine his concept of virtue because he did not conclude that nonviolent heretics should be deprived of their political rights. This chapter focuses on Augustine's justification of the coercion of the Donatists, which was a specific case that required his constant attention.[1] Although it is extremely difficult to derive general principles from political activities, this chapter provides evidence that Augustine justified coercion inasmuch as he saw it as a last resort for a sect that expressed its principles through violence. His general principles do not necessitate coercion, nor is it fully accurate to state that his "horrible doctrine"

---

1. Augustine's fullest justification for coercing heretics is found in *Ep.* 93 (written in 408). I focus on Augustine's arguments for coercing Donatist heretics instead of others such as the Pelagians (who denied original sin and the need for grace) or Rogatists (a Donatist faction) because these arguments reflect his most sustained justification of his position. He supported banning the Pelagian heresy because of false worship, and possibly because the Pelagians were associated with violent activity (Brown, *Augustine of Hippo,* 361). He also suspected the Rogatist heretics of plotting to commit acts of violence (*Ep.* 93.3.11).

(as Markus termed it) constitutes a "tragic" exception to his political thought that would otherwise admit of pluralism.[2]

Greater attention is instead given to Augustine's nuanced justification of the coercion of violent heretics and their leaders. In the disintegrating Roman empire, the distinction between belief and actions appeared to have dissolved, and it appears that Augustine thought the Donatist beliefs undermined the physical security of the empire. Furthermore, his justification of coercion is based on his view that the means of coercion must fit the end.[3] His position is usually interpreted as denying the heretic the knowledge of how the good that is enforced upon him actually shares with the proximate good the heretic loves. Rather, Augustine's view is that coercion takes the form of demonstrating to the heretic the insufficiency of that proximate good, while acknowledging that the proximate good intimates or shares in the highest good. Augustine's position on this affects his political theory, inasmuch as his position indicates reasons for the use of force to maintain civil peace.

According to Augustine, the purpose of coercion is not to enforce moral and religious conformity. He justified using coercion against Donatist heretics in order to curb their violence. He supported the banning of the Donatist heresy because he thought its doctrines were expressed in violence. He supported the banning of other, not always violent, heresies, because they had apparently emerged in North Africa, which could not be easily defined as either violent or nonviolent. Augustine's change of mind, from his initial advocacy of persuasion to his allowance of coercion, indicates that he first opposed the imperial policy in the *Theodosian Code*, which carried the pagan practice of enforcement of religion over to the Christian religion (see below for specifics on imperial law). That Augustine initially opposed this policy and the efforts of his Catholic colleagues to coerce heretics indicates his greater tolerance toward heretics. The

---

2. Those who view a direct link between Augustine's political views and coercion include: Deane, *Political and Social Ideas*, 215; Connolly, *Augustinian Imperative*, 66–73; William H. C. Frend, "Augustine and State Authority: The Example of the Donatists," 72; and Brian Tierney, who wrote that Augustine's theory of coercion shaped Church policy on the suppression of religious dissent ("Religious Rights: An Historical Perspective," 20–21). For the "tragic" view, see Markus, *Saeculum*, 134–46; Fortin, "St. Augustine," 198; and Thomas Heilke, "On Being Ethical without Moral Sadism: Two Readings of Augustine and the Beginnings of the Anabaptist Revolution." Milbank argues that Augustine's "ontology of peace" collapses at this point on the rocks of a "moment of 'pure violence' " between the Church and the heretic. For him, Augustine ends up presenting coercion not as a matter of persuasion or education, but as a battle of wills based on a "moment of 'pure violence,' externally and arbitrarily related to the end one has in mind" (*Theology and Social Theory*, 420). Markus's interpretation has been challenged by John R. Bowlin ("Augustine on Justifying Coercion").

3. A point that Bowlin argues but that is ultimately lost when he says that depriving one of freedom does not fit the end of coercion ("Augustine on Justifying Coercion," 66–67).

imperial policy of coercion, which caused chaos and dissent, put Augustine into the situation of having to justify the use of coercion as a last resort. His final position, however, placed him in a tenuous situation. On the one hand, he often had to exhort reluctant imperial officials (who themselves feared Donatist violence) to apply imperial law. On the other hand, evidence indicates that they used excessive, and even unlawful, violence when they finally applied the law (see *Ep.* 114.1). Augustine, therefore, was caught in the position of having to diffuse a situation in which it was difficult to have the law applied in a moderate and just way. He negotiated this dilemma by urging imperial officials to be clement, and, to heretics themselves, by utilizing the rhetoric of Roman authority, a mode of discourse in Roman culture that took an authoritative and prosecutorial tone.[4] As a result of his letters to the latter, his name would forever after be associated with the kind of immoderate persecution that he himself attempted to restrain.

Augustine changed his position when he saw that the laws could bring heretics to act virtuously. Coercion, he thought, can give people the opportunity, but only the opportunity, to live more virtuous lives. What really convinced Augustine of the efficacy of coercion is that it "liberated" people who stayed in the Donatist Church, due to their ignorance of the principles of the Catholic Church. As well, coercion enabled them to overcome the fear they had of leaving the Donatist Church, which coerced many of its members to stay. According to Augustine, therefore, coercion and law have an educative function. However, the scope of this function is limited; Augustine thought that law can force people only to *act* virtuously. *It cannot make them virtuous.* He did not think that coercion constitutes a sufficient cause of conversion.

## DEFINITION OF HERESY

A heretic is a professed member of the Church who obstinately rejects Church teaching by asserting an insufficient, proximate good as the proper object of worship: "So those in the church of Christ who have a taste *(sapiunt)* for something morbid and depraved, if they receive correction, so that they may

---

4. This dilemma was due, in part, to the relative ease with which parties manipulated the imperial law to their own advantage. The ability of the powerful in the late Roman empire to use their patronage to "use" the law made the law difficult to enforce. According to Jill Harries, "'[U]sing' the law was all-important [for Augustine], enforcing it, to the letter, was not" (*Law and Empire in Late Antiquity,* 92). This meant that Augustine, like other Roman patrons, reinterpreted and applied the law to help their clients. In the case of Augustine and other bishops, however, such "use" had the effect of checking the abuses of power by imperial officials.

know (*sapiant,* or relish) something sound and right, stubbornly resist and are unwilling to emend their pestilent and deadly dogmas, but persist in defending them, become heretics and leave the church and are counted among the enemies who exercise the church" (*CD* 18.51).[5] Augustine calls lower goods "morbid and depraved," which appears to suggest that they absolutely oppose the good. Augustine appears to invoke a kind of Manichaean dualism by dismissing these things in this way, in that his language suggests that those objects do not in any way share in the good. However, Augustine actually considered them proximate goods insofar as he thought that everything participates in the good. Heretics make the mistake of replacing the good with a proximate good, and stubbornly continue to worship that proximate good despite having its nature as a proximate good pointed out to them. Augustine does not use the language of "proximate" or "insufficient" goods, but he does treat the objects of Donatist worship in this way.

This definition indicates that only those in the Church of Christ can ever be heretics. The category does not include Jews, atheists, or children of heretics. In this sense, the category finds its political analogy in the traitor who betrays the principles of his or her country and acts seditiously (see *Ep.* 93.1.2, 185.6.23, 10.43). Furthermore, the heretic is not merely one who is incorrect about Church teaching. Because heretics are said to relish something morbid and depraved, they are said to persist in worshiping a good that is not appropriately worshiped. For example, heretics might be those who seek salvation exclusively through ritual observation, as in the case of the Donatists (as shown below). Augustine considered the Donatists as puritanical legalists who sought perfection exclusively through ritual and group membership. Ritual or legal purity "satisfies" their desire for perfection, whereas group membership "satisfies" their desire for the fruits of community. Ritual or legal purity and group membership combine to fulfill their desire to "see" the fruits of God. They sought the fruits of grace by law rather than through habits of virtue.

## HISTORICAL BACKGROUND AND DONATIST PRINCIPLES

Donatist principles expressed themselves in violence, and contributed to the disintegration of the western Roman empire. Before turning to the principles

---

5. "Qui ergo in ecclesia Christi morbidum aliquid pravumque sapiunt, si correpti, ut sanum rectumque sapiant, resistunt contumaciter suaque pestifera et mortifera dogmata emendare nolunt, sed defensare persistunt, haeretici fiunt et foras exeuntes habentur in exercentibus inimicis."

of Donatism, it is first necessary to examine the historical background to the Donatist controversy in order to show how Augustine found himself in a situation in which he finally had to admit that the distinction between violent and nonviolent heretics was insignificant.

The historical and political situation in which Augustine found himself was one episode in Rome's long, bloody history of religious persecution among pagans, Christians, and other groups.[6] Emperor Diocletian persecuted Christian sects until 305 A.D., at which time some of the bishops and priests surrendered sacred Scriptures rather than die as martyrs. They were branded *traditores* for having "handed over" the Scriptures. These *traditores* were considered traitorous by various Christians and deemed by some unsuitable to hold Church office. The event that sparked the Donatist scandal was the appointment by *traditores* of Caecilianus as bishop of Carthage. The Donatists, whose input in the decision was ignored and who opposed the tainted choice of the *traditores*, appealed to the emperor who then rejected their appeal, partly because he thought it inappropriate for him to handle the affairs of the Church.[7] The African bishops held more synods, and each one maintained the original decision; the Donatists persisted and then finally broke with the Church. Their subsequent violent activity (such as the attacks by the Circumcellions and the Battle of Bagai in 347) and the fact that they disobeyed the emperor led to their suppression, which involved the exile of bishops and confiscation of Church property.[8] The Donatists' invocation of imperial authority to settle the dispute later provided Augustine with a weapon to remind them, when they complained about coercion, that they were the first to appeal (repeatedly) to the emperors, including Constantine, to hear their case against the appointment of Caecilianus (see *Ep.* 43.2.4, written in 397). Augustine also reminded them of their attempts to use imperial authority to punish their own dissidents (*Ep.* 51.3, written in 399 or 400).[9] The dispute set Catholics and Donatists against one another, but they eventually reached a modus vivendi between 321 and 346, which ended when Julian the Apostate became emperor. He tolerated Donatism partly in order to weaken Christianity, which he opposed. Julian persecuted Catholics

---

6. See the following accounts of the suppression of Donatism: W. H. C. Frend, "Donatism-Donatists" and *The Donatist Church: A Movement of Protest in North Africa*; Peter Brown, "St. Augustine's Attitude to Religious Coercion"; Geoffrey Grimshaw Willis, *Saint Augustine and the Donatist Controversy*; Maureen A. Tilley, *Donatist Martyr Stories: The Church in Conflict in Roman North Africa*, x–xvii; and Deane, *Political and Social Ideas*, chap. 6.

7. Roman law generally allowed the Church to conduct its own affairs, especially to define doctrine (Tony Honoré, *Law and the Crisis of Empire, 379–455 A.D.*, 3).

8. Tilley, *Donatist Martyr Stories*, xv. See also *Ep.* 185.1.4, written in 417.

9. See Willis, *Augustine and the Donatist Controversy*, 34.

by transferring Catholic churches to the Donatists.[10] In 373, Emperor Valentian I banned Donatism again; nevertheless, the Donatist Church expanded in Africa. Around 374, under Optatus of Thamugadi in Numidia, they became allied with Gildo, an African count who rebelled against Emperor Honorius and his regent Stilicho with a view to transferring Africa to the eastern empire. Donatism was useful for Gildo's political ambitions because it was a conduit for African nationalist agitation against Rome. The revolt was serious, particularly since Gildo cut off corn supplies to Italy; this was considered an act of war, as Africa was Italy's sole source for corn. In response, Donatist property was confiscated.[11] Donatism, which had already attracted local resentment against Rome, became allied with forces intent on the disintegration of the Roman Empire. About this time, and until 390 when it was led by Parmenius, the Donatist Church grew to be as popular as Catholicism in North Africa. By the time Augustine began fighting it in the 390s, it had become a major force that threatened the security of the Roman Empire.

By the time Augustine turned his attention to the controversy, Catholic Christianity had been declared the official religion: "We command that those persons who follow this law shall embrace the name of Catholic Christians. The rest, however, whom We adjudge demented and insane, shall sustain the infamy of heretical dogmas, their meeting places shall not receive the name of churches, and they shall be smitten first by divine vengeance and secondly by the retribution of Our own initiative."[12] The imperial laws suppressing heresy also need to be seen in light of one of the political purposes of the *Theodosian Code*—an attempt to prevent the disintegration of the western empire.[13] This explains the imperial readiness to persecute heretics, who would have been seen as threats to imperial unity. The empire suppressed heretics by removing heretical priests from their churches (*CT* 16.1.3, proclaimed in 381), confiscating their property (*CT* 16.5.7–8, May 8, 381), forbidding them from holding assembly (*CT* 16.5.6.3, January 10, 381), fining people ten pounds of gold for permitting heretical groups to meet on their property (or beating them with clubs and deporting them if they could not afford to pay) (*CT* 16.5.21, June 15, 392), deporting those who threatened Catholics (*CT* 16.4.3, July 18, 392; explicated below), fining any heretic ten pounds of gold for securing ordination

10. Augustine, *Against the Letters of Petilian, the Donatist*, in *Writings against the Manichaeans and Donatists*, 2.84.184, written ca. 400. See also F. Van der Meer, *Augustine the Bishop*, 83.

11. Willis, *Augustine and the Donatist Controversy*, 62.

12. Clyde Parr, trans., *The Theodosian Code and Novels and Sirmordian Constitutions*, 16.1.2 (proclaimed in 380). Hereinafter *CT (Codex Theodosianus)*.

13. Honoré, *Law and the Crisis of Empire*, 97.

(*CT* 165.21, June 15, 392), and requiring everyone to hold the Catholic faith in every detail (*CT* 16.5.28, September 3, 395). Most historians argue that despite these laws against Donatists and heretics in general, they were laxly enforced, and the imperial government was powerless to impose its will. As Tony Honoré argues, provincial governors often failed to execute the laws because doing so would have caused unrest. Any magistrate who tried "would have been a fool."[14] Changes in imperial law, the Church's position, and Augustine's position are considered in greater detail below.

Donatist doctrine lent itself to being expressed through violence, and its hardness led its leaders and followers to believe that God had given them special authority to cleanse the world through means that otherwise would be morally wrong. Donatist doctrines and beliefs derived from a set of writings called the *Acts*, which provided descriptions of persecution by Catholics. Peter Brown reports that these "martyr stories" reflect the Donatists' dedication to ritual and legal purity:

> In the Acts, the Donatists admired an attitude such as the orthodox Jew had to the Torah. Their religion also was thought of as a "Law." Like the Macabees, whose example moved them profoundly, their martyrs died for "their holy laws." "I care for nothing but the Law of God, which I have learnt. This I guard, for this I die; in this I shall be burnt up. There is nothing in life other than this Law." The feeling of having defended something precious, of preserving a "Law" that had maintained the identity of a group in a hostile world, these are potent emotions. . . . Such a church was *"catholic"* in what the Donatists regarded as the most profound sense of the word: for it was the only church that had preserved the *"total"* Christian Law. A church could only preserve the Christian "Law" in its entirety by remaining "pure."[15]

The Donatists maintained ritual purity and understood their religion as Law. They saw themselves as the true keepers of virtue in a hostile world. Brown indicates that they saw the source of their own purity as different from that of Augustine and the Catholics: "It was the purity of the group in its relationship to God, that mattered. This group, like the ancient Israel, enjoyed a special relationship with God: for its prayers only were heard by Him. The anxiety, that genuinely haunted the Donatist bishops, was that, by tolerating any breach in a narrow and clearly defined order of ritual behavior, they might alienate

---

14. Ibid., 26, 133; see also Willis, *Augustine and the Donatist Controversy*, 30.
15. Brown, *Augustine of Hippo*, 218. He quotes from various Donatist sources and Augustine's own observations found in his letter against Pettilian (2.8.17, 2.38.90). Brown refers to *Monumenta ad Donatistarum historiam pertinentia*, P.L. viii, 673–784.

God from His church." This communal desire for purity demanded that rituals be followed precisely, and asserted that any breach of ritual would result in losing God's favor. Despite this, Donatist basilicas were often scenes of drunkenness and dancing, which frequently led Augustine to express doubts that the Donatists truly believed what they preached (*Ep.* 23.6–7, written in 392; 29.2, ca. 395 [on the feast called "Laetitia, vainly attempting to disguise their revels under a fair name"]; 35.2 [sexual licence]; 43.8.24; 108.5.14; 134.2).[16]

Augustine criticizes Donatist legalism and inordinate ritual purity, which (in his view) led to absurd consequences for liturgical practice. The Donatists exhibited the characteristics of a legalistic morality in their claim that only those who are part of the true Church can be saved. Membership, as they saw it, entailed following the Church's precepts to the letter:

> You think that you make a very acute remark when you affirm the name catholic to mean universal, not in respect to the communion as embracing the whole world, but in respect to the observance of all Divine precepts and of all the sacraments as if we (even accepting the position that the church is called catholic because it honestly holds the whole truth, of which parts here and there are found in some heresies) relied upon the testimony of this name *(huius nominis testimonio nitamur)*, and not upon the promises of God, and so many indisputable testimonies of the truth itself, our demonstration of the existence of the church of God in all nations. (*Ep.* 93.7.23)

The term *catholic,* that is, universal, meant different things to Catholics and Donatists (who considered themselves truly catholic). For the Donatists, being catholic entailed perfect observance of ritual and the Law, which guaranteed one's purity. For the Catholics, being catholic entailed worldwide communion, which includes the virtuous and depraved. For Augustine, rituals express, rather than constitute, virtue.

The Donatist claim that salvation comes through ritual observation of Law led them to believe that salvation could be gained only by communion with Donatist bishops and clergy, such as Vincentius in his hometown of Cartenna: "Meanwhile do all you can to proclaim and to maintain, that even though the gospel be published in Persia and India, as indeed it has been for a long time, no one who hears it can be in any degree cleansed from his sins, unless he come to Cartenna, or to the neighborhood of Cartenna! If you have not expressly said this, it is evidently through fear lest men should laugh at you" (*Ep.* 93.7.22; see

16. Willis, *Augustine and the Donatist Controversy,* 29.

also 93.6.21). Ritual purity required communion with pure bishops in their hometowns. The sacredness of locale combined with their African nationalism and anti-Roman sentiment, and Augustine criticizes them for restricting God's church to Africa alone (see *Ep.* 185.1.3). Donatist legalism, combined with their insistence that communion with God take place in the bishops' hometowns, led them to reject other forms of worship. For Augustine, this meant that they broke themselves off from the worldwide Christian communion: "[H]ow do you know that in the Christian society, which is spread so far and wide, there may not have been some in a very remote place, from which the fame of their righteousness could not reach you, who had already, before the date of your separation, separated themselves for some just cause from the communion of the whole world? How could the church in that case be found in your sect, rather than in those who were separated before you?" (*Ep.* 93.8.25). This statement indicates that the Donatists, by insisting on their own purity, separated themselves from the worldwide communion. For instance, they acted like a separate society, forbidding members from meeting with Catholics, sharing the same space (as in a room), intermarrying, answering their letters, responding to their letters, or letting them into their churches.[17]

Like a late Roman version of *Billy Budd,* this communal desire for purity appears to have resulted in violent acts, intended to cleanse the impure Catholics whom they saw polluted by the world: "The Donatist enthusiasts carried clubs called 'Israels'; they would 'purify' Catholic basilicas with coats of whitewash; they would destroy the altars of others."[18] Augustine reports various violent acts such as murder and the destruction of houses; he used these reports to argue for the need to restrain the Donatists (*Ep.* 88.7, written in 406; see also 133.1, written in 412).[19] He tells of the violence suffered by Maximianus, the Catholic bishop of Bagai, after one of the trials against the Donatists:

> [T]hey rushed upon him as he was standing at the altar, with fearful violence and cruel fury, beat him savagely with cudgels and weapons of every kind, and at last with the very boards of the broken altar. They also wounded him with a dagger in the groin so severely, that the effusion of blood would have soon put an end to his life, had not their further cruelty proved of service for his preservation; for, as they were dragging him along the ground thus severely wounded, the dust forced into the spouting vein stanched

17. Ibid., 28–29.
18. Brown, *Augustine of Hippo,* 219. See *EnP* 10.5; *Ep.* 29.12.
19. For other examples of Donatist violence, see *Ep.* 51.3, 88.6, 89.1, 133.1, 185.3–4, 185.7, 185.13, 185.27, 185.30). See also Brown, *Augustine of Hippo,* 241.

with blood, whose effusion was rapidly on the way to cause his death. (*Ep.* 185.7.27, written in 417)

The Donatists also used violence to dissuade their own members from becoming Catholics. For example, Augustine reports of Donatists who beat a presbyter who had left them for the Catholics (*Ep.* 88.6, written in 406) and later of the intimidation of members: "[T]hey were living among men among whom those who wished to be Catholics could not be so through the infirmity of fear, seeing that if anyone there said a single word in favor of the Catholic church, he and his house were utterly destroyed at once" (*Ep.* 185.4.13, written in 417).[20]

The Donatists' violence was often meant to bait authorities into persecuting them, which would enable them to view themselves as martyrs, thus solidifying their own position as the pure who are persecuted by an impure world. One of the reasons Augustine rejected the death penalty is that it provided the Donatists with even more martyrs (*Ep.* 139.2, written in 412). He mentions that Donatists often threatened authorities with violence if those authorities did not put them to death. If threats did not work, Donatists would often commit suicide (*Ep.* 185.3.12).

Leaders played a crucial role in Donatist ecclesiology, and Augustine's advocacy of coercion targets them. Augustine also suspected that Donatist leaders, though feigning a belief in moderation, actually encouraged Donatist violence.[21] In Donatist ecclesiology, the bishops and priests constituted an unbroken line of martyrs and the pure that originated in the handing over (*traditio*), or the sacrificing, of the Christian Law:

> [The Donatist] caste of "pure" bishops were often eminent men in Roman towns that had maintained their prestige. In the eyes of their congregations, these bishops stood for the uninterrupted succession of the "church of the Martyrs": a Donatist priest would be told by an angel the precise "line of descent of Christianity" that culminated in the bishop of his town. In a society that valued sheer physical continuity in life and death, these bishops were thought of as the "sons of the martyrs" as surely as the despised Catholics were the "sons of Caecilian [the original *traditore*]."[22]

The Donatist Church, then, appears to have been centered on the symbol of the procession of the martyrs, represented by the bishops and priests.

---

20. Brown, *Augustine of Hippo*, 223; see also *Ep.* 83.1, 85.29, 93.1.3, 3.10; *EnP* 54.16.

21. See Peter Iver Kaufman, *Redeeming Politics*, 139–40. Augustine elsewhere complains about intellectual elites who stir up crowds to attack Christians (*CD* 4.1, 6.pref., 18.51; see also 2.1, 5.26).

22. Brown, *Augustine of Hippo*, 220.

The fruits of community and grace were sought by the ritual purity of the priests. However, this ritual purity did not extend to the general congregation. The Donatist Church was based on a core of pure elites who constituted the procession of the martyrs; the general congregation would have been purified by observing the rituals conducted by the bishops and priests. In Augustine's view, because the Donatists advocated the purity of the Church as opposed to the Catholic "impurity," they sought the fruits of God prematurely. The Donatists sought the fruits of God with an insufficient good. They sought a perfect good through ritual observance and through their ecclesiology, but according to Augustine, those are only proximate and insufficient goods (my terms). For Augustine, loving an insufficient good as if it were a perfect good produces ill effects. It forces individuals to grasp the insufficient good, which leads them to lash out and destroy either it or other things, when the insufficient good fails to produce the good for which the heretics hope. The Donatists turned to violence in order to "purify" worldly objects, because they themselves sought purification from their attachment to worldly things.

As was shown in the previous chapter, Augustine understood that love of God or worship *(latreia)* is possible outside the sacramental order of the Church. The Catholic Church differed most significantly from the Donatists in that it sought the fruits of God not in ritual purity or in the procession of the martyrs, but in the vision of God that can be seen only "through an enigma" or mixed in with sins while the Catholic Church maintains temporal existence. This theory is reflected most directly in Augustine's view that the city of God and the earthly city exist intermingled in this life, that the Church will be filled with both the virtuous and the sinful who seek salvation (CD 1.35, 10.32, 11.1, 14.28, 15.1, 18.1). For example, he calls these two cities "mystical *(mystice)*," meaning that they must be interpreted figuratively (CD 15.1; DDC 2.62). In practice, this means that they seek the fruits of God in the actual virtues of their members (inside and outside the official sacramental order). Augustine states this principle when he explains the success of the early Church:

> [I]t is incredible that a very few men, of mean birth and the lowest rank, and no education, should have been able so effectually to persuade the world, and even its learned men, of so incredible a thing. . . . But if [skeptics] do not believe that these miracles were wrought by Christ's apostles to gain credence to their preaching of His resurrection and ascension, this one grand miracle suffices for us, that the whole world has believed without any miracles. (CD 22.5; see also 16.2)

Augustine's understanding of unity is governed by the Matthean idea that "By their fruits ye shall know them" (*CD* 16.2 [Matt. 7:20]; see also *CD* 5.15). The Catholic Church is united by the ability of its members to observe and practice virtue, and to see the miraculous in the unexpected and mundane, in the way that the apostles miraculously converted people to Christianity without the use of miracles. Adherence to this principle would have required great virtue and patience among Catholics because it required them to seek the fruits of God in unexpected places. Contrary to the views of the Donatists, the virtue required of the Catholics may have been even greater than that required of the Donatists themselves, who sought the fruits of God in the "physical" continuation of the martyrs, in the ritual and legal purity of their Church, and in their lust for persecution and martyrdom.

## LAW AND PUNISHMENTS

The year 408 A.D. marks a major break in Augustine's thinking. Before that, he had supported the use of imperial power only inasmuch as it could prevent Donatist violence against the Catholics. As we shall see, this included suppressing their activities, since these religious activities were linked to violence. Political instability had prevented both Augustine and the imperial powers from distinguishing the sect from the violence that it engendered. Until 408, Augustine rejected imperial laws compelling Donatists to become Catholic (for example, see *CT* 16.5.28), but he changed his mind once he appreciated the efficacy of these laws. Augustine's position changed in response to the changes in imperial and ecclesiastical policy. As shown below, he was reluctant to agree with the increasing tendency of the Church and the empire to compel Donatists to enter the Church; however, he consistently supported them once he agreed with their positions. The one exception to this is his rejection of the death penalty and his ambiguous rhetoric exhorting imperial officials to apply the law. Changes in imperial and Church policy can be divided into three periods: (1) the years 395 to 400, marked by the Church's appeal to the empire to protect it from Donatist attack, (2) the years 400 to 405, marked by the Church's declaration that the Donatists were heretics, and imperial suppression, and (3) the years 405 to 411, marked by the move toward coercing Donatists into the Catholic Church.

### The Years 395 to 400

As shown above, the period up to 390 was marked by imperial efforts to suppress Donatism and its accompanying violence; by 380, membership in the

Catholic Church was compulsory. The Church until then generally appealed to the emperor only to protect it from Donatist violence, and to enforce unity. This was the prevailing attitude of the Church until the period following the Edict of Unity of 405 (see below).[23] The Church differed from the emperor, who had declared all non-Catholics as heretics as early as 395 (*CT* 16.5.28). During this period Augustine, like other churchmen, was willing to appeal to the emperor to protect the Catholics from Donatist violence, but not to coerce them into communion with the Catholics.[24] That being the case, it has been noted that the "germ" of Augustine's idea of coercion lay in the writings of this period.[25] For instance, he appears to consider heresy in the same class as violent and sinful activities, as defined by Paul and punishable by imperial authorities (Gal. 5:19–21): "iniquity, fornication, moral corruption *(immunditiae)*, contentiousness, ambition, animosity, dissension, heresy, envy, drunkenness, and offenses."[26] Drawing on the words of Paul, Augustine understood heresy as a species of moral corruption that accompanied other kinds of moral pollution, particularly violence, of which the Donatists were guilty. Nevertheless, Augustine did not at this time advocate coercing the Donatists into becoming Catholics, but instead urged the use of imperial power to prevent them from attacking the Catholics.

### The Years 400 to 405

The period between 400 and 405 is characterized by increased persecution of the Donatists by the empire, and by appeals by the Church. At the Synod of Carthage in June 405, the Church pressured the empire to enforce its antiheretical laws by declaring the Donatists heretics.[27] Although the Church moved to categorize the Donatists as heretics, it stopped short of calling for enforced unity, although some bishops (not yet including Augustine) did.[28] The empire continued to consider the Donatists heretical and actually exceeded the Church's demands by declaring (in advance of the Church's appeal to the emperor) that all must become Catholic, and by disbanding Donatist churches (*CT* 16.5.37–38). *CT* 16.5.38, decreed on February 12, 405, is generally known as the "Edict

---

23. Ibid., 234; Willis, *Augustine and the Donatist Controversy*, 23–24.

24. Augustine, *The Retractions*, 2.31, commenting on (the lost work) *Contra partem Donati libri duo*, written about 397–400; "Against the Letter of Parmenian," in *Works of Saint Augustine*, ed. John E. Rotelle, O.S.A., vol. 18 (New York: New City Press, 1990), 8.15 (51, 35); see also Brown, "Augustine's Attitude," 265–66.

25. Brown, "Augustine's Attitude," 266.

26. Augustine, "Against the Letter of Parmenian," 1.10.16.

27. Willis, *Augustine and the Donatist Controversy*, 130.

28. Van der Meer, *Augustine the Bishop*, 88–89.

of Unity"; it transferred churches over to the Catholics, forbade rebaptism and other Donatist practices, and, even though it declared that all must be Catholic, stopped short of coercing heretics into their communion. As Brown argues, "For all its bombast, this Edict was faithful to the general principle of Roman legislation on religion. It touched only externals. No Donatist, as yet, was forced to join the Catholic church. Rather, the Donatist church was 'disbanded,' like a modern political party that has been declared illegal."[29]

During this period, Augustine supported the use of exile and fines to suppress Donatists. He does not appear to have supported the Church's position on the Edict of Unity. He maintained the pre-405 position by appealing merely for protection:

> Our brethren indeed demand help from the powers which are ordained, not to persecute you, but to protect themselves against the lawless acts of violence perpetrated by individuals of your party, which you yourselves, who refrain from such things, bewail and deplore; just as before the Roman Empire became Christian, the Apostle Paul took measures to secure that the protection of armed Roman soldiers should be granted him against the Jews who had conspired to kill him. (*Ep.* 87.8, written in 405)

Markus observes that Augustine's reluctance to adopt a policy of coercion may have played a part in delaying the African bishops from adopting such a strategy.[30] Indeed, that there was a problem of overzealous enforcement that exceeded Church policy is evidenced by Augustine's subsequent expressions of displeasure at actual enforcement as well as that advocated by some of his fellow Catholics: "Finally, if some of our party transgress the bounds of Christian moderation in this matter, it displeases us" (*Ep.* 87.8). Augustine's support of the Edict of Unity must have been lukewarm at best, since he consented to its principles only sometime in the subsequent three-year period, prior to his writing a letter recording his justification for his change of mind in 408.[31]

As shown above, Augustine thought that the Donatists had separated themselves from the worldwide Christian communion and believed, therefore, that the most appropriate punishment would be exile rather than corporal punishment: "But what shall I say against those whose fatal obstinacy is such that

29. Brown, *Augustine of Hippo*, 234.
30. Markus, *Saeculum*, 137.
31. According to Markus, the evidence is only sufficient to identify his change of mind sometime between 405 and 408: "At any rate within a year or two of the Edict of Unity, having seen its working, his doubts were dispelled.... Some time between 405 and 408 his consent followed, and thereafter he never wavered" (ibid., 138).

it is either coerced only by fear of losses, or is taught by exile *(vel damnorum terrore coercetur, vel docetur exsilio)* how universal (as had been foretold) is the diffusion of the church which they prefer to attack rather than to acknowledge?" (*Ep.* 89.2 (written in 406); see also 185.7.26 (written in 417).[32] Exile would make that removal concrete, since heresy is an expression of one's rejection of communion (with God and neighbor). Thus, the proper punishment is to deprive the heretic, whose physical violence can no longer be tolerated, of communal life (a punishment that his actions intend to achieve anyway). Such a justification is consistent with Augustine's theory of virtue. Just as being virtuous is enjoyable and being vicious unenjoyable, entailing as it does separation from God, so too is heresy punished by making concrete what the heretic has already chosen. What is crucial for this idea of exile is that, for Augustine, it is intended for leaders of movements whose violent activities have become impossible for others to tolerate. It is not, for Augustine (as it was for imperial law), a tool simply to ensure orthodoxy. We shall see presently, however, that Augustine found himself in a situation in which even exile was insufficient to maintain physical security.

Augustine's writings do not clarify the location to which the Donatists would be exiled. His failure to specify a location indicates that he assumed his readers would know that the Donatists would be exiled according to imperial law (although not completely, as shown presently). The *Theodosian Code* arranged to have heretics merely removed from cities and sent into the surrounding country, but it also decreed that more dangerous heretics be sent to outer provinces and islands; its authors presumably thought that the exile should fit the crime. For instance, the support of subversive hermits, who often entered town from their desert caves and engaged in political agitation, was punished by expulsion into the country to those same caves, which was another way of forcing them to adhere to their own self-proclaimed principles (*CT* 16.4.3, September 2, 390). Similarly, the code expels the Manichaean heretic Jovinian, who had engaged in heretical rites outside the city:

> Therefore, We command that the aforesaid person shall be arrested and beaten with leaden whips and that he shall be forced into exile along with the remaining adherents and ministers. He himself, as the instigator, shall be transported with all haste to the island of Boa; the rest, as seems best, provided only that the band of superstitious conspirators shall be dissolved

32. *Damnare* in classical and early medieval Latin means passing judgment, to sentence to pay. It derives from *damnum*, which is a loss of money or other possessions (Souter, *Glossary of Later Latin*, 87). Only later did it come to mean exclusively eternal damnation.

by the separation of exile, shall be deported for life to solitary islands situated at a great distance from each other. (*CT* 16.5.53, March 6, 412 [although the editor argues it was proclaimed in 398])

The author of this law thought it appropriate for Jovinian's heretical activities, which took place outside of Rome, to be punished with exile and beatings. The law goes further than Augustine's principles in calling for harsh beatings, and in exiling Jovinian's followers. Augustine, on the other hand, advocated exile only for leaders, and only pecuniary fines for violent followers. Earlier laws against the Donatists were more lenient than later ones. For example, one law (*CT* 16.5.34, March 4, 398) sent them into the country, and sent them farther only when they persisted in reentering Rome. In 407, a proclamation declared that Donatists and other heretics "shall have no customs and no laws in common with the rest of mankind" (*CT* 16.5.40, February 22, 407). The law itself does not specify location or conditions of exile, but lists a host of ways the heretics were to be deprived of their rights. This law reflects the general principles of punishment of heretics, and also reflects the chaotic condition of the western empire; the eastern empire continued to permit heretics to take offices such as that of a local councillor (*CT* 16.5.48, February 21, 410).[33] In 414, a severe proclamation was issued exiling Donatist bishops and priests to separate islands and provinces (*CT* 16.5.54.1, January 17, 414). That it lists outer provinces indicates that exile did not entail physical removal from the empire as a whole, which may have been impossible in any case, given its size. However, the principle behind the exile was to remove heretics from communion with others; exile to outer islands and provinces effectively cut them off from the empire. Imperial policy on heretics in general, therefore, gave Augustine a spectrum of types of exile to advocate for violent heretics: from mere banishment from the city, to expulsion to the outer limits of the empire. However, he does not appear to have advocated exile for followers. Furthermore, imperial policy understood exile as appropriate to the crime of heresy, which is consistent with Augustine's theory of punishment.

Augustine also advocated fines for heretical leaders and violent heretics. Heretics most commonly found themselves fined under the *Theodosian Code*. Social elites in particular were often fined ten pounds of gold (*CT* 16.5.21, proclaimed in 392),[34] and Circumcellions were fined ten pounds of silver

33. Honoré, *Law and the Crisis of Empire*, 131.
34. The translator considers this amount exceedingly high (454 n. 48), although Deane considers it "extraordinarily mild," considering the enormity of the crime (*Political and Social Ideas*, 188).

(*CT* 16.5.52, January 30, 412). Augustine warned a Donatist bishop, Crispinus, for instance, that he would be fined ten pounds of gold by the empire for rebaptizing people (*Ep.* 66.1, written in 402). His case was prosecuted by Augustine's friend Possidius, and Crispinus was found guilty; however, the fine was remitted at Possidius's behest (*Ep.* 88.7, written in 406). Augustine thought such fines were appropriate for heretics who committed acts of violence (see below), but that elites should be the only nonviolent heretics who should be fined. For example, he argued that heretical bishops or clergymen should be fined ten pounds of gold in those districts where the Catholic Church suffered violence from their clergy, Circumcellions, or "at the hands of any of their people" (*Ep.* 185.7.25, written in 417; see also 88.7). Augustine instead recommended fining such heretics the amount that would prevent them from leading wicked lives (*Ep.* 91.9, written in 408). The principle behind this was to prevent heretics from supporting their sect, but Augustine adamantly states that this should not involve their poverty, destitution, or dependence on others for their daily bread: "Neither was there any ground for your apprehending our inflicting a life of indigence and of dependence upon others for daily bread on those regarding whom I had said that we desired to secure to them the second of the possessions named above, vis., the means of supporting life" (*Ep.* 104.2.5, written in 409; see also 104.1.4). Such deprivation does not entail dependence on others for basic subsistence. Augustine contrasts this deprivation with the much more extreme poverty of the Roman dictators Cincinnatus and Fabricius. For example, he advocates fining a group of heretics ten pounds of silver for burning down a Catholic church: "But as to their third possession, viz. the means and opportunities of living wickedly, that is to say—passing over other things—their silver with which they constructed those images of their false gods, in whose protection or adoration or unhallowed worship an attempt was made even to destroy the church of God by fire" (*Ep.* 104.2.5). He thought the fine of ten pounds of silver was appropriate because it prevented the heretics who had burned down a Catholic church from furthering their impiety.

However, Augustine's optimal solution to violent heresy was not practical in the end because the threat of political dissolution in North Africa was too high and because Donatist leaders retained their followers by habit and by intimidation. He describes, in 417, the failure of the Edict of Unity to preserve the peace after 405:

> For a law had already been published, that the heresy of the Donatists, being of so savage a description that mercy towards it really involved a greater cruelty than its very madness wrought, should for the future be prevented

not only from being violent, but from existing with impunity at all; but yet no capital punishment was imposed upon it, that even in dealing with those who were unworthy, Christian gentleness might be observed, but a pecuniary fine was ordained, and sentence of exile was pronounced against their bishops or ministers.[35] (*Ep.* 185.7.26, written in 417)

Ultimately, Donatist numbers were too high, and their violence too severe, for exile and fines to be sufficiently effective penalties. The emperor reissued many decrees, which, as mentioned above, reflected the inability of magistrates to enforce the laws.[36] Thus, the empire, the Church, and Augustine lagging not far behind moved to eliminate the sect outright and use imperial power to incorporate it into the Church. This process culminated in the Synod of Carthage of 411, which was meant to conclude the century-old problem by allowing each side to compare each other's claims, in order to identify the true Catholic Church.[37]

### The Years 405 to 411

This period sees Augustine's final acceptance of coercion against the Donatists, and his support of the Edict of Unity of 405. Magistrates were too weak to enforce the edict; the Donatist Church grew and its violence intensified. Further, imperial decrees were issued, such as one proscribing the partisans of Gildo (which was an attempt to prevent sedition against Roman rule in North Africa) (*CT* 9.40.19, November 11, 408), forbidding heretical assemblies (*CT* 16.5.45, November 27, 408), punishing those who destroyed basilicas (*CT* 16.2.31, January 13, 409), and removing magistrates who neglected to carry out imperial orders (*CT* 16.5.46, 16.5.47, January 15 and June 26, 409). At the same time, the African proconsul punished heretics with death, which Augustine opposed (*Ep.* 100, written in 409; see below). Under earlier imperial law, heretics had received capital punishment for attacking Catholic churches and priests (*CT* 16.2.31, August 25, 398; 16.4.1, January 13, 386) and for disobeying their sentence of exile (*CT* 16.5.34, March 4, 398). After the Synod of Carthage in 409, however, heresy by itself (whether or not it involved violent acts) became a capital crime (*CT* 16.5.51, August 25, 410; 16.5.56, August 25, 410, and repeated in 415).

---

35. See Markus, *Saeculum,* 138; and Brown, *Augustine of Hippo,* 334. Capital punishment was proclaimed in 410 and again in 415 (*CT* 16.5.51, 16.5.56) (see below).

36. Willis, *Augustine and the Donatist Controversy,* 131; Honoré, *Law and the Crisis of Empire,* 26, 133.

37. Brown, *Augustine of Hippo,* 330–34.

The Synod of Carthage, chaired by Augustine's friend Marcellinus, lasted for three days and concluded with a proclamation to ban the Donatist heresy. The Donatists, as expected, rejected its conclusion and increased their violent activity, and were answered by increased imperial suppression. The ensuing violence was so widespread that Augustine commented on the fear that civil authorities had of the Donatist influence (*Ep.* 185.4.15). For instance, his friend Marcellinus, to whom the *City of God* is dedicated, appears to have been condemned to death and executed as a result of Donatist plots or pressure to avenge his role in the conference.[38] This fear was further justified: Augustine himself barely escaped assassination on one occasion.[39] The widespread influence of Donatism and the violence associated with it indicate that the optimal punishment for heretics, banishment, was unavailable to Augustine and the Church at the time.[40]

This account of efforts by the Church and the empire to suppress Donatism provides the background for Augustine's change of mind from initially rejecting to finally advocating coercion, as documented in Epistle 93. In the letter, he compares the compulsion of heretics to Christ's commanding the apostles to enter the house of his feast: "[C]ompel them to enter *(Quoscomque inveneritis cogite intrare)*" (*Ep.* 93.2.5, citing Luke 14:23). He states that he opposed coercion because he thought it would result in feigned conversions (*Ep.* 93.5.17). His rejection of coercion was the result of underestimating heretical violence and wickedness if left unpunished, and the extent to which heretics could benefit from the application of discipline. He also underestimated the ability of coercion to bring Donatists into the Catholic fold. The picture we have of Augustine's justifications, in their political context, is one of him facing a strong and violent sect that posed a threat not only to Catholics, but also to the physical integrity of the Roman Empire. His justification cannot be taken as a sanction to impose orthodoxy for its own sake, but rather because this sect held principles that expressed themselves in violence. Augustine was faced with the further difficulty of exhorting reluctant Roman authorities to carry out the imperial laws, but then having to restrain their violence when the application of the law became excessive. He wanted the authorities to enforce most of the imperial laws, but tried, often vainly, to make them stop short of capital punishment (permitted by law) and other excessively violent punishments.

---

38. T. D. Barnes, "Aspects of the Background of the *City of God*," 65 n. 6.
39. Brown, *Augustine of Hippo*, 330; Van der Meer, *Augustine the Bishop*, 88.
40. Brown, *Augustine of Hippo*, 240; Van der Meer, *Augustine the Bishop*, 80.

Augustine justified different types of coercion in this period. He maintained that exile and fines for leaders (when effective) were justified but changed his mind in advocating the coercion of Donatists to join the Catholic Church (instead of merely preventing Donatists from attacking Catholics), and in assenting to corporal punishment for violent heretics (but not for nonviolent ones). I have not found evidence that he advocated punishment for nonviolent Donatist followers, other than small fines (see *Ep.* 104.1–2, written in 409). He judged that the success of the Edict of Unity of 405 was based on the fact that most Donatist followers remained in the Church due to sloth, habit, and intimidation by their leaders. For these people, he provides a somewhat Aristotelian account of why coercion appears to have successfully effected "conversions": "Yet these same persons, under force of custom *(vi consuetudinis)*, would in no way have thought of being changed to a better condition, had they not, under the terror of this danger *(nisi hoc terrore perculisi)*, directed their minds earnestly to the study of truth" (*Ep.* 93.1.1). He reiterates this point later in the same letter:

> How many were bound, not by truth—for you [Vincentius, Donatist bishop] never pretended to that as yours—but by the chains of inveterate custom *(obduratae consuetudinis)* . . . ! How many supposed the sect of Donatus to be the true church, merely because ease had made them too listless, or conceited, or sluggish, to take pains to examine Catholic truth! How many would have entered earlier had not the calumnies of slanderers, who declared that we offered something else than we do upon the altar of God, shut them out! How many, believing that it mattered not to which party a Christian might belong, remained in the schism of Donatus only because they had been born into it, and no one was compelling them to forsake it and pass over into the Catholic church! (*Ep.* 93.5.17)

This statement reflects Augustine's view that law may force a certain number of people to change their actions and habits, in order to give them the opportunity to act virtuously. He observes that such people were held to heresy out of old habits and by misunderstanding the practices of the Catholic Church. As mentioned above, Donatists and Catholics had little contact with one another, since Donatists strove to separate themselves from "impure" Catholics. Their views of one another were incomplete, and followers in both camps were ignorant of one another, and, therefore, easily misled. Some Donatists remained because of intimidation by their leaders (see *Ep.* 83.1, 85.29, 93.1.3, 3.10). Thus, according to Augustine, the chains of bad habit developed because Donatist followers were ignorant of Catholics, and removing their leaders was the only way to convert them.

Augustine's understanding of the coercive aspect of law, as shown here, is similar to Aristotle's account of how law forces wicked people to act virtuously so that at least some of them will then become virtuous. Coercion in these circumstances is a necessary but not a sufficient cause of conversion. The role of bad habit in sin is a constant theme, especially in Augustine's *Confessions* where he narrates the ways in which his bad habits prevented him from fully loving God. Elsewhere, he points out the extent to which habits shape our perspectives: "For it is not for nothing that custom is called a sort of second and fitted-on nature. But we see new senses in the judging of these kinds of corporeal things, built by custom, by another custom disappear" (*DM* 6.7.19). Custom, as a kind of second nature, shapes our perceptions of right and wrong in ways that we may forget what is natural and not according to custom. Thus, Augustine uses terms such as *terror* and *shock* to indicate the means of breaking these habits in people's minds.

Augustine uses violent language in his rhetoric toward the Donatist bishop, and this harshness gives the impression of a gap between the habits of the heretic and the purposes of punishment. In other words, it gives the impression that coercion is detached from persuasion, since the means of coercion are disconnected from the understanding of the coerced. Coercion appears as a battle of wills, containing "a moment of 'pure violence.'" Augustine's rhetoric toward the Donatist bishops certainly includes an element of coercion. But is this his final view on the matter? Evidence indicates that it is not. A more substantive account of coercion lies beneath Augustine's excessive rhetoric directed toward Vincentius, the Donatist bishop and recipient of the infamous letter. However, Augustine was unsuccessful in ensuring that his substantive teaching was influential.

It is not surprising that Augustine's rhetoric veils a deeper meaning. His antipolitical rhetoric in the *City of God*, for example, covers his substantive political teaching. He did not wish to make this teaching explicit because he did not want to give his audience any reason to think that they could gain salvation through political means. The Donatists would certainly have been targeted by this rhetoric because they, like the pagans who constituted part of Augustine's audience in the *City of God*, sought perfect blessedness in this life. As with his strategy in the *City of God*, in his letters to the Donatists Augustine uses rhetoric to belittle worldly ambition and pride.

Peter Brown, in an essay called "The Limits of Intolerance," has recently explained that modern readers often overestimate the intolerance and "pure violence" of Christian apologists such as Augustine. He points out that, in the late empire, moral and religious order was preserved through a distinctive "style of command," such as unchallenged authority, fear, and force, which was accepted by the upper classes (to govern both themselves and the lower classes):

> For modern persons, it is not an altogether pleasant glimpse. If authority was to work without overt violence, it had to seem "natural"; it had to relay commands with quiet certainty from a position of unchallenged superiority to persons whose inferiority, also, was to be taken for granted. As a result of the religious changes of the age, the social hierarchy became even more high pitched. . . . Among the upper classes, a combination of browbeating and cajolery was the stuff of late Roman politics.[41]

Elites in the late Roman empire governed themselves through a network of patronage and honor. It was socially dangerous to overstep the bounds of what was permissible in these kinds of debates. Thus, Brown notes, it is a mistake to assert straightforwardly that the persecutions in which Augustine participated provided the principles of later persecutions: "In this manner, the opening of the modern debate on religious tolerance was fueled by a characteristically late Roman betrayal of a breach in decorum." Brown alerts the reader of the unspoken social conventions that structured Augustine's rhetoric. Historical scholarship on Roman legal rhetoric confirms Brown's thesis by comparing the rhetoric of religious disputes to the tone of legal battles: "Repeatedly, orators 'used' the law to wrong-foot opponents, not only in real life, as Augustine did, but also in leading a case, as it were a case at law. In this quasi-courtroom, 'they,' the enemy, were the law-breakers, while the speaker, invariably, was the champion of right, justice and the lawful authority of emperors." It was common to imitate the rhetorical style of command of the emperor, as well as to portray themselves as "victims" of their more "powerful" opponents.[42] According to this view, Augustine used the rhetoric of Roman law and of aristocratic manner to shame Vincentius and the Donatists for their base actions. Such shaming also belittles the shamed, and portrays them as incapable of reasoning and amenable to persuasion, which explains his imitation of the emperor's rhetoric that utilizes command rather than persuasion. Such a relationship between "shamer" and "shamed" would contain the aforementioned "moment of 'pure violence.' " However, the scholarship of Brown and Harries indicates that this

---

41. Brown, "The Limits of Intolerance," in *Authority and the Sacred: Aspects of Christianisation of the Roman World*, 44–45.

42. Ibid., 46; Harries, *Law and Empire*, 96, 2–5.

moment is rooted in the rhetoric of social decorum and not necessarily in the substance of Augustine's argument.

Since fines and exile of heretics did not appear to be working, a certain kind of violent coercion was required. This necessity, however, presented a conflict for Augustine. He felt compelled to exhort imperial authorities to enforce laws, but those authorities were often prone to excessive violence in their enforcement of those laws. Augustine's letters show that he strove to convince civil authorities to be more lenient. For example, he outlines the above principles for removing property in a letter (*Ep.* 104, written in 409) responding to Nectarius of Calama, a pagan philosopher, who had charged him with being responsible for the violent measures used by imperial authorities against a population in which there were religious riots (*Ep.* 103.4). Augustine denies responsibility and further states his opposition to violent measures; he advocates instead removal of property: "Far be it from us to demand the infliction, either by ourselves or by anyone, of such hardships upon any of our enemies . . . ! Examine more carefully my letter, to which you have so reluctantly sent a reply, for I have in it made my views sufficiently plain" (*Ep.* 104.1-2, referring to 93). That imperial authorities used violence in this way indicates that Augustine was unable to restrain them. It also shows his awareness that people misinterpreted his views. As Brown observes, Augustine's "interventions by letter, therefore, should be treated as exceptions to the usual routine of suppression: they reflect circumstances where the application of the laws had passed beyond his immediate control and, so, called for correspondence."[43]

Augustine's attempt to restrain officials is seen in a letter in which he asks Apringius, proconsul of Africa and Marcellinus's brother: "[W]hy do you not commute your sentence to a more prudent and more lenient one, as judges have the liberty of doing even in non-ecclesiastical cases?" (*Ep.* 134, written in 412). Even after his notorious change of heart in 408 when he stated that compulsion is rightful, Augustine always opposed the death penalty.[44] He told Donatus (a civil authority unrelated to the founder of Donatism) that the Catholics would stop bringing cases to his tribunal if he used capital punishment. In one letter, Augustine objects to the capital punishment of a murderous heretic and reminds his friend Marcellinus that the purpose of punishment is to turn men "from their insane disquiet to the quietness of men in their sound judgment, and

43. Brown, "Augustine's Attitude," 275 n. 2.
44. Brown observes Augustine was unable to prevent many executions (*Augustine of Hippo*, 242). Augustine opposed the death penalty because it prevents repentance (see *Ep.* 153.18, written ca. 414; see also 139.2 [written in 412], where he argues that capital punishment dishonors the blood of the martyrs). The Donatists claimed to be martyrs on account of their being persecuted.

betake themselves to some useful labour. This is indeed called a penal sentence" (*Ep.* 133.1, written in 412). Augustine argues that murderers' lives should be spared, and, further, that they should be tortured "not by stretching them on the rack, not by furrowing their flesh with iron claws, not by scorching them with flames, but by beating them with wooden rods *(sed virgarum verberibus eruisti)*— a mode of correction used by schoolmasters *(magistris artium liberalium)*, and by parents themselves in chastising children, and often by bishops in the sentences awarded by them" (*Ep.* 133.1–2). Although people today might wince at Augustine's general acceptance of torture as a method of discovering the perpetrator of a crime (he and other Romans thought it worked), it should be noted that he states that the actual punishment should be lighter. He also advocates beating the murderers with wooden rods, a method of discipline used by teachers, parents, and bishops. In its cultural context, Augustine's view of punishment was relatively mild; for instance, imperial law called for the use of leaden whips (*CT* 16.5.53, March 6, 412). In other words, the maximum penalty that a heretic who committed murder could expect, in Augustine's doctrine of compulsion, would be the same that a schoolboy would receive from his teachers.[45]

At one point Augustine appears to advocate violent methods for coercing heretics who had not engaged in violent activities; however, this is misleading. It should be noted that he uses a double-voice rhetoric to exhort Boniface, an imperial official, to apply the law. He uses violent and figurative language to exhort the official to keep the Donatists in awe of the law, but he fails to give a specific recommendation on the type of punishment; despite Augustine's intention, however, he failed to restrain the official. In a letter that has come down to us as a treatise titled "On the Correction of Donatists," he apparently asserts that beating heretics with rods is appropriate (*Ep.* 185.6.22–23, written in 417). He advocates this course after arguing that the persistence of Donatist violence shows that verbal persuasion, which up until then had failed, must be supplemented by coercion. This is the case because heretics lack the fear that one has of being separate from God (*Ep.* 185.6.21); instead, they fear only temporal punishments. However, Augustine's apparent advocacy of violent coercion constitutes an example of what Brown has called his "two voices *(duos voces)*" that reflect the scriptural polarities of "severity and mildness, of fear and love";[46] closer examination of the letter shows that he treats punishment by

45. This is a punishment that Augustine himself received from his schoolmasters. See *Conf.* 1.9–10; *CD* 22.22.
46. Brown, "Augustine's Attitude," 272.

rods as a figurative representation of the awe of imperial authority that heretics should fear. The *Theodosian Code* itself provided Augustine with a precedent for using figurative language. For instance, one law proclaims that heretics would be punished *(urere)* by deportation *(CT* 16.2.40). *Urere* means literally "to brand" or "to burn," as in "to be branded a traitor." However, the term is used figuratively here, since the punishment referred to is deportation rather than burning or branding.

Augustine speaks literally of using rods only for heretics who have committed violent acts. He invokes a passage from Proverbs to justify violent methods: " 'You will beat him with the rod *(percutis eum virga)*, and will free his soul from death' (Prov. 23:14); and elsewhere he says, 'He who spares the rod *(parcit baculo)* hates his son' (Prov. 23:24)" *(Ep.* 185.6.21). However, here again he speaks in a double voice. His rhetoric seems to encourage the authority to use violence to coerce all heretics to return to the fold. After having made his case, however, he concludes that he has been discussing heretics who have used violence *(Ep.* 185.6.23). He uses the example of Paul (which I discuss again below) to illustrate his point. Christ compelled Paul to love Christ by striking him down and by afterward consoling him:

> Let them recognize in his case Christ first compelling *(prius cogentem)*, and afterwards teaching *(postea docentem)*; first striking *(prius ferientem)*, and afterwards consoling *(postea consolantem)*. For it is wonderful how he who entered the service of the gospel in the first instance under the compulsion of bodily punishment *(poena corporis)*, afterwards labored more in the gospel than all they who were called by word only; and he who was compelled by the greater influence of fear to love, displayed that perfect love which casts out fear. *(Ep.* 185.6.22)

Augustine concludes from the example of Paul that the Church should use force in compelling violent heretics to return to the fold: "Why, therefore *(ergo)*, should not the church use force in compelling *(cogeret)* her lost sons to return, if the lost sons compelled *(coegerunt)* others to their destruction?" *(Ep.* 185.6.23). The Latin *ergo* indicates that Augustine considers this statement a conclusion based on the previous passage. The lesson he draws from Christ striking Paul is that those who persecute the Church, as did Paul, and who violently coerced others to remain Donatist, deserve to be coerced with violence.

Augustine reiterates this point when he compares the Church to a shepherd who brings sheep back to the fold "by fear or even the pain of the whip *(flagellorum terroribus)*, if [sheep and heretics] show symptoms of resistance; especially since, if they multiply with growing abundance among the fugitive slaves and robbers (*praesertim quoniam si apud fugitivos servos et praedones fecunditate multiplicentur*), he has the more right in that the mark of the master is recognized on them, who is not outraged in those whom we receive but do not rebaptise." The term *especially (praesertim)* in this quote reflects Augustine's emphasis on curbing the violence of heretics. In general, *praesertim* means "especially" or "above all," which makes it possible to interpret Augustine here as making a comparison of degree instead of kind. He may be arguing that all heretics deserve violent methods of coercion but that heretics who commit violent atrocities deserve it especially. However, *praesertim* here needs to be interpreted in the context he has previously established. This context involves the recommendation to Boniface, the Roman official and recipient of this letter, that imperial law must stop the violence of the heretics, and that this be achieved only by banning the sect. Augustine emphasizes the awe engendered by the violence of the imperial law. He then hints, however, that he is referring to violent methods for perpetrators of violence, and that lesser penalties are suitable for heretics not engaged in violent acts. *Praesertim*, therefore, means not so much the comparative "especially" or "above all," but, rather, constitutes the rhetorical hammer with which Augustine emphasizes the necessity of having Roman law instill awe in order to dissuade violent and nonviolent heretics, even though he believed that nonviolent heretics do not deserve violent punishments. Unfortunately, this kind of rhetoric was taken literally, and thus it failed to restrain imperial authorities and future generations of inquisitors.

Finally, Augustine's understanding of coercion as educative is illuminated in his discussion of the way the trials of heretics should be conducted:

> You will, however, most effectively help us to secure the fruit of our labours and dangers, if you take care that the imperial laws for the restraining of their sect, which is full of conceit and of impious pride, be so used that they may not appear either to themselves or to others to be suffering hardship in any form for the sake of truth and righteousness; but suffer them, when this is requested at your hands, to be convinced and instructed (*convinci atque instrui*) of certain things by the most manifest documentation (*rerum certarum manifestissimis documentis*) in the presence of your Excellency or of inferior judges, in order that those who are arrested by your command may themselves incline their stubborn will to the better part, and may read these things profitably to others in their party. (*Ep.* 100.2)

The proceedings of the trial should be public so that the individual understands clearly the purpose of the charges. Since the Donatists were making what he saw as false claims to martyrdom, Augustine thought that the purpose of the charges ought to be made public. This would prevent the Donatists from claiming that they had been falsely accused, and thus from portraying themselves as victims, a portrayal that would otherwise support their martyrology. Making the charges public also had the effect of explaining the purpose of the charges to others in the sect, which would act both as a clarification and as a warning. The public nature of the trial is important for a right-by-nature theory of punishment, since the form of the trial requires that the prosecutors attempt to convince and instruct the accused that the criminal charge is based on reasonable grounds, and not on reasons of political convenience for the authorities. This quotation alone does not prove that the trial aims to convince and instruct the accused on reasonable grounds. However, Augustine's theory of the purpose of punishment—to educate and to form virtue—indicates that the trial would have to speak to the accused's intellect in order for punishment, in the case of established guilt, to harmonize with its purpose. The requirement for the proceedings to be recorded and given to the sect at large is consistent with this general purpose of punishment, in that it attempts to teach others in the sect about the purpose of the accusation.

## PRINCIPLES OF COERCION

One of the purposes of coercing heretics is to preserve the physical security of church members. Augustine thought that one of the duties of a ruler is preserving the safety of the city (or church in Augustine's case) as a place in which citizens can, to an extent, fulfill their particular perfections. He draws from the example of Paul who sought assistance from the emperor when he discovered there were conspiracies against his life: "He sought assistance, therefore, not so much with any desire of revenging himself, as with the view of defending the church entrusted to his charge. And if he had omitted to do this, he would have deserved not to be praised for his patience (patientia), but to be blamed for negligence (negligentia)" (Ep. 185.7.28, citing Acts 23:17–32). This passage shows that the ruler shirks his duty when he neglects to defend his city or church. The precarious position of the Church in North Africa made this concern paramount. A common criticism of this kind of reasoning is that it appears to apply the standards of the world to the life of the Church. For instance, would it not have been saintly for Paul to have been martyred? Does Christ not teach one to reject the ways of emperors and soldiers, and instead entrust oneself and one's church to God? This view is critical of

Augustine's apparent impatience, which led him to distrust God's providence and, consequently, to intervene in God's plan. Augustine might be accused of failing to trust that God's work will be done regardless of one's actions. The above passage, however, indicates that he considered this to be negligence because, as a ruler or bishop, one would neglect those entrusted to one's charge. He would have neglected those for whose souls he is in some way (although not completely) responsible. It would be unjust to keep faith at the expense of safety in this instance. In this sense, the case of Augustine's justification of coercion is comparable to his discussion of whether it was rightful for the city of Sagentum to keep faith with the gods and the Romans and cause its own destruction (*CD* 22.6; discussed in Chapter 2 of this study). In that instance, it was shown that Augustine hints that Sagentum would have been justified in preserving itself. It is not that Augustine chooses the safety of the Church at the expense of virtue or keeping faith, but rather that he understands the love of God and of neighbor as being expressed in the cultivation of the virtue of those under the governor.

The main principle animating Augustine's understanding of coercion is reflected in his statement that the heretic should be threatened with deprivation of the proximate or inferior good that masquerades as the greatest good: "[O]ffenders must be deprived of that which they most fear to lose" (*Ep.* 104.1.2). What the heretic most fears to lose is that which he falsely thinks will bring salvation:

> [T]he thing to be considered when any one is coerced *(cogitur)*, is not the mere fact of the coercion, but the nature of that to which he is coerced, whether it be good or bad: not that any one can be good in spite of his own will, but that, through fear of suffering what he does not desire *(sed timendo quod non vult pati)*, he either renounces his hostile prejudices *(impedientem animositatem)*, or is compelled to examine truth of which he had been contentedly ignorant; so that through fearing, repudiate falsehood that he had contended, or seek truth of which he had been ignorant, and desiring to hold now what he had rejected *(ut timens vel respuat falsam de quo contendebat, vel quaerat verum quod nesciebat, et volens teneat jam quod nolebat)*. (*Ep.* 93.5.16)

These passages appear to reflect the "moment of 'pure violence,'" as described by Milbank. Augustine seems merely to state that the heretic will lose that which he most fears losing; if this is all he says, then the relation between the authority and the heretic is merely a battle of wills, since Augustine does not explain how the miserable heretic is then to love the real good and not just his proximate good. One suspects that Brown's comments on the Roman "style of command" are applicable here; Augustine had previously stated that the purpose of coercion is not to return evil for evil (*Ep.* 93.1.2). If coercion entails merely depriving a heretic of what he most fears to lose, then coercion would in fact be a return of evil for evil. Augustine does not appear to explain what to be the necessary next step. Neglecting to do this does not necessarily indicate that his theory of coercion contains this "moment of 'pure violence,'" however. Rather, neglecting to do this is consistent with Brown's view of the style of command among Roman elites. Authority does not need to justify itself to those it commands, and Augustine incorporates this idea into his rhetoric.

Furthermore, the second passage quoted above implies an Aristotelian understanding of punishment and law that transcends this moment of pure violence. The purpose of law is to enable citizens to choose the right and the good. Whether they do so lies beyond the power of the law. This is reflected in Augustine's statement that coercion puts the heretic into the position of either renouncing his "hostile prejudices" or actively turning to the search for truth. The purpose of coercion is to clarify Church doctrine to the heretic. After having done so, the individual heretic, freed from his initial ignorance, would have to decide whether to love the truth (and enter the Church). Force, in this circumstance, is a necessary but not a sufficient cause of conversion. The purpose of coercion, according to this passage, is to show the heretic the insufficiency of his object of worship and to teach him about the Church in order to prevent his hostility toward it. To use a popular metaphor, the heretic is brought to water but is not forced to drink.

## COERCION AS HEALING

Augustine's method of relating means to ends is explained more completely in his discussion of Christian healing. Spiritual healing parallels God's way of healing the sins of human beings. God's healing is based on what Augustine calls the principles of contrariety and similarity (*DDC* 1.27), which work in the following way. The principle of contrariety shows the heretic how opposed his proximate cause is to his proper end. The principle is insufficient because, taken by itself, it contains the "moment of 'pure violence.'" This principle is seen in Augustine's dictum of "removing that which the heretic fears most to lose." This is why Augustine adds the principle of similarity, by which the heretic learns that his proximate good masquerading as the highest good actually intimates the highest good.

Augustine compares these principles to those a doctor follows in healing a wound: "A doctor treating a physical wound applies some medications that are contrary—a cold one to a hot wound, a dry one to a wet wound, and so on—and also some that are similar, such as a round bandage to a round wound and a rectangular bandage to a rectangular wound, and he does not apply the same ligature to all wounds, but matches like with like" (*DDC* 1.28). The principle of contrariety is applied in order to moderate the extremes of a wound. The principle of similarity is applied so as to suit the wound. He uses this analogy in explaining how the principle of contrariety is present in God's healing activity:

> Because human beings fell through pride, [God's wisdom] used humility in healing them. We were deceived by the wisdom of the serpent; we are freed by the foolishness of God. But just as that was called wisdom yet was foolishness to those who despise God, so this so-called foolishness is wisdom to those who overcome the devil. We made base use of immortality, and so we died; Christ made good use of mortality, so we live. The disease entered through a corrupted female mind; healing emerged from an intact female body. Also relevant to the principle of contrariety is the fact that our vices too are treated by the example of his virtues. (*DDC* 1.29)

God applies the contrary aspects of our vice to bring that extreme to a condition of health: God's humility heals pride; God's "foolishness" heals false wisdom. Each contrary element opposes the extreme of the particular vice.

Augustine proposes that the principle of similarity prevents the vice from lapsing into its opposite vice. He then explains the principle of similarity in God's healing activity: "Examples of similarity in the kinds of bandages (as it were) applied to our limbs and wounds are these: it was one born of a woman that freed those deceived by a woman; it was a mortal man that freed mortals; and it was by death that he freed the dead" (*DDC* 1.30). The principle of similarity complements the principle of contrariety by showing the heretic how his proximate good actually intimates the highest good, even though he actually opposes the highest good in his obstinate and inordinate love of the proximate good. This is seen in Augustine's suggestions that Donatist heretics should lose only enough property to prevent them from harming Catholics. Augustine also applies the principle of similarity in his acknowledgment that Donatist criticisms of Catholic corruption contain an element of truth, and that these criticisms reflect the way that both sides share in truth (see *Ep.* 43.8.23). The operation of this principle is illustrated in the context of Augustine's strategy of internal Church reformation below.

In this context, Augustine's principles of similarity and contrariety compare with Aristotle's understanding of forming desires by finding the mean between extremes. For Aristotle, sometimes an inordinate desire can find the mean by applying its opposite (for example, forcing a coward to commit rash deeds), but the individual must also recognize that the opposing action, and its accompanying desire, also shares in the mean. Therefore, Augustine's theory of coercion lacks the "moment of 'pure violence' " by which the greatest good is completely alien to the good loved by the heretic. The principles of similarity and contrariety show sinful human beings how to reach the final goal that their sins purport to achieve, and also demonstrate how far their sins are from reaching their goal. The principles can be related to Augustine's statement, in Epistle 93, that the heretic is coerced by losing what he most fears losing. One loses one's greatest possession by understanding how short it falls in securing happiness (the principle of contrariety), but one is possibly led to see how that possession intimates the greater principle that needs to be fulfilled for happiness (the principle of similarity). For instance, exile is appropriate for one whose own purported purity alienates him from other human beings (thus showing how such purity is false); one has one's silver idols taken away and thus sees how one's reliance on those idols is misplaced.

These principles are reflected in Augustine's example of the conversion of Paul, used in order to demonstrate the principle of coercion:

> You also read how he who was at first Saul, and afterwards Paul, was compelled by the great violence *(magna violentia . . . compulsum)* with which Christ coerced him, to know and to embrace the truth; for you cannot but think that the light which your eyes enjoy is more precious to men than money or any other possession *(quamlemlibet possessionem)*. This light, lost suddenly by him when he was cast to the ground by the heavenly voice, he did not recover until he became a member of the Holy church. *(Ep. 93.1.5)*

This example shows that Augustine's principle of coercion involves the punishment of deprivation of one's proximate good, which still shares with the highest good. The Lord blinded Saul, but the Lord also gave him a vision of the "third heaven," which convinced him to enter the Church. Saul's blindness in sight enabled him to focus on what the Lord wanted him to see in his mind. Paul suffered the opposite (or contrariety) of sight, blindness, and was healed through similarity by the light of the third heaven of his spiritual vision. The agent who coerces does not return sight, as this example might suggest; rather, he teaches the heretic about the insufficiency of his proximate good, and attempts to convince him of the goodness of the highest good, by showing him that his previous understanding of the highest good was false. At this point, coercion must end and the heretic must be left to himself to decide whether to enter the Church or, at the very least, refrain from attacking it. Both principles, contrariety and similarity, are important for Augustine's theory; the principle of contrariety, applied by depriving the heretic of his possession, is insufficient if taken by itself, since, unless the heretic is taught, through the principle of similarity, to move beyond his possession, he will not know how his possession can be fulfilled.

## REFORMATION STRATEGY

Augustine's strategy of coercing heretics is not entirely one-sided, but it is accompanied by a reformation strategy on the part of the Church. The problem of maintaining virtue within the Church, and specifically of preventing scandal, was a paramount concern for Augustine. This in part explains his reluctance to embrace coercion because he was afraid of the effect of false conversions.[47]

In his letters, Augustine emphasizes the necessity for heretics to reform. This makes a certain amount of sense given the nature of his rhetoric, as discussed above. His reformation strategy, though not explicitly addressed in his polemical letters to the Donatists, is presented in his theoretical *City of God*. For example, there he discloses his concern for scandal when he emphasizes that Christians must truly be Christians and not just be Christians in name only: "Where therefore who are, and are called, Christians *(qui sumus vocamurque Christiani)* believe not in Peter, but in him in whom Peter believed" (CD 18.54; see also 1.35). Augustine's ecclesiology is based on the view that the Church will consist of reprobates as well as Christians, since it will experience the intermingling of the cities of God and of man:

> In this evil world, therefore, in these evil days, when amid present humilia-
> tion the church is preparing for her future high estate, and is schooled by the
> goads of fear, the tortures of sorrow, the vexations of toil and the dangers
> of temptation, rejoicing only in hope, in so far as her joy is wholesome,
> many reprobates are mingled with the good, and both kinds are gathered
> together as it were into the dragnet of the gospel. And in this world, as it
> were in a sea, both swim indiscriminately enclosed in nets until shore is
> reached, where the evil are to be separated from the good, and "God is to
> be all in all" (1 Cor. 15:28). (CD 18.49)

47. Markus, *Saeculum*, 138.

Augustine rejects the view that one can be saved merely by partaking in the sacrament; he maintains that one must also steadfastly practice virtue (*CD* 21.20). Those who sin and persist in sinning without asking forgiveness actually separate themselves from the body of Christ: "[Christ] shows what it is to eat the body of Christ and drink His blood, not only in the sacrament, but in reality, for to remain in Christ is to have Christ also remaining in him. For this is the same as if He said: 'He who does not remain in me, and in whom I do not remain, may not say or think that he is eating my body or drinking my blood.' So those who are not his members do not remain in Christ" (*CD* 21.25; citing John 6:56). These sins include not only explicit heresy such as that of the Donatists, but also other iniquities. The key is that one separates oneself from the body of Christ when one perseveres in sin: "For if they persevere in these sins until the end of this life, they cannot be said to persevere in Christ till the end." Such sins can be committed both by heretics and by those who, being Christians in name only, merely engage in ritual observance rather than attempt to be virtuous, thus bringing scandal to the Church. Such people are heretics inasmuch as they persevere in cutting themselves off from the body of Christ while calling themselves Christians. This requires that the Church reform itself by cultivating the virtues of its members, rather than by persecuting them (as the Donatists did with their own) when they do not cause scandal by leading others astray. If it does not reform itself in this way, then the Donatist charge that the Catholic Church is irreparably corrupt is justified. Although Augustine does not appear explicitly to grant the Donatists this point in the letters, he implicitly grants it when he points to the danger that merely nominal Christians pose to the Church. His reformation strategy requires that the Church experience the intermingling of heavenly and earthly cities, without succumbing either to Donatist-type legalism and hypermoralism or to an earthly organization of *traditores*.

Augustine points out that the success of the Church in satisfying the longings of human beings has led to the entry into the Church of many people who have only feigned love. He states this only to prevent Christians from becoming prideful about their identity and about the success of the Church: "But the devil, seeing the temples of the demons deserted and the human race running to the name of the Mediator who sets men free, stirred up heretics to resist the Christian doctrine under Christian guise *(sub vocabulo Christiano)*, as if they could be kept indifferently in the city of God without any reproof, even as the city of confusion kept indifferently the philosophers who held diverse and conflicting beliefs" (*CD* 18.51). Later in the chapter he reiterates: "For [heretics] are the cause of railing against the Christian and catholic name *(nomen);* and the dearer this name is to those who wish to live a godly life in Christ, the more they grieve that evildoers within the church make it less attractive than the minds of the godly desire" (*CD* 18.51). The success of the Church creates a new danger; whereas before it was persecuted by outsiders, it is now persecuted from within by those who seek to destroy it by giving it a bad name.

Augustine argues that the existence of heretics is important if weaker members of the Church are to recognize true Church doctrine, and thus virtue. Defending the Church against heresies provides leaders of the Church with the opportunity to clarify doctrine and to instruct: "No doubt many matters pertaining to the catholic faith are not only more diligently investigated when they are attacked by the feverish restlessness of the heretics, but are more clearly understood and more fervently expounded for the sake of defending them against these enemies. Thus the controversy stirred up by the adversary affords an opportunity for instruction" (*CD* 16.2; see also *Conf.* 7.9; *DDC* 3.104–5; *DVR* 8.15). Defending the ecclesiastical body against heretics is useful because it enables its members to understand virtue. This situation is analogous to the political situation in which citizens gain deeper insight into the principles of their regime when they are faced by a political crisis or enemy. For example, one possible explanation for the current "malaise" or dilemma in Western constitutional republics is that their citizens now lack an ideological enemy, communism, against which to organize. Augustine makes a similar point when he observes that Scipio opposed the destruction of Carthage, because such destruction would eventually undermine Rome: "He feared security, that enemy of weak minds, and he perceived that a wholesome fear would be a fit guardian for the citizens" (*CD* 1.30). Augustine's account of group identity is not reducible to hostility to the enemy; he points out, rather, that heresies help to clarify Church doctrine. In other words, the initial premise of the Church remains constant, but heretics or a crisis can provide members of the Church with deeper understanding of that premise.

This strategy of using heresy to reform the Church with its internal "heretics" illuminates Augustine's general use of *exempla.* Chapters 1, 5, and 6 showed that Augustine treats the *exempla* of the city of God and the city of man in two ways. On the one hand, the Church represents the perfect virtue of the city of God, whereas earthly cities filled with the reprobate represent the city of man. On the other hand, the world, which includes the political city and the Church, experiences these two cities as intermingled and intermixed, just as most human beings experience their wills as divided. As a result, Augustine also treats these *exempla* as models for each other, and treats the Church and heretics in an analogous manner.

According to Augustine, the principles of similarity and contrariety teach the heretic that the object of his love is insufficient, but that this object nevertheless shares with the highest good. He argues also that an intra-Church reformation strategy complements the coercion of heretics. Although Augustine does not appear to have admitted explicitly to the Donatists that the Catholic Church was filled with heretics, he insists in his theoretical treatise, the *City of God*, that it was disrupted by those who called themselves Catholic but whose perseverance in sin had caused them to separate from the body of Christ. This implicitly constitutes a partial agreement with the Donatist charge that some Catholics were corrupt (see *Ep.* 43). The difference between the Catholics and the Donatists was, however, that the Catholic Church, as viewed by Augustine, consists of the intermingling of the cities of God and of man, and that the body of Christ is more than the sum total of its members' virtues.

Augustine's theory of coercion is situated to some extent within a historical context. He changed his mind to justify coercion only after long holding the hope that the Donatists could be persuaded to join the Catholic Church and to cease their violent activities. In addition, he hoped that virtue could be instilled by persuasion; however, a combination of Donatist principles and Roman politics made that impossible. Coercion is a last resort to be applied only after the possibility of persuasion is exhausted. Augustine's insistence on an internal reformation strategy on the part of the Church indicates that he believed such violence involved corruption within the Church. Such reformation does not end even when the possibility of persuading heretics (which includes showing the heretics how much the Church has reformed) has been exhausted. Once it has been exhausted, Augustine considered that exile and fines become the optimal forms of coercion, and then only for leaders.

The exile of Donatist leaders from the community makes heresy concrete, since heresy entails spiritual separation. This means that the optimal form of coercion entails depriving heretics of the fruits of community. In Augustine's case, exile was not practical because the Donatists constituted the majority of the population in North Africa. The second-best form of coercion was to deprive the heretics of property, but only to the extent of depriving them of the means of false worship and of harming Catholics. Augustine opposed depriving heretics of the means of sustenance, since he did not want to make them dependent on others. From the evidence I have found, Augustine advocated physical punishments only for heretics who murdered; he does not appear to have prescribed beatings for those who did not commit acts of violence.[48] Augustine opposed the death penalty, believing, rather, that murderers deserved only the kind of beatings that schoolboys received. The important point here is that Augustine insisted that coercion be educative, even for murderers, and that he shared this view with the ancient world in general, and certainly with the Roman world. Unfortunately, Augustine's rhetoric, intended to exhort reluctant authorities to apply the law, albeit without excess, was taken in later ages to justify ruthless persecution.

48. See Deane, *Political and Social Ideas,* 206.

# CONCLUSION

I N THE INTRODUCTION, two preliminary observations were offered regarding the implications of this study of Augustine's report of his meditations: first, that Augustine's philosophical anthropology, because it can account for the full range of longings that human beings experience in this world, provides a coherent basis on which to understand political life, and second, and more specifically, his political thought can be drawn upon to affirm and to stand in judgment of liberal democracy. With regard to the first implication, this study shows how Augustine reasoned about politics in terms of right-by-nature, and virtue in terms of ordinate loving *(ordo amoris)*. It shows how he regarded politics as the establishment and maintenance of a "little world" in which human beings seek shelter from the disruptive forces that confront them. Politics is not merely about maintaining peace and security—although those certainly are valuable and difficult to obtain goods—but also about maintaining "a kind" of good life; according to this view, its goodness pales in comparison to the glory of the city of God, but, analogously, it is a real human good, nevertheless, which directs the multiplicity of human longings toward their various perfections without necessarily succumbing to the Caesarian temptation. Politics can satisfy human longings for political friendship, according to which participants recognize each other within an experienced—although not necessarily articulated—whole. Political friendship is experienced because a *populus* is unified by the objects of its love, and the better objects of love strengthen those bonds. The *populus* is best expressed when embodied by those who personify those objects. Thus, a society is bound together by the ritual reenactments and glorifications of the actions of those who best exemplify a people's loves that foster a civic attitude of gratitude. As such, a good society is grounded in the recognition that its bonds are determined in the first place "as if by lot," to recall Augustine's words, indicating that citizens' habits and civic virtues are formed by human conventions, which are in some sense arbitrary, but conventions that serve as a "second nature."

Although acknowledging the concrete achievements obtainable by political activity, this view of politics is also rooted in a salutary skepticism toward the possibilities of political life. Human beings are meant to establish and maintain their little world of order, but must remain mindful to the partial and historical nature of their achievements. Such mindfulness derives from reflecting on the longings that can never be completely satisfied by political activity, and from their recognition that what has been granted to them "as if by lot" could have been otherwise. Their political freedom consists in their collectively negotiating and fashioning their future out of the materials that constitute their past. Always present to them is the fact that their being is not completely of their own making, and that it is experienced as a gift. Only by recognizing, in a civic sense of gratitude, the miracle that has brought them forth, against the multiplicity of factors that could have prevented this, can they obtain the elevated and moderated political life that Augustine saw as necessary for human flourishing. Like refugees finally finding sanctuary, and like those described by and addressed by Augustine in his *City of God* in his day and in our own, neighbors love each other despite the great odds that would have prevented them from so doing. In doing so, their love reflects the plenitude, not the blind force, of creation.

A good portion of this study has been used to explain how Augustine's antipolitical rhetoric, his dialectic of "excess over excess" as it was called in Chapter 1, often obscures his affirmation of politics as a positive good. He uses this rhetoric to tame his audience's inordinate ambitions, which delude them into thinking that political activity can satisfy the totality of human beings' longings. However, his rhetoric is not merely negative. It is also pastoral because it tells the saving tale he discovered in his meditations and that needed to be preserved against the deformations of his and future times. The saving tale is about the truth of human beings' relationship with the ground of being and each other, and why the just and the unjust suffer equally. These truths were known in the classical world (often fleetingly or partially), and Augustine's achievement was in articulating them and in giving them public expression. He was thus one with true piety and the science of ruling peoples to whom he refers in book 5 of the *City of God*. That the "second founder of the faith," as Jerome called him, could appear at Rome's darkest hour would have made even the most committed pagan pause to wonder whether indeed the gods care for human affairs after all. The answer was obvious to Jerome, for whom Augustine's foundation was the way he engaged in pastoral care. Augustine's antipolitical rhetoric, therefore, serves to preserve in history the institution—the Church—that could care for those who wonder why the just and unjust suffer equally, and administer the sacraments that prepare them for eternal life.

Augustine's reflections on political life are timely in the context of the current state of liberalism and liberal democracy. Liberal states currently have difficulty confronting the forces of globalization, not only of the economy but also of issues generally signified as "humanitarian," and of localism that include ethnicity, culture, race, and religion. The structure and basis of various bodies politic are open to question; as things presently stand, the "heads" of societies are concerned with various modes of neutral proceduralism, whose legitimacy derives purportedly from consent. The basis for such consent is under strain as people increasingly see international organizations as more effective at handling issues such as the environment and the regulation of the international economy. Conversely, the autonomous individual who consents to these measures finds himself increasingly vulnerable to the effects of his freedoms, and is tempted to seek shelter in a myriad of local cultures, quite often defined in terms of ethnicity or religion. The body politic cannot decide whether to locate its head in the airy space of neutral proceduralism or in some "nonrational" part of the body such as the color of one's skin, for example.

Augustine's political thought, rooted in a philosophical anthropology more robust than that offered in various modern accounts, avoids this disease of the body politic. Its view of love of God and of neighbor is more satisfying than shallow proceduralism, and more respectful of meaningful pluralism and religion than is humanitarianism. The cultivation of a civic attitude of gratitude (whose grounds were explicated in Chapter 6) within a context of meaningful pluralism can tame liberal democracy's inordinate *pleonexia* and individualism with, to recall Hobbes, its endless quest for power that ceases only in death. This attitude can help to prevent the present regime of tolerance from degenerating into a regime of secularism by providing a constant reminder that nothing in the saeculum can fully satisfy human longings. A civic attitude of gratitude can also moderate and elevate the tendency to root politics in "nonrational" realms by reminding us to avoid reducing the foundation of political reality to one element.

Augustine's political thought, therefore, reminds us of the contingency of political achievements, and that any outcome will not likely endure as long as expected or longed for. Human beings are permanently caught in the tragic situation of longing for true happiness, but they face the mysterious impossibility of not being fully capable of attaining it. This does not mean that political activity is fruitless; it means only that the fruition of our greatest longings lies elsewhere, an insight achieved only by thinking and acting in the world, and by discovering that such longing reorients our being in the world. Between our political activities and that fruition, we long and live in hope.

# BIBLIOGRAPHY

PRIMARY

"Answer to Maximinus the Arian." In *Arianism and Other Heresies*, trans. Roland J. Teske. Hyde Park, N.Y.: New City Press, 1995.

*Anti-Pelagian Writings*. Trans. Peter Holmes, Rev. Robert Ernest Wallis, and Benjamin B. Warfield. Nicene and Post-Nicene Fathers, vol. 5, 1st ser. Peabody, Mass.: Hendrickson Publishers, 1994.

*Augustine on the Romans: Propositions from the Epistle to the Romans and Unfinished Commentary on the Epistle to the Romans*. Trans. Paula Fredriksen Landes. Chico, Calif.: Scholars Press, 1982.

*The Catholic and Manichaean Ways of Life*. Trans. Donald A. Gallagher and Idella J. Gallagher. Fathers of the Church, vol. 56. Washington, D.C.: Catholic University of America Press, 1966.

*De Civitate Dei* (City of God). Trans. G. E. McCracken et al. Bilingual ed. 7 vols. Cambridge: Harvard University Press, 1969–1988.

*De Civitate Dei* (City of God against the Pagans). Trans. R. W. Dyson. Cambridge: Cambridge University Press, 1998.

*Confessions*. Trans. F. J. Sheed. Indianapolis: Hackett Publishing, 1970.

*Confessions*. Trans. William Watts. Bilingual ed. 2 vols. Cambridge: Harvard University Press, 1989.

*Contra Academicos* (Against the Academics). Trans. John J. O'Meara. Ancient Christian Writers, vol. 12. New York: Newman Press, 1951.

*De Doctrina Christiana* (On Christian Teaching). Trans. R. P. H. Green. Oxford: Clarendon Press, 1995.

263

*Eighty-three Different Questions.* Trans. David L. Mosher. Fathers of the Church, vol. 70. Washington, D.C.: Catholic University of America Press, 1982.

*Enarrationes in Psalmos* (Expositions on the Book of Psalms). Trans. A. Cleveland Coxe. Nicene and Post-Nicene Fathers, vol. 8. Grand Rapids, Mich.: Wm. B. Eerdmans Publishing, 1989.

*Epistolarum* (The confessions and letters of St. Augustin). Trans. J. G. Pilkington and J. G. Cunningham. Grand Rapids, Mich.: Wm. B. Eerdmans Publishing, 1994.

*Epistolarum Classes Quatuor.* Opera Omnia, vol. 2. Paris: Apud Gaume Fratres, 1836.

*"The Greatness of the Soul" and "The Teacher."* Trans. Joseph M. Colleran, C.SS.R. Ancient Christian Writers, vol. 9. New York: Newman Press, 1978.

*Homilies on the Gospel of John, Homilies on the First Epistle of John, Soliloquies.* Trans. Rev. John Gibb and Rev. James Innis. Nicene and Post-Nicene Fathers, vol. 7, 1st ser. Grand Rapids, Mich.: Wm. B. Eerdmans Publishing, 1956.

*Letters.* Trans. Wilfrid Parsons et al. Fathers of the Church, vols. 9–13. New York: Fathers of the Church, 1951.

*De Libero Arbitrio.* "The Free Choice of the Will." In *The Teacher, the Free Choice of the Will, Grace and Free Will,* trans. Robert P. Russell. Fathers of the Church, vol. 59. Washington, D.C.: Catholic University of America Press, 1968.

*The Literal Meaning of Genesis.* Trans. John Hammond Taylor, S.J. Ancient Christian Writers, vols. 41–42. New York: Newman Press, 1982.

*Lord's Sermon on the Mount.* Trans. John J. Jepson, S.S. Ancient Christian Writers, vol. 5. New York: Newman Press, 1949.

*De Magistro, De Libero Arbitrio.* Ed. F. J. Thonnard. Oeuvres de Saint Augustin. Bilingual ed. Paris: Bibliothèques Augustinienne, 1941.

*De Musica.* "On Music." In *Writings of Saint Augustine,* trans. Robert Catesby Taliaterro. Fathers of the Church, vol. 2. New York: Cima Publishing, 1947.

*De Ordine.* "Divine Providence and the Problem of Evil." In *Happy Life, Answer to Skeptics, Divine Providence and the Problem of Evil, Soliloquies,* trans. Robert P. Russell, O.S.A. Fathers of the Church, vol. 1. New York: Cima Publishing, 1948.

*The Retractions.* Trans. Sister Mary Inez Bogan. Fathers of the Church, vol. 60. Washington, D.C.: Catholic University of America Press, 1968.

*Sermons on the Liturgical Seasons.* Trans. Sister Mary Sarah Muldowney, R.S.M. Fathers of the Church, vol. 17. New York: Fathers of the Church, 1959.

*Treatises on Various Subjects.* Trans. Sister Mary Sarah Muldowney, S.S.J., et al. Fathers of the Church, vol. 16. New York: Fathers of the Church, 1952.

*De Trinitate* (On the Trinity). Ed. W. J. Mountain. Corpus Christianorum Series Latina, vols. 50–50A. Turnholti, Belgium: Typographi Brepols Editores Pontificii, 1968.

*The Trinity.* Trans. Edmund Hill, O.P. Brooklyn: New City Press, 1991.

*The Trinity.* Trans. Stephen McKenna. Fathers of the Church, vol. 45. Washington, D.C.: Catholic University of America Press, 1963.

*De Vera Religione.* "On True Religion." In *Augustine: Earlier Writings,* trans. John H. S. Burleigh. Philadelphia: Westminster Press, 1953.

*Writings against the Manichaeans and against the Donatists.* Ed. Philip Schaff. Nicene and Post-Nicene Fathers, vol. 4. Grand Rapids, Mich.: Wm. B. Eerdmans Publishing, 1989.


SECONDARY


Adams, Jeremy Duquesnay. *The "Populus" of Augustine and Jerome: A Study in the Patristic Sense of Community.* New Haven: Yale University Press, 1971.

Ambrose, Bishop of Milan. *On Virginity.* Trans. Daniel Callam. Toronto: Peregrina Publishing, 1980.

Anastaplo, George. *The Constitution of 1787: A Commentary.* Baltimore: Johns Hopkins University Press, 1989.

Aquinas, Saint Thomas. *Summa Theologiae.* Trans. Fathers of the English Dominican Province. 5 vols. Westminster, Md.: Christian Classics, 1948.

Arendt, Hannah. *Lectures on Kant's Political Philosophy.* Ed. Ronald Beiner. Chicago: University of Chicago Press, 1982.

———. *Love and Saint Augustine.* Ed. Joanna Vecchiarelli Scott and Judith Chelius Stark. Chicago: University of Chicago Press, 1996.

Aristotle. *Nicomachean Ethics.* Trans. W. D. Ross. Oxford: Oxford University Press, 1988.

Arquillière, H.-X. *L'Augustinisme politique: Essai sur la formation des theories politiques du moyen âge.* 2d ed. Paris: Vrin, 1955.

Ayres, Lewis. "Between Athens and Jerusalem: Prolegomena to Anthropology in *De Trinitate.*" *Modern Theology* 8:1 (January 1992): 53–73.

———. "The Christological Context of Augustine's *De Trinitate* XIII: Toward Relocating Books VIII–XV." *Augustinian Studies* 29:1 (1998): 111–39.

———. "The Discipline of Self-Knowledge in Augustine's *De Trinitate* Book X." In *The Passionate Intellect: Essays on the Transformation of Classical Traditions, Presented to Professor I. G. Kidd,* 261–96. New Brunswick, N.J.: Transaction Publishers, 1995.

Balz, Horst, and Gerhart Schneider, eds. *Exegetical Dictionary of the New Testament*. Vol. 2. Grand Rapids, Mich.: Wm. B. Eerdmans Publishing, 1990.

Barnes, T. D. "Aspects of the Background of the *City of God*." *Revue de l'Université d'Ottawa* 52 (1982): 64–80.

Barr, Robert R. "The Two Cities in Saint Augustine." *Laval theologique et philosophique* 18 (1962): 211–29.

Becker, Carl L. *The Heavenly City of the Eighteenth-Century Philosophers*. New Haven: Yale University Press, 1932.

Berger, Adolf. "Encyclopedic Dictionary of Roman Law." *Transactions of the American Philosophical Society* 43:2 (1953): 333–808.

Berger, Peter. "On the Obsolescence of the Concept of Honor." In *Revisions: Changing Perspectives in Moral Philosophy*, ed. Stanley Hauerwas and Alasdair MacIntyre, 172–81. Notre Dame: University of Notre Dame Press, 1983.

Black, Antony. "Christianity and Republicanism: From St. Cyprian to Rousseau." *American Political Science Review* 91:3 (September 1997): 647–56.

Blumenberg, Hans. *The Legitimacy of the Modern Age*. Cambridge: MIT Press, 1983.

Bok, Sissela. *Lying*. New York: Vintage Books, 1989.

Bowlin, John R. "Augustine on Justifying Coercion." *Annual of the Society of Christian Ethics* 17 (1997): 49–70.

Brown, Peter. *Augustine of Hippo*. London: Faber and Faber, 1967.

———. *Authority and the Sacred: Aspects of Christianisation of the Roman World*. Cambridge: Cambridge University Press, 1995.

———. "Political Society." In *Augustine: A Collection of Essays*, ed. R. A. Markus, 331–35. New York: Anchor Books, 1972.

———. "St. Augustine's Attitude to Religious Coercion." In *Religion and Society in the Age of St. Augustine*, 262–78. New York: Harper and Row, 1972.

Burnell, Peter J. "The Problem of Service to Unjust Regimes in Augustine's *City of God*." *Journal of the History of Ideas* 54:2 (1993): 177–88.

———. "The Status of Politics in St. Augustine's *City of God*." *History of Political Thought* 13:1 (spring 1992): 13–29.

Camus, Albert. "Entre Plotin et Saint Augustin." In *Essais*, ed. R. Quilliot and L. Faucon, 1220–1313. Paris: Gallimard, 1965.

Carlyle, A. J. *A History of Medieval Political Theory in the West*. Vol. 1. Edinburgh: William Blackwood and Sons, 1903.

Cavadini, John. "The Structure and Intention of Augustine's *De Trinitate*." *Augustinian Studies* 23 (1992): 103–23.

Chroust, Anton. "St. Augustine's Philosophical Theory of Law." *Notre Dame Lawyer* 25:1 (1949): 285–315.

Cicero. *De Amicitia*. Trans. W. A. Falconer. Cambridge: Harvard University Press, 1992.

———. *De Finibus Bonorum et Malorum*. Trans. H. Rackham. Cambridge: Harvard University Press, 1983.

———. *"De Natura Deorum" and "Academica."* Trans. H. Rackham. London: Heinemann, 1933.

———. *De Officiis*. Trans. Walter Miller. Cambridge: Harvard University Press, 1990.

———. *"De Re Publica" and "De Legibus."* Trans. C. W. Keyes. Cambridge: Harvard University Press, 1988.

———. *Philippics*. Trans. Walter C. A. Ker. Cambridge: Harvard University Press, 1926.

Clark, Mary T. "Augustine on Person: Divine and Human." In *Augustine: Presbyter Factus Sum*, ed. Joseph T. Lienhard et al., 99–120. New York: Peter Lang, 1993.

Cochrane, Charles. *Christianity and Classical Culture*. Oxford: Oxford University Press, 1957.

Connolly, William. *The Augustinian Imperative: A Reflection on the Politics of Morality*. Newbury Park, Calif.: Sage, 1993.

Cooper, Barry. *The End of History: An Essay on Modern Hegelianism*. Toronto: University of Toronto Press, 1984.

Crosson, Frederick. "Religion and Faith in St. Augustine's *Confessions*." In *Rationality and Religious Faith*, ed. C. F. Delaney, 152–68. Notre Dame: University of Notre Dame Press, 1979.

———. "Show and Tell: The Concept of Teaching in St. Augustine's *De Magistro*." In *De Magistro di Agostino d'Ippona*, 13–65. Pavia, Italy: Editioni Augustinus, 1993.

———. "Structure and Meaning in St. Augustine's *Confessions*." In *The Augustinian Tradition*, ed. Gareth B. Matthews, 27–38. Berkeley: University of California Press, 1999.

Crouse, R. D. " 'In Aenigmate Trinitas' (*Confessions*, XIII, 5, 6): The Conversion of Philosophy in Augustine's *Confessions*." *Dionysius* 11 (December 1987): 53–62.

Deane, Herbert. *The Political and Social Ideas of St. Augustine*. New York: Columbia University Press, 1963.

Deferrari, Roy J., and M. Jerome Keeler, O.S.B. "St. Augustine's *City of God*: Its Plan and Development." *American Journal of Philology* 50 (1929): 109–37.

Dihle, Albrecht. *The Theory of Will in Classical Antiquity.* Berkeley: University of California Press, 1982.

Elshtain, Jean Bethke. *Augustine and the Limits of Politics.* Notre Dame: University of Notre Dame Press, 1995.

Figgis, John N. *The Political Aspects of St. Augustine's "City of God."* London: Longmans, Green, 1921.

Fortescue, Sir John. "In Praise of the Laws of England." In *On the Laws and Governance of England,* ed. Shelley Lockwood. Cambridge: Cambridge University Press, 1997.

Fortin, E. L. "Augustine and the Problem of Goodness." *University of Dayton Review* 22:3 (summer 1994): 177–92.

———. *Collected Essays.* Ed. J. Brian Benestad. 3 vols. Lanham, Md.: Rowman and Littlefield, 1996.

———. "Justice as the Foundation of the Political Community: Augustine and His Pagan Models (Book IV.4)." In *Augustinus: De Civitate Dei,* ed. Christoph Horn, 41–62. Berlin: Akademie Verlag, 1997.

———. Review of *Augustine and the Limits of Politics,* by Jean Bethke Elshtain. In *Review of Politics* 59:2 (spring 1997): 365–67.

———. "St. Augustine." In *History of Political Philosophy,* ed. Leo Strauss and Joseph Cropsey, 176–205. 3rd ed. Chicago: University of Chicago Press, 1987.

Frend, William H. C. "Augustine and State Authority: The Example of the Donatists." In *Agostino D'Ippona "Quaestiones Disputatae,"* 49–74. Palermo: Edizioni Augustinus, 1987.

———. "Donatism-Donatists." In *Encyclopedia of the Early Church,* trans. Adrian Walford, 1:246–49. New York: Oxford University Press, 1992.

———. *The Donatist Church: A Movement of Protest in North Africa.* Oxford: Clarendon Press, 1952.

Gadamer, Hans-Georg. "Articulating Transcendence." In *The Beginning and the Beyond: Papers from the Gadamer and Voegelin Conferences, Supplementary Issue of Lonergan Workshop,* ed. Fred Lawrence, 4:1–12. Chico, Calif.: Scholars Press, 1984.

Gebhardt, Jürgen. *Americanism: Revolutionary Order and Societal Self-Interpretation in the American Republic.* Trans. Ruth Hein. Baton Rouge: Louisiana State University Press, 1993.

Goerner, E. A. "On Thomistic Natural Law: The Bad Man's View of Thomistic Natural Right." *Political Theory* 7:1 (February 1979): 101–22.

———. *Peter and Caesar.* New York: Herder and Herder, 1965.

———. "Thomistic Natural Right: The Good Man's View of Thomistic Natural Law." *Political Theory* 11:3 (August 1983): 393–418.

Grant, George Parkin. *Technology and Justice.* Toronto: Anansi, 1986.

Griffiths, Paul J. "The Gift and the Lie: Augustine on Lying." *Communio* 26 (spring 1999): 3–30.

Guy, Jean-Claude, S.J. *Unité et structure logique de la "Cité de Dieu" de saint Augustin.* Paris: Études Augustiniennes, 1961.

Hagendahl, Harald. *Augustine and the Latin Classics.* 2 vols. Göteborg, Sweden: Erlanders Boktryckeri Aktiebolag, 1958.

Harries, Jill. *Law and Empire in Late Antiquity.* Cambridge: Cambridge University Press, 1999.

Hawkins, Peter S. "Polemical Counterpoint in *De Civitate Dei.*" *Augustinian Studies* 6 (1975): 97–106.

Heidegger, Martin. "Augustinus und der Neuplatonismus." In *Phänomenologie des Religiösen Lebens, Gesamtausgabe,* 60:160–302. Frankfurt am Main: Vittorio Klostermann, 1995.

———. "Question Concerning Technology." In *Basic Writings,* ed. David Farrell Krell, 283–318. San Francisco: Harper and Row, 1977.

Heilke, Thomas. "On Being Ethical without Moral Sadism: Two Readings of Augustine and the Beginnings of the Anabaptist Revolution." *Political Theory* 24:3 (August 1996): 495–507.

Honoré, Tony. *Law and the Crisis of Empire, 379–455 A.D.* Oxford: Clarendon Press, 1998.

Horace. *The Odes in Latin and English.* Trans. Philip Francis. London: Unit Library, 1902.

John of Salisbury. *Policraticus.* Trans. Cary J. Nederman. Cambridge: Cambridge University Press, 1990.

Johnson, Penelope D. "*Virtus:* Transition from Classical Latin to the *De Civitate Dei.*" In *The "City of God": A Collection of Critical Essays,* ed. Dorothy F. Donnelly, 233–40. New York: Peter Lang, 1995.

Jonas, Hans. *Augustin und das paulinische Freiheitsproblem.* 1930. Reprint, Göttingen: Vandenhoeck and Ruprecht, 1965.

Jordan, Mark. "Words and Word: Incarnation and Signification in Augustine's *De Doctrina Christiana.*" *Augustinian Studies* 11 (1980): 177–96.

Justinian. *Justinian's "Institutes."* Trans. Peter Birks and Grant McLeod. With Latin text by Paul Krueger. Ithaca: Cornell University Press, 1987.

Kaufman, Peter Iver. *Redeeming Politics.* Princeton: Princeton University Press, 1990.

Kemp, Kenneth W., and Thomas Sullivan. "Speaking Falsely and Telling Lies." *Proceedings of the Catholic Philosophical Association* 67 (1993): 151–70.

Kempshall, M. S. *The Common Good in Late Medieval Political Thought.* Oxford: Clarendon Press, 1999.

Kisiel, Theodore. *The Genesis of Heidegger's "Being and Time."* Berkeley: University of California Press, 1993.

Krell, David Farrell, ed. *Basic Writings.* San Francisco: Harper and Row, 1977.

Lendon, J. E. *Empire of Honour: The Art of Government in the Roman World.* Oxford: Clarendon Press, 1997.

Lewis, Ewart, ed. *Medieval Political Ideas.* New York: Alfred A. Knopf, 1954.

Liddell, H. G., and Robert Scott. *An Intermediate Greek-English Lexicon.* Oxford: Clarendon Press, 1994.

Livy. *Ab urbe condita* (The History of Rome). Trans. D. Spillan. 2 vols. New York: Harper and Bros., 1880.

Lossky, Vladimir. "Les éléments de 'Théologie négative' dans la pensée de saint Augustin." In *Augustinus Magister: Congrès International Augustinien,* 575–82. Paris: Études Augustiniennes, 1954.

Löwith, Karl. *Meaning in History.* Chicago: University of Chicago Press, 1949.

MacIntyre, Alasdair. *After Virtue.* Notre Dame: University of Notre Dame Press, 1984.

———. *Whose Justice? Which Rationality?* Notre Dame: University of Notre Dame Press, 1988.

MacQueen, D. J. "The Origin and Dynamics of Society and the State according to St. Augustine." *Augustinian Studies* 4 (1973): 73–101.

Manent, Pierre. *The City of Man.* Trans. Marc A. LePain. Princeton: Princeton University Press, 1998.

Markus, R. A. *The End of Ancient Christianity.* Cambridge: Cambridge University Press, 1990.

———. *Saeculum: History and Society in the Theology of St. Augustine.* Cambridge: Cambridge University Press, 1970.

McIlwain, C. H. *The Growth of Political Thought in the West.* New York: Macmillan, 1932.

Milbank, John. "Sacred Triads: Augustine and the Indo-European Soul." *Modern Theology* 13:4 (October 1997): 451–74.

———. *Theology and Social Theory.* Oxford: Blackwell, 1993.

Minogue, Kenneth. *Alien Powers: The Pure Theory of Ideology.* New York: St. Martin's Press, 1985.

Mommsen, Theodor. *A History of Rome under the Emperors.* New York: Routledge, 1996.

Nederman, Cary J., and Kate Langdon Forhan, eds. *Medieval Political Theory—A*

*Reader: The Quest for the Body Politic, 1100–1400.* New York: Routledge, 1993.

Nicgorski, Walter. "Cicero's Focus: From the Best Regime to the Model Statesman." *Political Theory* 19:2 (May 1991): 230–51.

Nicholas, Barry. *An Introduction to Roman Law.* Oxford: Oxford University Press, 1962.

Niebuhr, Reinhold. "Augustine's Political Realism." In *The Essential Reinhold Niebuhr,* ed. Robert McAfee Brown, 123–41. New Haven: Yale University Press, 1986.

Niemeyer, Gerhart. "Augustine's Political Philosophy?" In *Aftersight and Foresight: Selected Essays,* 267–88. Lanham, Md.: University Press of America, 1988.

Oakeshott, Michael. *On Human Conduct.* Oxford: Clarendon Press, 1975.

Ocker, Christopher. "Augustine, Episcopal Interests, and the Papacy in Late Roman Africa." *Journal of Ecclesiastical History* 42:2 (April 1991): 179–201.

O'Connell, Robert J., S.J. *St. Augustine's "Confessions": The Odyssey of Soul.* 1969. Reprint, New York: Fordham University Press, 1989.

O'Donnell, James J. "Augustine's Classical Readings." *Recherches Augustinienes* 15 (1980): 144–75.

O'Donovan, Oliver. "Augustine's *City of God* XIX and Western Political Thought." *Dionysius* 11 (1987): 89–110.

———. "*Usus* and *Fruitio* in Augustine, *De Doctrina Christiana* I." *Journal of Theological Studies,* n.s., 33:2 (October 1982): 361–97.

Parr, Clyde, trans. *The Theodosian Code and Novels and the Sirmondian Constitutions.* Princeton: Princeton University Press, 1952.

Petropulous, William. "The Person as *Imago Dei:* Augustine and Max Scheler in Eric Voegelin's *Herrschaftslehre* and *Political Religions.*" In *The Politics of the Soul: Eric Voegelin on Religious Experience,* ed. Glenn Hughes, 87–114. Lanham, Md.: Rowman and Littlefield, 1999.

Plato. *The "Republic" of Plato.* Trans. Allan Bloom. New York: Basic Books, 1968.

Rhodes, James M. "Right by Nature." *Journal of Politics* 53:2 (May 1991): 318–38.

Riley, Patrick. Review of *Morality and Politics in Modern Europe: The Harvard Lectures* and *Religion, Politics, and the Moral Life,* by Michael Oakeshott. *American Political Science Review* 88:3 (September 1994): 746–78.

Rist, John M. *Augustine: Ancient Thought Baptized.* Cambridge: Cambridge University Press, 1994.

Rossiter, Clinton. *Constitutional Dictatorship: Crisis Government in the Modern Democracies.* New York: Harcourt, Brace, and World, 1963.

Sallust. *The Histories.* Trans. Patrick McGushin. New York: Oxford University Press, 1992.

———. *"Jugurthine War" and "The Conspiracy of Catiline."* Trans. S. A. Handford. New York: Penguin Books, 1963.

Schall, James V. "A Latitude for Statesmanship? Strauss on St. Thomas." In *Leo Strauss: Political Philosopher and Jewish Thinker,* ed. Kenneth L. Deutsch and Walter Nicgorski, 211–30. Lanham, Md.: Rowman and Littlefield, 1994.

Scheler, Max. *On the Eternal in Man.* Trans. Bernard Noble. Hamden, Conn.: SCM Press, 1960.

Schofield, Malcolm. "Cicero's Definition of *Res Publica.*" In *Cicero the Philosopher,* ed. J. G. F. Powell, 63–84. Oxford: Clarendon Press, 1995.

Simon, Yves R. *A General Theory of Authority.* Notre Dame: University of Notre Dame Press, 1980.

Souter, Alexander. *A Glossary of Later Latin to 600* A.D. Oxford: Clarendon Press, 1949.

Starnes, Colin. "Augustine's Audience in the First Ten Books of the *City of God* and the Logic of His Argument." In *Studia Patristica,* ed. Elizabeth Livingstone, 27:388–93. Louvain, Belgium: Peeters, 1993.

Strauss, Leo. *Natural Right and History.* Chicago: University of Chicago Press, 1953.

Swift, Louis J. "Defining *Gloria* in Augustine's *City of God.*" In *Diakonia: Studies in Honor of Robert T. Mayer,* ed. Thomas Halton and Joseph P. Williman, 133–44. Washington, D.C.: Catholic University of America Press, 1986.

———. "Pagan and Christian Heroes in Augustine's *City of God.*" *Augustinianum* 27 (1987): 507–22.

Taylor, Charles. *Multiculturalism and the "Politics of Recognition."* Ed. Amy Gutmann. Princeton: Princeton University Press, 1992.

Teselle, Eugene. *Living in Two Cities: Augustinian Trajectories in Political Thought.* Scranton, Pa.: University of Scranton Press, 1998.

Thiele, Leslie Paul. "Heidegger on Freedom: Political Not Metaphysical." *American Political Science Review* 88:2 (June 1994): 278–91.

Tierney, Brian. "Religious Rights: An Historical Perspective." In *Religious Human Rights in Global Perspective: Religious Perspectives,* ed. John Witte Jr. and Johan D. van der Vyver, 17–46. Boston: Martinus Nijhoff Publishers, 1996.

Tilley, Maureen A. *Donatist Martyr Stories: The Church in Conflict in Roman North Africa.* Liverpool: Liverpool University Press, 1996.

Tuveson, E. L. *Redeemer Nation.* Chicago: University of Chicago Press, 1968.

Van Bavel, T. J., O.S.A. "God in between Affirmation and Negation according to Augustine." In *Augustine: Presbyter Factus Sum,* ed. Joseph T. Lienhard et al., 73–97. New York: Peter Lang, 1993.

Van der Meer, F. *Augustine the Bishop.* New York: Sheed and Ward, 1961.

Van Oort, Johannes. *Jerusalem and Babylon: A Study into Augustine's "City of God" and the Sources of His Doctrine of the Two Cities.* Leiden, Holland: E. J. Brill, 1991.

Virgil. *The Aeneid.* Trans. C. Day Lewis. Oxford: Oxford University Press, 1986.

Voegelin, Eric. *Anamnesis.* Trans. Gerhart Niemeyer. Columbia: University of Missouri Press, 1978.

———. *The Ecumenic Age.* Vol. 4 of *Order and History.* Baton Rouge: Louisiana State University Press, 1974.

———. *History of Political Ideas.* Vols. 1–4. Columbia: University of Missouri Press, 1997–1998.

———. *The New Science of Politics.* Chicago: University of Chicago Press, 1952.

———. *Race and State.* Trans. Ruth Hein. 1933. Reprint, Baton Rouge: Louisiana State University Press, 1997.

Weithman, Paul J. "Toward an Augustinian Liberalism." *Faith and Philosophy* 8:4 (October 1991): 461–80.

White, Michael J. "Pluralism and Secularism in the Political Order: St. Augustine and Theoretical Liberalism." *University of Dayton Review* 22:3 (summer 1994): 137–53.

Williams, Rowan. "The Paradoxes of Self-Knowledge in the *De Trinitate.*" In *Augustine: Presbyter Factus Sum, Collecteana Augustiniana,* ed. Joseph T. Lienhard, S.J., et al., 121–34. New York: Peter Lang, 1993.

———. "Politics and the Soul: A Reading of the *City of God.*" *Milltown Studies* 19/20 (1987): 55–72.

———. "*Sapientia* and the Trinity: Reflections on the *De Trinitate.*" In *Collecteana Augustiniana: Mélanges T. J. Van Bavel,* 317–32. Louvain, Belgium: Louvain University Press, 1990.

Williams, Stephen, and Gerard Friell. *Theodosius: The Empire at Bay.* New Haven: Yale University Press, 1995.

Willis, Geoffrey Grimshaw. *Saint Augustine and the Donatist Controversy.* Cambridge: Cambridge University Press, 1950.

Worthington, Glenn. "Michael Oakeshott and the *City of God.*" *Political Theory* 28:3 (June 2000): 377–98.

# INDEX